The Complete Book of Crochet Stitch Designs

The Complete Book of Crochet Stitch Designs

500 Classic & Original Patterns

Revised Edition

Linda P. Schapper

LARK CRAFTS
Asheville

Editor: Susan Mowery Kieffer

Technical Editor: Karen Manthey

Art Director: Shannon Yokeley

Cover Designer: Cindy LaBreacht

Assistant Designer: Travis Medford

Art Production Assistant: Jeff Hamilton

Editorial Assistance: Delores Gosnell, Dawn Dillingham, Rosemary Kast

Art Intern: Marshall Hudson

Editorial Intern: Katrina Usher

Illustrator: Orrin Lundgren

Photographer: Steve Mann

An Imprint of Sterling Publishing
387 Park Avenue South
New York, NY 10016

If you have questions or comments about
this book, please visit: larkcrafts.com

The Library of Congress has cataloged the hardcover edition as follows:

Schäpper, Linda.
  The Complete book of crochet stitch designs : 500 classic & original patterns
/ Linda P. Schäpper. -- Rev. ed.
       p. cm.
  Includes index.
  ISBN-13: 978-1-57990-915-4 (hc-plc with jacket : alk. paper)
  ISBN-10: 1-57990-915-9 (hc-plc with jacket : alk. paper)
  1. Crocheting--Patterns. I. Title.
  TT820.S28 2007
  746.43'4041--dc22
                          2006102075

20 19 18 17 16 15 14 13 12 11 10

Revised Edition

Published by Lark Crafts
An Imprint of Sterling Publishing Co., Inc.
387 Park Avenue South, New York, NY 10016

First Paperback Edition 2011
Text © 2007, Linda P. Schapper
Photography and illustrations © 2007, Lark Crafts, an Imprint of Sterling Publishing Co., Inc.
First published in 1985 by Sterling Publishing Co., Inc.

Distributed in Canada by Sterling Publishing, c/o Canadian Manda Group, 165 Dufferin Street, Toronto, Ontario, Canada M6K 3H6

Distributed in the United Kingdom by GMC Distribution Services, Castle Place, 166 High Street, Lewes, East Sussex, England BN7 1XU

Distributed in Australia by Capricorn Link (Australia) Pty Ltd., P.O. Box 704, Windsor, NSW 2756 Australia

Manufactured in China

ISBN 13: 978-1-57990-915-4 (hardcover) 978-1-4547-0137-8 (paperback)

For information about custom editions, special sales, and premium and corporate purchases, please contact Sterling Special Sales Department at 800-805-5489 or specialsales@sterlingpub.com.

Requests for information about desk and examination copies available to college and university professors must be submitted to academic@larkbooks.com.
Our complete policy can be found at www.larkcrafts.com.

◼ Contents ◼

■ Introduction ■

Although crochet is thought to have originated as early as the Stone Age, when there were no needles available to join clothing and a rough crude hook was used, very little about early crochet has survived in the way of a written record. It is possible that we have adopted the French word for hook—*crochet*—as the name of the craft because the French did more than any other group to record crochet patterns.

Patterns were passed down through families, and new patterns were copied by examining the design with a magnifying glass. In the 19th century, written instructions became more popular as reading levels of women improved. Instructions, however, often can be long and tedious and, although perfectly clear to the writer, frequently difficult for the crocheter.

Crochet itself is based on a few simple stitches used in endless variation. It begins with a chain, and the way the stitches are formed determines the pattern. You need only a hook, your hand, and the thread. It's easy to carry with you and can be done anywhere. Unlike knitting and weaving, it is difficult to make a mistake which cannot be corrected immediately.

Crochet is versatile. It can make generous lace patterns, mimic knitting, patchwork, or weaving, and it can form any number of textile patterns. I found the challenge of making 500 different patterns with the same white thread exhilarating.

This book includes an extensive list of the symbols used in the International Crochet Symbols system. It's easy to read after you have worked out the four or five basic stitches, and it makes crocheting easier. This system allows you to see the whole pattern in proportion, and it's a nice experience to be able to pick up a crochet book in Russian and understand the crochet symbols. The symbols themselves look a great deal like the actual crochet stitches and, as you will see, are not at all difficult to follow. These start on page 16.

The pages that follow give instructions for the basic stitches referred to in the designs. On page 18 a Pictorial Index begins. This provides a small-size, overall view of each crochet design, along with the page number on which it can be found.

I hadn't thought much about crochet in the 20 years between the time my original *Crochet Stitch Designs* was published and when I was asked to update the book to have it re-issued. I was pleased to hear that crochet was undergoing a huge revival in interest and that a new generation was using the old techniques, both for expressive and utilitarian purposes.

As I sat down to work on the new publication, I discovered that many of the original crochet samples were missing, that photographs were not available, and that I would have to redo the samples. I had a few days of panic. I had forgotten how to crochet in the intervening years, and I had neither the time nor the patience to sit still in a chair and redo countless blocks of white wool.

Finding no other way around it, I did sit down and let my own old instructions teach me how to crochet again. And, I was immediately hooked! There is something so soothing and relaxing and challenging about crochet. After twenty years, I had rediscovered an old friend. I hope with this book, that you will discover or perhaps even rediscover the joy of crochet.

Notes for those using the written instructions
- Stitch is always counted from the last stitch used.
- The abbreviations used are the American ones. British readers should keep this in mind since a few British abbreviations are different.
- The diagrams are easier once you have learned them. When in doubt, check the diagrams.

▪ Basic Stitches ▪

SLIP KNOT

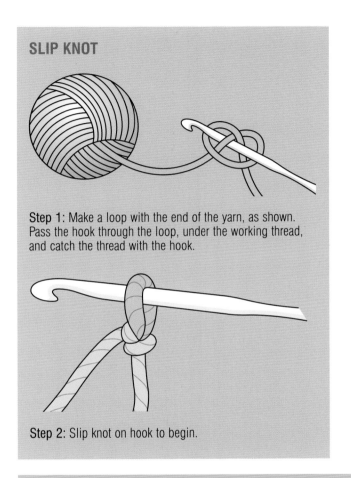

Step 1: Make a loop with the end of the yarn, as shown. Pass the hook through the loop, under the working thread, and catch the thread with the hook.

Step 2: Slip knot on hook to begin.

CHAIN (CH)

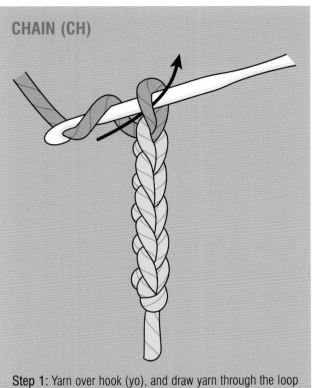

Step 1: Yarn over hook (yo), and draw yarn through the loop on hook (ch made). Repeat as required.

SLIP STITCH (SL ST)

Step 1: Insert hook in designated stitch.

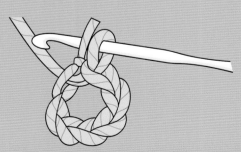

Step 2: Yo, draw yarn through stitch and the loop on hook (sl st made).

SINGLE CROCHET (SC)
This is a short, tight stitch.

Make a chain of desired length.
Step 1: Insert hook in designated st (2nd ch from hook for first sc).

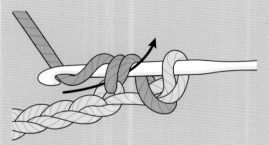

Step 2: Draw yarn through stitch.

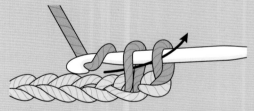

Step 3: Yo, draw yarn through 2 loops on hook (sc made).

Step 4: Insert hook in next chain, and repeat steps to create another single crochet.

HALF DOUBLE CROCHET (HDC)
This stitch gives a lot of body and structure and resembles knitting.

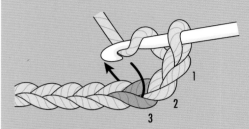

Make a chain of desired length.
Step 1: Yo, insert hook in designated st (3rd ch from hook for first hdc).

Step 2: Yo, draw through stitch (3 loops on hook).

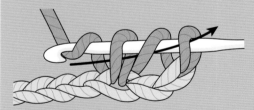

Step 3: Yo, draw yarn through 3 loops on hook (hdc made).

Step 4: You will have one loop left on the hook. Yo, insert hook in next ch, and repeat sequence across row.

DOUBLE CROCHET (DC)

This is perhaps the most popular and frequently used crochet stitch.

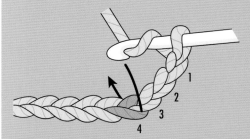

Make a chain of desired length.
Step 1: Yo, insert hook in designated st (4th ch from hook for first dc).

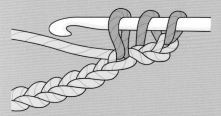

Step 2: Yo, draw through stitch (3 loops on hook).

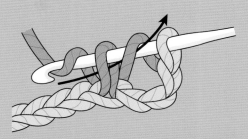

Step 3: Yo, draw yarn through first 2 loops on hook.

Step 4: Yo, draw yarn through last 2 loops on hook (dc made).

Step 5: Yo, insert hook in next st, and repeat steps to continue across row. Repeat steps 2-4 to work next dc.

TREBLE CROCHET (TR)

Make a chain of desired length.

Step 1: Yo twice, insert hook in designated st (5th ch from hook for first tr).

Step 2: Yo, draw through stitch (4 loops on hook).

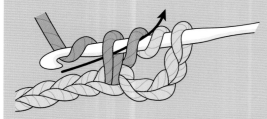

Step 3: Yo, draw yarn through 2 loops on hook (3 loops on hook).

Step 4: Yo, draw yarn through 2 loops on hook (2 loops on hook).

Step 5: Yo, draw yarn through 2 loops on hook (tr made).

Step 6: Yo twice, and repeat steps in next ch st.

BOBBLE (SHOWN FOR 4-LOOPED BOBBLE)

Can be made with 2 to 6 loops. Shown for 4 loops.

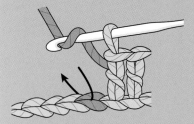

Step 1: Yo, insert hook in designated st.

Step 2: Yo, draw yarn through st and up to level of work (first loop).

Step 3: (Yo, insert hook in same st, yo, draw yarn through st) as many times as required (3 more times for 4-looped bobble st—11 loops on hook).

Step 4: Yo, draw yarn through all loops on hook (bobble made).

PUFF STITCH (SHOWN FOR 3-DC PUFF STITCH)

Can be made with 2 to 6 sts. Shown for 3 dc.

Step 1: Yo, insert hook in designated st (4th ch from hook for first puff st), yo, draw yarn through st, yo, draw yarn through 2 loops on hook (half-closed dc made—2 loops remain on hook).

Step 2: Yo, insert hook in same st, yo, draw yarn through st, yo, draw yarn through 2 loops on hook for each additional dc required (2 more times for 3-dc puff stitch—4 loops on hook).

Step 3: Yo, draw yarn through all loops on hook (puff stitch made).

POPCORN (POP)

Can be made with 2 to 6 sts. Shown with 5 dc.

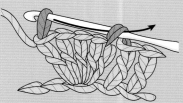

Pop on RS rows:
Step 1: Work 5 dc in designated st (4th ch from hook for first pop).

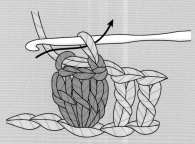

Step 2: Drop loop from hook, insert hook from front to back in top of first dc of group, pick up dropped loop, and draw through st, ch 1 tightly to secure (pop made).

Pop on WS rows:
Step 1: Work 5 dc in designated st (4th ch from hook for first pop).

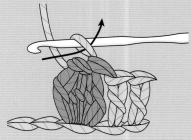

Step 2: Drop loop from hook, insert hook from back to front in top of first dc of group, pick up dropped loop, and draw through st, ch 1 tightly to secure (pop made).

CLUSTER

Shown for 4-dc cluster.

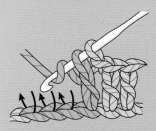

Step 1: Yo, insert hook in designated st, yo, draw yarn through st, yo, draw yarn through 2 loops on hook (half-closed dc made—2 loops remain on hook).

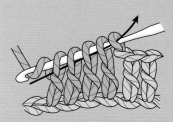

Step 2: Yo, insert hook in next designated st, yo, draw yarn through st, yo, draw yarn through 2 loops on hook) as many times as required (3 more times for 4-dc cluster—4 half-closed dc made—5 loops on hook).

Step 3: Yo, draw yarn through all loops on hook (cluster made).

PICOT
Shown for ch-3 picot.

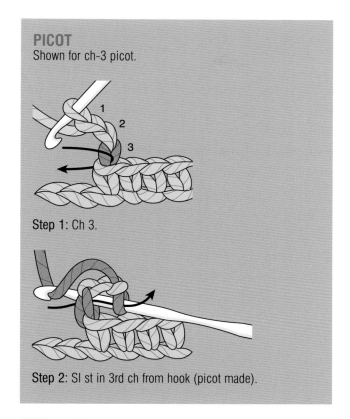

Step 1: Ch 3.

Step 2: Sl st in 3rd ch from hook (picot made).

CROSSED STITCH (CROSSED TR SHOWN)

Step 1: Skip required number of sts (skip 2 sts shown), tr in next st, ch required number of sts (ch 1 shown), working behind tr just made, tr in first skipped st.

Y-STITCH (Y-ST)

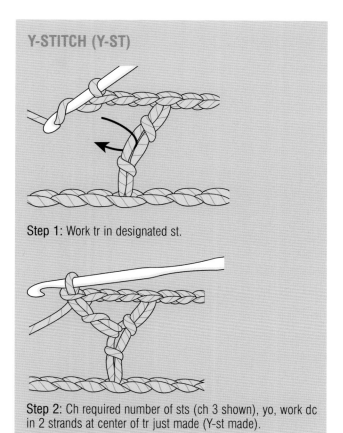

Step 1: Work tr in designated st.

Step 2: Ch required number of sts (ch 3 shown), yo, work dc in 2 strands at center of tr just made (Y-st made).

V-STITCH (V-ST), OR SHELL
A designated number of stitches (frequently worked with double crochet stitches) worked in same stitch (shown for 4-dc shell). V-sts are comprised of 2 dc (with or without a ch space). Shells can be made with 3 or more dc (with or without ch spaces).

Work 4 dc in designated st (shell made).

X-STITCH (X-ST)
Shown for tr X-st.

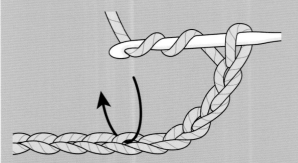

Make a chain of desired length.
Step 1: Yo twice, insert hook in designated st (6th ch from hook for first X-st), yo, draw yarn through st.

Step 2: Yo, draw yarn through 2 loops on hook (3 loops remain on hook), yo, skip designated number of sts (skip 2 ch shown), insert hook in next st, yo, draw yarn through st (5 loops on hook).

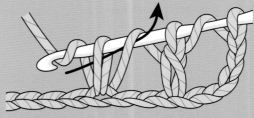

Step 3: Yo, draw yarn through 2 loops on hook (4 loops remain on hook).

Step 4: Yo, draw yarn through 2 loops on hook three times (1 loop remains on hook) (inverted Y shape made).

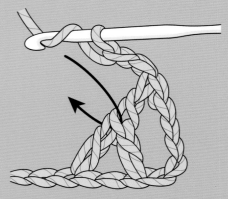

Step 5: Ch required number of sts (ch 2 shown), yo, insert hook in 2 strands at center of "cluster" just made, yo, draw yarn through st (3 loops on hook).

Step 6: Yo, draw yarn through 2 loops on hook (twice) (X-st made).

FRONT POST DOUBLE CROCHET (FPDC)
Stitch is raised to front side of work.

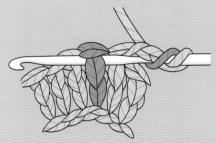

Step 1: Yo, insert hook from front to back to front again, around the post of next designated st.

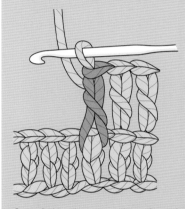

Step 2: Yo, draw yarn through st, (yo, draw yarn through 2 loops on hook) twice (FPdc made).

BACK POST DOUBLE CROCHET (BPDC)
Stitch is raised to back side of work.

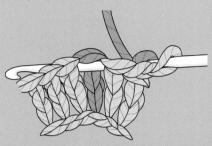

Step 1: Yo, insert hook from back to front to back again, around the post of next designated st.

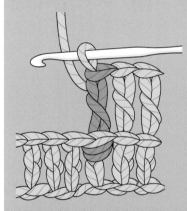

Step 2: Yo, draw yarn through st, (yo, draw yarn through 2 loops on hook) twice (BPdc made).

■ International Crochet Symbols ■

chain stitch (ch)	⬯	⬯⬯⬯⬯⬯
slip stitch (sl st)	•	• • • • •
single crochet (sc)	X	X X X X X
half double crochet (hdc)	T	T T T T T
double crochet (dc)	Ŧ	Ŧ Ŧ Ŧ Ŧ Ŧ
treble crochet (tr)	ŧ	ŧ ŧ ŧ ŧ ŧ
front Post double crochet (FPdc)	∫	∫ ∫ ∫ ∫ ∫
back Post double crochet (BPdc)	∫	∫ ∫ ∫ ∫ ∫
picot	⌒	⌒ ⌒ ⌒ ⌒ ⌒
3-dc popcorn (pop)	⬯	⬯ ⬯ ⬯ ⬯ ⬯
4-dc popcorn (pop)	⬯	⬯ ⬯ ⬯ ⬯ ⬯
5-dc popcorn (pop)	⬯	⬯ ⬯ ⬯ ⬯ ⬯
2-looped bobble	⬭	⬭ ⬭ ⬭ ⬭ ⬭
3-looped bobble	⬭	⬭ ⬭ ⬭ ⬭ ⬭
4-looped bobble	⬭	⬭ ⬭ ⬭ ⬭ ⬭
5-looped bobble	⬭	⬭ ⬭ ⬭ ⬭ ⬭
2-dc puff st	⬭	⬭ ⬭ ⬭ ⬭ ⬭
3-dc puff st	⬭	⬭ ⬭ ⬭ ⬭ ⬭

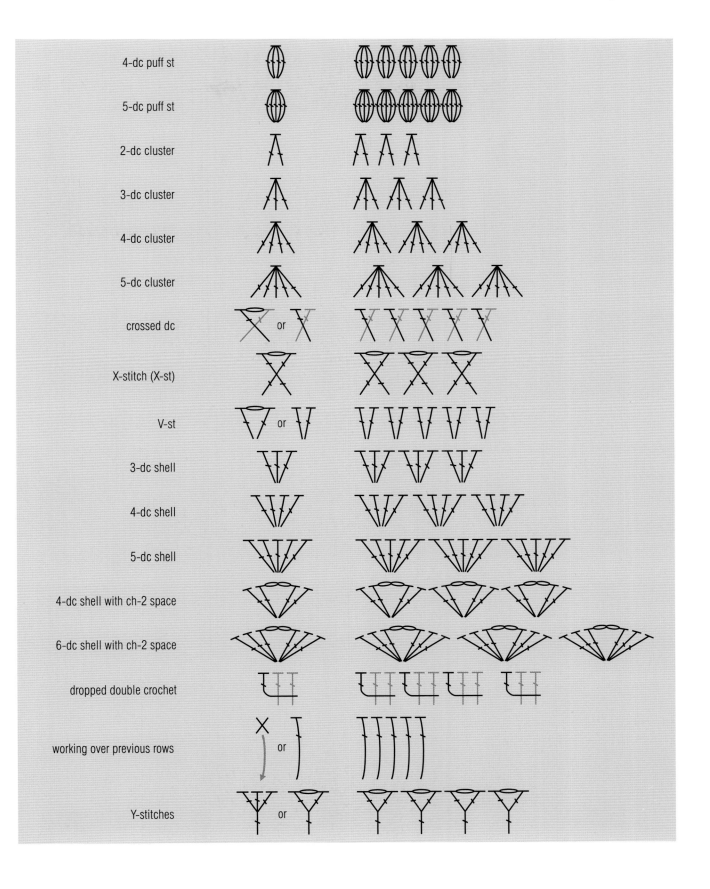

4-dc puff st

5-dc puff st

2-dc cluster

3-dc cluster

4-dc cluster

5-dc cluster

crossed dc

X-stitch (X-st)

V-st

3-dc shell

4-dc shell

5-dc shell

4-dc shell with ch-2 space

6-dc shell with ch-2 space

dropped double crochet

working over previous rows

Y-stitches

■ Pictorial Index ■

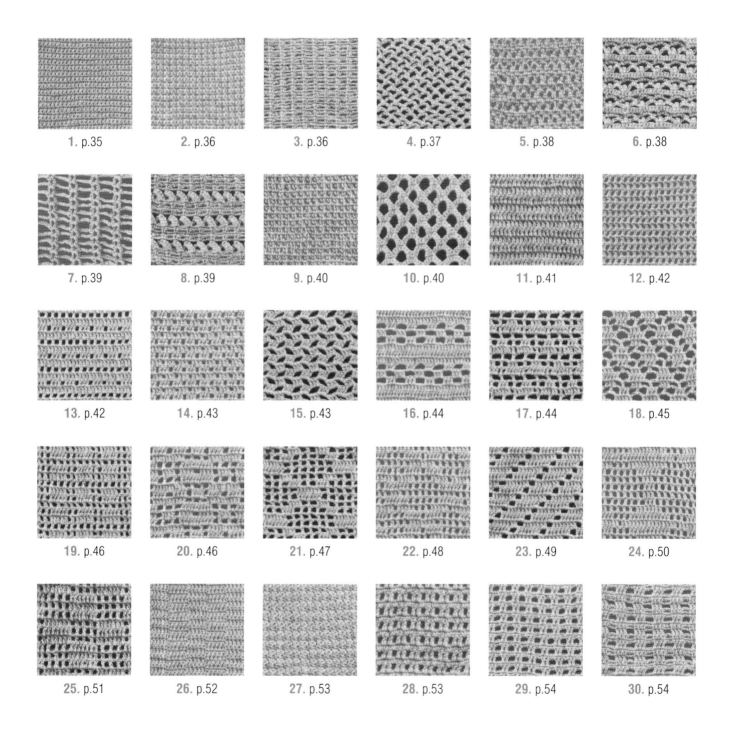

1. p.35   2. p.36   3. p.36   4. p.37   5. p.38   6. p.38

7. p.39   8. p.39   9. p.40   10. p.40   11. p.41   12. p.42

13. p.42   14. p.43   15. p.43   16. p.44   17. p.44   18. p.45

19. p.46   20. p.46   21. p.47   22. p.48   23. p.49   24. p.50

25. p.51   26. p.52   27. p.53   28. p.53   29. p.54   30. p.54

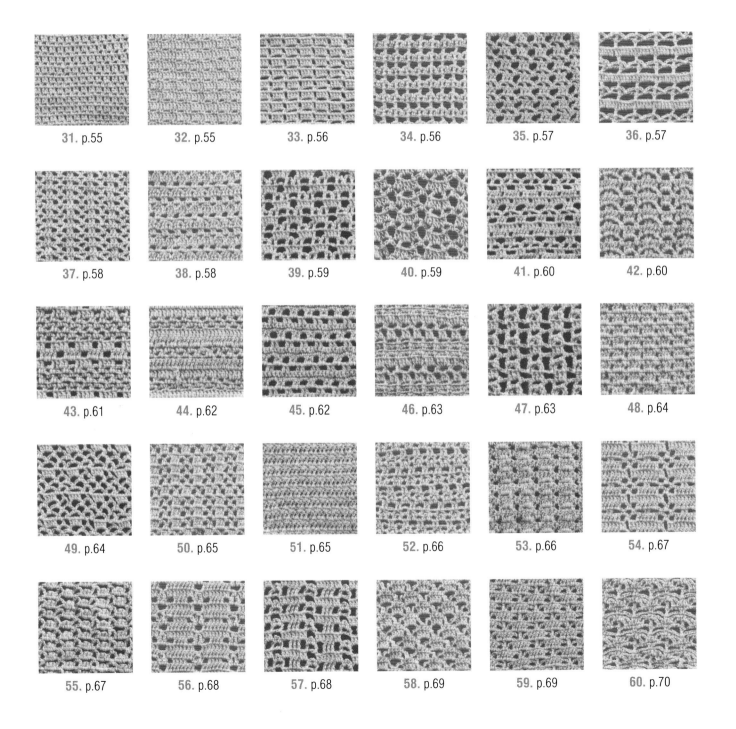

31. p.55   32. p.55   33. p.56   34. p.56   35. p.57   36. p.57

37. p.58   38. p.58   39. p.59   40. p.59   41. p.60   42. p.60

43. p.61   44. p.62   45. p.62   46. p.63   47. p.63   48. p.64

49. p.64   50. p.65   51. p.65   52. p.66   53. p.66   54. p.67

55. p.67   56. p.68   57. p.68   58. p.69   59. p.69   60. p.70

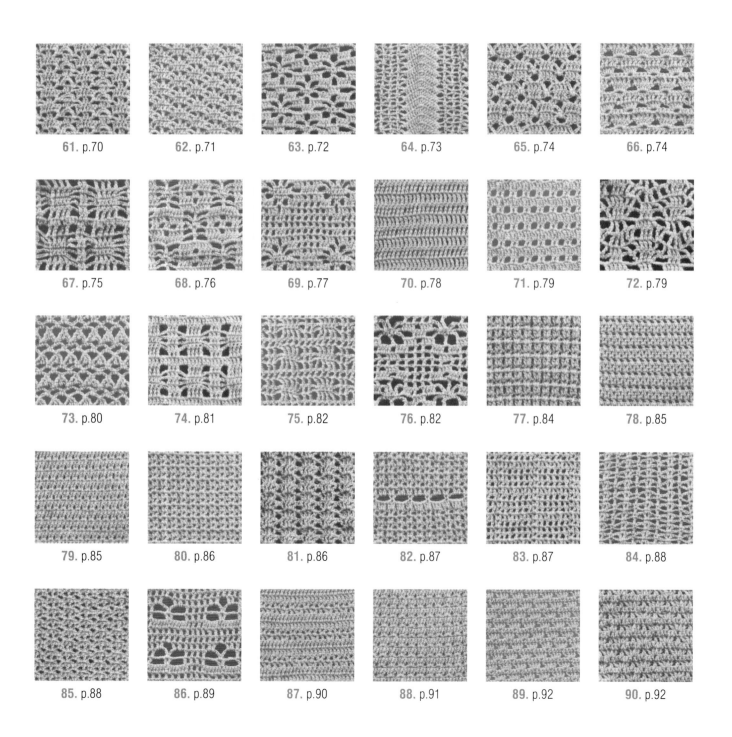

61. p.70 **62.** p.71 **63.** p.72 **64.** p.73 **65.** p.74 **66.** p.74

67. p.75 **68.** p.76 **69.** p.77 **70.** p.78 **71.** p.79 **72.** p.79

73. p.80 **74.** p.81 **75.** p.82 **76.** p.82 **77.** p.84 **78.** p.85

79. p.85 **80.** p.86 **81.** p.86 **82.** p.87 **83.** p.87 **84.** p.88

85. p.88 **86.** p.89 **87.** p.90 **88.** p.91 **89.** p.92 **90.** p.92

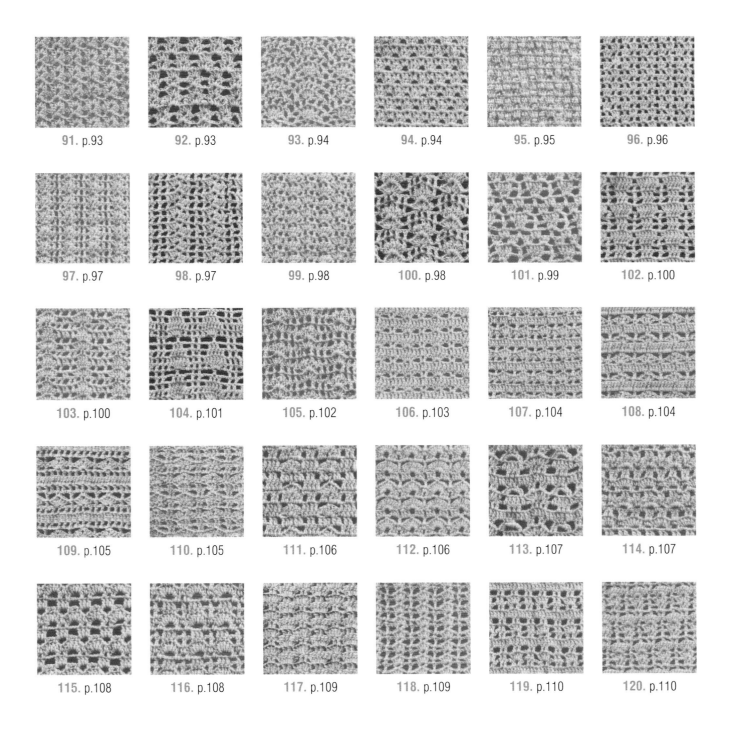

91. p.93   **92.** p.93   **93.** p.94   **94.** p.94   **95.** p.95   **96.** p.96

97. p.97   **98.** p.97   **99.** p.98   **100.** p.98   **101.** p.99   **102.** p.100

103. p.100   **104.** p.101   **105.** p.102   **106.** p.103   **107.** p.104   **108.** p.104

109. p.105   **110.** p.105   **111.** p.106   **112.** p.106   **113.** p.107   **114.** p.107

115. p.108   **116.** p.108   **117.** p.109   **118.** p.109   **119.** p.110   **120.** p.110

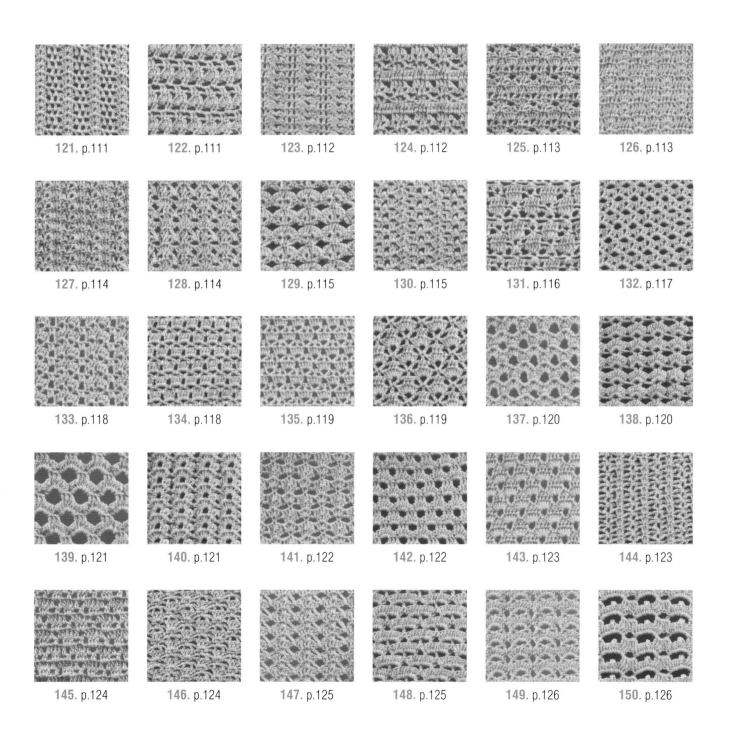

121. p.111 122. p.111 123. p.112 124. p.112 125. p.113 126. p.113

127. p.114 128. p.114 129. p.115 130. p.115 131. p.116 132. p.117

133. p.118 134. p.118 135. p.119 136. p.119 137. p.120 138. p.120

139. p.121 140. p.121 141. p.122 142. p.122 143. p.123 144. p.123

145. p.124 146. p.124 147. p.125 148. p.125 149. p.126 150. p.126

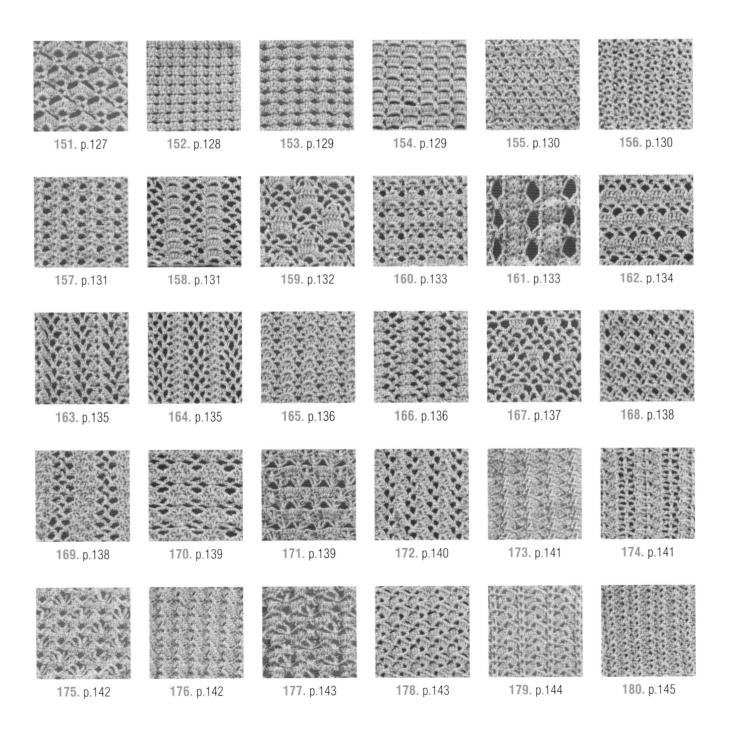

151. p.127   152. p.128   153. p.129   154. p.129   155. p.130   156. p.130

157. p.131   158. p.131   159. p.132   160. p.133   161. p.133   162. p.134

163. p.135   164. p.135   165. p.136   166. p.136   167. p.137   168. p.138

169. p.138   170. p.139   171. p.139   172. p.140   173. p.141   174. p.141

175. p.142   176. p.142   177. p.143   178. p.143   179. p.144   180. p.145

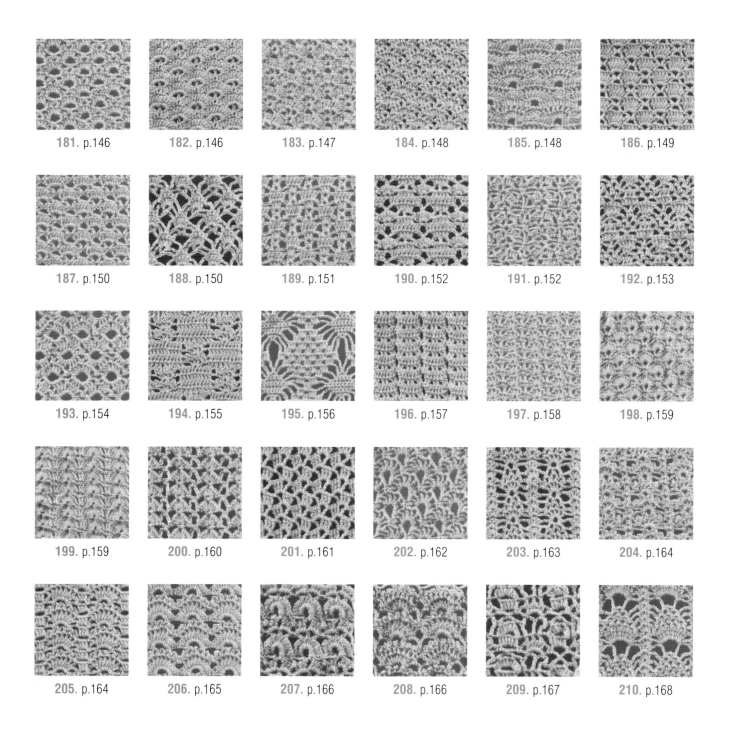

181. p.146   182. p.146   183. p.147   184. p.148   185. p.148   186. p.149

187. p.150   188. p.150   189. p.151   190. p.152   191. p.152   192. p.153

193. p.154   194. p.155   195. p.156   196. p.157   197. p.158   198. p.159

199. p.159   200. p.160   201. p.161   202. p.162   203. p.163   204. p.164

205. p.164   206. p.165   207. p.166   208. p.166   209. p.167   210. p.168

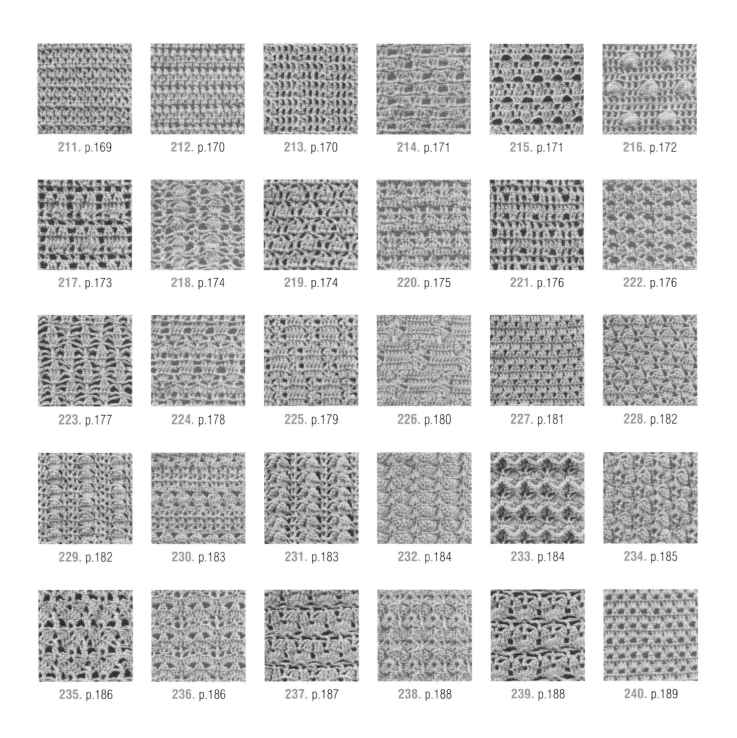

211. p.169 212. p.170 213. p.170 214. p.171 215. p.171 216. p.172

217. p.173 218. p.174 219. p.174 220. p.175 221. p.176 222. p.176

223. p.177 224. p.178 225. p.179 226. p.180 227. p.181 228. p.182

229. p.182 230. p.183 231. p.183 232. p.184 233. p.184 234. p.185

235. p.186 236. p.186 237. p.187 238. p.188 239. p.188 240. p.189

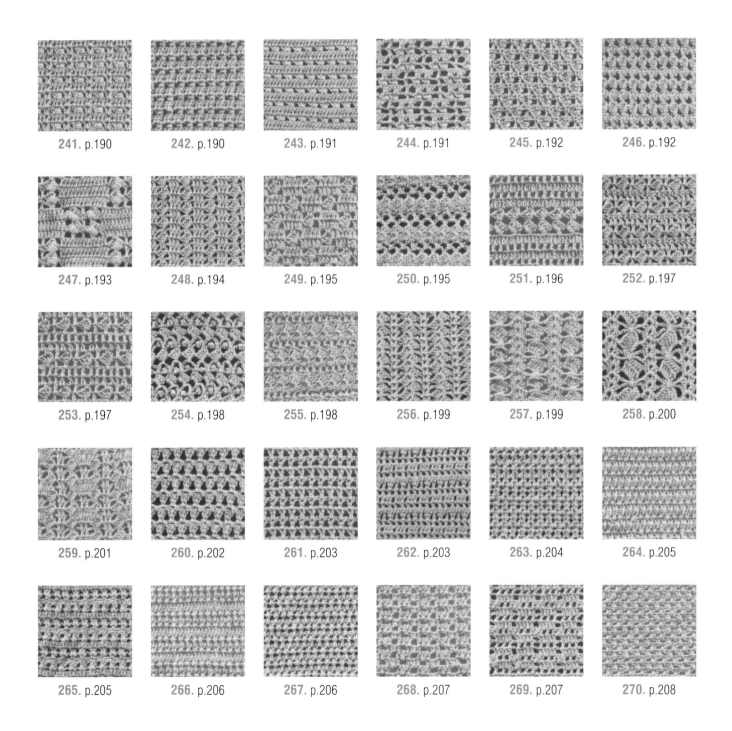

241. p.190

242. p.190

243. p.191

244. p.191

245. p.192

246. p.192

247. p.193

248. p.194

249. p.195

250. p.195

251. p.196

252. p.197

253. p.197

254. p.198

255. p.198

256. p.199

257. p.199

258. p.200

259. p.201

260. p.202

261. p.203

262. p.203

263. p.204

264. p.205

265. p.205

266. p.206

267. p.206

268. p.207

269. p.207

270. p.208

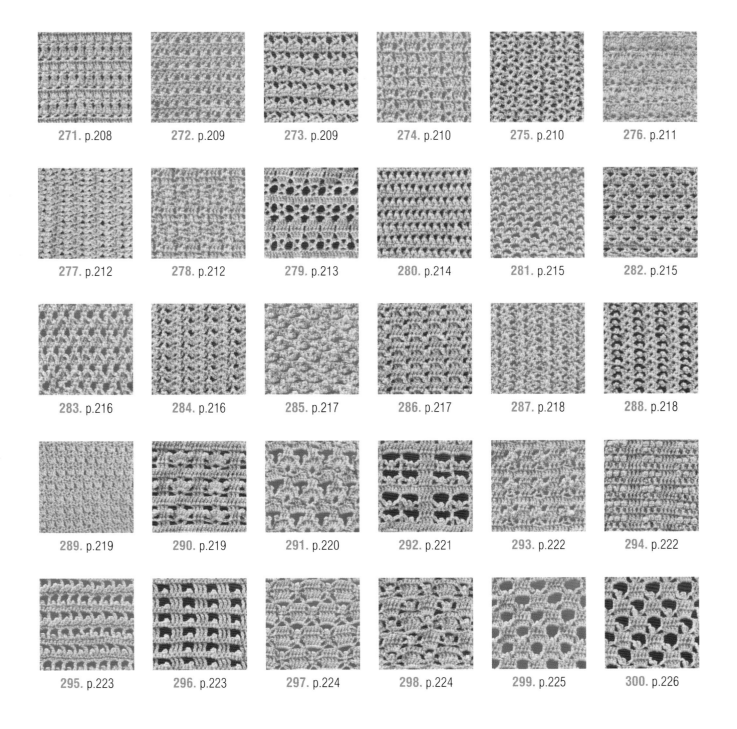

271. p.208 272. p.209 273. p.209 274. p.210 275. p.210 276. p.211

277. p.212 278. p.212 279. p.213 280. p.214 281. p.215 282. p.215

283. p.216 284. p.216 285. p.217 286. p.217 287. p.218 288. p.218

289. p.219 290. p.219 291. p.220 292. p.221 293. p.222 294. p.222

295. p.223 296. p.223 297. p.224 298. p.224 299. p.225 300. p.226

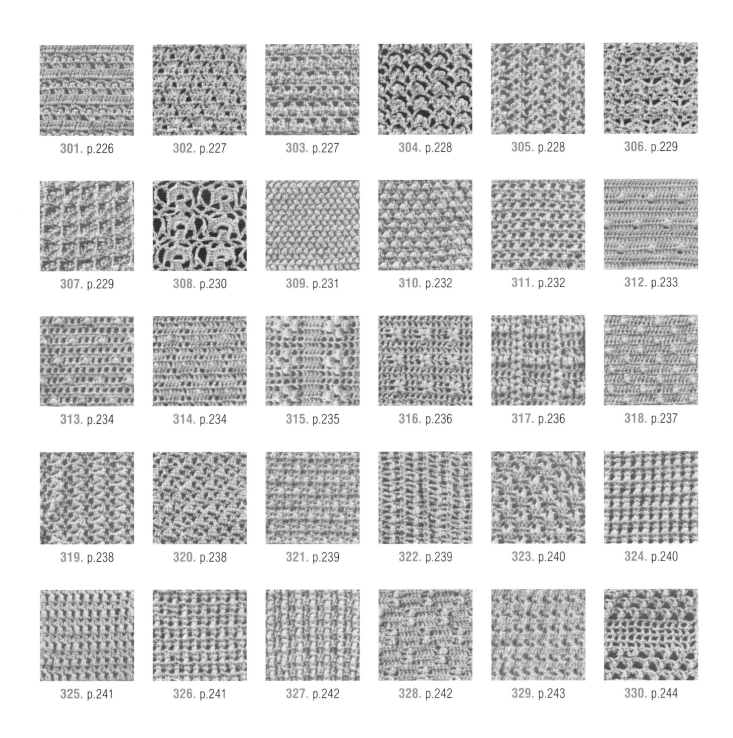

301. p.226   302. p.227   303. p.227   304. p.228   305. p.228   306. p.229

307. p.229   308. p.230   309. p.231   310. p.232   311. p.232   312. p.233

313. p.234   314. p.234   315. p.235   316. p.236   317. p.236   318. p.237

319. p.238   320. p.238   321. p.239   322. p.239   323. p.240   324. p.240

325. p.241   326. p.241   327. p.242   328. p.242   329. p.243   330. p.244

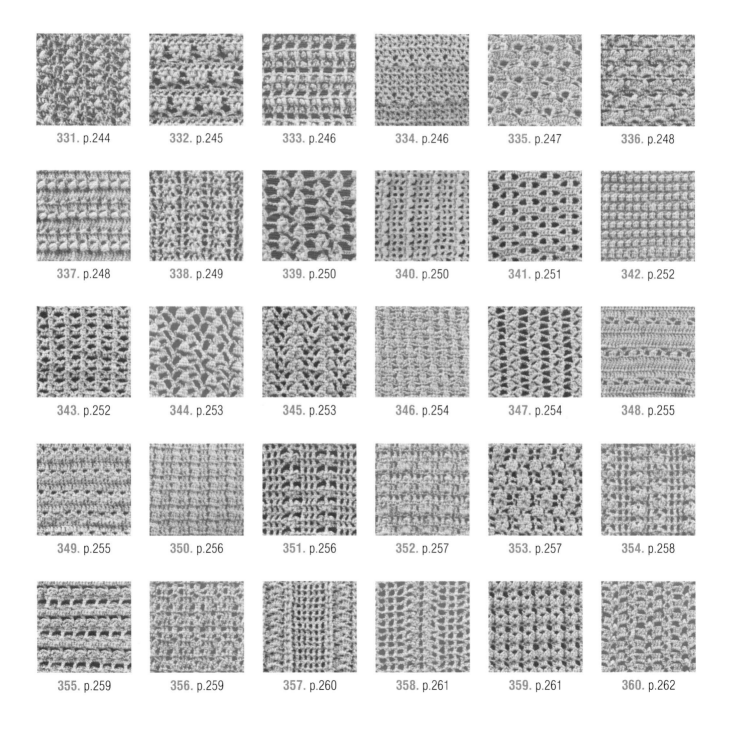

331. p.244

332. p.245

333. p.246

334. p.246

335. p.247

336. p.248

337. p.248

338. p.249

339. p.250

340. p.250

341. p.251

342. p.252

343. p.252

344. p.253

345. p.253

346. p.254

347. p.254

348. p.255

349. p.255

350. p.256

351. p.256

352. p.257

353. p.257

354. p.258

355. p.259

356. p.259

357. p.260

358. p.261

359. p.261

360. p.262

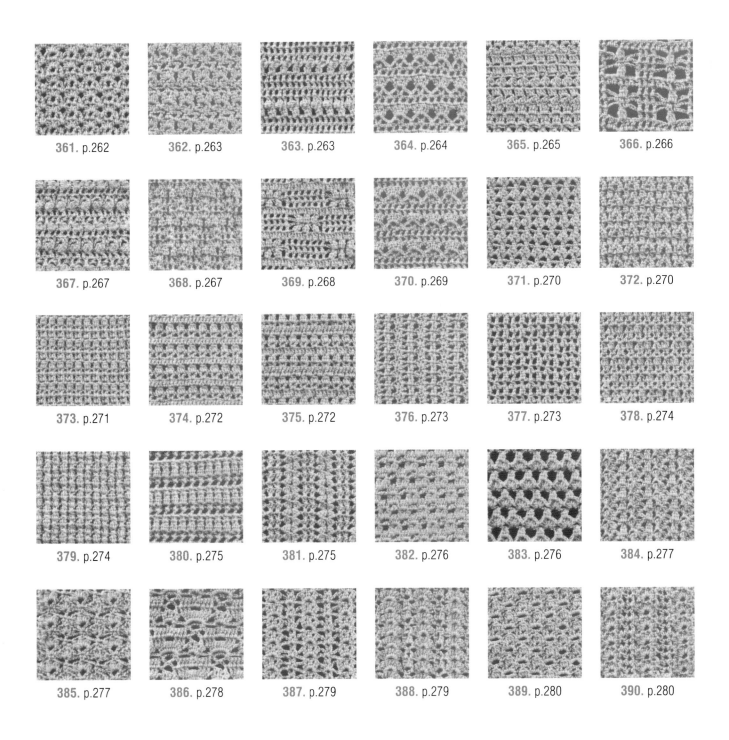

361. p.262 **362**. p.263 **363**. p.263 **364**. p.264 **365**. p.265 **366**. p.266

367. p.267 **368**. p.267 **369**. p.268 **370**. p.269 **371**. p.270 **372**. p.270

373. p.271 **374**. p.272 **375**. p.272 **376**. p.273 **377**. p.273 **378**. p.274

379. p.274 **380**. p.275 **381**. p.275 **382**. p.276 **383**. p.276 **384**. p.277

385. p.277 **386**. p.278 **387**. p.279 **388**. p.279 **389**. p.280 **390**. p.280

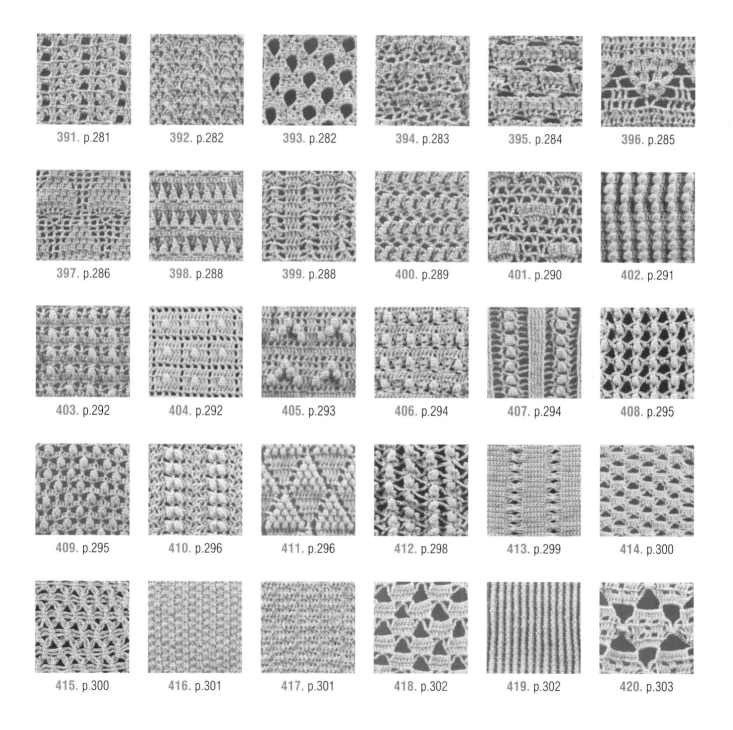

391. p.281

392. p.282

393. p.282

394. p.283

395. p.284

396. p.285

397. p.286

398. p.288

399. p.288

400. p.289

401. p.290

402. p.291

403. p.292

404. p.292

405. p.293

406. p.294

407. p.294

408. p.295

409. p.295

410. p.296

411. p.296

412. p.298

413. p.299

414. p.300

415. p.300

416. p.301

417. p.301

418. p.302

419. p.302

420. p.303

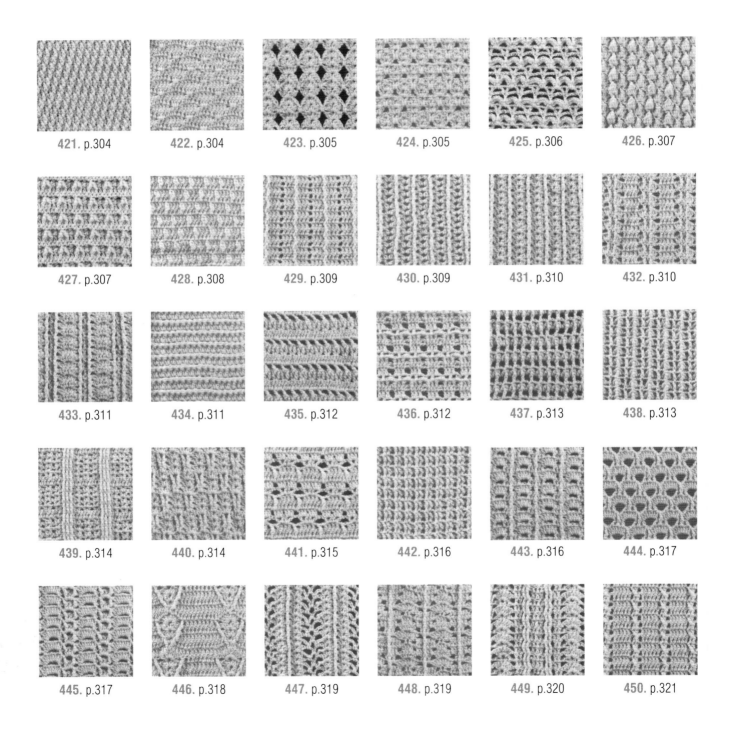

421. p.304

422. p.304

423. p.305

424. p.305

425. p.306

426. p.307

427. p.307

428. p.308

429. p.309

430. p.309

431. p.310

432. p.310

433. p.311

434. p.311

435. p.312

436. p.312

437. p.313

438. p.313

439. p.314

440. p.314

441. p.315

442. p.316

443. p.316

444. p.317

445. p.317

446. p.318

447. p.319

448. p.319

449. p.320

450. p.321

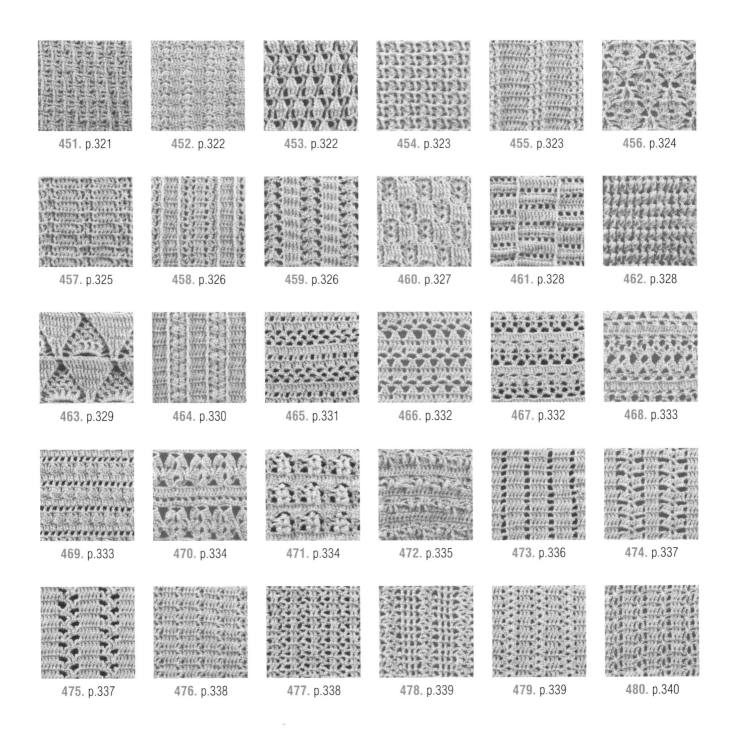

451. p.321 452. p.322 453. p.322 454. p.323 455. p.323 456. p.324

457. p.325 458. p.326 459. p.326 460. p.327 461. p.328 462. p.328

463. p.329 464. p.330 465. p.331 466. p.332 467. p.332 468. p.333

469. p.333 470. p.334 471. p.334 472. p.335 473. p.336 474. p.337

475. p.337 476. p.338 477. p.338 478. p.339 479. p.339 480. p.340

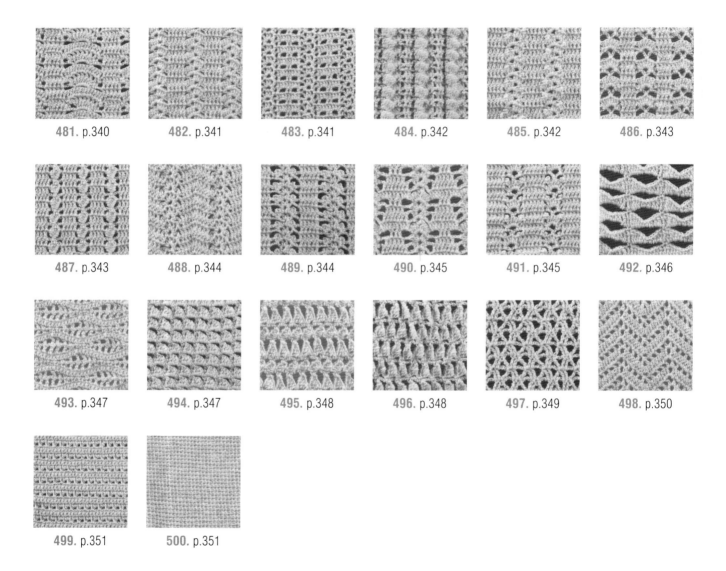

481. p.340   **482.** p.341   **483.** p.341   **484.** p.342   **485.** p.342   **486.** p.343

487. p.343   **488.** p.344   **489.** p.344   **490.** p.345   **491.** p.345   **492.** p.346

493. p.347   **494.** p.347   **495.** p.348   **496.** p.348   **497.** p.349   **498.** p.350

499. p.351   **500.** p.351

.1.
Single Crochet

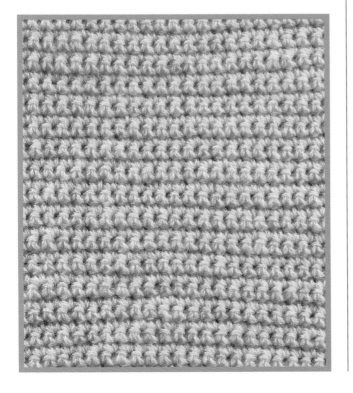

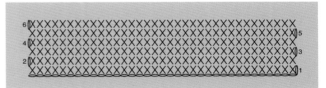

Chain any multiple plus 1.

Row 1: Sc in 2nd ch from hook, turn.

Row 2: Ch 1, sc in each sc across, turn.

Rep Row 2 for pattern.

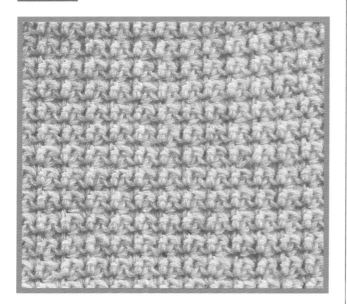

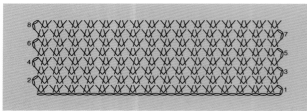

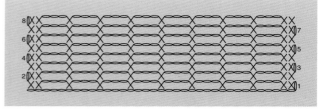

Chain multiples of 2.

Row 1: 2 sc in 4th ch from hook, *skip next ch, 2 sc in next ch; rep from * across, turn.

Row 2: Ch 2, skip first sc, 2 sc in next sc, *skip next sc, 2 sc in next sc; rep from * across, turn.

Rep Row 2 for pattern.

Chain multiples of 4.

Row 1: Sc in 2nd ch from hook, sc in next ch, *ch 3, skip next 3 ch, sc in next ch; rep from * across to within last ch, sc in last ch, turn.

Row 2: Ch 1, sc in first 2 sc, *ch 3, skip next ch-3 space, sc in next sc; rep from * across to within last ch, sc in last sc, turn.

Rep Row 2 for pattern.

.2.

Single Crochet & Chains

4

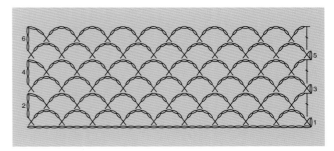

Chain multiples of 4 plus 2.

Row 1: Sc in 2nd ch from hook, *ch 5, skip next 3 ch, sc in next ch; rep from * across, turn.

Row 2: Ch 5 (counts as dc, ch 2), (sc, ch 5) in each ch-5 loop across to within last ch-5 loop, sc in next ch-5 loop, ch 2, dc in last sc, turn.

Row 3: Ch 1, sc in first dc, (ch 5, sc) in each ch-5 loop across, ending with sc in 3rd ch of turning ch, turn.

Rep Rows 2-3 for pattern.

5

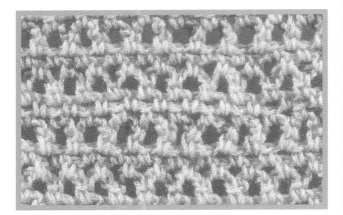

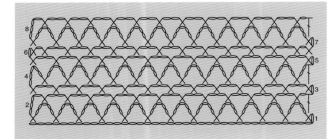

Chain multiples of 3 plus 2.

Row 1: Sc in 2nd ch from hook, *ch 5, skip next 2 ch, sc in next ch; rep from * across, turn.

Row 2: Ch 4 (counts as dc, ch 1), (sc, ch 2) in each ch-5 loop across to within last ch-5 loop, sc in next ch-5 loop, ch 1, dc in last sc, turn.

Row 3: Ch 1, sc in first dc, skip next ch-1 space, (ch 2, sc) in each ch-5 loop across, ending with last sc in 3rd ch of turning ch, turn.

Row 4: Ch 5 (counts as dc, ch 2), sc in first ch-2 space, (ch 5, sc) in each ch-2 space across to last ch-2 space, ch 2, dc in last sc, turn.

Row 5: Ch 1, sc in first dc, (ch 2, sc) in each ch-5 loop across, ending with last sc in 3rd ch of turning ch, turn.

Row 6: Ch 1, sc in first sc, ch 1, sc in next ch-2 space, (ch 2, sc) in each ch-2 space across to last ch-2 space, ch 1, sc in last sc, turn.

Row 7: Ch 1, sc in first sc, skip next ch-1 space, (ch 5, sc) in each ch-2 space across to last ch-2 space, ch 5, skip next ch-1 space, sc in last sc, turn.

Rep Rows 2-7 for pattern.

6

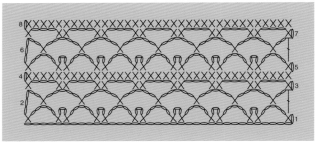

Chain multiples of 5 plus 1.

Row 1: Sc in 2nd ch from hook, *ch 5, skip next 3 ch, sc in next ch, ch 3, sc in next ch; rep from * across to within last 4 ch, ch 5, skip next 3 ch, sc in last ch, turn.

Row 2: Ch 5 (counts as dc, ch 2), sc in next ch-5 loop, *ch 5, skip next ch-3 loop, sc in next ch-5 loop; rep from * across to last ch-5 loop, ch 2, dc in last sc, turn.

Row 3: Ch 1, sc in first dc, (ch 3, 2 sc) in each ch-5 loop across to last ch-5 loop, ch 3, sc in 3rd ch of turning ch, turn.

Row 4: Ch 1, sc in first sc, *3 sc in next ch-3 loop, sc in each of next 2 sc; rep from * across, ending with sc in last sc, turn.

Row 5: Ch 1, sc in first sc, *ch 5, skip next 3 sc, sc in next sc**, ch 3, sc in next sc; rep from * across, ending last rep at **, turn.

Rep Rows 2-5 for pattern.

7

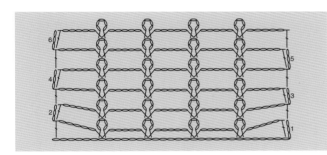

Chain multiples of 6 plus 4.

Row 1: Dc in 4th ch from hook, *ch 5, skip next 5 ch (sc, ch 5, sc) in next ch; rep from * across to within last 6 ch, ch 5, skip next 5 ch, dc in last ch, turn.

Row 2: Ch 3, dc in first dc, *ch 5, skip next ch-5 loop, (sc, ch 5, sc) in next ch-5 loop; rep from * across to last (sc, ch 5, sc) loop, ch 5, skip next ch-5 loop, skip next dc, dc in 3rd ch of turning ch, turn.

Rep Row 2 for pattern.

8

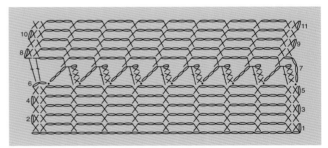

Chain multiples of 4.

Row 1: Sc in 2nd ch from hook, sc in next ch, *ch 3, skip next 3 ch, sc in next ch; rep from * across to within last ch, sc in last ch, turn.

Row 2: Ch 1, sc in first 2 sc, *ch 3, skip next ch-3 loop, sc in next sc; rep from * across to within last sc, sc in last sc, turn.

Rows 3-5: Rep row 2.

Row 6: Ch 2, skip first 2 sc, sl st in next ch-3 loop, *ch 3, dc in next sc, ch 1, work 3 sc around the post of last dc made, sl st in next ch-3 loop; rep from * across to last ch-3 loop, ch 3, dc in next sc, work 3 sc around the post of last dc made, sl st in last sc, turn.

Row 7: Ch 4, *sc in next ch-3 loop, ch 3; rep from * across to last ch-3 loop, 2 dc in last ch-2 space, turn.

Row 8: Ch 1, sc in each of first 2 dc, *ch 3, skip next ch-3 space, sc in next sc; rep from * across, sc in last ch-4 space, turn.

Rep Rows 3-8 for pattern.

9

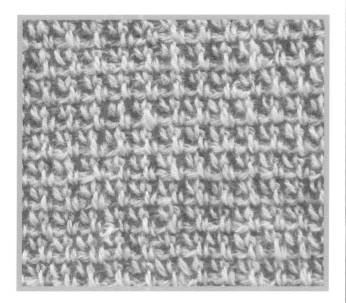

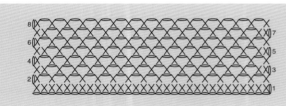

Chain multiples of 2.

Row 1: Sc in 2nd ch from hook, sc in each ch across, turn.

Row 2: Ch 1, sc in first sc, *ch 1, skip next sc, sc in next sc; rep from * across, turn.

Row 3: Ch 1, sc in first sc, sc in next ch-1 space, (ch 1, sc) in each ch-1 space across to last ch-1 space, sc in last sc, turn.

Rep Rows 2-3 for pattern.

10

Chain multiples of 6 plus 2.

Row 1: Sc in 2nd ch from hook, *ch 6, skip next 5 ch, sc in next ch; rep from * across, turn.

Row 2: Ch 1, sc in first sc, *7 sc in next ch-6 loop, sc in next sc; rep from * across, turn.

Row 3: Ch 7 (counts as tr, ch 3), skip in first sc, skip next 2 sc, sc in each of next 3 sc, *ch 6, skip next 5 sc, sc in each of next 3 sc; rep from * across to within last 3 sc, ch 3, skip next 2 sc, tr in last sc, turn.

Row 4: Ch 1, sc in first tr, 3 sc in next ch-3 loop, skip next sc, sc in next sc, skip next sc, *7 sc in next ch-6 loop, skip next sc, sc in next sc, skip next sc; rep from * across to ch-7 turning ch, 3 sc in ch-3 loop of turning ch, sc in 4th ch of turning ch, turn.

Row 5: Ch 1, sc in first 2 sc, *ch 6, skip next 5 sc, sc in each of next 3 sc; rep from * across, ending with sc in each of last 2 sc, turn.

Row 6: Ch 1, sc in first sc, *skip next sc, work 7 sc in next ch-6 loop, skip next sc, sc in next sc; rep from * across, turn.

Rep Rows 3-6 for pattern.

.3.
Double Crochet & Chains

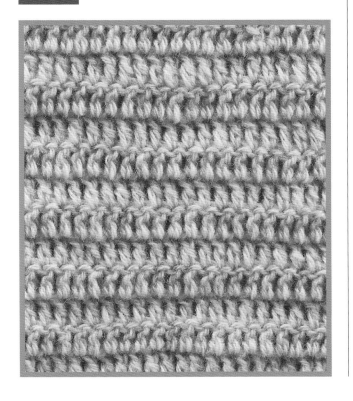

11

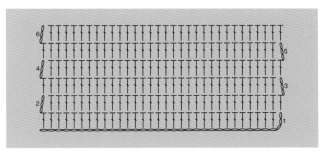

Chain any multiple plus 3.

Row 1: Dc in 4th ch from hook, dc in each ch across, turn.

Row 2: Ch 3 (counts as dc), skip first dc, dc in each dc across, ending with dc in 3rd ch of turning ch, turn.

Rep Row 2 for pattern.

12

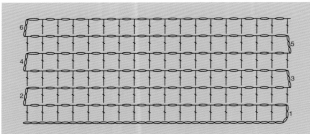

Chain multiples of 2.

Row 1: Dc in 6th ch from hook, *ch 1, skip next ch, dc in next ch; rep from * across, turn.

Row 2: Ch 4 (counts as dc, ch 1), skip next ch-1 space, dc in next dc, *ch 1, skip next ch-1 space, dc in next dc; rep from * across, ending with dc in 3rd ch of turning ch, turn.

Rep Row 2 for pattern.

13

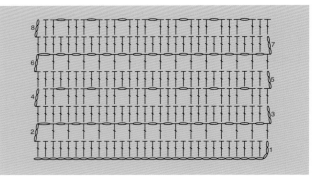

Chain multiples of 4 plus 1.

Row 1: Dc in 4th ch from hook, dc in each ch across, turn.

Row 2: Ch 4 (counts as dc, ch 1), skip next dc, dc in next dc, *ch 1, skip next dc, dc in next dc; rep from * across, ending with dc in 3rd ch of turning ch, turn.

Row 3: Ch 3 (counts as dc), *dc in next ch-1 space, dc in next dc; rep from * across, ending with dc in 3rd ch of turning ch, turn.

Row 4: Ch 3 (counts as dc), skip first dc, dc in each of next 2 dc, *ch 1, skip next dc, dc in each of next 3 dc; rep from * across, ending with last dc in 3rd ch of turning ch, turn.

Row 5: Ch 3 (counts as dc), skip first dc, dc in each of next 2 dc, *dc in next ch-1 space, dc in each of next 3 dc; rep from * across, ending with dc in 3rd ch of turning ch, turn.

Rep Rows 2-5 for pattern.

14

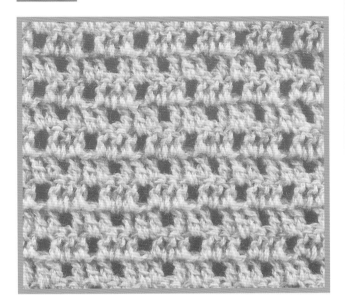

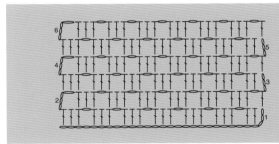

Chain multiples of 4 plus 1.

Row 1: Dc in 4th ch from hook, dc in next ch, *ch 1, skip next ch, dc in each of next 3 ch; rep from * across, turn.

Row 2: Ch 4 (counts as dc, ch 1), skip first dc, skip next dc, *dc in next dc, dc in next ch-1 space, dc in next dc, ch 1, skip next dc; rep from * across to within last st, dc in 3rd ch of turning ch, turn.

Row 3: Ch 3 (counts as dc), *dc in next ch-1 space, dc in next dc, ch 1, skip next dc, dc in next dc; rep from * across to turning ch, dc in next ch-1 space of turning ch, dc in 3rd ch of turning ch, turn.

Rep Rows 2-3 for pattern.

15

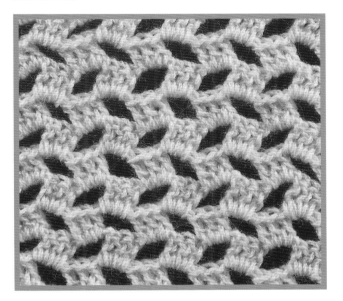

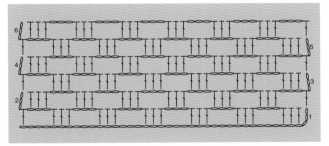

Chain multiples of 6 plus 4.

Row 1: Dc in 4th ch from hook, dc in each of next 2 ch, *ch 3, skip next 3 ch, dc in each of next 3 ch; rep from * across to within last 4 ch, ch 3, skip next 3 ch, dc in last ch, turn.

Row 2: Ch 3 (counts as dc), skip first dc, *3 dc in next ch-3 loop, ch 3; rep from * across to last ch-3 loop, dc in 3rd ch of turning ch, turn.

Rep Row 2 for pattern.

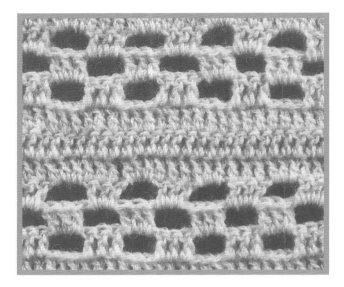

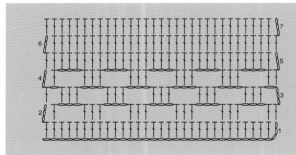

Rows 6-7: Ch 3 (counts as dc), skip first dc, dc in each dc across, ending with dc in 3rd ch of turning ch, turn.

Rep Rows 2-7 for pattern.

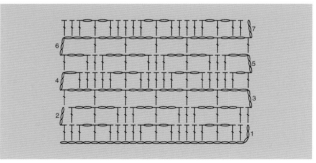

Chain multiples of 6 plus 3.

Row 1: Dc in 4th ch from hook, dc in each ch across, turn.

Row 2: Ch 3 (counts as dc), skip first dc, dc in next dc, *ch 3, skip next 3 dc, dc in each of next 3 dc; rep from * across to within last 5 sts, ch 3, skip next 3 dc, dc in next dc, dc in 3rd ch of turning ch, turn.

Row 3: Ch 4 (counts as dc, ch 1), 3 dc in next ch-3 loop, *ch 3, 3 dc in next ch-3 loop; rep from * across to last ch-3 loop, ch 1, dc in 3rd ch of turning ch, turn.

Row 4: Ch 3 (counts as dc), dc in next ch-1 space, *ch 3, 3 dc in next ch-3 loop; rep from * across to last ch-3 loop, ch 3, skip next 3 dc, dc in ch-1 space of turning ch, dc in 3rd ch of turning ch, turn.

Row 5: Ch 3 (counts as dc), skip first dc, dc in next dc, * 3 dc in next ch-3 loop, dc in each of next 3 dc; rep from * across to last ch-3 loop, ending with dc in last dc, dc in 3rd ch of turning ch, turn.

Chain multiples of 8 plus 3.

Row 1: Dc in 4th ch from hook, dc in next ch, *ch 1, skip next ch, dc in next ch, ch 1, skip next ch, dc in each of next 5 ch; rep from * across, ending with dc in each of last 3 ch, turn.

Row 2: Ch 3 (counts as dc), skip first dc, dc in next dc, ch 2, skip next ch-1 space, dc in next dc, ch 2, skip next dc, *dc in each of next 3 dc, ch 2, skip next ch-1 space, dc in next dc, ch 2, skip next dc; rep from * across to last 2 sts, dc in next dc, dc in 3rd ch of turning ch, turn.

Row 3: Ch 6 (counts as dc, ch 3), skip first dc, *ch 3, skip next 3 sts, dc in next dc; rep from * across, ending with dc in 3rd ch of turning ch, turn.

Row 4: Ch 4 (counts as dc, ch 1), *2 dc in next ch-3 loop, dc in next dc, 2 dc in next ch-3 loop, ch 1**, dc in next dc, ch 1; rep from * across, ending last rep at **, dc in 3rd ch of turning ch, turn.

Row 5: Ch 5 (counts as dc, ch 2), skip first dc, *skip next dc, dc in each of next 3 dc, ch 2, skip next ch-1 space**, dc in next dc, ch 2; rep from * across, ending last rep at **, dc in 3rd ch of turning ch, turn.

Row 6: Rep Row 3.

Row 7: Ch 3 (counts as dc), 2 dc in next ch-3 loop, *ch 1, dc in next dc, ch 1, 2 dc in next ch-3 loop, dc in next dc, 2 dc in next ch-3 loop; rep from * across, ending with dc in 3rd ch of turning ch, turn.

Rep Rows 2-7 for pattern.

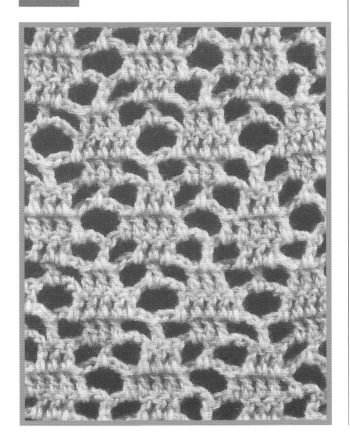

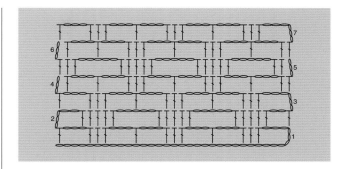

Chain multiples of 10 plus 6.

Row 1: Dc in 10th ch from hook, dc in each of next 2 ch, *ch 3, skip next 3 ch, dc in next ch**, ch 3, skip next 3 ch, dc in each of next 3 ch; rep from * across, ending last rep at **, turn.

Row 2: Ch 5 (counts as dc, ch 2), dc in next ch-3 loop, dc in each of next 3 dc, dc in next ch-3 loop, *ch 5, dc in next ch-3 loop, dc in each of next 3 dc, dc in next ch-3 loop; rep from * across to last ch-3 loop, ch 2, dc in 3rd ch of turning ch, turn.

Row 3: Ch 6 (counts as dc, ch 3), skip next dc, dc in each of next 3 dc, ch 3, *dc in next ch-5 loop, ch 3, skip next dc, dc in each of next 3 dc, ch 3; rep from * across, ending with dc in 3rd ch of turning ch, turn.

Row 4: Ch 3 (counts as dc), dc in next ch-3 loop, ch 3, skip next dc, dc in next dc, ch 3, dc in next ch-3 loop, *dc in next dc, dc in next ch-3 loop, ch 3, skip next dc, dc in next dc, ch 3, dc in next ch-3 loop; rep from * across, dc in 3rd ch of turning ch, turn.

Row 5: Ch 3 (counts as dc), skip first dc, dc in next dc, dc in next ch-3 loop, ch 5, *dc in next ch-3 loop, dc in each of next 3 dc, dc in next ch-3 loop, ch 5; rep from * across to within last ch-3 loop, dc in next ch-3 loop, dc in next dc, dc in 3rd ch of turning ch, turn.

Row 6: Ch 3 (counts as dc), skip first dc, dc in next dc, ch 3, dc in next ch-5 loop, ch 3, skip next dc, *dc in each of next 3 dc, ch 3, dc in next ch-5 loop, ch 3, skip next dc; rep from * across to within last 2 sts, dc in next dc, dc in 3rd ch of turning ch, turn.

Row 7: Ch 6 (counts as dc, ch 3), dc in next ch-3 loop, dc in next dc, dc in next ch-3 loop, ch 3, skip next dc, dc in next dc; rep from * across, ending with last dc in 3rd ch of turning ch, turn.

Rep Rows 2-7 for pattern.

19

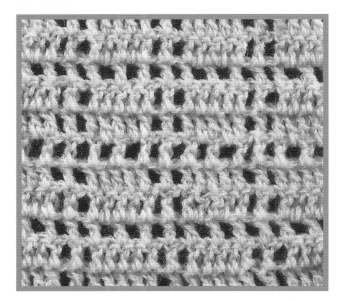

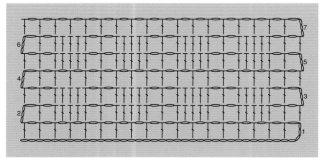

Chain multiples of 8 plus 6.

Row 1: Dc in 6th ch from hook, *ch 1, skip next ch, dc in next ch; rep from * across, turn.

Row 2: Ch 4 (counts as dc, ch 1), skip next ch-1 space, dc in next dc, ch 1, dc in next dc, *(dc in next ch-1 space, dc in next dc) twice, (ch 1, dc) in each of next 2 dc; rep from * across, skip next ch of turning ch, dc in next ch of turning ch, turn.

Row 3: Ch 4 (counts as dc, ch 1), skip next ch-1 space, dc in next dc, *ch 1, dc in each of next 5 dc, (ch 1, dc) in each of next 2 dc; rep from * across, skip next ch of turning ch, dc in next ch of turning ch, turn.

Row 4: Ch 4 (counts as dc, ch 1), skip next ch-1 space, dc in next dc, *ch 1, skip next st, dc in next dc; rep from * across, ending with last dc in 3rd ch of turning ch, turn.

Rep Rows 2-4 for pattern.

20

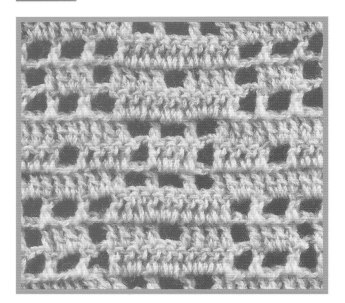

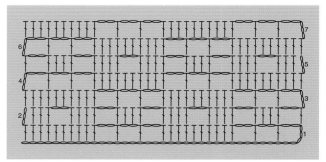

Chain multiples of 18 plus 5.

Row 1: Dc in 8th ch from hook, (ch 2, skip next 2 ch, dc in next ch) twice, *dc in each of next 9 ch**, (ch 2, skip next 2 ch, dc in next ch) 3 times; rep from * across, ending last rep at **, turn.

Row 2: Ch 3 (counts as dc), skip first dc, dc in each of next 3 dc, ch 2, skip next 2 dc, dc in each of next 4 dc, *ch 2, skip next ch-2 space, dc in next dc, 2 dc in next ch-2 space, dc in next dc, ch 2, skip next ch-2 space**, dc in each of next 4 dc, ch 2, skip next 2 dc, dc in each of next 4 dc; rep from * across, ending last rep at **, dc in 3rd ch of turning ch, turn.

Row 3: Ch 5 (counts as dc, ch 2), skip next ch-2 space, (dc in next dc, ch 2, skip next 2 sts) twice, *dc in each of next 4 dc, 2 dc in next ch-2 space, dc in each of next 4 dc**, (ch 2, skip 2 sts, dc in next dc) 3 times; rep from * across, ending last rep at **, with last dc in 3rd ch of turning ch, turn.

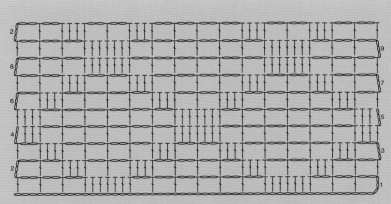
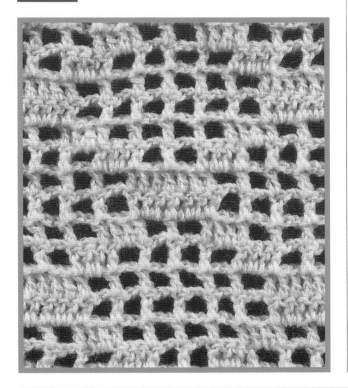

Row 4: Ch 5 (counts as dc, ch 2), skip first 3 dc, (dc in next dc, ch 2, skip next 2 dc) twice, *(dc in next dc, 2 dc in next ch-2 space) 3 times**, (dc in next dc, ch 2, skip next 2 dc) 3 times; rep from * across, ending last rep at **, dc in 3rd ch of turning ch, turn.

Rep Rows 2-4 for pattern.

Chain multiples of 24 plus 5.

Row 1: Dc in 8th ch from hook, (ch 2, skip next 2 ch, dc in next ch) twice, dc in each of next 6 ch, *(ch 2, skip next 2 ch, dc in next ch) 6 times, dc in each of next 6 dc; rep from * across to within last 9 ch sts, (ch 2, skip next 2 ch, dc in next ch) 3 times, turn.

Row 2: Ch 5 (counts as dc, ch 2), skip next ch-2 space, dc in next dc, ch 2, skip next 2 sts, dc in next dc, 2 dc in next ch-2 space, dc in next dc, (ch 2, skip next 2 sts, dc in next dc) twice, 2 dc in next ch-2 space, dc in next dc, *(ch 2, skip next 2 sts, dc in next dc) 4 times, dc in next dc, 2 dc in next ch-2 space, dc in next dc, (ch 2, skip next 2 sts, dc in next dc) twice, dc in next dc, 2 dc in next ch-2 space, dc in next dc; rep from * across to within last 6 sts, ch 2, skip next 2 sts, dc in next dc, ch 2, skip next 2 ch, dc in 3rd ch of turning ch, turn.

Row 3: Ch 5 (counts as dc, ch 2), skip first 3 sts, dc in next dc, 2 dc in next ch-2 space, dc in next dc, (ch 2, skip next 2 sts, dc in next dc) 4 times, dc in next dc, 2 dc in next ch-2 space, dc in next dc, *(ch 2, skip next 2 sts, dc in next dc) twice, 2 dc in next ch-2 space, dc in next dc, (ch 2, skip next 2 sts, dc in next dc) 4 times, 2 dc in next ch-2 space, dc in next dc; rep from * across to within last 3 sts, ch 2, skip next 2 sts, dc in 3rd ch of turning ch, turn.

Row 4: Ch 3 (counts as dc), 2 dc in next ch-2 space, dc in next dc, *(ch 2, skip next 2 sts, dc in next dc) 6 times, 2 dc in next ch-2 space**, dc in next dc, 2 dc in next ch-2 space, dc in next dc; rep from * across, ending last rep at **, dc in 3rd ch of turning ch, turn.

Row 5: Ch 3 (counts as dc), skip first dc, dc in each of next 3 dc, *(ch 2, dc) in each of next 6 dc**, dc in each of next 6 dc; rep from * across, ending last rep at **, dc in each of next 2 dc, dc in 3rd ch of turning ch, turn.

Row 6: Rep Row 3.

Row 7: Rep Row 2.

Row 8: Ch 5 (counts as dc, ch 2), skip next ch-2 space, dc in next dc, (ch 2, skip next 2 sts, dc in next dc) twice, (2 dc in next ch-2 space, dc next dc) twice, *(ch 2, skip next 2 sts, dc in next dc) 6 times, (2 dc in next ch-2 space, dc next dc) twice; rep from * across to within last 9 sts, (ch 2, skip next 2 sts, dc in next dc) 3 times, ending with last dc in 3rd ch of turning ch, turn.

Row 9: Ch 5 (counts as dc, ch 2), skip next ch-2 space, dc in next dc, (ch 2, skip next 2 sts, dc in next dc) twice, dc in each of next 6 dc, *(ch 2, skip next 2 sts, dc in next dc) 6 times, dc in each of next 6 dc; rep from * across to within last 9 sts, (ch 2, skip next 2 sts, dc in next dc) 3 times, ending with dc in 3rd ch of turning ch, turn.

Rep Rows 2-9 for pattern.

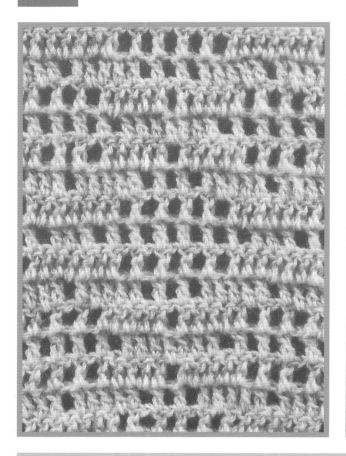

Chain multiples of 16 plus 2.

Row 1: Dc in 6th ch from hook, (ch 1, skip next ch, dc in next ch) 6 times, dc in each of next 2 ch, *(ch 1, skip next ch, dc in next ch) 7 times, dc in each of next 2 ch; rep from * across to within last 14 ch sts, (ch 1, skip next ch, dc in next ch) 7 times, turn.

Row 2: Ch 4 (counts as dc, ch 1), skip next ch-1 space, dc in next dc, *(ch 1, skip next st, dc in next dc) 5 times, dc in each of next 6 sts; rep from * across to within last 12 sts, (ch 1, skip next ch-1 space, dc in next dc) 6 times, ending with last dc in next ch of turning ch, turn.

Row 3: Ch 4 (counts as dc, ch 1), skip next ch-1 space, dc in next dc, (ch 1, skip next st, dc in next dc) 4 times, *dc in each of next 4 sts, ch 1, skip next st, dc in each of next 5 sts, (ch 1, skip next st, dc in next dc) 3 times; rep from * across to within last 4 sts, (ch 1, skip next st, dc in next dc) twice, ending with last dc in 3rd ch of turning ch, turn.

Row 4: Ch 4 (counts as dc, ch 1), skip next ch-1 space, dc in next dc, (ch 1, skip next st, dc in next dc) 3 times, *dc in each of next 4 sts, (ch 1, skip next st, dc in next dc) 3 times, dc in each of next 4 sts, ch 1, skip next st, dc in next dc; rep from * across to within last 9 sts, (ch 1, skip next st, dc in next dc) 3 times, ending with dc in 3rd ch of turning ch, turn.

Row 5: Ch 4 (counts as dc, ch 1), skip next ch-1 space, dc in next dc, (ch 1, skip next ch-1 space, dc in next dc) twice, *dc in each of next 4 sts, (ch 1, skip next st, dc in next dc) 5 times, dc in each of next 2 sts; rep from * across to within last 8 sts, dc in each of next 2 sts, (ch 1, skip next st, dc in next dc) 3 times, ending with last dc in 3rd ch of turning ch, turn.

Row 6: Rep Row 4.

Row 7: Rep Row 3.

Row 8: Rep Row 2.

Row 9: Ch 4 (counts as dc, ch 1), skip next ch-1 space, dc in next dc, (ch 1, skip next st, dc in next dc) 6 times, *dc in each of next 2 sts, (ch 1, skip next st, dc in next dc) 7 times; rep from * across, ending with last dc in 3rd ch of turning ch, turn.

Rep Rows 2-9 for pattern.

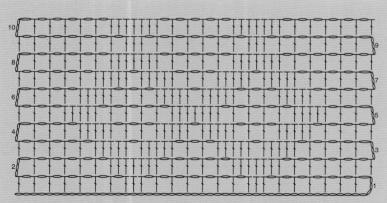

23

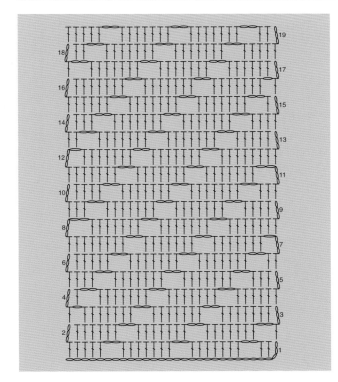

Chain multiples of 9 plus 3.

Row 1: Dc in 4th ch from hook, dc in next ch, *ch 2, skip next 2 ch, dc in each of next 7 ch; rep from * across, ending with dc in each of last 5 ch, turn.

Row 2: Ch 3 (counts as dc), skip first dc, dc in each of next 6 sts, *ch 2, skip next 2 sts, dc in each of next 7 sts; rep from * across to within last 3 sts, ch 2, skip next 2 sts, dc in 3rd ch of turning ch, turn.

Row 3: Ch 3 (counts as dc), skip first dc, dc in each of next 7 sts, *ch 2, skip next 2 sts, dc in each of next 7 sts; rep from * across to within last 2 sts, ch 1, skip next dc, dc in 3rd ch of turning ch, turn.

Row 4: Ch 3 (counts as dc), skip first dc, dc in next st, *ch 2, skip next 2 sts, dc in each of next 7 sts; rep from * across to within last 8 sts, ch 2, skip next 2 sts, dc in each of next 5 dc, dc in 3rd ch of turning ch, turn.

Row 5: Ch 3 (counts as dc), skip first dc, dc in each of next 3 dc, *ch 2, skip next 2 sts, dc in each of next 7 sts; rep from * across to within last 6 sts, ch 2, skip next 2 sts, dc in each of next 3 sts, dc in 3rd ch of turning ch, turn.

Row 6: Ch 3 (counts as dc), skip first dc, dc in each of next 5 sts, *ch 2, skip next 2 sts, dc in each of next 7 sts; rep from * across to within last 4 sts, ch 2, skip next 2 dc, dc in next st, dc in 3rd ch of turning ch, turn.

Row 7: Ch 4 (counts as dc, ch 1), skip first 2 dc, *dc in each of next 7 sts, ch 2, skip next 2 sts; rep from * across to within last 8 sts, dc in each of next 7 sts, dc in 3rd ch of turning ch, turn.

Row 8: Ch 5 (counts as dc, ch 2), skip first 3 dc, *dc in each of next 7 sts, ch 2, skip next 2 sts; rep from * across to within last 7 sts, dc in each of next 6 sts, dc in 3rd ch of turning ch, turn.

Row 9: Ch 3 (counts as dc), skip first dc, dc in each of next 4 sts, *ch 2, skip next 2 sts, dc in each of next 7 sts; rep from * across to within last 5 sts, ch 2, skip next 2 dc, dc in each of next 2 sts, dc in 3rd ch of turning ch, turn.

Row 10: Rep Row 9.

Row 11: Rep Row 8.

Row 12: Rep Row 7.

Row 13: Rep Row 6.

Row 14: Rep Row 5.

Row 15: Rep Row 4.

Row 16: Rep Row 3.

Row 17: Rep Row 2.

Row 18: Ch 3 (counts as dc), skip first dc, dc in each of next 2 sts, *ch 2, skip next 2 sts, dc in each of next 7 sts; rep from * across to within last 7 sts, ch 2, skip next 2 sts, dc in each of next 4 sts, dc in 3rd ch of turning ch, turn.

Row 19: Rep Row 18.

Rep Rows 2-19 for pattern.

24

Chain multiples of 16 plus 6.

Row 1: Dc in 6th ch from hook, (ch 1, skip next ch, dc in next ch) 3 times, dc in each of next 2 ch, *(ch 1, skip next ch, dc in next ch) 7 times, dc in each of next 2 ch; rep from * across to within last 8 ch sts, (ch 1, skip next ch, dc in next ch) 4 times, turn.

Rows 2-4: Ch 4 (counts as dc, ch 1), skip next ch-1 space, dc in next dc, (ch 1, skip next st, dc in next dc) 3 times, dc in each of next 2 dc, *(ch 1, skip next st, dc in next dc) 7 times, dc in each of next 2 dc; rep from * across to within last 8 sts, (ch 1, skip next ch-1 space, dc in next dc) 4 times, ending with last dc in next ch of turning ch, turn.

Row 5: Ch 4 (counts as dc, ch 1), skip next ch-1 space, dc in next dc, (ch 1, skip next ch-1 space, dc in next dc) twice, dc in each of next 6 sts, *(ch 1, skip next st, dc in next dc) 5 times, dc in each of next 6 sts; rep from * across to within last 6 sts, (ch 1, skip next st, dc in next dc) 3 times, ending with dc in 3rd ch of turning ch, turn.

Row 6: Ch 4 (counts as dc, ch 1), skip next ch-1 space, dc in next dc, ch 1, skip next ch-1 space, dc in next dc, dc in each of next 10 sts, *(ch 1, skip next st, dc in next dc) 3 times, dc in each of next 10 sts; rep from * across to last 4 sts, (ch 1, skip next st, dc in next dc) twice, ending with last dc in 3rd ch of turning ch, turn.

Row 7: Ch 4 (counts as dc, ch 1), skip next ch-1 space, dc in each of next 15 sts, *ch 1, skip next st, dc in each of next 15 sts; rep from * across to within last 2 sts, ch 1, skip next st, dc in 3rd ch of turning ch, turn.

Row 8: Rep Row 6.

Row 9: Rep Row 5.

Row 10: Rep Row 2.

Rep Rows 2-10 for pattern.

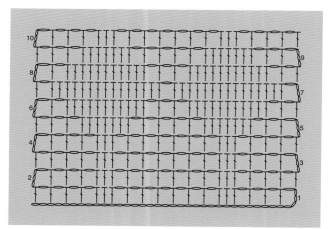

25

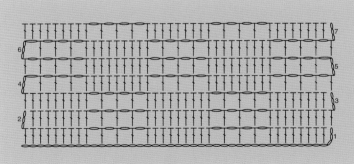

Chain multiples of 16 plus 11.

Row 1: Dc in 4th ch from hook, dc in each of next 7 ch, *(ch 1, skip next ch, dc in next ch) 4 times, dc in each of next 8 ch; rep from * across, turn.

Rows 2-3: Ch 3 (counts as dc), skip first dc, dc in each of next 8 dc, (ch 1, skip next st, dc in next dc) 4 times, dc in each of next 8 dc; rep from * across, ending with last dc in 3rd ch of turning ch, turn.

Row 4: Ch 4 (counts as dc, ch 1), skip first 2 sts, dc in next dc, (ch 1, skip next st, dc in next dc) 3 times, dc in each of next 8 sts, (ch 1, skip next st, dc in next dc) 4 times; rep from * across, ending with last dc in 3rd ch of turning ch, turn.

Rows 5-6: Rep Row 4.

Row 7: Rep Row 2.

Rep Rows 2-7 for pattern.

.4.
Single Crochet, Double Crochet & Chains

26

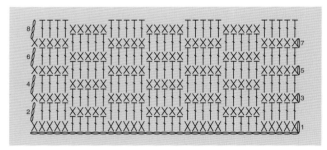

Chain multiples of 10 plus 6.

Row 1: Sc in 2nd ch from hook, sc in each of next 4 ch, *dc in each of next 5 sc, sc in each of next 5 ch; rep from * across, turn.

Row 2: Ch 3 (counts as dc), skip first sc, dc in each of next 4 sc, sc in each of next 5 dc, dc in each of next 5 sc; rep from * across, turn.

Row 3: Ch 1, sc in each of first 5 dc, *dc in each of next 5 sc, sc in each of next 5 dc; rep from * across, ending with last sc in 3rd ch of turning ch, turn.

Rep Rows 2-3 for pattern.

27

Chain multiples of 2 plus 1.

Row 1: Sc in 2nd ch from hook, dc in next ch, *sc in next ch, dc in next ch; rep from * across, turn.

Row 2: Ch 1, sc in first dc, dc in next sc, *sc in next dc, dc in next sc; rep from * across, turn.

Rep Row 2 for pattern.

28

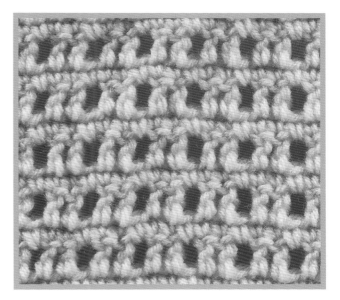

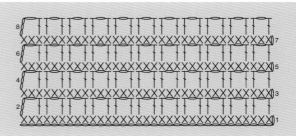

Chain multiples of 3 plus 1.

Row 1: Sc in 2nd ch from hook, sc in each ch across, turn.

Row 2: Ch 4 (counts as dc, ch 1), skip first 2 sc, dc in each of next 2 sc, *ch 1, skip next sc, dc in each of next 2 sc; rep from * across to within last 2 sc, ch 1, skip next sc, dc in last sc, turn.

Row 3: Ch 1, sc in each dc and each ch-1 space across, ending with sc in 3rd ch of turning ch, turn.

Rep Rows 2-3 for pattern.

29

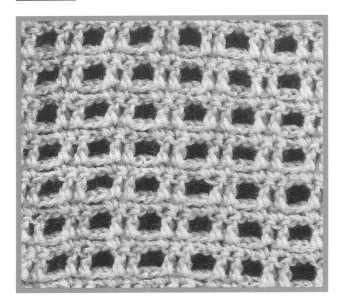

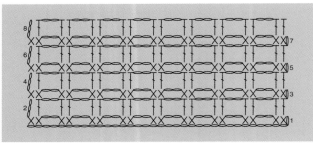

Chain multiples of 4 plus 3.

Row 1: Sc in 2nd ch from hook, sc in next ch, *ch 2, skip next 2 ch, sc in each of next 2 ch; rep from * across, turn.

Row 2: Ch 3 (counts as dc), skip first sc, dc in next sc, *ch 2, skip next ch-2 space, dc in each of next 2 sc; rep from * across, turn.

Row 3: Ch 1, sc in each of first 2 dc, *ch 2, skip next ch-2 space, sc in each of next 2 dc; rep from * across, ending with last sc in 3rd ch of turning ch, turn.

Rep Rows 2-3 for pattern.

30

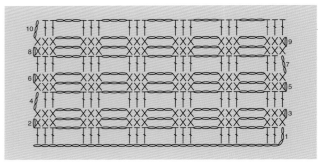

Chain multiples of 6 plus 5.

Row 1: Dc in 4th ch from hook, dc in next ch, *ch 3, skip next 3 ch, dc in each of next 3 ch; rep from * across, turn.

Row 2: Ch 1, sc in each of first 3 dc, *ch 3, skip next ch-3 loop, sc in each of next 3 dc; rep from * across, ending with last sc in 3rd ch of turning ch, turn.

Row 3: Ch 1, sc in each of first 3 sc, *ch 3, skip next ch-3 space, sc in each of next 3 sc; rep from * across, turn.

Row 4: Ch 3, (counts as dc), skip first sc, dc in each of next 2 sc, *ch 3, skip next ch-3 space, dc in each of next 3 sc; rep from * across, turn.

Rep Rows 2-4 for pattern.

31

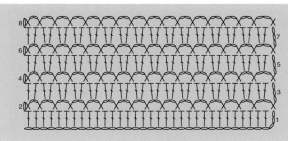

Chain multiples of 2 plus 1.

Row 1: Dc in 4th ch from hook, dc in each ch across, turn.

Row 2: Ch 1, sc in first dc, ch 2, skip next dc, sc in space bet last skipped and next dc, *ch 2, skip next 2 dc, sc in space bet last skipped and next dc; rep from * across, ending with sc in 3rd ch of turning ch, turn.

Row 3: Ch 3 (counts as dc), 2 dc in each ch-2 space across to last ch-2 space, dc in last ch-2 space, dc in last sc, turn.

Rep Rows 2-3 for pattern.

32

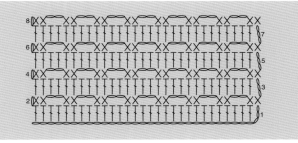

Chain multiples of 4.

Row 1: Dc in 4th ch from hook, dc in each ch across, turn.

Row 2: Ch 1, sc in first dc, sc in next dc, *ch 2, skip next 2 dc, sc in each of next 2 dc; rep from * across, ending with last sc in 3rd ch of turning ch, turn.

Row 3: Ch 3 (counts as dc), dc in next sc, *2 dc in next ch-2 space, dc in each of next 2 sc; rep from * across, turn.

Rep Rows 2-3 for pattern.

33

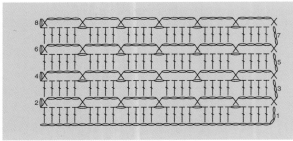

Chain multiples of 5 plus 3.

Row 1: Dc in 4th ch from hook, dc in each of next 3 ch, *ch 1, skip next ch, dc in each of next 4 ch; rep from * across to within last ch, dc in last ch, turn.

Row 2: Ch 1, sc in first dc, *ch 4, skip next 4 dc, sc in next ch-1 space; rep from * across, ending with sc in 3rd ch of turning ch, turn.

Row 3: Ch 3 (counts as dc), 4 dc in each ch-4 loop across, dc in last sc, turn.

Rep Rows 2-3 for pattern.

34

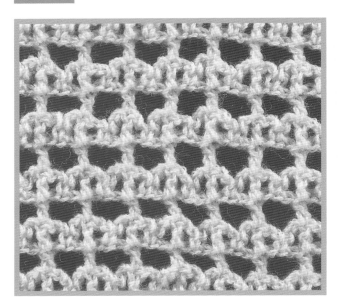

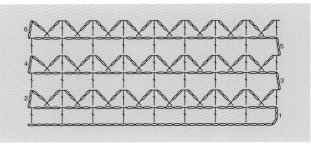

Chain multiples of 4 plus 2.

Row 1: Dc in 10th ch from hook, *ch 3, skip next 3 ch, dc in next ch; rep from * across, turn.

Row 2: Ch 5 (counts as dc, ch 2), sc in next ch-3 loop, ch 2, dc in next dc, *ch 2, sc in next ch-3 loop, ch 2, dc in next dc; rep from * across, ending with last dc in next ch of turning ch, turn.

Row 3: Ch 6 (counts as dc, ch 3), skip next 2 ch-2 spaces, dc in next dc, *ch 3, skip next 2 ch-2 spaces, dc in next dc; rep from * across, ending with last dc in 3rd ch of turning ch, turn.

Rep Rows 2-3 for pattern.

35

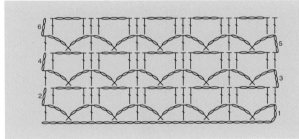

Chain multiples of 6.

Row 1: Sc in 9th ch from hook, ch 3, skip next 2 ch, dc in next ch, *ch 3, skip next 2 ch, sc in next ch, ch 3, skip next 2 ch, dc in next ch; rep from * across, turn.

Row 2: Ch 3 (counts as dc), *dc in next ch-3 loop, ch 3, dc in next ch-3 loop, dc in next dc; rep from * across, ending with last dc in next ch of turning ch, turn.

Row 3: Ch 6 (counts as dc, ch 3), skip next dc, sc in next ch-3 loop, ch 3, skip next dc, dc in next dc, *ch 3, sc in next ch-3 loop, ch 3, skip next dc, dc in next dc; rep from * across, ending with last dc in 3rd ch of turning ch, turn.

Rep Rows 2-3 for pattern.

36

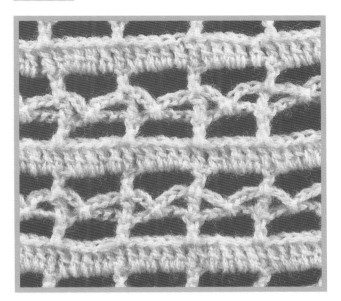

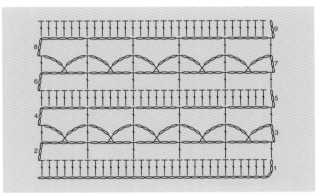

Chain multiples of 6 plus 3.

Row 1: Dc in 4th ch from hook, dc in each ch across, turn.

Row 2: Ch 8 (counts as dc, ch 5), skip first 6 dc, dc in next dc, *ch 5, skip next 5 dc, dc in next dc; rep from * across, ending with last dc in 3rd ch of turning ch, turn.

Row 3: Ch 6 (counts as dc, ch 3), sc in next ch-5 loop, ch 3, dc in next dc, *ch 3, sc in next ch-5 loop, ch 3, dc in next dc; rep from * across, ending with last dc in 3rd ch of turning ch, turn.

Rep Rows 2-3 for pattern.

37

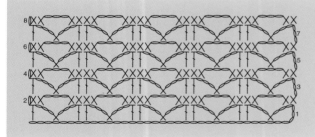

Chain multiples of 7 plus 5.

Row 1: Sc in 9th ch from hook, ch 3, skip next 2 ch, *dc in each of next 2 ch, ch 3, skip next 2 ch, sc in next ch, ch 3, skip next 2 ch; rep from * across to last ch, dc in last ch, turn.

Row 2: Ch 1, sc in first dc, sc in next ch-3 loop, ch 3, sc in next ch-3 loop, *sc in each of next 2 dc, sc in next ch-3 loop, ch 3, sc in next ch-3 loop; rep from * across to last ch-3 loop of turning ch, sc in next ch of turning ch, turn.

Row 3: Ch 6 (counts as dc, ch 3), skip first 2 sc, sc in next ch-3 loop, ch 3, skip next sc, *dc in each of next 2 sc, ch 3, sc in next ch-3 loop, ch 3, skip next sc; rep from * across to last st, dc in last sc, turn.

Rep Rows 2-3 for pattern.

38

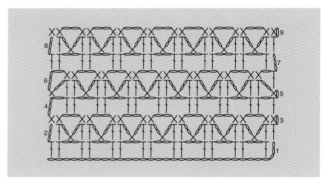

Chain multiples of 4.

Row 1: Dc in 4th ch from hook, *ch 2, skip next 2 ch, dc in each of next 2 ch; rep from * across, turn.

Row 2: Ch 3 (counts as dc), skip first dc, dc in next dc, *ch 2, sc in next ch-2 space, ch 2, dc in each of next 2 dc; rep from * across, ending with last dc in 3rd ch of turning ch, turn.

Row 3: Ch 1, sc in each of first 2 dc, *ch 2, skip next 2 ch-2 spaces, sc in each of next 2 dc; rep from * across, ending with last sc in 3rd ch of turning ch, turn.

Row 4: Ch 4 (counts as dc, ch 1), (2 dc, ch 2) in each ch-2 space across to within last ch-2 space, 2 dc in next ch-2 space, ch 1, dc in last sc, turn

Row 5: Ch 1, sc in first dc, *ch 2, dc in each of next 2 dc, ch 2, sc in next ch-2 space; rep from * across, ending with last sc in 3rd ch of turning ch, turn.

Row 6: Ch 4 (counts as dc, ch 1), *sc in each of next 2 dc, ch 2, skip next 2 ch-2 spaces; rep from * across to within last 2 dc, sc in each of next 2 dc, ch 1, skip next ch-2 space, dc in last sc, turn.

Row 7: Ch 3 (counts as dc), dc in next ch-1 space, ch 2, (2 dc, ch 2) in each ch-2 space across to last ch-2 space, dc in next ch-1 space of turning ch, dc in 3rd ch of turning ch, turn.

Rep Rows 2-7 for pattern.

Chain multiples of 8 plus 7.

Row 1: Dc in 4th ch from hook, dc in each of next 3 ch, *ch 3, skip next ch, sc in next ch, ch 3, skip next ch, dc in each of next 5 ch; rep from * across, turn.

Row 2: Ch 6 (counts as dc, ch 3), skip first 2 dc, sc in next dc, ch 3, skip next dc, *dc in next dc, ch 3, skip next 2 ch-3 loops, dc in next dc, ch 3, skip next dc, sc in next dc, ch 3, skip next dc; rep from * across to last st, dc in 3rd ch of turning ch, turn.

Row 3: Ch 6 (counts as dc, ch 3), skip next 2 ch-3 loops, dc in next dc, *3 dc in next ch-3 loop, dc in next dc, ch 3, skip next 2

ch-3 loops, dc in next dc; rep from * across, ending with last dc in 3rd ch of turning ch, turn.

Row 4: Ch 3 (counts as dc), 3 dc in next ch-3 loop, dc in next dc, *ch 3, skip next dc, sc in next dc, ch 3, skip next dc, dc in next dc, 3 dc in next ch-3 loop, dc in next dc; rep from * across, ending with last dc in 3rd ch of turning ch, turn.

Rep Rows 2-4 for pattern.

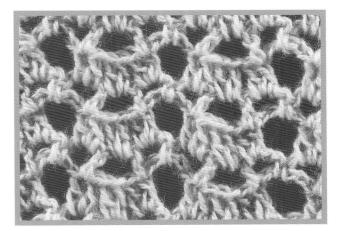

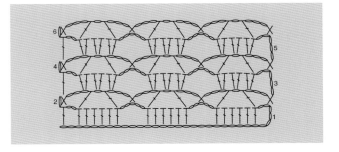

Chain multiples of 9 plus 5.

Row 1: Dc in 7th ch from hook, dc in each of next 5 ch, *ch 5, skip next 3 ch, dc in each of next 6 ch; rep from * across to within last 2 ch, ch 2, skip next ch, dc in last ch, turn.

Row 2: Ch 1, sc in first dc, *ch 3, dc in next dc, ch 1, skip next 4 dc, dc in next dc, ch 3**, sc in next ch-5 loop, ch 3; rep from * across, ending last rep at **, ch 3, skip next 2 ch, sc in next ch of turning ch, turn.

Row 3: Ch 5 (counts as dc, ch 2),*2 dc in next ch-3 loop, 2 dc in next ch-1 space, 2 dc in next ch-3 loop**, ch 5; rep from * across to within last sc, dc in last sc, turn.

Rep Rows 2-3 for pattern.

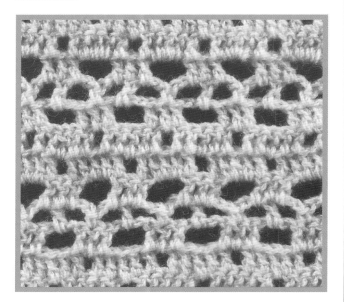

Row 5: Ch 5 (counts as tr, ch 1), dc in next ch-3 loop, dc in next dc, dc in next ch-3 loop, *ch 3, dc in next ch-3 loop, dc in next dc, dc in next ch-3 loop; rep from * across to last ch-3 loop, ch 1, tr in last sc, turn.

Row 6: Ch 3 (counts as dc), dc in next ch-1 space, dc in next dc, *ch 1, skip next dc, dc in next dc**, 3 dc in next ch-3 loop, dc in next dc; rep from * across, ending last rep at **, dc in next ch-1 space of turning ch, dc in 3rd ch of turning ch, turn.

Rep Rows 2-6 for pattern.

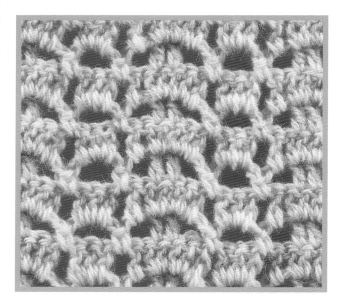

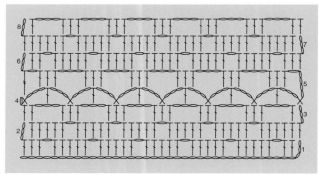

Chain multiples of 6 plus 3.

Row 1: Dc in 4th ch from hook, dc in next ch, *ch 1, skip next ch, dc in each of next 5 ch; rep from * across to last 4 ch, ch 1, skip next ch, dc in each of last 3 ch, turn.

Row 2: Ch 3 (counts as dc), skip first dc, dc in each of next 2 dc, dc in next ch-1 space, dc in each of next 2 dc, *ch 1, skip next dc, dc in each of next 2 dc, dc in next ch-1 space, dc in each of next 2 dc; rep from * across to last st, dc in 3rd ch of turning ch, turn.

Row 3: Ch 3 (counts as dc), skip first dc, *dc in next dc, ch 3, skip next 3 dc, dc in next dc, dc in next ch-1 space; rep from * across, ending with last dc in 3rd ch of turning ch, turn.

Row 4: Ch 1, sc in first dc, *ch 3, dc in next ch-3 loop, ch 3, skip next dc, sc in next dc; rep from * across, ending with last sc in 3rd ch of turning ch, turn.

Chain multiples of 11 plus 5.

Row 1: Sc in 9th ch from hook, *ch 5, skip next 3 ch, sc in next ch, ch 3, skip next 2 ch**, dc in each of next 2 ch, ch 3, skip next 2 ch, sc in next ch; rep from * across, ending last rep at **, dc in last ch, turn.

Row 2: Ch 3 (counts as dc), dc in first dc, dc in next ch-3 loop, ch 1, 3 dc in next ch-5 loop, ch 1, dc in next ch-3 loop, 2 dc in next dc, *2 dc in next dc, dc in next ch-3 loop, ch 1, 3 dc in next ch-5 loop, ch 1, dc in next ch-3 loop, 2 dc in next dc; rep from * across, ending with last 2 dc in next ch of turning ch, turn.

Row 3: Ch 6 (counts as dc, ch 3), sc in next ch-1 space, ch 5, sc in next ch-1 space, ch 3, skip next 2 dc, dc in next dc, *dc in next dc, ch 3, sc in next ch-1 space, ch 5, sc in next ch-1 space, ch 3, skip next 2 dc, dc in next dc; rep from * across, ending with last dc in 3rd ch of turning ch, turn.

Rep Rows 2-3 for pattern.

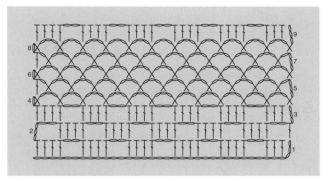

43

Chain multiples of 6.

Row 1: Dc in 4th ch from hook, dc in each of next 2 ch, *ch 2, skip next 2 ch, dc in each of next 4 ch; rep from * across, turn.

Row 2: Ch 5 (counts as dc, ch 2), skip first 3 dc, dc in next dc, *2 dc in next ch-2 space, dc in next dc, ch 2, skip next 2 dc, dc in next dc; rep from * across, ending with last dc in 3rd ch of turning ch, turn.

Row 3: Ch 3 (counts as dc), 2 dc in next ch-2 space, dc in next dc, *ch 2, skip next 2 dc, dc in next dc, 2 dc in next ch-2 space, dc in next dc; rep from * across, ending with last dc in 3rd ch of turning ch, turn.

Row 4: Ch 1, sc in first dc, ch 3, skip next 2 dc, sc in next dc, *ch 3, skip next ch-2 space, sc in next dc, ch 3, skip next 2 dc, sc in next dc; rep from * across, ending with last sc in 3rd ch of turning ch, turn.

Row 5: Ch 4 (counts as dc, ch 1), sc in next ch-3 loop, (ch 3, sc) in each ch-3 loop across to last ch-3 loop, ch 1, dc in last sc, turn.

Row 6: Ch 1, sc in first dc, (ch 3, sc) in each ch-3 loop across, ending with last sc in 3rd ch of turning ch, turn.

Rows 7-8: Rep Rows 5-6.

Row 9: Ch 3 (counts as dc), 2 dc in next ch-3 loop, dc in next sc, *ch 2, skip next ch-3 loop, dc in next sc, 2 dc in next ch-3 loop, dc in next sc; rep from * across, turn.

Rep Rows 2-9 for pattern.

44

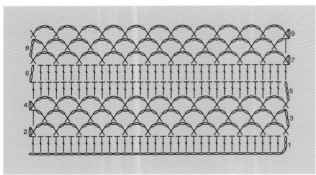

Chain multiples of 3.

Row 1: Dc in 4th ch from hook, dc in each ch across, turn.

Row 2: Ch 1, sc in first dc, *ch 3, skip next 2 dc, sc in next dc; rep from * across, ending with last sc in 3rd ch of turning ch, turn.

Row 3: Ch 3 (counts as hdc, ch 1), sc in next ch-3 loop, (ch 3, sc) in each ch-3 loop across to last ch-3 loop, ch 1, hdc in last sc, turn.

Row 4: Ch 1, sc in first hdc, (ch 3, sc) in each ch-3 loop across, ending with last sc in 2nd ch of turning ch, turn.

Row 5: Ch 3 (counts as dc), *2 dc in next ch-3 loop, dc in next sc; rep from * across, turn.

Row 6: Ch 3 (counts as dc), skip first dc, dc in each dc across, ending with last dc in 3rd ch of turning ch, turn.

Rep Rows 2-6 for pattern.

45

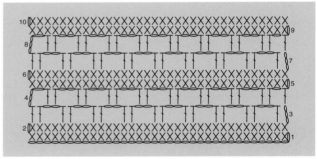

Chain multiples of 4 plus 3.

Row 1: Sc in 2nd ch from hook, sc in each ch across, turn.

Row 2: Ch 1, sc in each sc across, turn.

Row 3: Ch 3 (counts as dc), skip first sc, dc in next sc, *ch 2, skip next 2 sc, dc in each of next 2 sc; rep from * across, turn.

Row 4: Ch 4 (counts as dc, ch 1), 2 dc in next ch-2 space, (ch 2, 2 dc) in each ch-2 space across to last ch-2 space, ch 1, skip next dc, dc in 3rd ch of turning ch, turn.

Row 5: Ch 1, sc in first dc, sc in next ch-1 space, sc in each of next 2 dc, *2 sc in next ch-2 space, sc in each of next 2 dc; rep from * across to within last ch-1 space, sc in ch-1 space, sc in 3rd ch of turning ch, turn.

Rep Rows 2-5 for pattern.

46

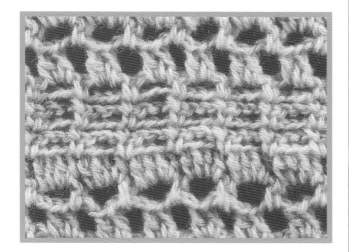

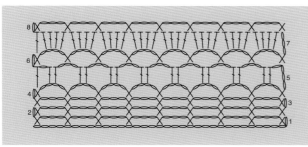

Chain multiples of 4 plus 2.

Row 1: Sc in 2nd ch from hook, *ch 3, skip next 3 ch, sc in next ch; rep from * across, turn.

Rows 2-3: Ch 1, sc in first sc, *ch 3, skip next ch-3 loop, sc in next sc; rep from * across, turn.

Row 4: Ch 1, sc in first sc, *ch 4, skip next ch-3 loop, sc in next sc; rep from * across, turn.

Row 5: Ch 4 (counts as dc, ch 1), 2 dc in next ch-4 loop, (ch 3, 2 dc) in each ch-4 loop across to last ch-4 loop, ch 1, dc in last sc, turn.

Row 6: Ch 1, sc in first dc, skip next ch-1 space, *ch 4, sc in next ch-4 loop; rep from * across, ending with last sc in 3rd ch of turning ch, turn.

Row 7: Ch 3 (counts as dc), 4 dc in each ch-4 loop across, dc in last sc, turn.

Row 8: Ch 1, sc in first dc, *skip next 4 dc, sc in space bet last skipped and next dc; rep from * across, ending with last sc in 3rd ch of turning ch, turn.

Rep Rows 2-8 for pattern.

47

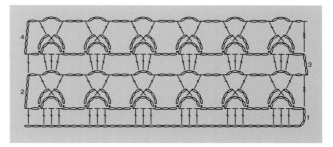

Double Treble Crochet (dtr): Yo (3 times), insert hook in next st, yo, draw yarn through st, (yo, draw yarn through 2 loops on hook) 4 times.

Chain multiples of 6 plus 4.

Row 1: Dc in 6th ch from hook, dc in each of next 2 ch, ch 5, turn, sl st in ch-1 space of turning ch, ch 3, turn, sc in next ch-5 loop, ch 3, sl st in last dc made before ch-5 loop, *ch 3, skip next 3 ch, dc in each of next 3 ch, ch 5, turn, sl st in last ch-3 loop, ch 3, turn, sc in next ch-5 loop, ch 3, sl st in last dc made; rep from * across to last 2 ch, ch 1, skip next ch, dc in last ch, turn.

Row 2: Ch 6 (counts as dtr, ch 1), dc in next ch-3 loop, ch 3, dc in next ch-3 loop, *ch 2, skip next ch-3 loop, dc in next ch-3 loop, ch 3, dc in next ch-3 loop; rep from * across to last ch-3 loop, ch 1, dtr in next ch of turning ch, turn.

Row 3: Ch 4 (counts as dc, ch 1), 3 dc in next ch-3 loop, ch 5, turn, sl st in last ch-1 space of turning ch, ch 3, turn, sc in next ch-5 loop, ch 3, sl st in last dc made, *ch 3, skip next ch-2 space, 3 dc in next ch-3 loop, ch 5, turn, sl st in last ch-3 loop, ch 3, turn, sc in next ch-5 loop, ch 3, sl st in last dc made; rep from * across to last ch-3 loop, ch 1, dc in 5th ch of turning ch, turn.

Rep Rows 2-3 for pattern.

48

Chain multiples of 4 plus 3.

Row 1: Sc in 2nd ch from hook, sc in next ch, *ch 2, skip next 2 ch, sc in each of next 2 ch; rep from * across, turn.

Row 2: Ch 3 (counts as dc), 4 dc in each ch-2 space across to last ch-3 loop, skip next sc, dc in last sc, turn.

Row 3: Ch 1, sc in first dc, sc bet first 2 dc, *ch 2, skip next 4 dc, sc bet last skipped dc and next dc; rep from * across, ending with sc bet last 2 sts, sc in 3rd ch of turning ch, turn.

Rep Rows 2-3 for pattern.

49

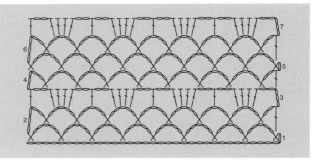

Chain multiples of 8 plus 2.

Row 1: Sc in 2nd ch from hook, *ch 5, skip next 3 ch, sc in next ch; rep from * across, turn.

Row 2: Ch 5 (counts as dc, ch 2), sc in next ch-5 loop, (ch 5, sc) in each ch-5 loop across to last ch-5 loop, ch 2, dc in last sc, turn.

Row 3: Ch 5 (counts as dc, ch 2), skip next ch-2 space, 4 dc in next ch-5 loop, *ch 2, dc in next ch-5 loop, ch 2, 4 dc in next ch-5 loop; rep from * across to last ch-5 loop, ch 2, dc in 3rd ch of turning ch, turn.

Row 4: Ch 5 (counts as dc, ch 2), sc in next ch-2 space, (ch 5, sc) in each ch-2 space across to last ch-2 space, ch 2, dc in 3rd ch of turning ch, turn.

Row 5: Ch 1, sc in first dc, (ch 5, sc) in each ch-5 loop across, ending with last sc in 3rd ch of turning ch, turn.

Rep Rows 2-5 for pattern.

50

Chain multiples of 6 plus 4.

Row 1: Sc in 5th ch from hook, *ch 3, skip next 2 ch, sc in next ch; rep from * across to within last 2 ch, ch 1, skip next ch, hdc in last ch, turn.

Row 2: Ch 3 (counts as dc), dc in next ch-1 space, ch 3, sc in next ch-3 loop, ch 3, *3 dc in next ch-3 loop, ch 3, sc in next ch-3 loop, ch 3; rep from * across to turning ch, dc in ch-1 space of turning ch, dc in next ch of turning ch, turn.

Row 3: Ch 3 (counts as hdc, ch 1), sc in next ch-3 loop, (ch 3, sc) in each ch-3 loop across to last ch-3 loop, ch 1, skip next dc, hdc in 3rd ch of turning ch, turn.

Rows 4-7: Rep Rows 2-3 (twice).

Row 8: Ch 1, sc in first hdc, ch 3, 3 dc in next ch-3 loop, *ch 3, sc in next ch-3 loop, ch 3, 3 dc in next ch-3 loop; rep from * across to last ch-3 loop, ch 3, sc in 2nd ch of turning ch, turn.

Row 9: Ch 4 (counts as dc, ch 1), sc in next ch-3 loop, (ch 3, sc) in each ch-3 loop across to last ch-3 loop, ch 1, dc in last sc, turn.

Rep Rows 2-9 for pattern.

51

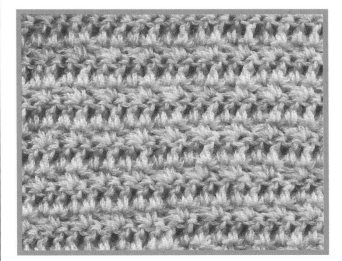

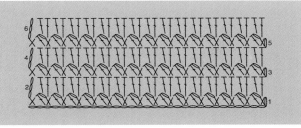

Chain multiples of 6 plus 4.

Row 1: (Sc, ch 1, dc) in 2nd ch from hook, *skip next ch (sc, ch 1, dc) in next ch; rep from * across to within last 2 ch, skip next ch, sc in last ch, turn.

Row 2: Ch 3 (counts as dc), dc in next ch-1 space, dc in next sc; rep from * across, turn.

Row 3: Ch 1, (sc, ch 1, dc) in first dc, *skip next dc (sc, ch 1, dc) in next dc; rep from * across to within last 2 sts, skip next dc, sc in 3rd ch of turning ch, turn.

Rep Rows 2-3 for pattern.

52

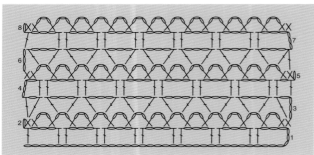

Chain multiples of 5.

Row 1: Dc in 10th ch from hook, *dc in next ch, ch 3, skip next 3 ch, dc in next ch; rep from * across, turn.

Row 2: Ch 1, sc in first dc, (sc, ch 3, sc, ch 3) in each ch-3 loop across to within last ch-3 loop, (sc, ch 3, sc) in last ch-3 loop, sc in 3rd ch of turning ch, turn.

Row 3: Ch 4 (counts as dc, ch 1), dc in first sc, skip next ch-3 loop, *(dc, ch 3, dc) in next ch-3 loop, skip next ch-3 loop; rep from * across to within last 2 sc, skip next sc, (dc, ch 1, dc) in last sc, turn.

Row 4: Ch 4 (counts as dc, ch 1), skip next ch-1 space, dc in each of next 2 dc, *ch 3, skip next ch-3 loop, dc in each of next 2 dc; rep from * across to turning ch, ch 1, skip next ch, dc in 3rd ch of turning ch, turn.

Row 5: Ch 1, sc in first dc, sc in next ch-1 space, ch 3, (sc, ch 3, sc, ch 3) in each ch-3 loop across to turning ch, sc in next ch-1 space of turning ch, sc in 3rd ch of turning ch, turn.

Row 6: Ch 3 (counts as dc), *(dc, ch 3, dc) in next ch-3 loop, skip next ch-3 loop; rep from * across to within last ch-3 loop, dc in next ch-3 loop, ch 3, 2-dc cluster worked across same ch-3 loop and last sc, turn.

Row 7: Ch 6 (counts as dc, ch 3), skip next ch-3 loop, *dc in each of next 2 dc, ch 3, skip next ch-3 loop; rep from * across to last 2 sts, skip next dc, dc in 3rd ch of turning ch, turn.

Rep Rows 2-7 for pattern.

53

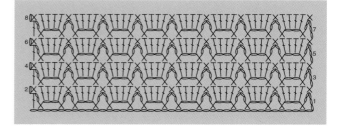

Chain multiples of 5 plus 1.

Row 1: Sc in 7th ch from hook, ch 2, skip next 2 ch, sc in next ch, *ch 4, skip next ch, sc in next ch, ch 2, skip next 2 ch, sc in next ch; rep from * across to within last ch, ch 2, dc in last ch, turn.

Row 2: Ch 1, sc in first dc, *4 dc in next ch-2 space, sc in next ch-4 loop; rep from * across, ending with last sc in 3rd ch of turning ch, turn.

Row 3: Ch 5 (counts as dc, ch 2), sc in next dc, ch 2, skip next 2 dc, *ch 4, skip next sc, sc in next dc, ch 2, skip next 2 dc, sc in next dc; rep from * across to within last sc, ch 2, dc in last sc, turn.

Rep Rows 2-3 for pattern.

54

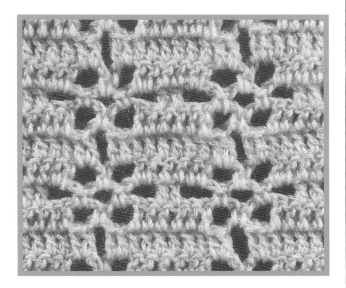

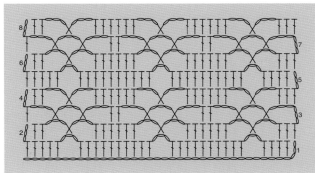

Chain multiples of 12 plus 2.

Row 1: Dc in 4th ch from hook, dc in each of next 3 ch, ch 3, skip next 2 ch, *dc in each of next 10 ch, ch 3, skip next 2 ch; rep from * across to within last 5 ch, dc in each of last 5 ch, turn.

Row 2: Ch 3 (counts as dc), skip first dc, dc in each of next 2 dc, ch 3, sc in next ch-3 loop, ch 3, skip next 2 dc, *dc in each of next 6 dc, ch 3, sc in next ch-3 loop, ch 3, skip next 2 dc; rep from * across to within last 3 sts, dc in each of next 2 dc, dc in 3rd ch of turning ch, turn.

Row 3: Ch 6 (counts as dc, ch 3), *(sc, ch 3) in each of next 2 ch-3 loops, skip next 2 dc**, dc in each of next 2 dc; rep from * across, ending last rep at **, dc in 3rd ch of turning ch, turn.

Row 4: Ch 3 (counts as dc), *2 dc in next ch-3 loop, ch 3, sc in next ch-3 loop, ch 3**, 2 dc in next ch-3 loop, dc in each of next 2 dc; rep from * across, ending last rep at **, 2 dc in ch-3 loop of turning ch, dc in 3rd ch of turning ch, turn.

Row 5: Ch 3 (counts as dc), skip first dc, dc in each of next 2 dc, 2 dc in next ch-3 loop, ch 3, 2 dc in next ch-3 loop, *dc in each of next 6 dc, 2 dc in next ch-3 loop, ch 3, 2 dc in next ch-3 loop; rep from * across to last ch-3 loop, dc in next 2 dc, dc in 3rd ch of turning ch, turn.

Rep Rows 2-5 for pattern.

55

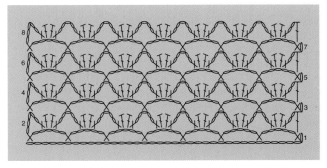

Chain multiples of 5 plus 2.

Row 1: Sc in 2nd ch from hook, *ch 5, skip next 4 ch, sc in next ch; rep from * across, turn.

Row 2: Ch 5 (counts as dc, ch 2), (sc, 2 dc, sc) in next ch-5 loop, (ch 5, sc, 2 dc, sc) in each ch-5 loop across to last ch-5 loop, ch 2, dc in last sc, turn.

Row 3: Ch 1, sc in first dc, (ch 5, sc) in each ch-5 loop across, ending with last sc in 3rd ch of turning ch, turn.

Rep Rows 2-3 for pattern.

56

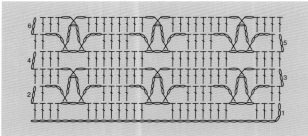

Chain multiples of 11 plus 2.

Row 1: Dc in 4th ch from hook, dc in each of next 2 ch, ch 3, skip next 3 ch, *dc in each of next 8 ch, ch 3, skip next 3 ch; rep from * across to within last 4 ch, dc in each of last 4 ch, turn.

Row 2: Ch 3 (counts as dc), skip first dc, dc in next dc, *ch 4, (sc, ch 7, sc) in next ch-3 loop, ch 4, skip next 2 dc**, dc in each of next 4 dc; rep from * across, ending last rep at **, dc in next dc, dc in 3rd ch of turning ch, turn.

Row 3: Ch 3 (counts as dc), skip first dc, dc in next dc, *2 dc in next ch-4 loop, ch 1, sc in next ch-7 loop, ch 1, 2 dc in next ch-4 loop**, dc in each of next 4 dc; rep from * across, ending last rep at **, dc in next dc, dc in 3rd ch of turning ch, turn.

Row 4: Ch 3 (counts as dc), skip first dc, dc in each of next 3 dc, ch 3, skip next 2 ch-1 spaces, *dc in each of next 8 dc, ch 3, skip next 2 ch-1 spaces; rep from * across to within last 4 sts, dc in each of next 3 dc, dc in 3rd ch of turning ch, turn.

Rep Rows 2-4 for pattern.

57

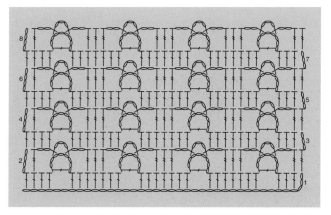

Chain multiples of 9 plus 3.

Row 1: Dc in 4th ch from hook, dc in each of next 2 ch, ch 8, dc in 8th ch from hook, skip next 2 ch, *dc in each of next 7 ch, ch 8, dc in 8th ch from hook, skip next 2 ch; rep from * across to within last 4 ch, dc in each of last 4 ch, turn.

Row 2: Ch 4 (counts as tr), skip first dc, tr in next dc, *ch 2, (sc, ch 3, sc) in next ch-8 loop, ch 2, skip next 2 dc**, tr in each of next 3 dc; rep from * across, ending last rep at **, tr in next dc, tr in 3rd ch of turning ch, turn.

Row 3: Ch 3 (counts as dc), skip first dc, dc in next dc, *2 dc in next ch-2 space, ch 8, dc in 8th ch from hook, skip next ch-3 loop, 2 dc in next ch-2 space**, dc in each of next 3 tr; rep from * across, ending last rep at **, dc in next tr, dc in 4th ch of turning ch, turn.

Rep Rows 2-3 for pattern.

58

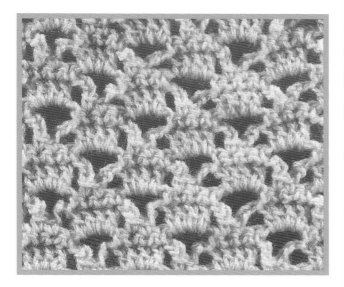

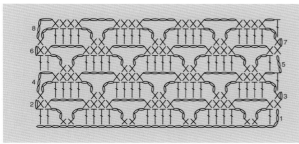

Chain multiples of 8 plus 2.

Row 1: Dc in 4th ch from hook, *ch 3, skip next ch, sc in each of next 2 ch, ch 3, skip next ch, dc in each of next 4 ch; rep from * across, ending with dc in each of last 2 ch, turn.

Row 2: Ch 1, sc in first 2 dc, *ch 4, skip next 2 ch-3 loops**, sc in each of next 4 dc; rep from * across, ending last rep at **, sc in next dc, dc in 3rd ch of turning ch, turn.

Row 3: Ch 1, *sc in sc, ch 3, 4 dc in next ch-4 loop, ch 3, skip next sc, sc in next sc; rep from * across, turn.

Row 4: Ch 4 (counts as dc, ch 1), skip next ch-3 loop, sc in each of next 4 dc, *ch 4, skip next ch-3 loops, sc in each of next 4 dc; rep from * across to within last ch-3 loop, ch 1, skip next ch-3 loop, dc in last sc, turn.

Row 5: Ch 3, dc in next ch-1 space, ch 3, skip next sc, sc in each of next 2 sc, ch 3, *4 dc in next ch-4 loop, ch 3, skip next sc, sc in each of next 2 sc, ch 3; rep from * across to turning ch, dc in next ch-1 space of turning ch, dc in 3rd ch of turning ch, turn.

Rep Rows 2-5 for pattern.

59

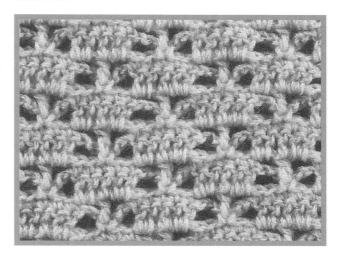

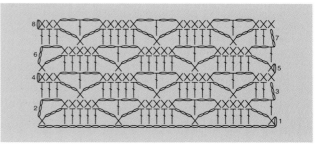

Chain multiples of 10 plus 2.

Row 1: Sc in 2nd ch from hook, *ch 3, skip next 2 ch, dc in each of next 5 ch, ch 3, skip next 2 ch, sc in next ch; rep from * across, turn.

Row 2: Ch 5 (counts as dc, ch 2), skip next ch-3 loop, sc in each of next 5 dc, *ch 2, skip next ch-3 loop, dc in next sc, ch 2, skip next ch-3 loop, sc in each of next 5 dc; rep from * across to within last ch-3 loop, ch 2, skip next ch-3 loop, dc in last sc, turn.

Row 3: Ch 3 (counts as dc), *2 dc in next ch-2 space, ch 3, skip next 2 sc, sc in next sc, ch 3, 2 dc in next ch-2 space, dc in next dc; rep from * across, ending with dc in 3rd ch of turning ch, turn.

Row 4: Ch 1, sc in each of first 3 dc, *ch 2, skip next ch-3 loop, dc in next sc, ch 2, skip next ch-3 loop**, sc in each of next 5 dc; rep from * across, ending last rep at **, sc in each of next 2 dc, sc in 3rd ch of turning ch, turn.

Row 5: Ch 1, sc in first sc, *ch 3, 2 dc in next ch-2 space, dc in next dc, 2 dc in next ch-2 space, ch 3, skip next 2 sc, sc in next sc; rep from * across, turn.

Rep Rows 2-5 for pattern.

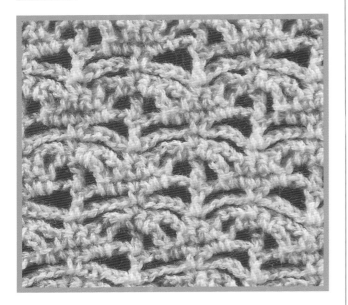

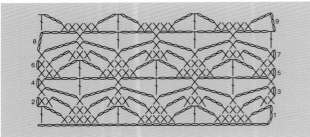

Chain multiples of 10 plus 6.

Row 1: Sc in 9th ch from hook, sc in each of next 4 ch, *ch 3, skip next 2 ch, dc in next ch**, ch 3, skip next 2 ch, sc in each of next 5 ch; rep from * across, ending last rep at **, turn.

Row 2: Ch 1, sc in first dc, *sc in next ch-3 loop, ch 3, skip next sc, sc in each of next 3 sc, ch 3, sc in next ch-3 loop, sc in next dc; rep from * across, ending with last sc in next ch of turning ch, turn.

Row 3: Ch 1, sc in first sc, *ch 5, skip next ch-3 loop, skip next sc, sc in next sc; rep from * across, turn.

Row 4: Ch 1, sc in first sc, *ch 4, skip next ch-5 loop, dc in next sc, ch 4, skip next ch-5 loop, sc in next sc; rep from * across, turn.

Row 5: Ch 1, sc in first sc, *2 sc in next ch-4 loop, ch 3, dc in next dc, ch 3, 2 sc in next ch-4 loop, sc in next sc; rep from * across, turn.

Row 6: Ch 1, sc in each of first 2 sc, *ch 3, sc in next ch-3 loop, sc in next dc, sc in next ch-3 loop, ch 3, skip next sc, sc in each of next 3 sc; rep from * across, ending with sc in each of last 2 sc, turn.

Row 7: Rep Row 3.

Row 8: Ch 7 (counts as dc, ch 4), skip next ch-5 loop, sc in next sc, ch 4, skip next ch-5 loop, dc in next sc, *ch 4, skip next ch-5 loop, sc in next sc, ch 4, skip next ch-5 loop, dc in next sc; rep from * across, turn.

Row 9: Ch 6 (counts as dc, ch 3), *2 sc in next ch-4 loop, sc in next sc, 2 sc in next ch-4 loop, ch 3, dc in next dc**, ch 3; rep from * across, ending last rep at **, with last dc in 3rd ch of turning ch, turn.

Rep Rows 2-9 for pattern.

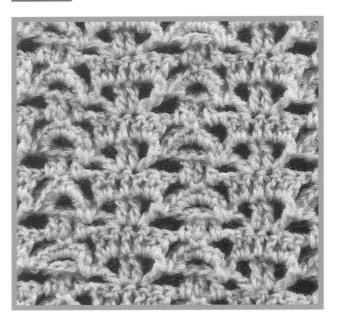

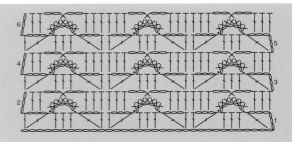

Chain multiples of 11 plus 6.

Row 1: Dc in 7th ch from hook, *skip next 3 ch, dc in each of next 3 ch, ch 5, turn, skip next 3 dc, sl st bet last skipped and next dc, turn, work 7 sc in ch-5 loop just made, sl st in dc at base of ch-5 loop, skip next 3 ch, (dc, ch 3, dc) in next ch**, (dc, ch 3, dc) in next ch; rep from * across, ending last rep at **, turn.

Row 2: Ch 3 (counts as dc), *2 dc in next ch-3 loop, ch 2, skip next 3 sc, sc in next sc, ch 2, 2 dc in next ch-3 loop**, dc in each of next 2 dc; rep from * across, ending last rep at **, dc in 3rd ch of turning ch, turn.

Row 3: Ch 6 (counts as dc, ch 3), dc in first dc, *dc in next ch-2 space, dc in next sc, dc in next ch-2 space, ch 5, turn, skip next 3 dc, sl st bet last skipped and next dc, turn, work 7 sc in ch-5 loop just made, sl st in dc at base of ch-5 loop, skip next 2 dc**, (dc, ch 3, dc) in next dc, (dc, ch 3, dc) in next dc; rep from * across, ending last rep at **, (dc, ch 3, dc) in 3rd ch of turning ch, turn.

Rep Rows 2-3 for pattern.

62

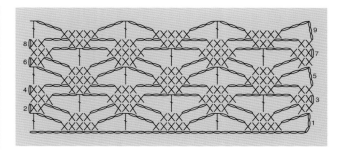

Chain multiples of 12 plus 6.

Row 1: Sc in 10th ch from hook, sc in each of next 4 ch, ch 3, skip next 3 ch, dc in next ch, *ch 3, skip next 3 ch, sc in each of next 5 ch, ch 3, skip next 3 ch, dc in next ch; rep from * across, turn.

Row 2: Ch 1, sc in first dc, *sc in next ch-3 loop, ch 3, skip next sc, sc in each of next 3 sc, ch 3, sc in next ch-3 loop, sc in next dc; rep from * across, ending with last sc in next ch of turning ch, turn.

Row 3: Ch 1, sc in each of first 2 sc, *sc in next ch-3 loop, ch 3, skip next sc, dc in next sc, ch 3, sc in next ch-3 loop, sc in each of next 3 sc; rep from * across, ending with sc in each of last 2 sc, turn.

Row 4: Ch 1, sc in each of first 2 sc, *ch 3, sc in next ch-3 loop, sc in next dc, sc in next ch-3 loop, ch 3, skip next sc, sc in each of next 3 sc; rep from * across, ending with sc in each of last 2 sc, turn.

Row 5: Ch 6 (counts as dc, ch 3), *sc in next ch-3 loop, sc in each of next 3 sc, sc in next ch-3 loop, ch 3, skip next sc, dc in next sc**, ch 3, sc in next ch-3 loop; rep from * across, ending last rep at **, turn.

Rep Rows 2-5 for pattern.

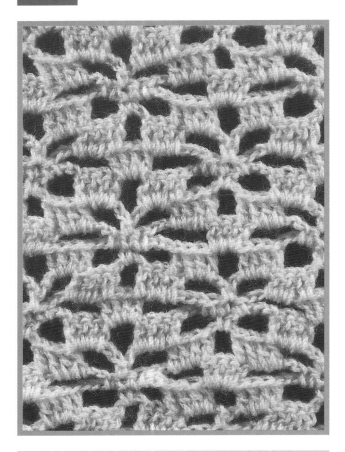

63

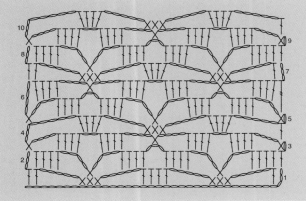

Chain multiples of 17 plus 2.

Row 1: Dc in 4th ch from hook, ch 5, skip next 5 ch, sc in each of next 3 ch, *ch 5, skip next 5 ch, dc in each of next 4 ch; rep from * across, ending with dc in each of last 2 ch, turn.

Row 2: Ch 3 (counts as dc), skip first dc, *dc in next dc, 3 dc in next ch-5 loop, ch 4, skip next sc, sc in next sc, ch 4, 3 dc in next ch-5 loop, dc in next dc**, ch 3 skip next 2 dc; rep from * across, ending last rep at **, dc in 3rd ch of turning ch, turn.

Row 3: Ch 1, sc in first dc, *ch 4, skip next 3 dc, dc in next dc, 3 dc in next ch-4 loop, ch 2, 3 dc in next ch-4 loop, dc in next dc, ch 4, sc in next ch-3 loop; rep from * across, ending with last sc in 3rd ch of turning ch, turn.

Row 4: Ch 8 (counts as dc, ch 5), skip next ch-4 loop, *4 dc in next ch-2 space, ch 5**, sc in next ch-4 loop, sc in next sc, sc in next ch-4 loop, ch 5; rep from * across, ending last rep at **, dc in last sc, turn.

Row 5: Ch 1, sc in first dc, *ch 4, 3 dc in next ch-5 loop, dc in next dc, ch 3, skip next 2 dc, dc in next dc, 3 dc in next ch-4 loop, ch 4, skip next sc, sc in next sc; rep from * across, ending with last sc in 3rd ch of turning ch, turn.

Row 6: Ch 4 (counts as tr), *3 dc in next ch-4 loop, dc in next dc, ch 4, sc in next ch-3 loop, ch 4, skip next 3 dc, dc in next dc, 3 dc in next ch-4 loop**, ch 2; rep from * across, ending last rep at **, tr in last sc, turn.

Row 7: Ch 3 (counts as dc), skip first tr, dc in next dc, ch 5, *sc in next ch-4 loop, sc in next sc, sc in next ch-4 loop, ch 5**, 4 dc in next ch-2 space, ch 5; rep from * across, ending last rep at **, skip next 3 dc, dc in next dc, dc in 4th ch of turning ch, turn.

Rep Rows 2-7 for pattern.

64

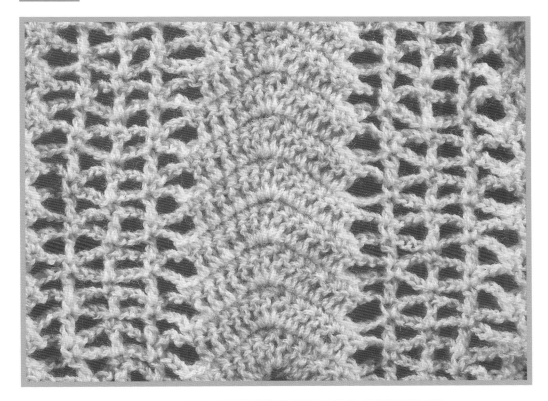

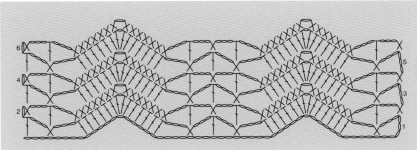

Chain multiples of 26 plus 6.

Row 1: Sc in 9th ch from hook, ch 3, skip next 4 ch, *dc in each of next 5 ch, (2 dc, ch 1, 2 dc) in next ch, dc in each of next 5 ch, ch 3, skip next 4 ch, sc in next ch, ch 3, skip next 2 ch, dc in next ch**, ch 3, skip next 2 ch, sc in next ch, ch 3, skip next 4 ch; rep from * across, ending last rep at **, turn.

Row 2: Ch 1, sc in first dc, *ch 3, skip next ch-3 loop, dc in next sc, ch 3, skip next ch-3 loop, sc in each of next 7 dc, ch 1, sc in each of next 7 dc, ch 3, skip next ch-3 loop, dc in next sc, ch 3, skip next ch-3 loop, sc in next dc; rep from * across, ending with last sc in 3rd ch of turning ch, turn.

Row 3: Ch 6 (counts as dc, ch 3), skip next ch-3 loop, *sc in next dc, ch 3, skip next 2 sc, dc in each of next 5 dc, (2 dc, ch 1, 2 dc) in next ch-1 space, dc in each of next 5 sc, ch 3, skip next ch-3 loop, sc in next dc, ch 3, skip next ch-3 loop, dc in next sc**, ch 3, skip next ch-3 loop; rep from * across, ending last rep at **, turn.

Rep Rows 2-3 for pattern.

65

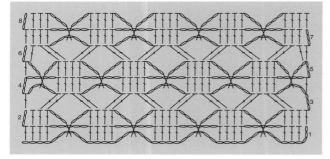

Chain multiples of 9 plus 6.

Row 1: Dc in 4th ch from hook, dc in each of next 2 ch, *ch 5, skip next 5 ch, dc in each of next 4 ch; rep from * across, turn.

Row 2: Ch 3 (counts as dc), skip first dc, dc in each of next 3 dc, *ch 3, sc over ch-5 loops in 2 rows below, ch 3, dc in each of next 4 dc; rep from * across, ending with last dc in 3rd ch of turning ch, turn.

Row 3: Ch 7 (counts as dc, ch 4), skip first dc, skip next dc, *dc in each of next 2 dc, skip next 2 ch-3 loops, dc in each of next 2 dc**, ch 5; rep from * across, ending last rep at **, ch 4, skip next dc, dc in 3rd ch of turning ch, turn.

Row 4: Ch 7 (counts as dc, ch 4), skip next ch-4 loop, dc in each of next 4 dc, *ch 5, skip next ch-5 loop, dc in each of next 4 dc; rep from * across to turning ch, ch 4, dc in 3rd ch of turning ch, turn.

Row 5: Ch 6 (counts as dc, ch 3), sc over ch-4 loops in 2 rows below, ch 3, *dc in each of next 4 dc, ch 3, sc over ch-5 loops in 2 rows below, ch 3; rep from * across, working last sc over ch-4 loops in 2 rows below, dc in 3rd ch of turning ch, turn.

Row 6: Ch 3 (counts as dc), dc in next ch-3 loop, skip next ch-3 loop, *dc in each of next 2 dc, ch 5, dc in each of next 2 dc**, skip next 2 ch-3 loops; rep from * across, ending last rep at **, skip next ch-3 loop, dc in next ch-3 loop, dc in 3rd ch of turning ch, turn.

Row 7: Ch 3 (counts as dc), skip first dc, dc in each of next 3 dc, *ch 5, skip next ch-5 loop, dc in each of next 4 dc; rep from * across, ending with last dc in 3rd ch of turning ch, turn.

Rep Rows 2-7 for pattern.

66

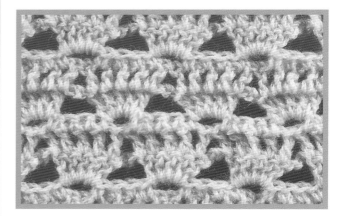

Chain multiples of 7 plus 3.

Row 1: Sc in 2nd ch from hook, sc in each of next 2 ch, ch 3, skip next 3 ch, sc in each of next 4 ch; rep from * across, ending with sc in each of last 3 ch, turn.

Row 2: Ch 4 (counts as dc, ch 1), (5 dc, ch 3) in each ch-3 loop across to within last ch-3 loop, 5 dc in last ch-3 loop, ch 1, skip next 2 sc, dc in last sc, turn.

Row 3: Ch 3 (counts as dc), skip next ch-1 space, *(dc, ch 1) in each of next 4 dc, dc in next dc**, skip next ch-3 loop; rep from * across, ending last rep at **, dc in 3rd ch of turning ch, turn.

Row 4: Ch 1, sc in first dc, ch 1, sc in each of next 4 ch-1 spaces, *ch 3, sc in each of next 4 ch-1 spaces; rep from * across to within last 2 sts, ch 1, skip next dc, sc in 3rd ch of turning ch, turn.

Row 5: Ch 3 (counts as dc), 2 dc in next ch-1 space, (ch 3, 5 dc) in each ch-3 loop across to within last ch-1 space, ch 3, 2 dc in next ch-1 space, dc in last sc, turn.

Row 6: Ch 4 (counts as dc, ch 1), skip first dc, dc in next dc, ch 1, dc in next dc, skip next ch-3 loop, *(dc, ch 1) in each of next 4 dc, dc in next dc, skip next ch-3 loop; rep from * across to within last 3 sts, (dc, ch 1) in each of next 2 dc, dc in 3rd ch of turning ch, turn.

Row 7: Ch 1, sc in first dc, sc in each of next 2 ch-1 spaces, ch 3, *sc in each of next 4 ch-1 spaces, ch 3; rep from * across to within last 2 ch-1 spaces, sc in each of last 2 ch-1 space, sc in 3rd ch of turning ch, turn.

Rep Rows 2-7 for pattern.

67

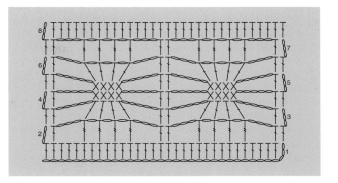

Chain multiples of 15 plus 4.

Row 1: Dc in 4th ch from hook, dc in each ch across, turn.

Row 2: Ch 3 (counts as dc), skip first dc, dc in next dc, *ch 3, skip next 3 dc, (tr in next dc, ch 1, skip next ch) 3 times, tr in next dc, ch 3, skip next 3 dc, dc in each of next 2 dc; rep from * across, ending with last dc in 3rd ch of turning ch, turn.

Row 3: Ch 3 (counts as dc), skip first dc, dc in next dc, *ch 5, skip next ch-3 loop, dc in each of next 4 tr, ch 5, skip next ch-3 loop, dc in each of next 2 dc; rep from * across, ending with last dc in 3rd ch of turning ch, turn.

Row 4: Ch 3 (counts as dc), skip first dc, dc in next dc, *ch 5, skip next ch-5 loop, sc in each of next 4 dc, ch 5, skip next ch-3 loop, dc in each of next 2 dc; rep from * across, ending with last dc in 3rd ch of turning ch, turn.

Row 5: Ch 3 (counts as dc), skip first dc, dc in next dc, *ch 5, skip next ch-5 loop, sc in each of next 4 sc, ch 5, skip next ch-3 loop, dc in each of next 2 dc; rep from * across, ending with last dc in 3rd ch of turning ch, turn.

Row 6: Ch 3 (counts as dc), skip first dc, dc in next dc, *ch 3, skip next ch-5 loop, (dc, ch 1) in each of next 3 sc, dc in next dc, ch 3, skip next ch-5 loop, dc in each of next 2 dc; rep from * across, ending with last dc in 3rd ch of turning ch, turn.

Row 7: Ch 3 (counts as dc), skip first dc, dc in next dc, *ch 3, skip next ch-3 loop, (tr, ch 1) in each of next 3 dc, tr in next dc, ch 3, skip next ch-3 loop, dc in each of next 2 dc; rep from * across, ending with last dc in 3rd ch of turning ch, turn.

Row 8: Ch 3 (counts as dc), skip first dc, dc in next dc, *3 dc in next ch-3 loop, (dc in next tr, dc in next ch-1 space) 3 times, dc in next tr, 3 dc in next ch-3 loop, dc in each of next 2 dc; rep from * across, ending with last dc in 3rd ch of turning ch, turn.

Rep Rows 2-8 for pattern.

68

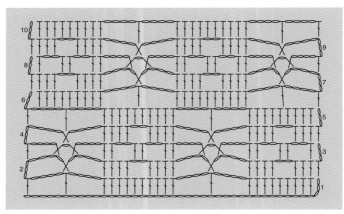

Chain multiples of 19 plus 3.

Row 1: Dc in 4th ch from hook, dc in each of next 8 ch, *ch 4, skip next 4 ch, dc in next ch, ch 4, skip next 4 ch**, dc in each of next 10 ch; rep from * across, ending last rep at **, dc in last ch, turn.

Row 2: Ch 7 (counts as dc, ch 4), skip next ch-4 loop, sc in next dc, ch 4, skip next ch-4 loop, *dc in each of next 4 dc, ch 2, skip next 2 dc, dc in each of next 4 dc**, ch 4, skip next ch-4 loop, sc in next dc, ch 4, skip next ch-4 loop; rep from * across, ending last rep at **, with last dc in 3rd ch of turning ch, turn.

Row 3: Ch 3 (counts as dc), skip first dc, dc in next dc, *ch 2, skip next 2 dc, 2 dc in next ch-2 space, ch 2, skip next 2 dc, dc in each of next 2 dc, ch 4, sc in next ch-4 loop, ch 1, sc in next ch-4 loop, ch 4**, dc in each of next 2 dc; rep from * across, ending last rep at **, dc in 3rd ch of turning ch, turn.

Row 4: Ch 7 (counts as dc, ch 4), skip next ch-4 loop, sc in next ch-1 space, ch 4, skip next ch-4 loop, *dc in each of next 2 dc, 2 dc in next ch-2 space, ch 2, 2 dc in next ch-2 space, dc in each of next 2 dc**, ch 4, skip next ch-4 loop, sc in next ch-1 space, ch 4, skip next ch-4 loop; rep from * across, ending last rep at **, with last dc in 3rd ch of turning ch, turn.

Row 5: Ch 3 (counts as dc), skip first dc, dc in each of next 3 dc, *2 dc in next ch-2 space, dc in each of next 4 dc, ch 4, skip next ch-4 loop, dc in next sc, ch 4, skip next ch-4 loop**, dc in each of next 4 dc; rep from * across, ending last rep at **, dc in 3rd ch of turning ch, turn.

Row 6: Ch 3 (counts as dc), *4 dc in each of next 2 ch-4 loops, ch 4, skip next 5 dc, dc bet last skipped and next dc, ch 4; rep from * across, skip next 4 dc, dc in 3rd ch of turning ch, turn.

Rep Rows 2-6 for pattern, ending with Row 5 of pattern.

69

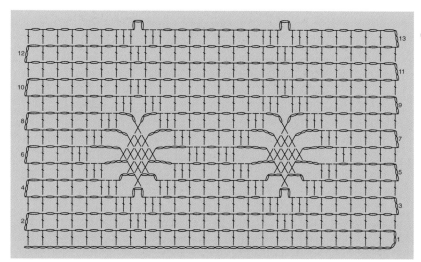

Chain multiples of 20 plus 14.

Row 1: Dc in 6th ch from hook, *ch 1, skip next ch, dc in next ch; rep from * across, turn.

Row 2: Ch 4 (counts as dc, ch 1), (dc, ch 1) in each of next 6 dc, *dc in next dc, dc in next ch-1 space, (dc, ch 1) in each of next 9 dc; rep from * across to within last 8 ch-1 spaces, dc in next dc, dc in next ch-1 space, (dc, ch 1) in each of next 7 dc, dc in 3rd ch of turning ch, turn.

Row 3: Ch 4 (counts as dc, ch 1), (dc, ch 1) in each of next 5 dc, *dc in next dc, dc in next ch-1 space, dc in next dc, ch 3, skip next dc, dc in next dc, dc in next ch-1 space**, (dc, ch 1) in each of next 7 dc; rep from * across, ending last rep at **, (dc, ch 1) in each of next 6 dc, dc in 3rd ch of turning ch, turn.

Row 4: Ch 4 (counts as dc, ch 1), (dc, ch 1) in each of next 4 dc, *dc in next dc, dc in next ch-1 space, dc in next dc, ch 3, sc in next ch-3 loop, ch 3, skip next 2 dc, dc in next dc, dc in next ch-1 space, (dc, ch 1) in each of next 5 dc; rep from * across, dc in 3rd ch of turning ch, turn.

Row 5: Ch 4 (counts as dc, ch 1), (dc, ch 1) in each of next 3 dc, *dc in next dc, dc in next ch-1 space, dc in next dc, ch 4, sc in next ch-3 loop, sc in next sc, sc in next ch-3 loop, ch 4, skip next 2 dc, dc in next dc, dc in next ch-1 space, (dc, ch 1) in each of next 3 dc; rep from * across, dc in next dc, ch 1, dc in 3rd ch of turning ch, turn.

Row 6: Ch 4 (counts as dc, ch 1), (dc, ch 1) in each of next 2 dc, *dc in next dc, dc in next ch-1 space, dc in next dc, ch 4, sc in next ch-4 loop, sc in each of next 3 sc, sc in next ch-4 loop, ch 4, skip next 2 dc, dc in next dc, dc in next ch-1 space, dc in next dc, ch 1; rep from * across, (dc, ch 1) in each of next 2 dc, dc in 3rd ch of turning ch, turn.

Row 7: Ch 4 (counts as dc, ch 1), (dc, ch 1) in each of next 3 dc, *skip next dc, dc in next dc, 2 dc in next ch-4 loop, ch 4, skip next sc, sc in each of next 3 sc, ch 4, 2 dc in next ch-4 loop, dc in next dc, ch 1, skip next dc, (dc, ch 1) in each of next 2 dc; rep from * across, dc in next dc, ch 1, dc in 3rd ch of turning ch, turn.

Row 8: Ch 4 (counts as dc, ch 1), (dc, ch 1) in each of next 4 dc, *skip next dc, dc in next dc, 2 dc in next ch-4 loop, ch 3, skip next sc, sc in next sc, ch 3, 2 dc in next ch-4 loop, dc in next dc, ch 1, skip next dc, (dc, ch 1) in each of next 4 dc; rep from * across, dc in 3rd ch of turning ch, turn.

Row 9: Ch 4 (counts as dc, ch 1), (dc, ch 1) in each of next 5 dc, *skip next dc, dc in next dc, 2 dc in next ch-3 loop, ch 1, 2 dc in next ch-3 loop, dc in next dc, ch 1, skip next dc**, (dc, ch 1) in each of next 6 dc; rep from * across, ending last rep at **, (dc, ch 1) in each of next 5 dc, dc in 3rd ch of turning ch, turn.

Row 10: Ch 4 (counts as dc, ch 1), (dc, ch 1) in each of next 6 dc, *skip next dc, dc in next dc, dc in next ch-1 space, dc in next dc, ch 1, skip next dc**, (dc, ch 1) in each of next 8 dc; rep from * across, ending last rep at **, (dc, ch 1) in each of next 6 dc, dc in next dc, turn.

Row 11: Ch 4 (counts as dc, ch 1), *dc in next dc, ch 1, skip next st; rep from * across, ending with dc in 3rd ch of turning ch, turn.

Rep Rows 2-11 for pattern.

.5.

Treble Crochet, Double Crochet, Single Crochet & Chains

70

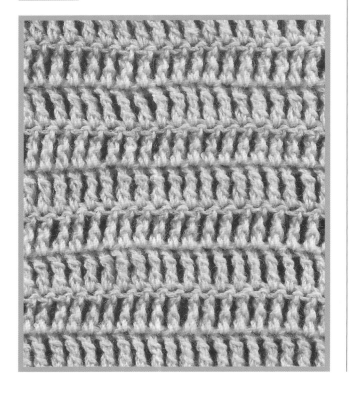

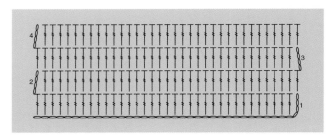

Chain any multiple plus 4.

Row 1: Tr in 5th ch from hook, tr in each ch across, turn.

Row 2: Ch 4 (counts as tr), skip first tr, tr in each tr across, ending with tr in 4th ch of turning ch, turn.

Rep Row 2 for pattern.

71

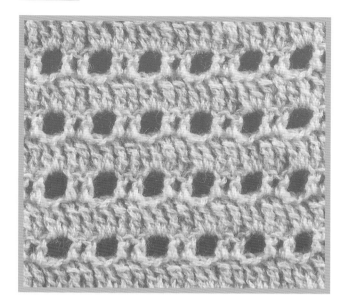

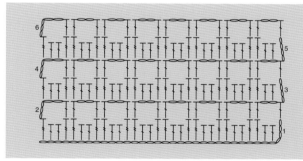

Chain multiples of 4 plus 3.

Row 1: Dc in 5th ch from hook, dc in next ch, *tr in each of next 2 ch, dc in each of next 2 ch; rep from * across to within last ch, tr in last ch, turn.

Row 2: Ch 5 (counts as dc, ch 2), skip first 3 sts, *dc in each of next 2 tr, ch 2, skip next 2 dc; rep from * across to last st, dc in 4th ch of turning ch, turn.

Row 3: Ch 4 (counts as tr), 2 dc in next ch-2 space, *tr in each of next 2 dc, 2 dc in next ch-2 space; rep from across to last st, tr in 3rd ch of turning ch, turn.

Rep Rows 2-3 for pattern.

72

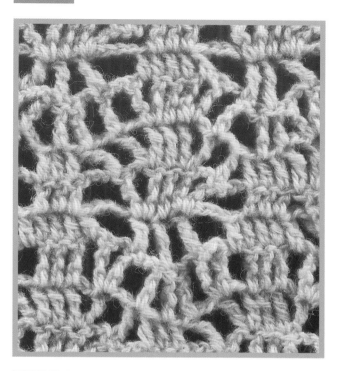

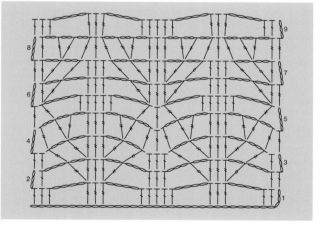

Chain multiples of 16 plus 3.

Row 1: Dc in 4th ch from hook, dc in next ch, *ch 4, skip next 4 ch, tr in each of next 3 ch, ch 4, skip next 4 ch, dc in each of next 5 ch; rep from * across, ending with dc in each of last 3 ch, turn.

Row 2: Ch 3 (counts as dc), skip first dc, dc in next dc, *ch 3, skip next ch-4 loop, (tr, ch 2, tr) in next tr, tr in next tr, (tr, ch 2, tr) in next tr, ch 3, skip next dc**, dc in each of next 3 dc; rep from * across, ending last rep at **, dc in next dc, dc in 3rd ch of turning ch, turn.

Row 3: Ch 3 (counts as dc), skip first dc, dc in next dc, *skip next ch-3 loop, tr in next tr, ch 2, skip next ch-2 space, (tr, ch 2, tr) in next tr, tr in next tr, (tr, ch 2, tr) in next tr, ch 2, skip next ch-2 space, tr in next tr, skip next ch-3 loop**, dc in each of next 3 dc; rep from across, ending last rep at **, dc in next dc, dc in 3rd ch of turning ch, turn.

Row 4: Ch 4 (counts as tr), skip first 2 dc, *tr in next tr, ch 2, skip next ch-2 space, (tr, ch 2, tr) in next tr, ch 2, skip next ch-2 space, tr in each of next 3 tr, ch 2, skip next ch-2 space, (tr, ch 2, tr) in next tr, ch 2, skip next ch-2 space, tr in next tr, skip next dc, tr in next dc, skip next dc; rep from * across, ending with last tr in 3rd ch of turning ch, turn.

Row 5: Ch 4 (counts as tr), *skip next ch-2 space, tr in next tr, ch 4, skip next ch-2 space, dc in next ch-2 space, dc in each of next 3 tr, dc in next ch-2 space, ch 4, skip next ch-2 space, tr in next tr, skip next tr, tr in next tr; rep from * across, ending with last tr in 4th ch of turning ch, turn.

Row 6: Ch 4 (counts as tr), skip first tr, *(tr, ch 2, tr) in next tr, ch 3, skip next dc, dc in each of next 3 dc, ch 3, skip next ch-4 loop, (tr, ch 2, tr) in next tr, tr in next tr; rep from * across to last st, tr in 4th ch of turning ch, turn.

Row 7: Ch 4 (counts as tr), skip first tr, *(tr, ch 2, tr) in next tr, ch 2, skip next ch-2 space, tr in next tr, skip next ch-3 loop, dc in each of next 3 dc, skip next ch-3 loop, tr in next tr, ch 2, skip next ch-2 space, (tr, ch 2, tr) in next tr, tr in next tr; rep from * across, ending with last tr in 4th ch of turning ch, turn.

Row 8: Ch 4 (counts as tr), skip first tr, tr in next tr, *ch 2, skip next ch-2 space, (tr, ch 2, tr) in next tr, ch 2, skip next ch-2 space, tr in next tr, skip next dc, tr in next dc, skip next dc, tr in next tr, ch 2, skip next ch-2 space, (tr, ch 2, tr) in next tr, ch 2, skip next ch-2 space**, tr in each of next 3 tr; rep from * across, ending last rep at **, tr in next tr, tr in 4th ch of turning ch, turn.

Row 9: Ch 3 (counts as dc), skip first dc, dc in next dc, *dc in next ch-2 space, ch 4, skip next 2 ch-2 spaces, tr in each of next 3 tr, ch 4, skip next 2 ch-2 spaces, dc in next ch-2 space**, dc in each of next 3 dc; rep from * across, ending last rep at **, dc in next dc, dc in 4th ch of turning ch, turn.

Rep Rows 2-9 for pattern.

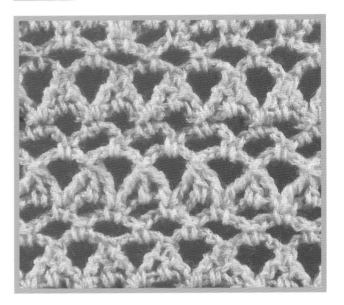

Chain multiples of 4 plus 2.

Row 1: Sc in 2nd ch from hook, *ch 5, skip next 3 ch, sc in next ch; rep from * across, turn.

Row 2: Ch 6 (counts as tr, ch 2), work half-closed tr in first sc, half-closed dc in next ch-5 loop, half-closed tr in next sc, yo, draw yarn through 4 loops on hook to complete cluster, *ch 5, work half-closed tr in last sc worked, half-closed dc in next ch-5 loop, half-closed tr in next sc, yo, complete cluster; rep from * across to last sc, ch 2, tr in last sc, turn.

Row 3: Ch 1, sc in first tr, (ch 5, sc) in each ch-5 loop across, ending with last sc in 4th ch of turning ch, turn.

Row 4: Ch 6 (counts as tr, ch 2), (sc, ch 5) in each ch-5 loop across to within last ch-5 loop, sc in next ch-5 loop, ch 2, tr in last sc, turn.

Row 5: Ch 2, skip next ch-2 space, tr in next sc, ch 5, work 1 cluster of (tr, dc, tr) across next (sc, ch 5, sc) as before; rep from * across to last sc, ch 5, work half-closed tr in last sc worked, work half-closed dc in 4th ch of turning ch, yo, complete end cluster, turn.

Row 6: Ch 6 (counts as tr, ch 2), (sc, ch 5) in each ch-5 loop across to last ch-5 loop, sc in next ch-5 loop, ch 2, tr in 2nd ch of turning ch, turn.

Row 7: Rep Row 3.

Rep Rows 2-7 for pattern.

74

Chain multiples of 11 plus 5.

Row 1: Dc in 4th ch from hook, dc in each ch across, turn.

Row 2: Ch 3 (counts as dc), skip first dc, dc in each of next 2 dc, *ch 3, skip next 2 dc, tr in each of next 4 dc, ch 3, skip next 2 dc, dc in each of next 3 dc; rep from * across, ending with last dc in 3rd ch of turning ch, turn.

Row 3: Ch 3 (counts as dc), skip first dc, dc in each of next 2 dc, *ch 3, skip next ch-3 loop, sc in each of next 4 tr, ch 3, skip next ch-3 loop, dc in each of next 3 dc; rep from * across, ending with last dc in 3rd ch of turning ch, turn.

Rows 4-5: Ch 3 (counts as dc), skip first dc, dc in each of next 2 dc, *ch 3, skip next ch-3 loop, sc in each of next 4 sc, ch 3, skip next ch-3 loop, dc in each of next 3 dc; rep from * across, ending with last dc in 3rd ch of turning ch, turn.

Row 6: Ch 3 (counts as dc), skip first dc, dc in each of next 2 dc, *ch 3, skip next ch-3 loop, tr in each of next 4 sc, ch 3, skip next ch-3 loop, dc in each of next 3 dc; rep from * across, ending with last dc in 3rd ch of turning ch, turn.

Row 7: Ch 3 (counts as dc), skip first dc, dc in each of next 2 dc, *2 dc in next ch-2 space, dc in each of next 4 tr, 2 dc in next ch-2 space, dc in each of next 3 dc; rep from * across, ending with last dc in 3rd ch of turning ch, turn.

Rep Rows 2-7 for pattern.

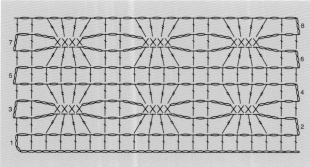

Chain multiples of 12 plus 6.

Row 1 (WS): Dc in 6th ch from hook, *ch 1, skip next ch, dc in next ch; rep from * across, turn.

Row 2: Ch 4 (counts as dc, ch 1), skip next ch-1 space, dc in next dc, *ch 3, tr in each of next 4 dc, ch 3, dc in next dc, ch 1, dc in next dc; rep from * across, ending with last dc in 3rd ch of turning ch, turn.

Row 3: Ch 4 (counts as dc, ch 1), skip next ch-1 space, dc in next dc, *ch 3, sc in each of next 4 tr, ch 3, dc in next dc, ch 1, dc in next dc; rep from * across, ending with last dc in 3rd ch of turning ch, turn.

Row 4: Ch 4 (counts as dc, ch 1), skip next ch-1 space, dc in next dc, *ch 1, (tr, ch 1) in each of next 4 sc, dc in next dc, ch 1, dc in next dc; rep from * across, ending with last dc in 3rd ch of turning ch, turn.

Row 5: Ch 4 (counts as dc, ch 1), skip next ch-1 space, *dc in next st, ch 1, skip next ch-1 space; rep from * across to last st, dc in 3rd ch of turning ch, turn.

Rep Rows 2-5 for pattern.

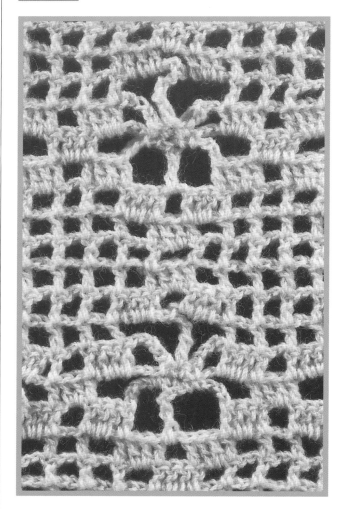

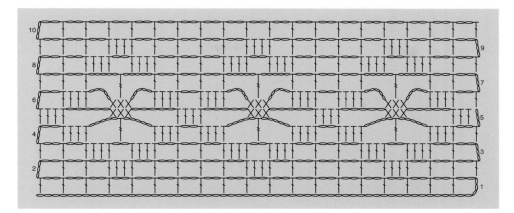

Chain multiples of 18 plus 8.

Row 1: Dc in 8th ch from hook, *ch 2, skip next 2 ch, dc in next ch; rep from * across, turn.

Row 2: Ch 5 (counts as dc, ch 2), skip next ch-2 space, (dc, ch 2) in each of next 2 dc, dc in next dc, 2 dc in next ch-2 space, *(dc, ch 2) in each of next 5 dc, dc in next dc, 2 dc in next ch-2 space; rep from * across to within last 3 ch-2 spaces, (dc, ch 2) in each of next 3 dc, skip next 2 ch, dc in next ch of turning ch, turn.

Row 3: Ch 5 (counts as dc, ch 2), skip next ch-2 space, dc in next dc, ch 2, *dc in next dc, 2 dc in next ch-2 space, dc in next dc, ch 2, skip next 2 dc, dc in next dc, 2 dc in next ch-2 space**, (dc, ch 2) in each of next 3 dc; rep from * across, ending last rep at **, (dc, ch 2) in each of next 2 dc, dc in 3rd ch of turning ch, turn.

Row 4: Ch 5 (counts as dc, ch 2), skip next ch-2 space, *dc in next dc, 2 dc in next ch-2 space, dc in next dc, ch 5, tr in next ch-2 space, ch 5, skip next 3 dc, dc in next dc, 2 dc in next ch-2 space, dc in next dc, ch 2; rep from * across to turning ch, dc in 3rd ch of turning ch, turn.

Row 5: Ch 3 (counts as dc), 2 dc in next ch-2 space, *dc in next dc, ch 5, sc in next ch-5 loop, sc in next tr, sc in next ch-5 loop, ch 5, skip next 3 dc, dc in next dc, 2 dc in next ch-2 space; rep from * across to last st, dc in 3rd ch of turning ch, turn.

Row 6: Ch 5 (counts as dc, ch 2), skip first dc, *skip next 2 dc, dc in next dc, 3 dc in next ch-5 loop, ch 5, sc in each of next 3 sc, ch 5, 3 dc in next ch-5 loop, dc in next dc, ch 2; rep from * across, dc in 3rd ch of turning ch, turn.

Row 7: Ch 5 (counts as dc, ch 2), skip next ch-2 space, *dc in next dc, ch 2, skip next 2 dc, dc in next dc, ch 5, skip next sc, tr in next sc, ch 5, skip next ch-5 loop, dc in next dc, ch 2, skip next 2 dc, dc in next dc, ch 2, skip next ch-2 space; rep from * across to turning ch, dc in 3rd ch of turning ch, turn.

Row 8: Ch 5 (counts as dc, ch 2), skip next ch-2 space, dc in next dc, ch 2, *dc in next dc, 3 dc in next ch-5 space, ch 2, 3 dc in next ch-5 loop**, (dc, ch 2) in each of next 3 dc; rep from * across, ending last rep at **, (dc, ch 2) in each of next 2 dc, dc in 3rd ch of turning ch, turn.

Row 9: Ch 5 (counts as dc, ch 2), skip next ch-2 space, (dc, ch 2) in each of next 2 dc, skip next 2 dc, dc in next dc, 2 dc in next ch-2 space, *dc in next dc, ch 2, skip next 2 dc, (dc, ch 2) in each of next 4 dc, skip next 2 dc, dc in next dc, 2 dc in next ch-2 space; rep from * across to within last 10 sts, dc in next dc, ch 2, skip next 2 dc, (dc, ch 2) in each of next 2 dc, dc in 3rd ch of turning ch, turn.

Row 10: Ch 5 (counts as dc, ch 2), skip next ch-2 space, dc in next dc, *ch 2, skip next 2 sts, dc in next dc; rep from * across, ending with last dc in 3rd ch of turning ch, turn.

Rep Rows 2-10 for pattern.

.6.
V-Stitches

77

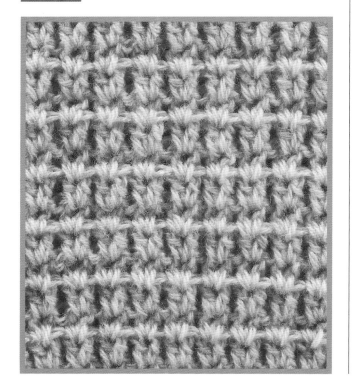

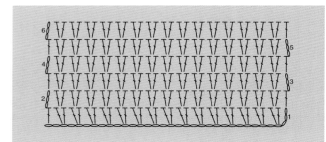

Chain multiples of 2.

Row 1: 2 dc in 4th ch from hook, skip next ch, *2 dc in next ch, skip next ch; rep from * across to within last ch, dc in last ch, turn.

Row 2: Ch 3 (counts as dc), skip first 2 dc, *2 bet last skipped and next dc, skip next 2 dc; rep from * across to within last 2 sts, skip next dc, dc in 3rd ch of turning ch, turn.

Rep Row 2 for pattern.

78

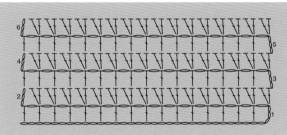

Chain multiples of 2.

Row 1: Dc in 6th ch from hook, *ch 1, skip next ch, dc in next ch; rep from * across, turn.

Row 2: Ch 3 (counts as dc), skip first dc, 2 dc in each dc across, ending with last 2 dc in 3rd ch of turning ch, turn.

Row 3: Ch 4 (counts as dc, ch 1), skip first 2 dc, *dc in next dc, ch 1, skip next dc; rep from * across to turning ch, dc in 3rd ch of turning ch, turn.

Rep Rows 2-3 for pattern.

79

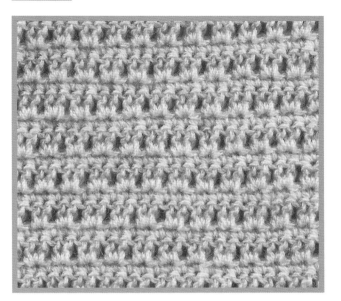

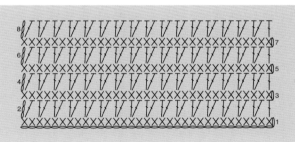

Chain multiples of 2.

Row 1: Sc in 2nd ch from hook, sc in each ch across, turn.

Row 2: Ch 3 (counts as dc), dc in first sc, skip next sc, *2 dc in next sc, skip next sc; rep from * across to within last sc, dc in last sc, turn.

Row 3: Ch 1, sc in each dc across, ending with last sc in 3rd ch of turning ch, turn.

Rep Rows 2-3 for pattern.

80

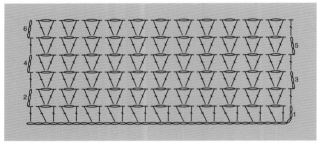

Chain multiples of 3 plus 1.

Row 1: Dc in 4th ch from hook, ch 1, dc in next ch, *skip next ch, dc in next ch, ch 1, dc in next ch; rep from * across to within last 2 ch, skip next ch, dc in last ch, turn.

Row 2: Ch 3 (counts as dc), (dc, ch 1, dc) in each ch-1 space across to last ch-1 space, dc in 3rd ch of turning ch, turn.

Rep Row 2 for pattern.

81

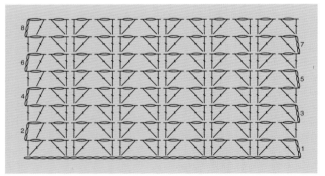

Chain multiples of 6 plus 4.

Row 1: Dc in 5th ch from hook, skip next 4 ch, *(dc, ch 1, dc) in each of next 2 ch, skip next 4 ch; rep from * across to within last ch, (dc, ch 1, dc) in last ch, turn.

Row 2: Ch 4 (counts as dc, ch 1), dc in next ch-1 space, skip next ch-1 space, *(dc, ch 1, dc) in each of next 2 dc, skip next 2 ch-1 spaces; rep from * across to turning ch, (dc, ch 1, dc) in 3rd ch of turning ch, turn.

Rep Row 2 for pattern.

82

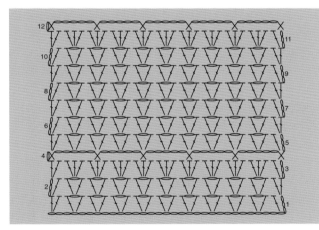

Chain multiples of 3 plus 1.

Row 1: Dc in 4th ch from hook, skip next 2 ch, *(dc, ch 1, dc) in next ch, skip next 2 ch; rep from * across to within last ch, 2 dc in last ch, turn.

Row 2: Ch 3 (counts as dc), dc in first dc, (dc, ch 1, dc) in each ch-1 space across to within last 3 sts, skip next 2 dc, 2 dc in 3rd ch of turning ch, turn.

Row 3: Ch 3 (counts as dc), dc in first dc, 3 dc in each ch-1 space across to within last 3 sts, skip next 2 dc, 2 dc in 3rd ch of turning ch, turn.

Row 4: Ch 1, sc in first dc, *ch 5, skip next 5 dc, sc in next dc; rep from * across, ending with last sc in 3rd ch of turning ch, turn.

Row 5: Ch 3 (counts as dc), dc in first dc, *(dc, ch 1, dc) in next ch-5 loop, (dc, ch 1, dc) in next sc; rep from * across, ending with 2 dc in last sc, turn.

Rows 7-10: Rep Row 2.

Rep Rows 3-10 for pattern.

83

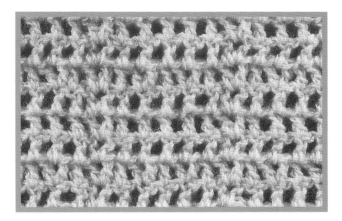

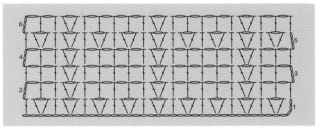

Chain multiples of 12 plus 3.

Row 1: (Dc, ch 1, dc) in 5th ch from hook, skip next ch, dc in next ch, *skip next ch, (dc, ch 1, dc) in next ch, skip next ch, dc in next ch; rep from * across, turn.

Row 2: Ch 4 (counts as dc, ch 1), dc in next ch-1 space, ch 1, dc in next dc, (dc, ch 1, dc) in next ch-1 space, skip next dc, dc in next dc, ch 1, dc in next ch-1 space, *ch 1, skip next dc, dc in next dc, ch 1, dc in next ch-1 space, ch 1, skip next dc, dc in next dc, (dc, ch 1, dc) in next ch-1, skip next dc, dc in next dc, ch 1, dc in next ch-1 space; rep from * across to last ch-1 space, ch 1, skip next dc, dc in 3rd ch of turning ch, turn.

Row 3: Ch 4 (counts as dc, ch 1), skip next ch-1 space, dc in next dc, ch 1, dc in next dc, (dc, ch 1, dc) in next ch-1 space, skip next dc, dc in next dc, *(ch 1, dc) in each of next 4 dc, (dc, ch 1, dc) in next ch-1 space, skip next dc, dc in next dc; rep from * across to within last 2 ch-1 spaces, ch 1, dc in next dc, ch 1, dc in 3rd ch of turning ch, turn.

Row 4: Rep Row 3.

Row 5: Ch 3 (counts as dc), *skip next ch-1 space, (dc, ch 1, dc) in next dc, dc in next dc, (dc, ch 1, dc) in next ch-1 space, skip next dc, dc in next dc, (dc, ch 1, dc) in next dc, dc in next dc; rep from * across, ending with last dc in 3rd ch of turning ch, turn.

Rep Rows 2-5 for pattern.

84

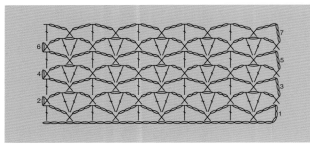

Chain multiples of 6.

Row 1: Sc in 9th ch from hook, ch 3, skip next 2 ch, dc in next ch, *ch 3, skip next 2 ch, sc in next ch, ch 3, skip next 2 ch, dc in next ch; rep from * across, turn.

Row 2: Ch 1, sc in first dc, *ch 2, (dc, ch 1, dc) in next sc, ch 2, sc in next dc; rep from * across, ending with last sc in 3rd ch of turning ch, turn.

Row 3: Ch 6 (counts as dc, ch 3), skip next ch-2 space, sc in next ch-1 space, ch 3, skip next ch-2 space, dc in next sc, *ch 3, skip next ch-2 space, sc in next ch-1 space, ch 3, skip next ch-2 space, dc in next sc; rep from * across, ending with last dc in 3rd ch of turning ch, turn.

Rep Rows 2-3 for pattern.

85

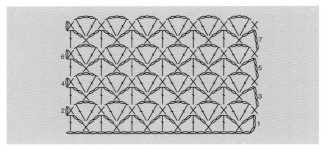

Chain multiples of 4 plus 1.

Row 1: Sc in 7th ch from hook, ch 2, skip next ch, dc in next ch, *ch 2, skip next ch, sc in next ch, ch 2, skip next ch, dc in next ch; rep from * across, turn.

Row 2: Ch 1, sc in first dc, *skip next ch-2 space, (dc, ch 3, dc) in next sc, skip next ch-2 space, sc in next dc; rep from * across, ending with last sc in 3rd ch of turning ch, turn.

Row 3: Ch 5 (counts as dc, ch 2), sc in next ch-3 loop, ch 2, dc in next sc, *ch 2, sc in next ch-3 loop, dc in next sc; rep from * across, turn.

Rep Rows 2-3 for pattern.

86

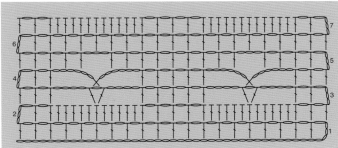

Chain multiples of 20 plus 4.

Row 1: Dc in 6th ch from hook, *ch 1, skip next ch, dc in next ch; rep from * across, turn.

Row 2: Ch 4 (counts as dc, ch 1), skip next ch-1 space, dc in next dc, ch 1, *(dc in next dc, dc in next ch-1 space) 6 times**, (dc, ch 1) in each of next 4 dc; rep from * across, ending last rep at **, (dc, ch 1) in each of next 2 dc, dc in 3rd ch of turning ch, turn.

Row 3: Ch 4 (counts as dc, ch 1), skip next ch-1 space, dc in next dc, ch 1, dc in next dc, *ch 4, skip next 5 dc, (dc, ch 1, dc) in next dc, ch 4, skip next 5 dc**, (dc, ch 1) in each of next 4 dc, dc in next dc; rep from * across, ending last rep at **, (dc, ch 1) in each of next 2 dc, dc in 3rd ch of turning ch, turn.

Row 4: Ch 4 (counts as dc, ch 1), skip next ch-1 space, dc in next dc, ch 1, dc in next dc, *ch 6, skip next ch-4 loop, sc in next ch-1 space, ch 6, skip next ch-4 loop**, (dc, ch 1) in each of next 4 dc, dc in next dc; rep from * across, ending last rep at **, (dc, ch 1) in each of next 2 dc, dc in 3rd ch of turning ch, turn.

Row 5: Ch 4 (counts as dc, ch 1), skip next ch-1 space, dc in next dc, ch 1, dc in next dc, *ch 1, (dc, ch 1, dc) in next ch-5 loop, ch 3, (dc, ch 1, dc) in next ch-5 loop, ch 1**, (dc, ch 1) in each of next 4 dc, dc in next dc; rep from * across, ending last rep at **, (dc, ch 1) in each of next 2 dc, dc in 3rd ch of turning ch, turn.

Row 6: Ch 4 (counts as dc, ch 1), skip next ch-1 space, (dc, ch 1) in each of next 4 dc, dc in next ch-3 loop, ch 1, *(dc, ch 1) in each of next 9 dc, dc in next ch-3 loop, ch 1; rep from * across to within last 4 ch-1 spaces, (dc, ch 1) in each of next 4 dc, dc in 3rd ch of turning ch, turn.

Rep Rows 2-6 for pattern.

87

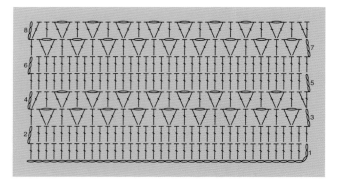

Chain multiples of 4 plus 3.

Row 1: Dc in 4th ch from hook, dc in each ch across, turn.

Row 2: Ch 3 (counts as dc), skip first dc, dc in each dc across, ending with last dc in 3rd ch of turning ch, turn.

Row 3: Ch 3 (counts as dc), skip first dc, *skip next dc, (dc, ch 1, dc) in next dc, skip next dc, dc in next dc; rep from * across, ending with last dc in 3rd ch of turning ch, turn.

Row 4: Ch 3 (counts as dc), dc in first dc, dc in next ch-1 space, *skip next dc, (dc, ch 1, dc) in next dc, dc in next ch-1 space; rep from * across to last ch-1 space, skip next dc, dc in 3rd ch of turning ch, turn.

Row 5: Ch 3 (counts as dc), skip first dc, dc in each of next 3 dc, *dc in next ch-1 space, dc in each of next 3 dc; rep from * across to within last st, dc in 3rd ch of turning ch, turn.

Rep Rows 2-5 for pattern.

.7.
Simple Shells

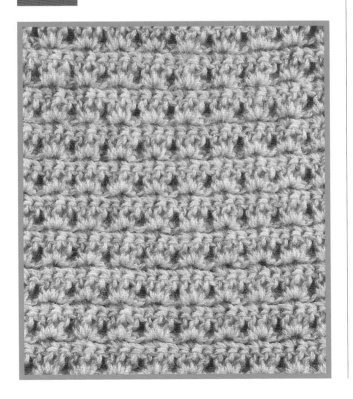

88

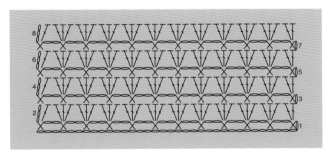

Chain multiples of 3 plus 2.

Row 1: Sc in 2nd ch from hook, *ch 2, skip next 2 ch sc in next ch; rep from * across, turn.

Row 2: Ch 3 (counts as dc), dc in first sc, 3 dc in each sc across, ending with 2 dc in last sc, turn.

Row 3: Ch 1, sc in first dc, *ch 2, skip next 2 dc, sc in next dc; rep from * across, ending with last sc in 3rd ch of turning ch, turn.

Rep Rows 2-3 for pattern.

89

Chain multiples of 4 plus 1.

Row 1: 4 dc in 5th ch from hook, *skip next 3 ch, 4 dc in next ch; rep from * across to within last 4 ch, skip next 3 ch, 3 dc in last ch, turn.

Row 2: Ch 1, sc in each dc across, ending with last sc in top of turning ch, turn.

Row 3: Ch 3 (counts as dc), skip first sc, 2 dc in next sc, *skip next 3 sc, 4 dc in next sc; rep from * across to within last 2 sc, skip next sc, dc in last sc, turn.

Row 4: Rep Row 2.

Row 5: Ch 3 (counts as dc), skip first 3 sc, *4 dc in next sc, skip next 3 sc; rep from * across to within last sc, 3 dc in last sc, turn.

Rep Rows 2-5 for pattern.

90

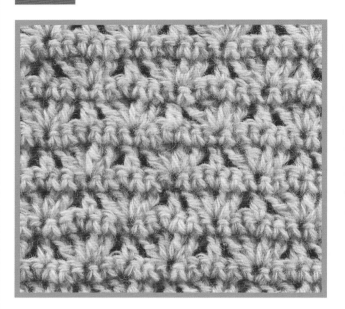

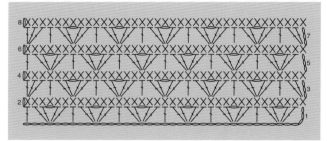

Chain multiples of 6 plus 3.

Row 1: (2 dc, ch 1, 2 dc) in 6th ch from hook, skip next 2 ch, dc in next ch, *skip next 2 ch, (2 dc, ch 1, 2 dc) in next ch, skip next 2 ch, dc in next ch; rep from * across, turn.

Row 2: Ch 1, sc in each dc and ch-1 space across, ending with last sc in top of turning ch, turn.

Row 3: Ch 3 (counts as dc), 2 dc in first sc, skip next 2 sc, dc in next sc, *skip next 2 sc, (2 dc, ch 1, 2 dc) in next sc, skip next 2 sc, dc in next sc; rep from * across to within last 3 sc, skip next 2 sc, 3 dc in last sc, turn.

Row 4: Rep Row 2.

Row 5: Ch 3 (counts as dc), skip first sc, *skip next 2 sc, (2 dc, ch 1, 2 dc) in next sc, skip next 2 sc, dc in next sc; rep from * across, turn.

Rep Rows 2-5 for pattern.

91

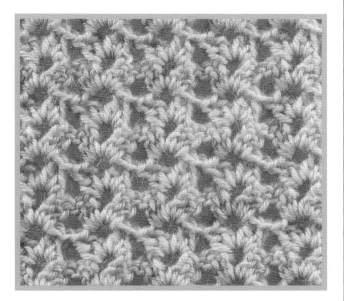

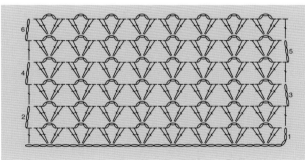

Chain multiples of 4 plus 1.

Row 1: (2 dc, ch 3, 2 dc) in 6th ch from hook, *skip next 3 ch, (2 dc, ch 3, 2 dc) in next ch; rep from * across to within last 3 ch, skip next 2 ch, dc in last ch, turn.

Row 2: Ch 3 (counts as dc), (2 dc, ch 3, 2 dc) in each ch-3 loop across to last ch-3 loop, skip next 2 dc, dc in 3rd ch of turning ch, turn.

Rep Row 2 for pattern.

92

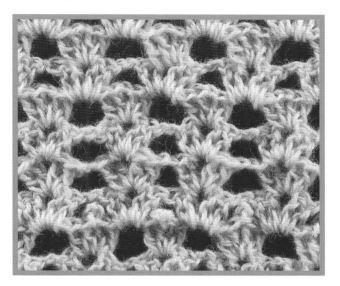

Chain multiples of 5 plus 4.

Row 1: 2 dc in 4th ch from hook, *ch 2, skip next 4 ch, (2 dc, ch 1, 2 dc) in next ch; rep from * across to within last 5 ch, ch 2, skip next 4 ch, 3 dc in last ch, turn.

Row 2: Ch 3 (counts as dc), 2 dc in first dc, *ch 2, skip next ch-2 space, (2 dc, ch 1, 2 dc) in next ch-1 space; rep from * across to last ch-1 space, ch 2, skip next ch-2 space, skip next 2 dc, 3 dc in 3rd ch of turning ch, turn.

Row 3: Ch 3 (counts as dc), *(2 dc, ch 1, 2 dc) in next ch-2 space**, ch 2, skip next ch-1 space; rep from * across, ending last rep at **, skip next 2 dc, dc in 3rd ch of turning ch, turn.

Row 4: Ch 3 (counts as dc), *(2 dc, ch 1, 2 dc) in next ch-1 space**, ch 2, skip next ch-2 space; rep from * across, ending last rep at **, skip next 2 dc, dc in 3rd ch of turning ch, turn.

Row 5: Ch 3 (counts as dc), *(2 dc, ch 3, sl st in 3rd ch from hook for picot, 2 dc) in next ch-1 space**, ch 2, skip next ch-2 space; rep from * across, ending last rep at **, skip next 2 dc, dc in 3rd ch of turning ch, turn.

Row 6: Ch 3 (counts as dc), 2 dc in first dc, *ch 2, skip next picot, (2 dc, ch 1, 2 dc) in next ch-2 space; rep from * across to last ch-2 space, ch 2, skip next picot, skip next 2 dc, 3 dc in 3rd ch of turning ch, turn.

Rows 7-9: Rep Row 2.

Rep Rows 3-9 for pattern.

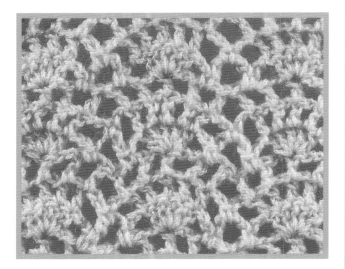

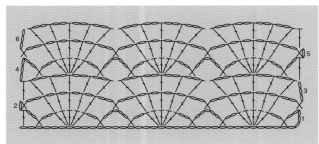

Chain multiples of 12 plus 5.

Row 1: Sc in 7th ch from hook, *ch 2, skip next 3 ch, 5 dc in next ch, ch 2, skip next 3 ch, sc in next ch**, ch 5, skip next 3 ch, sc in next ch; rep from * across, ending last rep at **, ch 2, skip next ch, dc in last ch, turn.

Row 2: Ch 1, sc in first dc, *ch 2, skip next 2 ch-2 spaces, (dc, ch 1) in each of next 4 dc, dc in next dc, ch 2, skip next ch-2

space**, sc in next ch-5 loop; rep from * across, ending last rep at **, skip next 2 ch, sc in next ch of turning ch, turn.

Row 3: Ch 3 (counts as dc), skip next ch-2 space, *(dc, ch 2) in each of next 4 dc, dc in next dc**, skip next 2 ch-2 spaces; rep from * across, ending last rep at **, skip next ch-2 space, dc in last sc, turn.

Row 4: Ch 5 (counts as dc, ch 2), *sc in next ch-2 space, ch 2, skip next ch-2 space, 5 dc in next dc, ch 2, skip next ch-2 space, sc in next ch-2 space**, ch 5; rep from * across, ending last rep at **, ch 2, dc in 3rd ch of turning ch, turn.

Rep Rows 2-4 for pattern.

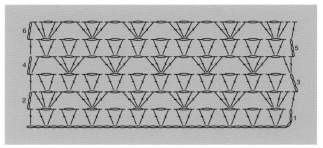

Chain multiples of 6 plus 1.

Row 1: (Dc, ch 1, dc) in 5th ch from hook, *skip next 2 ch, (dc, ch 1, dc) in next ch; rep from * across to within last 2 ch, skip next ch, dc in last ch, turn.

Row 2: Ch 3 (counts as dc), (2 dc, ch 1, 2 dc) in next ch-1 space, *ch 1, skip next ch-1 space, (2 dc, ch 1, 2 dc) in next ch-1 space; rep from * across to last ch-1 space, skip next dc, dc in 3rd ch of turning ch, turn.

Row 3: Ch 3 (counts as dc), (dc, ch 1, dc) in each ch-1 space across to last ch-1 space, skip next 2 dc, dc in 3rd ch of turning ch, turn.

Row 4: Ch 3 (counts as dc), dc in first dc, *ch 1, skip next ch-1 space, (2 dc, ch 1, 2 dc) in next ch-1 space; rep from * across to within last ch-1 space, ch 1, skip next ch-1 space, skip next dc, dc in 3rd ch of turning ch, turn.

Row 5: Ch 3 (counts as dc), (dc, ch 1, dc) in each ch-1 space across to last ch-1 space, skip next dc, dc in 3rd ch of turning ch, turn.

Rep Rows 2-5 for pattern.

95

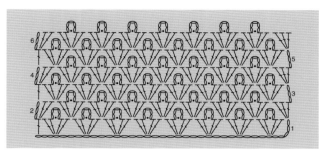

Picot: Ch 5, sl st in 5th ch from hook.

Double Treble Crochet (dtr): Yo (3 times), insert hook in next st, yo, draw yarn through st, (yo, draw yarn through 2 loops on hook) 4 times.

Chain multiples of 4 plus 1.

Row 1: (2 dc, picot, 2 dc) in 6th ch from hook for shell, *skip next 3 ch, (2 dc, picot, 2 dc) in next ch for shell; rep from * across to within last 3 ch, skip next 2 ch, dc in last ch, turn.

Row 2: Ch 3 (counts as dc), 2 dc in first dc, *skip next shell, (2 dc, picot, 2 dc) bet last skipped and next shell; rep from * across to within last shell, skip next shell, 3 dc in 3rd ch of turning ch, turn.

Row 3: Ch 3 (counts as dc), skip first 3 dc, *(2 dc, picot, 2 dc) bet last skipped dc and next shell, skip next shell; rep from * across to within last 3 dc, skip next 2 dc, dc in 3rd ch of turning ch, turn.

Rep Rows 2-3 for pattern.

.8.
Shells—Filet

96

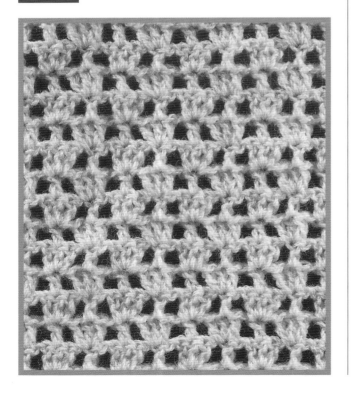

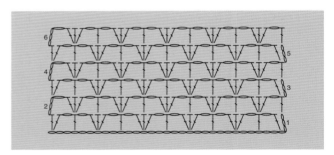

Chain multiples of 6 plus 4.

Row 1: Dc in 4th ch from hook, *ch 1, skip next 2 ch, dc in next ch, ch 1, skip next 2 ch, 3 dc in next ch; rep from * across, ending with 2 dc in last ch, turn.

Row 2: Ch 4 (counts as dc, ch 1), *skip next ch-1 space, 3 dc in next dc, ch 1, skip next dc, dc in next dc; rep from * across, ending with last dc in 3rd ch of turning ch, turn.

Row 3: Ch 3 (counts as dc), dc in first dc, *ch 1, skip next dc, dc in next dc, ch 1, skip next ch-1 space, 3 dc in next dc; rep from * across, ending with 2 dc in 3rd ch of turning ch, turn.

Rep Rows 2-3 for pattern.

97

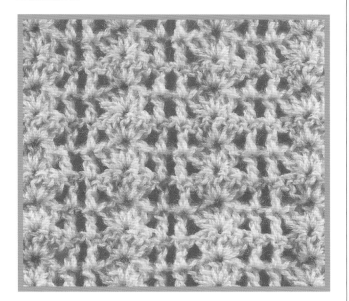

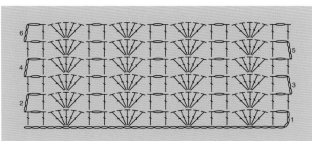

Chain multiples of 8 plus 6.

Row 1: Dc in 6th ch from hook, *skip next 2 ch, 5 dc in next ch, skip next 2 ch, dc in next ch, ch 1, skip next ch, dc in next ch; rep from * across, turn.

Row 2: Ch 4 (counts as dc, ch 1), skip next ch-1 space, dc in next dc, *skip next 2 dc, 5 dc in next dc, skip next 2 dc, dc in next dc, ch 1, skip next ch-1 space, dc in next dc; rep from * across, ending with last dc in next ch of turning ch, turn.

Rep Row 2 for pattern

98

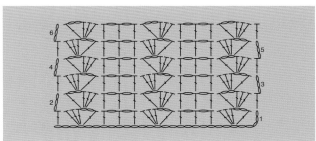

Chain multiples of 10 plus 9.

Row 1: (Dc, ch 2, 3 dc) in 6th ch from hook, skip next 2 ch, *(dc in next ch, ch 1, skip next ch) twice, dc in next ch, skip next 2 ch, (dc, ch 2, 3 dc) in next ch, skip next 2 ch; rep from * across to within last ch, dc in last ch, turn.

Row 2: Ch 3 (counts as dc), (dc, ch 2, 3 dc) in next ch-2 space, *skip next dc, (dc, ch 1) in each of next 2 dc, dc in next dc, (dc, ch 2, 3 dc) in next ch-2 space; rep from * across to last ch-2 space, dc in top of turning ch, turn.

Rep Row 2 for pattern.

99

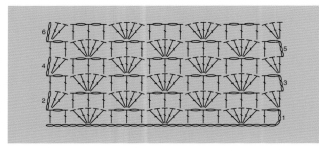

Chain multiples of 10 plus 4.

Row 1: Dc in 6th ch from hook, skip next 2 ch, 5 dc in next ch, skip next 2 ch, *(dc in next ch, ch 1, skip next ch) twice, dc in next ch, skip next 2 ch, 5 dc in next ch, skip next 2 ch; rep from * across to within last 3 ch, dc in next ch, ch 1, skip next ch, dc in last ch, turn.

Row 2: Ch 3 (counts as dc), 2 dc in first dc, skip next dc, (dc in next dc, ch 1, skip next dc) twice, dc in next dc, *skip next ch-1 space, 5 dc in next dc, skip next dc, (dc in next dc, ch 1, skip next dc) twice, dc in next dc; rep from * across to within last 3 sts, skip next ch-1 space of turning ch, 3 dc in next ch of turning ch, turn.

Row 3: Ch 4 (counts as dc, ch 1), skip first 2 dc, dc in next dc, skip next ch-1 space, 5 dc in next dc, skip next dc, *(dc in next dc, ch 1, skip next dc) twice, dc in next dc, skip next ch-1 space, 5 dc in next dc, skip next dc; rep from * across to within last 3 sts, dc in next dc, ch 1, skip next dc, dc in 3rd ch of turning ch, turn.

Rep Rows 2-3 for pattern.

100

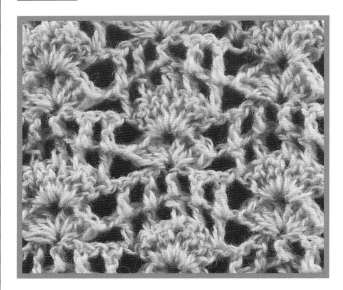

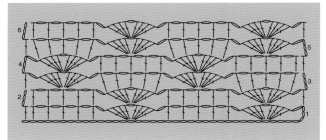

Chain multiples of 18 plus 5.

Row 1: (4 dc, ch 1, 4 dc) in 9th ch from hook, ch 1, skip next 4 ch, *(dc in next ch, ch 1, skip next ch) 4 times, dc in next dc**, ch 1, skip next 4 ch, (4 dc, ch 1, 4 dc) in next ch, ch 1, skip next 4 ch; rep from * across, ending last rep at **, dc in last ch, turn.

Row 2: Ch 3 (counts as dc), skip first dc, *dc in next dc, (ch 1, dc) in each of next 4 dc, ch 1, skip next ch-1 space, (4 dc, ch 1, 4 dc) in next ch-1 space, ch 1, skip next ch-1 space; rep from * across to turning ch, dc in next ch of turning ch, turn.

Row 3: Ch 3 (counts as dc), skip next ch-1 space, *(dc in next dc, ch 1, skip next dc) twice, dc in next ch-1 space, (ch 1, skip next dc, dc in next dc) twice, ch 1, skip next 3 ch-1 spaces, (4 dc, ch 1, 4 dc) in next dc, ch 1**, skip next 3 ch-1 spaces; rep from * across, ending last rep at **, skip next 2 ch-1 spaces, skip next dc, dc in 3rd ch of turning ch, turn.

Row 4: Ch 4 (counts as dc, ch 1), skip next ch-1 space, *(4 dc, ch 1, 4 dc) in next ch-1 space, ch 1, skip next ch-1 space, (dc, ch 1) in each of next 4 dc, dc in next dc**, ch 1, skip next ch-1 space; rep from * across, ending last rep at **, dc in 3rd ch of turning ch, turn.

Row 5: Ch 4 (counts as dc, ch 1), skip next 2 ch-2 spaces, *(4 dc, ch 1, 4 dc) in next dc, ch 1, skip next 3 ch-1 spaces, (dc in next dc, ch 1, skip next dc) twice, dc in next ch-1 space, (ch 1, skip next dc, dc in next dc) twice**, ch 1, skip next 3 ch-1 spaces; rep from * across, ending last rep at **, dc in 3rd ch of turning ch, turn.

Rep Rows 2-5 for pattern.

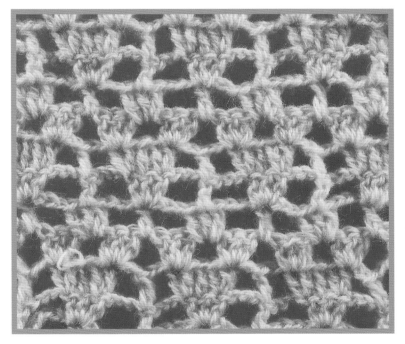

101

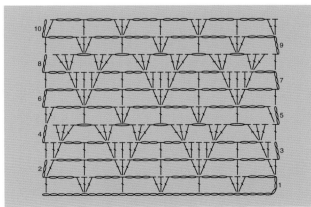

Chain multiples of 10 plus 6.

Row 1: 3 dc in 11th ch from hook, *ch 3, skip next 4 ch, dc in next ch**, ch 3, skip next 4 ch, 3 dc in next ch; rep from * across, ending last rep at **, turn.

Row 2: Ch 3 (counts as dc), dc in first dc, *ch 3, skip next dc, dc in next dc, ch 3, skip next ch-3 loop, 3 dc in next dc; rep from * across, ending with 2 dc in 3rd ch of turning ch, turn.

Row 3: Ch 3 (counts as dc), skip first dc, 2 dc in next dc, ch 2, dc in next dc, ch 2, 2 dc in next dc**, dc in next dc, 2 dc in next dc; rep from * across, ending last rep at **, dc in 3rd ch of turning ch, turn.

Row 4: Ch 3 (counts as dc), skip first 2 dc, *3 dc in next dc, ch 1, skip next 2 ch-2 spaces, 3 dc in next dc**, ch 1, skip next 3 dc; rep from * across, ending last rep at **, skip next dc, dc in 3rd ch of turning ch, turn.

Row 5: Ch 3 (counts as dc), dc in first dc, *ch 3, dc in next ch-1 space, ch 3**, 3 dc in next ch-1 space; rep from * across, ending last rep at **, skip next 3 dc, 2 dc in 3rd ch of turning ch, turn.

Row 6: Ch 6 (counts as dc, ch 3), skip next ch-3 loop, *3 dc in next dc, ch 3, skip next dc**, dc in next dc, ch 3, skip next ch-3 loop; rep from * across, ending last rep at **, dc in 3rd ch of turning ch, turn.

Row 7: Ch 5 (counts as dc, ch 2), skip next ch-3 loop, *2 dc in next dc, dc in next dc, 2 dc in next dc, ch 2**, dc in next dc, ch 2; rep from * across, ending last rep at **, dc in 3rd ch of turning ch, turn.

Row 8: Ch 3 (counts as dc), skip next ch-2 space, *3 dc in next dc, ch 1, skip next 3 dc, 3 dc in next dc**, ch 1, skip next 2 ch-2 spaces; rep from * across, ending last rep at **, dc in 3rd ch of turning ch, turn.

Row 9: Ch 6 (counts as dc, ch 3), *3 dc in next ch-1 space, ch 3**, dc in next ch-1 space, ch 3; rep from * across, ending last rep at **, skip next 3 dc, dc in 3rd ch of turning ch, turn.

Rep Rows 2-9 for pattern.

102

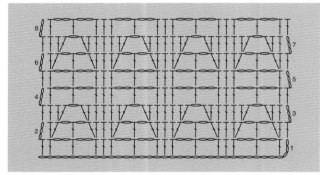

Chain multiples of 8 plus 3.

Row 1: Dc in 4th ch from hook, *ch 2, skip next 2 ch, dc in next ch, ch 2, skip next 2 ch**, dc in each of next 3 ch; rep from * across, ending last rep at **, dc in each of last 2 ch, turn.

Row 2: Ch 3 (counts as dc), skip first dc, 2 dc in next dc, *ch 1, dc in next dc, ch 1, 2 dc in next dc**, dc in next dc, 2 dc in next dc; rep from * across, ending last rep at **, dc in 3rd ch of turning ch, turn.

Row 3: Ch 3 (counts as dc), skip first dc, dc in next dc, 2 dc in next dc, *ch 1, skip next 2 ch-1 spaces, 2 dc in next dc**, dc in each of next 3 dc, 2 dc in next dc; rep from * across, ending last rep at **, dc in next dc, dc in 3rd ch of turning ch, turn.

Row 4: Ch 3 (counts as dc), skip first dc, dc in next dc, *ch 2, dc in next ch-1 space, ch 2, skip next 2 dc**, dc in each of next 3 dc; rep from * across, ending last rep at **, dc in next dc, dc in 3rd ch of turning ch, turn.

Row 5: Ch 3 (counts as dc), skip first dc, dc in next dc, *ch 2, dc in next dc, ch 2**, dc in each of next 3 dc; rep from * across, ending last rep at **, ch 2, dc in next dc, dc in 3rd ch of turning ch, turn.

Rep Rows 2-5 for pattern.

103

Chain multiples of 12 plus 3.

Row 1: 3 dc in 4th ch from hook, *ch 1, skip next 4 ch, dc in each of next 2 ch, ch 1, skip next 4 ch**, 4 dc in each of next 2 ch; rep from * across, ending last rep at **, 4 dc in last ch, turn.

Row 2: Ch 3 (counts as dc), 2 dc in first dc, *ch 1, dc in next ch-1 space, ch 2, dc in next ch-1 space, ch 1, skip next 3 dc**, 3 dc in each of next 2 dc; rep from * across, ending last rep at **, 3 dc in 3rd ch of turning ch, turn.

Row 3: Ch 3 (counts as dc), dc in first dc, *ch 1, dc in next ch-1 space, ch 1, 2 dc in next ch-2 space, ch 1, dc in next ch-1 space, ch 1, skip next 2 dc**, 2 dc in each of next 2 dc; rep from * across, ending last rep at **, 2 dc in 3rd ch of turning ch, turn.

Row 4: Ch 4 (counts as dc, ch 1), *dc in next ch-1 space, ch 1, dc in next ch-1 space, ch 2, (dc, ch 1) in each of next 2 ch-1 spaces, skip next dc**, dc in each of next 2 dc; rep from * across, ending last rep at **, dc in 3rd ch of turning ch, turn.

Row 5: Ch 3 (counts as dc), 3 dc in first dc, *ch 1, skip next ch-1 space, 2 dc in next ch-2 space, ch 1, skip next 2 ch-1 spaces**, 4 dc in each of next 2 dc; rep from * across, ending last rep at **, 4 dc in 3rd ch of turning ch, turn.

Rep Rows 2-5 for pattern.

104

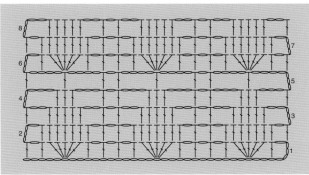

Chain multiples of 12 plus 2.

Row 1: Dc in 6th ch from hook, *skip next 2 ch, 5 dc in next ch, skip next 2 ch**, (dc in next ch, ch 1, skip next ch) 3 times, dc in next ch; rep from * across, ending last rep at **, dc in next ch, ch 1, skip next ch, dc in last ch, turn.

Row 2: Ch 4 (counts as dc, ch 1), skip first dc, *dc in each of next 7 dc**, ch 1, (dc, ch 1) in each of next 2 dc; rep from * across, ending last rep at **, ch 1, dc in 4th ch of turning ch, turn.

Row 3: Ch 5 (counts as dc, ch 2), skip next ch-1 space, skip next dc, *dc in each of next 5 dc, ch 2, skip next ch-1 space**, dc in next dc, ch 1, dc in next dc, ch 2, skip next dc; rep from * across, ending last rep at **, dc in 3rd ch of turning ch, turn.

Row 4: Ch 6 (counts as dc, ch 3), skip next ch-2 space, skip next dc, *dc in each of next 3 dc, ch 3, skip next ch-2 space**, dc in next dc, ch 1, dc in next dc, ch 3, skip next dc; rep from * across, ending last rep at **, dc in 3rd ch of turning ch, turn.

Row 5: Ch 7 (counts as dc, ch 4), skip next ch-3 loop, skip next dc, *dc in next dc, ch 4, skip next ch-3 loop**, dc in next dc, ch 1, dc in next dc, ch 4, skip next dc; rep from * across, ending last rep at **, dc in 3rd ch of turning ch, turn.

Row 6: Ch 4 (counts as dc, ch 1), *dc in next ch-4 loop, 5 dc in next dc, dc in next ch-4 loop, ch 1**, (dc, ch 1) in each of next 2 dc; rep from * across, ending last rep at **, dc in 3rd ch of turning ch, turn.

Rep Rows 2-6 for pattern.

105

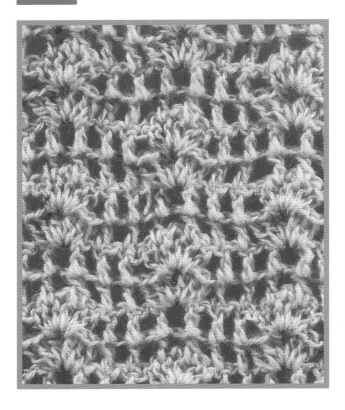

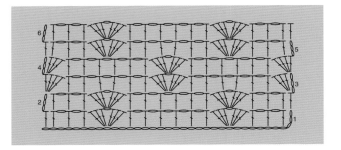

Chain multiples of 16 plus 3.

Row 1: Dc in 4th ch from hook, (ch 1, skip next ch, dc in next ch) twice, *skip next 2 ch, (3 dc, ch 1, 3 dc) in next ch, skip next 2 ch, dc in next ch**, (ch 1, skip next ch, dc in next ch) 5 times; rep from * across, ending last rep at **, (ch 1, skip next ch, dc in next ch) twice, dc in last ch, turn.

Row 2: Ch 3 (counts as dc), skip first dc, (dc, ch 1) in each of next 2 dc, dc in next dc, (3 dc, ch 1, 3 dc) in next ch-1 space, skip next 3 dc**, (dc, ch 1) in each of next 5 dc, dc in next dc; rep from * across, ending last rep at **, (dc, ch 1) in each of next 2 dc, dc in next dc, dc in 3rd ch of turning ch, turn.

Row 3: Ch 3 (counts as dc), 3 dc in first dc, skip next dc, (dc, ch 1) in each of next 2 dc, skip next 2 dc, (dc, ch 1) in each of next 2 dc, skip next 2 dc, dc in next dc, ch 1, dc in next dc, skip next ch-1 space**, (3 dc, ch 1, 3 dc) in next ch-1 space; rep from * across, ending last rep at **, 4 dc in 3rd ch of turning ch, turn.

Row 4: Ch 3 (counts as dc), 3 dc in first dc, skip next 3 dc, *(dc, ch 1) in each of next 5 dc, dc in next dc**, (3 dc, ch 1, 3 dc) in next ch-1 space, skip next 3 dc; rep from * across, ending last rep at **, skip next 3 dc, 4 dc in 3rd ch of turning ch, turn.

Row 5: Ch 3 (counts as dc), skip first dc, dc in next dc, ch 1, skip next 2 dc, dc in next dc, ch 1, dc in next dc, *skip next ch-1 space, (3 dc, ch 1, 3 dc) in next ch-1 space, skip next ch-1 space**, (dc, ch 1) in each of next 2 dc, skip next 2 dc, (dc, ch 1) in each of next 2 dc, skip next 2 dc, dc in next dc, ch 1, dc in next dc; rep from * across, ending last rep at **, (dc, ch 1) in each of next 2 dc, skip next 2 dc, dc in next dc, dc in 3rd ch of turning ch, turn.

Rep Rows 2-5 for pattern.

.9.
Shells—Symmetrical

106

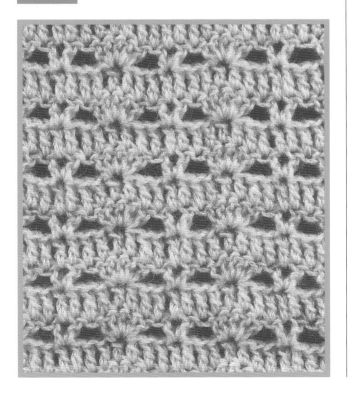

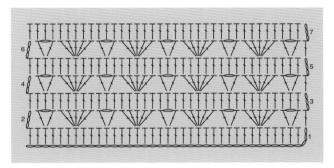

Chain multiples of 8 plus 7.

Row 1: Dc in 4th ch from hook, dc in each ch across, turn.

Row 2: Ch 3 (counts as dc), skip first 2 dc, *(dc, ch 1, dc) in next dc**, skip next 3 dc, 5 dc in next dc, skip next 3 dc; rep from * across, ending last rep at **, skip next dc, dc in 3rd ch of turning ch, turn.

Row 3: Ch 3 (counts as dc), skip first dc, dc in each dc and each ch-1 space across, ending with last dc in 3rd ch of turning ch, turn.

Rep Rows 2-3 for pattern.

107

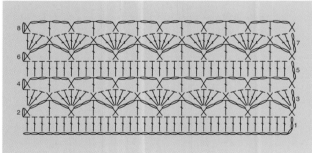

Chain multiples of 6 plus 3.

Row 1: Dc in 4th ch from hook, dc in each ch across, turn.

Row 2: Ch 1, sc in first dc, *ch 2, skip next 2 dc, dc in next dc, ch 2, skip next 2 dc, sc in next dc; rep from * across, ending with last sc in 3rd ch of turning ch, turn.

Row 3: Ch 3 (counts as dc), 2 dc in first sc, sc in next dc, *5 dc in next sc, sc in next dc; rep from * across to last dc, 3 dc in 3rd ch of turning ch, turn.

Row 4: Ch 1, sc in first dc, *ch 2, skip next 2 dc, dc in next sc, ch 2, skip next 2 dc, sc in next dc; rep from * across, ending with last sc in 3rd ch of turning ch, turn.

Row 5: Ch 3 (counts as dc), *2 dc in next ch-2 space, dc in next dc, 2 dc in next ch-2 space, dc in next sc; rep from * across, turn.

Rep Rows 2-5 for pattern.

108

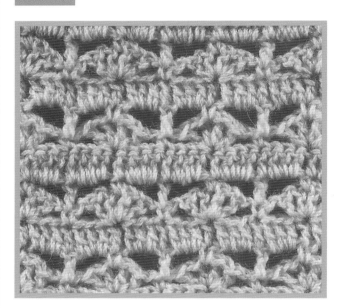

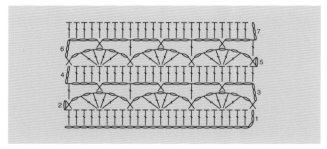

Chain multiples of 8 plus 3.

Row 1: Dc in 4th ch from hook, dc in each ch across, turn.

Row 2: Ch 1, sc in first dc, *ch 1, skip next 3 dc, (dc, ch 1, dc, ch 1, dc, ch 1, dc) in next dc, ch 1, skip next 3 dc, sc in next dc; rep from * across, ending with last sc in 3rd ch of turning ch, turn.

Row 3: Ch 6 (counts as dc, ch 3), skip next 2 ch-1 spaces, sc in next ch-1 space, ch 3, skip next 2 ch-1 spaces, dc in next sc, *ch 3, skip next 2 ch-1 spaces, sc in next ch-1 space, ch 3, skip next 2 ch-1 spaces, dc in next sc; rep from * across, turn.

Row 4: Ch 3 (counts as dc), *3 dc in next ch-3 loop, dc in next sc, 3 dc in next ch-3 loop, dc in next dc; rep from * across, ending with last dc in 3rd ch of turning ch, turn.

Rep Rows 2-4 for pattern.

109

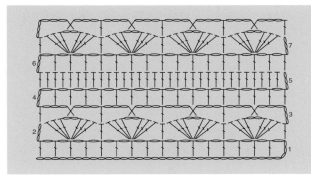

Chain multiples of 8 plus 4.

Row 1: Dc in 6th ch from hook, *ch 1, skip next ch, dc in next ch; rep from * across, turn.

Row 2: Ch 3 (counts as dc), *skip next 2 ch-1 spaces, (3 dc, ch 2, 3 dc) in next dc, skip next 2 ch-1 spaces, dc in next dc; rep from * across, ending with last dc in next ch of turning ch, turn.

Row 3: Ch 6 (counts as dc, ch 3), *sc in next ch-2 space, ch 3, skip next 3 dc**, dc in next dc, ch 3; rep from * across, ending last rep at **, dc in 3rd ch of turning ch, turn.

Row 4: Ch 4 (counts as dc, ch 1), *dc in next ch-3 loop, ch 1, dc in next sc, ch 1, dc in next ch-3 loop, ch 1**, dc in next dc, ch 1; rep from * across, ending last rep at **, dc in 3rd ch of turning ch, turn.

Row 5: Ch 3 (counts as dc), skip first dc, dc in each dc and ch-1 space across, ending with dc in 3rd ch of turning ch, turn.

Row 6: Ch 4 (counts as dc, ch 1), skip first 2 dc, dc in next dc, *ch 1, skip next dc, dc in next dc; rep from * across, ending with last dc in 3rd ch of turning ch, turn.

Rep Rows 2-6 for pattern.

110

Chain multiples of 10 plus 4.

Row 1: Dc in 8th ch from hook, dc in each of next 3 ch, *ch 2, skip next 2 ch, dc in each of next 2 ch, ch 2, skip next 2 ch, dc in each of next 4 ch; rep from * across to within last 3 ch, ch 2, skip next 2 ch, dc in last ch, turn.

Row 2: Ch 1, sc in first dc, *skip next 2 dc, (3 dc, ch 2, 3 dc) bet last skipped and next dc, skip next ch-2 space**, sc in each of next 2 dc; rep from * across, ending last rep at **, sc in next ch of turning ch, turn.

Row 3: Ch 6 (counts as dc, ch 3), *2 sc in next ch-2 space, ch 3, skip next 3 dc**, dc in each of next 2 sc, ch 3; rep from * across, ending last rep at **, dc in last sc, turn.

Row 4: Ch 5 (counts as dc, ch 2), *dc in next ch-3 loop, dc in each of next 2 sc, dc in next ch-3 loop, ch 2**, dc in each of next 2 dc; rep from * across, ending last rep at **, dc in 3rd ch of turning ch, turn.

Rep Rows 2-4 for pattern.

111

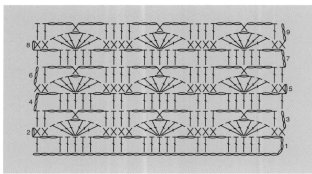

Chain multiples of 11 plus 4.

Row 1: Dc in 8th ch from hook, dc in each of next 4 ch, *ch 2, skip next 2 ch, dc in each of next 2 ch, ch 2, skip next 2 ch, dc in each of next 5 ch; rep from * across to within last 3 ch, ch 2, skip next 2 ch, dc in last ch, turn.

Row 2: Ch 1, sc in each of first 2 dc, *skip next 2 dc, (3 dc, ch 1, 3 dc) in next dc**, sc in next ch-2 space, sc in each of next 2 dc, sc in next ch-2 space; rep from * across, ending last rep at **, sc in next ch-2 space of turning ch, sc in next ch of turning ch, turn.

Row 3: Ch 3 (counts as dc), skip first sc, dc in next sc, *ch 3, sc in next ch-2 space, skip next 3 dc**, dc in each of next 4 sc; rep from * across, ending last rep at **, dc in each of last 2 sc, turn.

Row 4: Ch 5 (counts as dc, ch 2), *2 dc in next ch-3 loop, dc in next sc, 2 dc in next ch-3 loop, ch 2, skip next dc**, dc in each of next 2 dc, ch 2; rep from * across, ending last rep at **, dc in 3rd ch of turning ch, turn.

Rep Rows 2-4 for pattern.

112

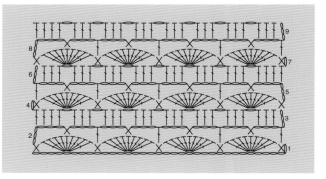

Chain multiples of 8 plus 2.

Row 1: Sc in 2nd ch from hook, skip next 3 ch, *9 dc in next ch, skip next 3 ch, sc in next ch; rep from * across, turn.

Row 2: Ch 6 (counts as dc, ch 3), skip first sc, skip next 4 dc, sc in next dc, *ch 3, skip next 4 dc, dc in next sc**, ch 3, skip next 4 dc, sc in next dc; rep from * across, ending last rep at **, turn.

Row 3: Ch 3 (counts as dc), 3 dc in next ch-3 space, *ch 1, 3 dc in next ch-3 space; rep from * across, dc in 3rd ch of turning ch, turn.

Row 4: Ch 1, sc in first dc, *9 dc in next ch-1 space, sc in next ch-1 space; rep from * across, ending with last sc in 3rd ch of turning ch, turn.

Rep Rows 2-4 for pattern.

113

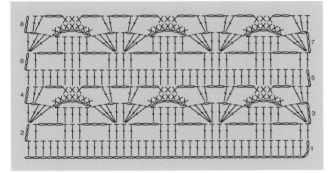

Chain multiples of 13 plus 2.

Row 1: Dc in 4th ch from hook, dc in each ch across, turn.

Row 2: Ch 3 (counts as dc), skip first dc, dc in next dc, *ch 3, skip next 3 dc, dc in each of next 3 dc, ch 3, skip next 3 dc**, dc in each of next 4 dc; rep from * across, ending last rep at **, dc in next dc, dc in 3rd ch of turning ch, turn.

Row 3: Ch 4 (counts as dc, ch 1), 3 dc in first dc, *dc in next ch-3 loop, dc in each of next 3 dc, dc in next ch-3 loop, ch 5, turn, skip next 5 dc, sl st bet last skipped and next dc, turn, work 7 sc in ch-5 loop, sl st in last ch of ch-5 loop, skip next dc**, (3 dc, ch 1, dc) in next dc, (dc, ch 1, 3 dc) in next dc; rep from * across, ending last rep at **, (3 dc, ch 1, dc) in 3rd ch of turning ch, turn.

Row 4: Ch 3 (counts as dc), 2 dc in next ch-1 space, *ch 2, skip next 3 dc and next 2 sc, sc in each of next 3 sc, ch 2, 2 dc in next ch-1 space**, ch 2, 2 dc in next ch-1 space; rep from * across, ending last rep at **, dc in 3rd ch of turning ch, turn.

Row 5: Ch 3 (counts as dc), skip first dc, dc in each st across, working 2 dc in each ch-2 space, ending with dc in 3rd ch of turning ch, turn.

Rep Rows 2-5 for pattern.

114

Chain multiples of 8 plus 4.

Row 1: Dc in 4th ch from hook, *ch 2, skip next 2 ch, dc in each of next 2 ch; rep from * across, turn.

Row 2: Ch 1, sc in first dc, ch 2, sc in next ch-2 space, (ch 3, sc) in each ch-2 pace across to last ch-2 space, ch 2, sc in 3rd ch of turning ch, turn.

Row 3: Ch 3 (counts as dc), 3 dc in next ch-2 space, sc in next ch-3 loop, *6 dc in next ch-3 loop, sc in next ch-3 loop; rep from * across to last ch-3 loop, 3 dc in next ch-2 space, dc in last sc, turn.

Row 4: Ch 3 (counts as dc), skip first dc, dc in next dc, *ch 2, skip next 2 dc, 2 dc in next sc, ch 2, skip next 2 dc, dc in each of next 2 dc; rep from * across, ending with last dc in 3rd ch of turning ch, turn.

Row 5: Rep Row 2.

Row 6: Ch 1, sc in first sc, skip next ch-2 space, 6 dc in next ch-3 loop, *sc in next ch-3 loop, 6 dc in next ch-3 loop; rep from * across to last ch-3 loop, skip next ch-2 space, sc in last sc, turn.

Row 7: Ch 3 (counts as dc), dc in first sc, *ch 2, skip next 2 dc, dc in each of next 2 dc, ch 2, skip next 2 dc, 2 dc in next sc; rep from * across, turn.

Rep Rows 2-7 for pattern.

115

Chain multiples of 6 plus 3.

Row 1: Dc in 4th ch from hook, *ch 3, skip next 3 ch, dc in each of next 3 ch; rep from * across, ending with dc in each of last 2 ch, turn.

Row 2: Ch 3 (counts as hdc, ch 1), skip first dc, sc in next dc, ch 5, sc in next dc, *ch 2, skip next dc, sc in next dc, ch 5, sc in next dc; rep from * across to within last st, ch 1, hdc in 3rd ch of turning ch, turn.

Row 3: Ch 1, sc in first dc, *5 dc in next ch-5 loop, sc in next ch-5 loop; rep from * across, ending with last sc in 2nd ch of turning ch, turn.

Row 4: Ch 4 (counts as dc, ch 1), skip first sc, skip next dc, sc in next dc, *ch 2, skip next dc, sc in next dc, ch 3, skip next 3 sts, sc in next dc; rep from * across to within last 2 sts, ch 1, skip next dc, dc in last sc, turn.

Row 5: Ch 3 (counts as dc), dc in next ch-1 space, *ch 3, skip next ch-2 space, 3 dc in next ch-3 loop; rep from * across to last ch-3 loop, ch 3, dc in next ch-1 space of turning ch, dc in 3rd ch of turning ch, turn.

Rep Rows 2-5 for pattern.

116

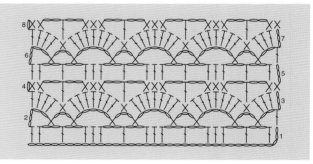

Chain multiples of 8 plus 3.

Row 1: Dc in 4th ch from hook, *ch 2, skip next 2 ch, dc in next ch, ch 2, skip next 2 ch, dc in each of next 3 ch; rep from * across, ending with dc in each of last 2 ch, turn.

Row 2: Ch 5 (counts as dc, ch 2), sc in next ch-2 space, ch 3, sc in next ch-2 space, *ch 5, sc in next ch-2 space, ch 3, sc in next ch-2 space; rep from * across to last ch-2 space, ch 2, skip next dc, dc in 3rd ch of turning ch, turn.

Row 3: Ch 3 (counts as dc), 3 dc in next ch-2 space, sc in next ch-3 loop, *7 dc in next ch-5 loop, sc in next ch-3 loop; rep from * across to last ch-3 loop, 3 dc in next ch-2 space of turning ch, dc in 3rd ch of turning ch, turn.

Row 4: Ch 1, sc in first 2 dc, *ch 2, skip next 2 dc, dc in next sc, ch 2, skip next 2 dc**, sc in each of next 3 dc; rep from * across, ending last rep at **, sc in next dc, sc in 3rd ch of turning ch, turn.

Row 5: Ch 3 (counts as dc), skip first sc, dc in next sc, *ch 2, dc in next dc, ch 2, dc in each of next 3 sc; rep from * across, ending with dc in each of last 2 sc, turn.

Rep Rows 2–5 for pattern.

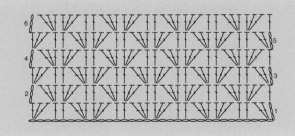

Chain multiples of 8 plus 3.

Row 1: 2 dc in 4th ch from hook, *skip next 2 ch, dc in each of next 2 dc, skip next 2 ch, 3 dc in next ch**, 3 dc in next ch; rep from * across, ending last rep at **, turn.

Row 2: Ch 3 (counts as dc), skip first 3 dc, *3 dc in each of next 2 dc, skip next 2 dc**, dc in each of next 2 dc; rep from * across, ending last rep at **, dc in 3rd ch of turning ch, turn.

Row 3: Ch 3 (counts as dc), 2 dc in first dc, skip next 2 dc, *dc in each of next 2 dc, skip next 2 dc**, 3 dc in next dc, 3 dc in next dc; rep from * across, ending last rep at **, 3 dc in 3rd ch of turning ch, turn.

Rep Rows 2–3 for pattern.

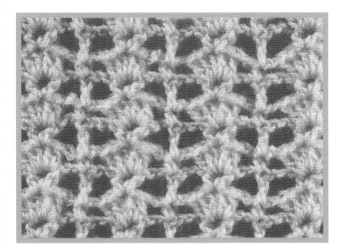

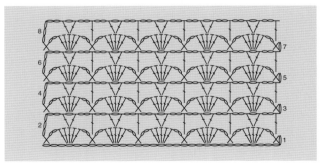

Chain multiples of 6 plus 2.

Row 1: Sc in 2nd ch from hook, *ch 2, skip next 2 ch, 5 dc in next ch, ch 2, skip next 2 ch, sc in next ch; rep from * across, turn.

Row 2: Ch 5 (counts as dc, ch 2), *skip next ch-2 space, skip next 2 dc, (dc, ch 1, dc) in next dc, ch 2, skip next ch-2 space, dc in next sc**, ch 2, skip next ch-2 space, skip next 2 dc; rep from * across, ending last rep at **, turn.

Row 3: Ch 1, sc in first dc, *ch 2, skip next ch-2 space, 5 dc in next ch-1 space, ch 2, skip next ch-2 space, sc in next dc; rep from * across, ending with last sc in 3rd ch of turning ch, turn.

Rep Rows 2–3 for pattern.

119

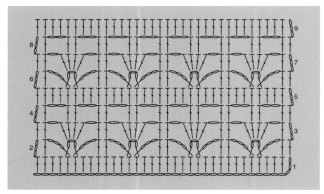

Chain multiples of 8 plus 4.

Row 1: Dc in 4th ch from hook, dc in each ch across, turn.

Row 2: Ch 3 (counts as dc), skip first dc, dc in next dc, *ch 3, skip next 2 dc, sc in next dc, ch 3, sc in next dc, ch 3, skip next 2 dc, dc in each of next 2 dc; rep from * across, ending with last dc in 3rd ch of turning ch, turn.

Row 3: Ch 3 (counts as dc), skip first dc, dc in next dc, *ch 1, skip next ch-3 loop, 4 dc in next ch-3 loop, ch 1, skip next ch-3 loop, dc in each next 2 dc; rep from * across, ending with last dc in 3rd ch of turning ch, turn.

Row 4: Ch 3 (counts as dc), skip first dc, dc in next dc, *ch 2, skip next ch-1 space, skip next dc, dc in each of next 2 dc, ch 2, skip next ch-1 space, dc in each of next 2 dc; rep from * across, ending with last dc in 3rd ch of turning ch, turn.

Row 5: Ch 3 (counts as dc), skip first dc, dc in next dc, *2 dc in next ch-2 space, dc in each of next 2 dc; rep from * across, ending with last dc in 3rd ch of turning ch, turn.

Rep Rows 2-5 for pattern.

120

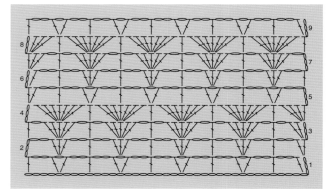

Chain multiples of 8.

Row 1: Dc in 4th ch from hook, ch 2, skip next 3 ch, dc in next ch, *ch 2, skip next 3 ch, (dc, ch 1, dc) in next ch, ch 2, skip next 3 ch, dc in next ch; rep from * across, turn.

Row 2: Ch 5 (counts as dc, ch 2), skip next ch-2 space, *3 dc in next ch-1 space, ch 2, skip next ch-2 space, dc in next dc, ch 2, skip next ch-2 space; rep from * across to last 2 sts, skip next dc, 2 dc in 3rd ch of turning ch, turn.

Row 3: Ch 3 (counts as dc), 2 dc in first dc, ch 1, skip next ch-2 space, dc in next dc, *ch 1, skip next dc, 5 dc in next dc, ch 1, skip next ch-2 space, dc in next dc; rep from * across, ending with last dc in 3rd ch of turning ch, turn.

Row 4: Ch 3 (counts as dc), *skip next ch-1 space, skip next 2 dc, 7 dc in next dc, skip next ch-1 space, dc in next dc; rep from * across to within last 4 sts, skip next ch-1 space, skip next 2 dc, 4 dc in 3rd ch of turning ch, turn.

Row 5: Ch 5 (counts as dc, ch 2), skip first 4 dc, *(dc, ch 1, dc) in next dc, ch 2, skip next 3 dc, dc in next dc, ch 2, skip next 3 dc; rep from * across to within last st, 2 dc in 3rd ch of turning ch, turn.

Row 6: Ch 3 (counts as dc), dc in first dc, *ch 2, skip next ch-2 space, dc in next dc, ch 2, skip next ch-2 space, 3 dc in next ch-1 space; rep from * across to turning ch, ch 2, dc in 3rd ch of turning ch, turn.

Row 7: Ch 4 (counts as dc, ch 1), skip next ch-2 space, skip next dc, *5 dc in next dc, ch 1, skip next ch-2 space, dc in next dc, ch 1, skip next ch-2 space, skip next dc; rep from * across to turning ch, 3 dc in 3rd ch of turning ch, turn.

Row 8: Ch 3 (counts as dc), 3 dc in first dc, skip next ch-1 space, *dc in next dc, skip next ch-1 space, skip next 2 dc, 7 dc in next dc, skip next ch-1 space; rep from * across to turning ch, dc in 3rd ch of turning ch, turn.

Row 9: Ch 3 (counts as dc), dc in first dc, skip next 3 dc, dc in next dc, *ch 2, skip next 3 dc, (dc, ch 1, dc) in next dc, ch 2, skip next 3 dc, dc in next dc; rep from * across, ending with last dc in 3rd ch of turning ch, turn.

Rep Rows 2-9 for pattern.

Chain multiples of 9 plus 4.

Row 1: 2 dc in 4th ch from hook, *skip next 2 ch, dc in next ch, ch 1, skip next ch, dc in next ch, ch 1, skip next 3 ch**, (2 dc, ch 1, 2 dc) in next ch; rep from * across, ending last rep at **, 3 dc in last ch, turn.

Row 2: Ch 3 (counts as dc), 2 dc in first dc, *(dc, ch 1) in each of next 2 ch-1 spaces**, (2 dc, ch 1, 2 dc) in next ch-1 space; rep from * across, ending last rep at **, skip next 3 dc, 3 dc in 3rd ch of turning ch, turn.

Rep Row 2 for pattern.

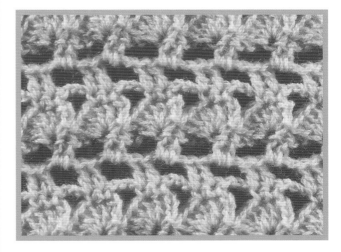

122

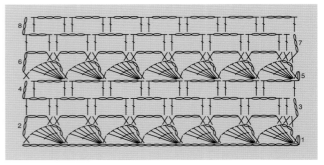

Chain multiples of 5 plus 2.

Row 1: (Sc, ch 3, 5 dc) in 2nd ch from hook, *skip next 4 ch, (sc, ch 3, 5 dc) in next ch; rep from * across to within last 5 ch, skip next 4 ch, sc in last ch, turn.

Row 2: Ch 5 (counts as dc, ch 2), skip first sc, skip next 4 dc, *sc in next dc, sc in next ch-3 loop, ch 3, skip next sc, skip next 4 dc; rep from * across, sc in next dc, 2 sc in next ch-3 loop, turn.

121

Row 3: Ch 3 (counts as dc), skip first sc, dc in each of next 2 sc, *ch 3, skip next ch-3 loop, dc in each of next 2 sc; rep from * across to turning ch, ch 2, dc in 3rd ch of turning ch, turn.

Row 4: Ch 3 (colunts as dc), dc in next ch-2 space, ch 3, (2 dc, ch 3) in each ch-3 loop across to last ch-3 loop, skip next 2 dc, dc in 3rd ch of turning ch, turn.

Row 5: Ch 1, (sc, ch 3, 5 dc) in first dc, skip next ch-3 loop, skip next dc, *(sc, ch 3, 5 dc) in next dc, skip next ch-3 loop, skip next dc; rep from * across to turning ch, sc in 3rd ch of turning ch, turn.

Rep Rows 2-5 for pattern.

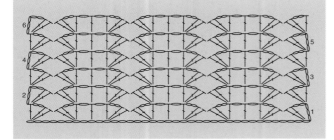

Chain multiples of 10 plus 2.

Row 1: 2 dc in 6th ch from hook, *skip next 5 ch, (2 dc, ch 2, dc) in next ch**, ch 1, skip next ch, dc in next ch, ch 1, skip next ch, (dc, ch 2, 2 dc) in next ch; rep from * across, ending last rep at **, turn.

Row 2: Ch 5 (counts as dc, ch 2), 2 dc in first dc, skip next 2 ch-2 spaces, *(2 dc, ch 2, dc) in next dc, ch 1, dc in next dc, ch 1, (dc, ch 2, 2 dc) in next dc, skip next 2 ch-2 spaces; rep from * across to turning ch, (2 dc, ch 2, dc) in 3rd ch of turning ch, turn.

Rep Row 2 for pattern.

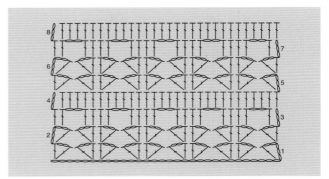

Chain multiples of 6 plus 5.

Row 1: Dc in 6th ch from hook, *skip next 4 ch, *(dc, ch 2, dc) in each of next 2 ch, skip next 4 ch; rep from * across to within last ch, (dc, ch 2, dc) in last ch, turn.

Row 2: Ch 5 (counts as dc, ch 2), dc in first dc, skip next 2 ch-2 spaces, *(dc, ch 2, dc) in each of next 2 dc, skip next 2 ch-2 spaces; rep from * across to turning ch, (dc, ch 2, dc) in 3rd ch of turning ch, turn.

Row 3: Ch 3 (counts as dc), dc in next ch-2 space, *ch 2, dc in next ch-2 space, dc in each of next 2 dc, dc in next ch-2 space; rep from * across to last ch-2 space, ch 2, dc in next ch-2 space of turning ch, dc in 3rd ch of turning ch, turn.

Row 4: Ch 3 (counts as dc), skip first dc, dc in next dc, *2 dc in next ch-2 space**, dc in each of next 4 dc; rep from * across, ending last rep at **, dc in next dc, dc in 3rd ch of turning ch, turn.

Row 5: Ch 5 (counts as dc, ch 2), dc in first dc, skip next 4 dc, *(dc, ch 2, dc) in each of next 2 dc, skip next 4 dc; rep from * across to turning ch, (dc, ch 2, dc) in 3rd ch of turning ch, turn.

Rep Rows 2-5 for pattern.

125

Chain multiples of 7 plus 2.

Row 1: 5 dc in 6th ch from hook, *skip next 2 ch, dc in each of next 2 dc, skip next 2 ch, 5 dc in next ch; rep from * across to within last 3 ch, skip next 2 ch, dc in last ch, turn.

Row 2: Ch 5 (counts as dc, ch 2), dc in first dc, skip next 5 dc, *(dc, ch 2, dc) in each of next 2 dc, skip next 5 dc; rep from * across to turning ch, (dc, ch 2, dc) in top of turning ch, turn.

Row 3: Ch 5 (counts as dc, ch 2), dc in first dc, skip next 2 ch-2 spaces, *(dc, ch 2, dc) in each of next 2 dc, skip next 2 ch-2 spaces; rep from * across to turning ch, (dc, ch 2, dc) in 3rd ch of turning ch, turn.

Row 4: Ch 4 (counts as dc, ch 1), skip first dc, *dc in next dc, ch 2, dc in next dc, ch 1**, skip next ch-2 space, dc in each of next 2 dc, ch 1, skip next ch-2 space; rep from * across, ending last rep at **, dc in 3rd ch of turning ch, turn.

Row 5: Ch 3 (counts as dc), *skip next ch-1 space, 5 dc in next ch-2 space, skip next ch-1 space**, dc in each of next 2 dc; rep from * across, ending last rep at **, dc in 3rd ch of turning ch, turn.

Rep Rows 2–5 for pattern.

126

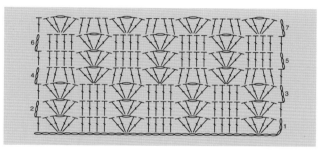

Chain multiples of 9.

Row 1: (2 dc, ch 1, 2 dc) in 6th ch from hook, skip next 2 ch, *dc in each of next 4 ch, skip next 2 ch, (2 dc, ch 1, 2 dc) in next ch, skip next 2 ch; rep from * across to within last ch, dc in last ch, turn.

Row 2: Ch 3 (counts as dc), skip first 3 dc, *(2 dc, ch 2, 2 dc) in next ch-1 space, skip next 2 dc**, dc in each of next 4 dc, skip next 2 dc; rep from * across, ending last rep at **, (dc, ch 2, dc) in top of turning ch, turn.

Row 3: Rep Row 2.

Row 4: Ch 3 (counts as dc), skip first dc, *dc in each of next 4 dc**, skip next 2 dc, (2 dc, ch 1, 2 dc) bet last skipped and next dc, skip next 2 dc; rep from * across, ending last rep at **, dc in 3rd ch of turning ch, turn.

Row 5: Ch 3 (counts as dc), skip first dc, *dc in each of next 4 dc**, skip next 2 dc, (2 dc, ch 1, 2 dc) in next ch-1 space, skip next 2 dc; rep from * across, ending last rep at **, dc in 3rd ch of turning ch, turn.

Row 6: Rep Row 5.

Row 7: Ch 3 (counts as dc), skip first 3 dc, *(2 dc, ch 1, 2 dc) bet last skipped and next dc, skip next 2 dc**, dc in each of next 4 dc, skip next 2 dc; rep from * across, ending last rep at **, dc in 3rd ch of turning ch, turn.

Rep Rows 2–7 for pattern.

127

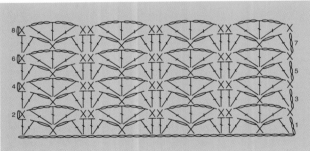

Chain multiples of 9 plus 3.

Row 1: Dc in 4th ch from hook, *ch 1, skip next 3 ch, sc in next ch, ch 1, skip next 3 ch, 2 dc in next ch**, 2 dc in next ch; rep from * across, ending last rep at **, turn.

Row 2: Ch 1, sc in first dc, *skip next ch-1 space, (dc, ch 3, dc, ch 3, dc) in next sc, skip next dc**, sc in each of next 2 dc; rep from * across, ending last rep at **, sc in 3rd ch of turning ch, turn.

Row 3: Ch 3 (counts as dc), dc in first sc, *ch 1, skip next ch-3 loop, sc in next dc, ch 1, skip next dc**, 2 dc in each of next 2 sc; rep from * across, ending last rep at **, 2 dc in last sc, turn.

Rep Rows 2-3 for pattern.

128

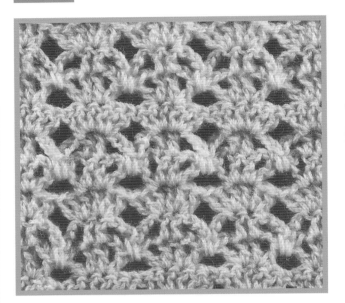

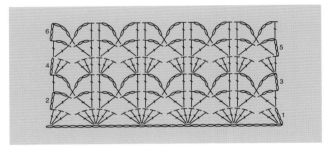

Chain multiples of 6 plus 4.

Row 1: 2 dc in 4th ch from hook, *skip next 5 ch, 6 dc in next ch; rep from * across, ending with 3 dc in last ch, turn.

Row 2: Ch 5 (counts as dc, ch 2), dc in first dc, skip next 4 dc, *(dc, ch 2, dc) in each of next 2 dc, skip next 4 dc; rep from * across to turning ch, (dc, ch 2, dc) in 3rd ch of turning ch, turn.

Row 3: Ch 6 (counts as dc, ch 3), skip first 2 dc, sc bet last skipped and next dc, *ch 3, skip next ch-2 space, dc in each of next 2 dc, ch 3, skip next dc, sc bet last skipped and next dc; rep from * across to turning ch, ch 3, dc in 3rd ch of turning ch, turn.

Row 4: Ch 3 (counts as dc), 2 dc in first dc, skip next 2 ch-3 loops, *3 dc in each of next 2 dc, skip next 2 ch-3 loops; rep from * across to turning ch, 3 dc in 3rd ch of turning ch, turn.

Rep Rows 2-4 for pattern.

129

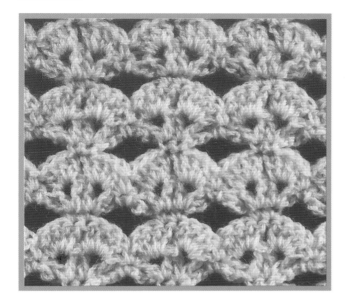

Chain multiples of 9 plus 2.

Row 1: Sc in 2nd ch from hook, *skip next 3 ch, (dc, ch 2, dc) in each of next 2 ch, skip next 3 ch, sc in next ch; rep from * across, turn.

Row 2: Ch 1, sc in first sc, *(hdc, 3 dc) in next ch-2 space, (3 dc, hdc) in next ch-2 space, sc in next sc; rep from * across, turn.

Row 3: Ch 7 (counts as tr, ch 3), skip first 4 sts, sc in each of next 2 dc, *ch 7, skip next 7 sts, sc in each of next 2 dc; rep from * across to within last 4 sts, ch 3, skip next 3 sts, tr in last sc, turn.

Row 4: Ch 1, sc in first tr, skip next ch-3 loop, (dc, ch 3, dc) in each of next 2 sc, sc in next ch-7 loop; rep from * across, ending with last sc in 4th ch of turning ch, turn.

Rep Rows 2-4 for pattern.

130

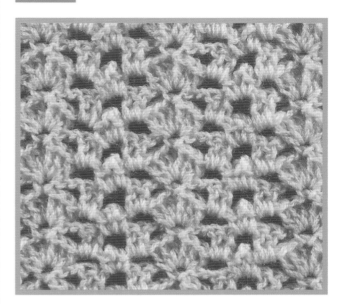

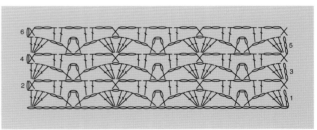

Chain multiples of 11 plus 4.

Row 1: 3 dc in 4th ch from hook, *ch 2, skip next 4 ch, sc in next ch, ch 3, sc in next ch, ch 2, skip next 4 ch**, (3 dc, ch 1, 3 dc) in next ch; rep from * across, ending last rep at **, 4 dc in last ch, turn.

Row 2: Ch 1, sc in first dc, *ch 2, 2 dc in next ch-2 space, ch 2, skip next ch-3 loop, 2 dc in next ch-2 space, ch 2, sc in next ch-1 space; rep from * across, ending with last sc in 3rd ch of turning ch, turn.

Row 3: Ch 3 (counts as dc), 3 dc in first sc, *ch 2, skip next ch-2 space, (sc, ch 3, sc) in next ch-2 space, ch 2, skip next ch-2 space**, (3 dc, ch 1, 3 dc) in next sc; rep from * across, ending last rep at **, 4 dc in last sc, turn.

Rep Rows 2-3 for pattern.

131

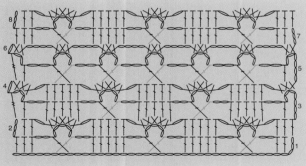

Chain multiples of 12 plus 3.

Row 1: Dc in 4th ch from hook, dc in next ch, *ch 2, skip next 4 ch, dc in next ch, ch 5, working over last dc made, skip 1 ch to the right of last ch worked, dc in next ch to the right (crossed dc), ch 2, skip 2 ch to the left of ch at base of first dc of crossed dc**, dc in each of next 5 ch; rep from * across, ending last rep at **, dc in each of last 3 ch, turn.

Row 2: Ch 3 (counts as dc), skip first dc, dc in each of next 2 dc, *ch 1, skip next ch-2 space, 5 sc in next ch-5 loop, ch 1, skip next ch-2 space**, dc in each of next 5 dc; rep from * across, ending last rep at **, dc in each of next 2 dc, dc in 3rd ch of turning ch, turn.

Row 3: Ch 7 (counts as tr, ch 3), skip first dc, dc in next dc, ch 2, skip next ch-1 space, dc in each of next 5 sc, *ch 2, skip next 3 dc, dc in next dc, ch 5, working over last dc made, skip 1 dc to the right of last dc worked, dc in next dc to the right, ch 2, skip next ch-1 space, dc in each of next 5 sc; rep from * across to within last 4 sts, ch 2, skip next dc, dc in next dc, ch 3, tr in 3rd ch of turning ch, turn.

Row 4: Ch 1, 3 sc in next ch-3 loop, *ch 1, skip next ch-2 space, dc in each of next 5 dc, ch 1, skip next ch-2 space**, 5 sc in next ch-5 loop; rep from * across, ending last rep at **, 3 sc in ch-3 loop of turning ch, turn.

Row 5: Ch 6 (counts as tr, ch 2), skip first sc, dc in next sc, ch 2, skip next ch-1 space, *skip next 3 dc, dc in next dc, ch 5, working over last dc made, skip 1 dc to the right of last dc worked, dc in next dc to the right, ch 2, skip next ch-1 space**, skip next 3 sc, dc in next sc, ch 5, working over last dc made, skip 1 sc to the right of last dc worked, dc in next sc to the right, ch 2, skip next ch-1 space; rep from * across, ending last rep at **, skip next sc, dc in next sc, ch 2, tr in last sc, turn.

Row 6: Ch 1, 2 sc in next ch-2 space, ch 4, skip next ch-2 space, *3 sc in next ch-5 loop, ch 4, skip next ch-2 space; rep from * across to turning ch, 2 sc in ch-2 space of turning ch, turn.

Row 7: Ch 3, skip first sc, dc in next sc, dc in next ch-4 loop, *ch 2, skip next 2 sc, dc in next sc, ch 5, working over last dc made, skip 1 sc to the right of last dc worked, dc in next sc to the right, ch 2, dc in next ch-4 loop**, dc in each of next 3 sc, dc in next ch-4 loop; rep from * across, ending last rep at **, dc in each of last 2 sc, turn.

Rep Rows 2-7 for pattern.

.10.
Shells—Overall Patterns

132

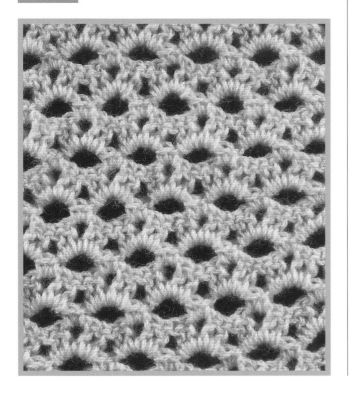

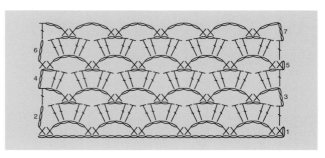

Chain multiples of 6 plus 3.

Row 1: Sc in 2nd ch from hook, sc in next ch, *ch 4, skip next 4 ch, sc in each of next 2 ch; rep from * across, turn.

Row 2: Ch 3 (counts as dc), (2 dc, ch 2, 2 dc) in each ch-4 loops across, dc in last sc, turn.

Row 3: Ch 5 (counts as dc, ch 2), (2 sc, ch 4) in each ch-2 space across to within last ch-2 space, 2 sc in last ch-2 space, ch 2, skip next 2 dc, dc in 3rd ch of turning ch, turn.

Row 4: Ch 4 (counts as dc, ch 1), 2 dc in next ch-2 space, (2 dc, ch 2, 2 dc) in each ch-4 loop across to last ch-4 loop, 2 dc in ch-2 space of turning ch, ch 1, dc in 3rd ch of turning ch, turn.

Row 5: Ch 1, sc in first dc, sc in next ch-1 space, ch 4, (2 sc, ch 4) in each ch-2 space across to turning ch, sc in last ch-1 space of turning ch, sc in 3rd ch of turning ch, turn.

Rep Rows 2-5 for pattern.

133

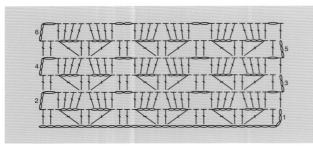

Chain multiples of 10 plus 4.

Row 1: Dc in 4th ch from hook, *skip next 3 ch, (dc, ch 3, dc) in each of next 2 ch, skip next 3 ch, dc in each of next 2 ch; rep from * across, turn.

Row 2: Ch 4 (counts as dc, ch 1), skip first 2 dc, *dc in next dc, 3 dc in each of next 2 ch-3 loops, dc in next dc**, ch 2, skip next 2 dc; rep from * across, ending last rep at **, ch 1, skip next dc, dc in 3rd ch of turning ch, turn.

Row 3: Ch 3 (counts as dc), dc in next ch-1 space, *skip next 3 dc, (dc, ch 3, dc) in each of next 2 dc, skip next 3 dc**, 2 dc in next ch-2 space; rep from * across, ending last rep at **, dc in ch-1 space of turning ch, dc in 3rd ch of turning ch, turn.

Rep Rows 2-3 for pattern.

134

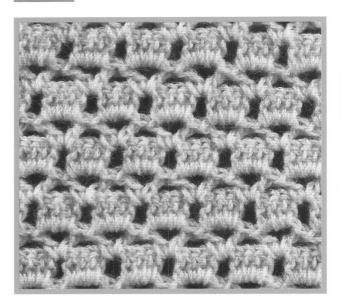

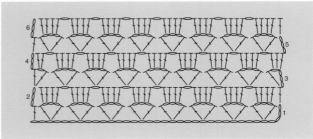

Chain multiples of 4 plus 3.

Row 1: (Dc, ch 3, dc) in 5th ch from hook, *skip next 3 ch, (dc, ch 3, dc) in next ch; rep from * across to within last 2 ch, skip next ch, dc in last ch, turn.

Row 2: Ch 3 (counts as dc), (4 dc, ch 1) in each ch-3 loop across to within last ch-3 loop, 4 dc in last ch-3 loop, dc in top of turning ch, turn.

Row 3: Ch 4 (counts as dc, ch 1), dc in first dc, (dc, ch 3, dc) in each ch-1 space across to last ch-1 space, skip next 4 dc, (dc, ch 1, dc) in 3rd ch of turning ch, turn.

Row 4: Ch 3 (counts as dc), 2 dc in next ch-1 space, ch 1 (4 dc, ch 1) in each ch-3 loop across to turning ch, 2 dc in ch-1 space of turning ch, dc in 3rd ch of turning ch, turn.

Row 5: Ch 3 (counts as dc), (dc, ch 3, dc) in each ch-1 space across to last ch-1 space, skip next 2 dc, dc in 3rd ch of turning ch, turn.

Rep Rows 2-5 for pattern.

135

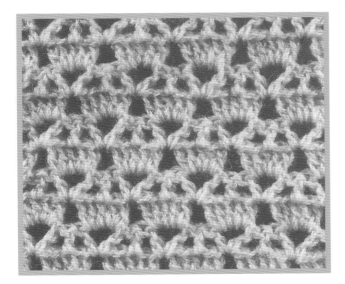

Chain multiples of 6 plus 3.

Row 1: 5 dc in 6th ch from hook, *ch 1, skip next 5 ch, 5 dc in next ch; rep from * across to within last 3 ch, skip next 2 ch, dc in last ch, turn.

Row 2: Ch 4 (counts as dc, ch 1), dc in first dc, skip next 2 dc, dc in next dc, *(dc, ch 3, dc) in next ch-1 space, skip next 2 dc, dc in next dc; rep from * across to within last 3 sts, skip next 2 dc, (dc, ch 1, dc) in top of turning ch, turn.

Row 3: Ch 3 (counts as dc), 2 dc in next ch-1 space, ch 1, (5 dc, ch 1) in each ch-3 loop across to last ch-3 loop, 2 dc in ch-1 space of turning ch, dc in 3rd ch of turning ch, turn.

Row 4: Ch 3 (counts as dc), *(dc, ch 3, dc) in next ch-1 space, skip next 2 dc, dc in next dc; rep from * across, ending with last dc in 3rd ch of turning ch, turn.

Row 5: Ch 3 (counts as dc), (5 dc, ch 1) in each ch-3 loop across to within last ch-3 loop, 5 dc in last ch-3 loop, dc in 3rd ch of turning ch, turn.

Rep Rows 2-5 for pattern.

136

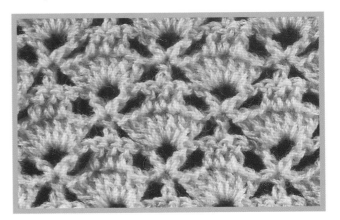

Chain multiples of 10 plus 4.

Row 1: 7 dc in 9th ch from hook, *ch 1, skip next 4 ch, dc in next ch**, ch 1, skip next 4 ch, 7 dc in next ch; rep from * across, ending last rep at **, turn.

Row 2: Ch 4 (counts as dc, ch 1), dc in first dc, *ch 1, skip next 2 dc, dc in each of next 3 dc, skip next ch-1 space**, (dc, ch 3, dc) in next dc; rep from * across, ending last rep at **, (dc, ch 1, dc) in next ch of turning ch, turn.

Row 3: Ch 3 (counts as dc), 3 dc in next ch-1 space, *ch 1, skip next ch-1 space, skip next dc, dc in next dc, ch 1, skip next ch-1 space**, 7 dc in next ch-3 loop; rep from * across, ending last rep at **, 3 dc in ch-1 space of turning ch, dc in 3rd ch of turning ch, turn.

Row 4: Ch 3 (counts as dc), skip first dc, dc in next dc, *ch 1, skip next ch-1 space, (dc, ch 3, dc) in next dc, ch 1, skip next 2 dc**, dc in each of next 3 dc; rep from * across, ending last rep at **, dc in next dc, dc in 3rd ch of turning ch, turn.

Row 5: Ch 4 (counts as dc, ch 1), skip next ch-1 space, *7 dc in next ch-3 loop, ch 1, skip next ch-1 space, skip next dc**, dc in next dc, ch 1, skip next ch-1 space; rep from * across, ending last rep at **, dc in 3rd ch of turning ch, turn.

Rep Rows 2-5 for pattern.

137

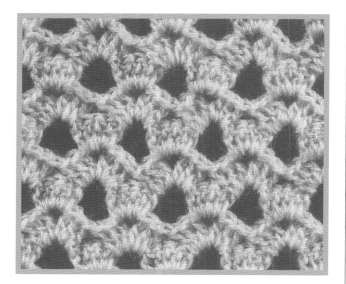

Chain multiples of 7 plus 2.

Row 1: (3 dc, ch 2, 3 dc) in 6th ch from hook, *skip next 6 ch, (3 dc, ch 2, 3 dc) in next ch; rep from * across to within last 3 ch, skip next 2 ch, dc in last ch, turn.

Row 2: Ch 3 (counts as dc), (5 dc, ch 2) in each ch-2 space across to last within ch-2 space, 5 dc in last ch-2 space, skip next 3 dc, dc in top of turning ch, turn.

Row 3: Ch 4 (counts as dc, ch 1), 3 dc in first dc, (3 dc, ch 2, 3 dc) in each ch-2 space across to last ch-2 space, skip next 5 dc, (3 dc, ch 1, dc) in 3rd ch of turning ch, turn.

Row 4: Ch 3 (counts as dc), 2 dc in first ch-1 space, ch 2, (5 dc, ch 2) in each ch-2 space across to turning ch, 2 dc in ch-1 space of turning ch, dc in 3rd ch of turning ch, turn.

Row 5: Ch 3 (counts as dc), (3 dc, ch 2, 3 dc) in each ch-2 space across to last ch-2 space, skip next 2 dc, dc in 3rd ch of turning ch, turn.

Rep Rows 2-5 for pattern.

138

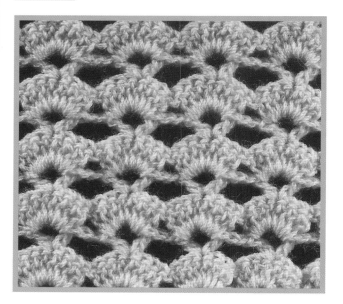

Chain multiples of 7 plus 5.

Row 1: Dc in 5th ch from hook, *ch 2, skip next 6 ch, (dc, ch 3, dc) in next ch; rep from * across to within last 7 ch, ch 2, skip next 6 ch, (dc, ch 1, dc) in last ch, turn.

Row 2: Ch 3 (counts as dc), 4 dc in next ch-1 space, skip next ch-2 space, *8 dc, in next ch-3 loop, skip next ch-2 space; rep from * across to within last ch-1 space of turning ch, 4 dc in ch-1 space of turning ch, dc in 3rd ch of turning ch, turn.

Row 3: Ch 4 (counts as dc, ch 1), dc in first dc, ch 2, skip next 8 dc, *(dc, ch 3, dc) bet last skipped and next dc, ch 2, skip next 8 dc; rep from * across to turning ch, (dc, ch 1, dc) in 3rd ch of turning ch, turn.

Rep Rows 2-3 for pattern.

139

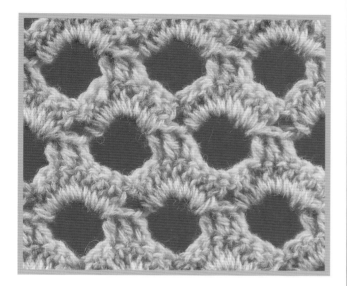

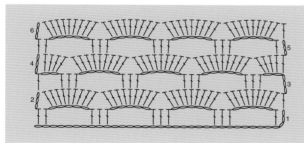

Chain multiples of 8 plus 3.

Row 1: Dc in 4th ch from hook, *ch 5, skip next 5 ch, dc in each of next 3 ch; rep from * across, ending with dc in each of last 2 ch, turn.

Row 2: Ch 3 (counts as dc), 9 dc in each ch-5 loop across to last ch-5 loop, skip next dc, dc in 3rd ch of turning ch, turn.

Row 3: Ch 5 (counts as dc, ch 2), skip first 4 dc, dc in each of next 3 dc, *ch 5, skip next 6 dc, dc in each of next 3 dc; rep from * across to within last 4 sts, ch 2, skip next 3 dc, dc in 3rd ch of turning ch, turn.

Row 4: Ch 3 (counts as dc), 4 dc in next ch-2 space, 9 dc in each ch-5 loop across to last ch-5 loop, 4 dc in in ch-2 space of turning ch, dc in 3rd ch of turning ch, turn.

Row 5: Ch 3 (counts as dc), skip first dc, dc in next dc, *ch 5, skip next 6 dc**, dc in each of next 3 dc; rep from * across, ending last rep at **, dc in next dc, dc in 3rd ch of turning ch, turn.

Rep Rows 2-5 for pattern.

140

Chain multiples of 7 plus 4.

Row 1: (2 dc, ch 1, 3 dc, ch 1, 2 dc) in 7th ch from hook, *skip next 6 ch, (2 dc, ch 1, 3 dc, ch 1, 2 dc) in next ch; rep from * across to within last 4 ch, skip next 3 ch, dc in last ch, turn.

Row 2: Ch 3 (counts as dc), *(dc, ch 2, 2 dc) in next ch-1 space, ch 2, (2 dc, ch 1, dc) in next ch-2 space; rep from * across to last ch-1 space, skip next 2 dc, dc in 3rd ch of turning ch, turn.

Row 3: Ch 3 (counts as dc), skip next ch-2 space, *(2 dc, ch 1, 3 dc, ch 1, 2 dc) in next ch-2 space**, skip next 2 ch-2 spaces; rep from * across, ending last rep at **, skip next ch-2 space, skip next dc, dc in 3rd ch of turning ch, turn.

Rep Rows 2-3 for pattern.

141

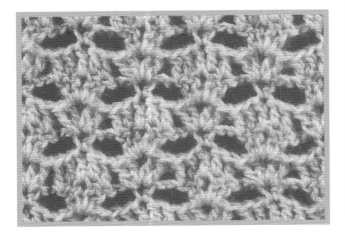

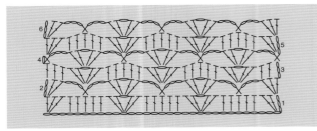

Chain multiples of 10 plus 4.

Row 1: 2 dc in 4th ch from hook, *skip next 2 ch, dc in each of next 5 ch, skip next 2 ch**, (2 dc, ch 1, 2 dc) in next ch; rep from * across, ending last rep at **, 3 dc in last ch, turn.

Row 2: Ch 3 (counts as dc), 2 dc in first dc, *ch 3, skip next 4 dc, sc in next dc, ch 3, skip next 4 dc**, (2 dc, ch 1, 2 dc) in next ch-1 space; rep from * across, ending last rep at **, 3 dc in 3rd ch of turning ch, turn.

Row 3: Ch 3 (counts as dc), skip first dc, dc in each of next 2 dc, *skip next ch-3 loop, (2 dc, ch 1, 2 dc) in next sc, skip next ch-3 loop, dc in each of next 2 dc**, dc in next ch-1 space, dc in each of next 2 dc; rep from * across, ending last rep at **, dc in 3rd ch of turning ch, turn.

Row 4: Ch 1, sc in first dc, *ch 3, skip next 4 dc, (2 dc, ch 1, 2 dc) in next ch-1 space, ch 3, skip next 4 dc, sc in next dc; rep from * across, ending with last sc in 3rd ch of turning ch, turn.

Row 5: Ch 3 (counts as dc), 2 dc in first sc, *skip next ch-3 loop, dc in each of next 2 dc, dc in next ch-1 space, dc in each of next 2 dc, skip next ch-3 loop**, (2 dc, ch 1, 2 dc) in next sc; rep from * across, ending last rep at **, 3 dc in last sc, turn.

Rep Rows 2-5 for pattern.

142

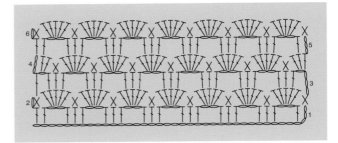

Chain multiples of 5 plus 3.

Row 1: Dc in 4th ch from hook, *ch 2, skip next 2 ch, dc in each of next 3 ch; rep from * across, ending with dc in each of last 2 ch, turn.

Row 2: Ch 1, sc in first dc, *5 dc in next ch-2 space, skip next dc, sc in next dc; rep from * across, ending with last sc in 3rd ch of turning ch, turn.

Row 3: Ch 4 (counts as dc, ch 1), skip first sc, skip next dc, dc in each of next 3 dc, *ch 2, skip next 3 sts, dc in each of next 3 dc; rep from * across to within last 2 sts, ch 1, skip next dc, dc in last sc, turn.

Row 4: Ch 3 (counts as dc), 2 dc in next ch-1 space, skip next dc, sc in next dc, *5 dc in next ch-2 space, skip next dc, sc in next dc; rep from * across to within last 3 sts, skip next dc, 2 dc in ch-1 space of turning ch, dc in 3rd ch of turning ch, turn.

Row 5: Ch 3 (counts as dc), skip first dc, dc in next dc, *ch 2, skip next 3 sts, dc in each of next 3 dc; rep from * across to within last 5 sts, ch 2, skip next 3 sts, dc in next dc, dc in 3rd ch of turning ch, turn.

Rep Rows 2-5 for pattern.

143

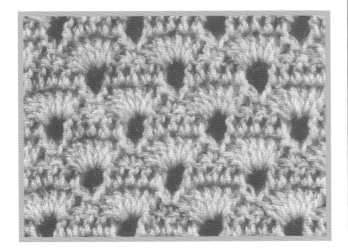

Chain multiples of 6 plus 2.

Row 1: Sc in 2nd ch from hook, *skip next 2 ch, 7 dc in next ch, skip next 2 ch, sc in next ch; rep from * across, turn.

Row 2: Ch 4 (counts as tr), skip first sc, skip next dc, *dc in each of next 5 dc**, skip next 3 sts; rep from * across, ending last rep at **, skip next dc, tr in last sc, turn.

Row 3: Ch 3 (counts as dc), 3 dc in first dc, skip next 2 dc, sc in next dc, *skip next 2 dc, 7 dc bet last skipped and next dc, skip next 2 dc, sc in next dc; rep from * across to within last 3 sts, skip next 2 dc, 4 dc in 4th ch of turning ch, turn.

Row 4: Ch 3 (counts as dc), skip first dc, dc in each of next 2 dc, *skip next 3 sts, dc in each of next 5 dc; rep from * across to within last 6 sts, skip next 3 sts, dc in each of next 2 dc, dc in 3rd ch of turning ch, turn.

Row 5: Ch 1, sc in first dc, *skip next 2 dc, 7 dc bet last skipped and next dc, skip next 2 dc, sc in next dc; rep from * across, ending with last sc in 3rd ch of turning ch, turn.

Rep Rows 2-5 for pattern.

144

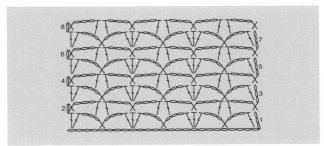

Chain multiples of 8 plus 4.

Row 1: Dc in 4th ch from hook, *ch 3, skip next 3 ch, sc in next ch, ch 3, skip next 3 ch, 3 dc in next ch; rep from * across, ending with 2 dc in last ch, turn.

Row 2: Ch 1, sc in first dc, *ch 3, skip next dc, dc in each of next 2 ch-3 loops, ch 3, skip next dc, sc in next dc; rep from * across, ending with last sc in 3rd ch of turning ch, turn.

Row 3: Ch 3 (counts as dc), dc in first sc, *skip next ch-3 loop, sc bet next 2 dc, ch 3, skip next ch-3 loop, 3 dc in next sc; rep from * across, ending with 2 dc in last sc, turn.

Rep Rows 2-3 for pattern.

145

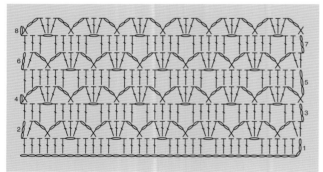

Chain multiples of 6 plus 3.

Row 1: Dc in 4th ch from hook, dc in each of next 4 ch, *ch 1, skip next ch, dc in each of next 5 ch; rep from * across to within last ch, dc in last ch, turn.

Row 2: Ch 3 (counts as dc), dc in first dc, *ch 2, skip next 2 dc, sc in next dc, ch 2**, 3 dc in next ch-1 space; rep from * across, ending last rep at **, skip next 2 dc, dc in 3rd ch of turning ch, turn.

Row 3: Ch 3 (counts as dc), skip first dc, dc in next dc, dc in next ch-2 space, *ch 1, dc in next ch-2 space**, dc in each of next 3 dc, dc in next ch-2 space; rep from * across, ending last rep at **, dc in next dc, dc in 3rd ch of turning ch, turn.

Row 4: Ch 1, sc in first dc, *ch 2, 3 dc in next ch-1 space, ch 2, skip next 2 dc, sc in next dc; rep from * across, ending with last sc in 3rd ch of turning ch, turn.

Row 5: Ch 3 (counts as dc), *dc in next ch-2 space, dc in each of next 3 dc, dc in next ch-2 space**, ch 1; rep from * across, ending last rep at **, tr in last sc, turn.

Rep Rows 2-5 for pattern

146

Chain multiples of 10 plus 3.

Row 1: Dc in 4th ch from hook, *ch 3, skip next 2 ch, sc in next ch, ch 1, skip next ch, sc in next ch, ch 3, skip next 2 ch, dc in next ch**, ch 1, skip next ch, dc in next ch; rep from * across, ending last rep at **, dc in last ch, turn.

Row 2: Ch 1, sc in first dc, *ch 3, skip next ch-3 loop, (dc, ch 1, dc, ch 1, dc) in next ch-1 space, ch 3, skip next ch-3 loop, sc in next ch-1 space; rep from * across, ending with last sc in 3rd ch of turning ch, turn.

Row 3: Ch 1, sc in first sc, sc in next ch-3 loop, *ch 3, dc in next ch-1 space, ch 1, dc in next ch-1 space, ch 3, sc in next ch-3 loop**, ch 1, sc in next ch-3 loop; rep from * across, ending last rep at **, sc in last sc, turn.

Row 4: Ch 4 (counts as dc, ch 1), dc in first sc, *ch 3, skip next ch-3 loop, sc in next ch-1 space, ch 3, skip next ch-3 loop**, (dc, ch 1, dc, ch 1, dc) in next ch-1 space; rep from * across, ending last rep at **, skip next sc, (dc, ch 1, dc) in last sc, turn.

Row 5: Ch 3 (counts as dc), *dc in next ch-1 space, ch 3, sc in next ch-3 loop, ch 1, sc in next ch-3 loop, ch 3, dc in next ch-1 space**, ch 1; rep from * across, ending last rep at **, dc in 3rd ch of turning ch, turn.

Rep Rows 2-5 for pattern.

147

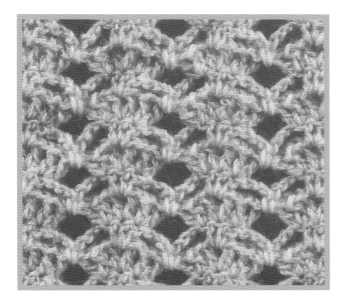

Chain multiples of 8 plus 2.

Row 1 (WS): Sc in 2nd ch from hook, *ch 3, skip next 3 ch, 3 dc in next ch, ch 3, skip next 3 ch, sc in next ch; rep from * across, turn.

Row 2: Ch 4 (counts as tr), *skip next ch-3 loop, (dc, ch 1, dc, ch 1) in each of next 2 dc, (dc, ch 1, dc) in next dc**, skip next 2 ch-3 loops; rep from * across, ending last rep at **, skip next ch-3 loop, tr in last sc, turn.

Row 3: Ch 1, sc in first tr, *ch 3, skip next 2 ch-1 spaces, 3 dc in next ch-1 space, ch 3, skip next 2 ch-1 spaces, sc bet next 2 dc; rep from * across, ending with last sc in 3rd ch of turning ch, turn.

Rep Rows 2-3 for pattern.

148

Chain multiples of 8 plus 6.

Row 1: Sc in 7th ch from hook, *ch 5, skip next 4 ch, sc in next ch**, ch 5, skip next 2 ch, sc in next ch; rep from * across, ending last rep at **, ch 2, skip next ch, dc in last ch, turn.

Row 2: Ch 1, sc in first dc, skip next ch-2 space, *9 dc in next ch-5 loop, sc in next ch-5 loop; rep from * across, ending with last sc in top of turning ch, turn.

Row 3: Ch 5 (counts as dc, ch 2), skip first sc, *skip next 2 dc, sc in next dc, ch 5, skip next 2 dc, sc in next dc, ch 2, skip next 3 dc, dc in next sc**, ch 2; rep from * across, ending last rep at **, turn.

Row 4: Ch 3 (counts as dc), 4 dc in next ch-2 space, sc in next ch-5 loop, *4 dc in next ch-2 space, dc in next dc, 4 dc in next ch-2 space, sc in next ch-5 loop; rep from * across to last ch-5 loop, 4 dc in ch-2 space of turning ch, dc in 3rd ch of turning ch, turn.

Row 5: Ch 5 (counts as dc, ch 2), skip first dc, *sc in next dc, ch 2, skip next 3 dc, dc in next sc, ch 2, skip next 2 dc, sc in next dc**, ch 5, skip next 2 dc; rep from * to * across, ending last rep at **, ch 2, skip next dc, dc in 3rd ch of turning ch, turn.

Rep Rows 2-5 for pattern.

149

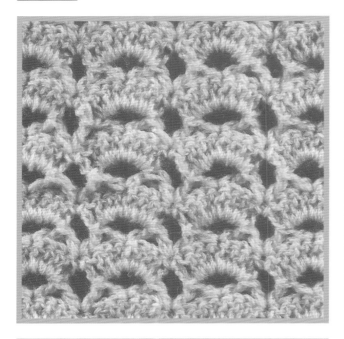

Chain multiples of 8 plus 7.

Row 1: Work 1 cluster of 2 dc, working first half-closed dc in 7th ch from hook, skip next 3 ch, work 2nd half-closed dc in next ch, yo, complete cluster, ch 5, *work 1 cluster of 2 dc, working first half-closed dc in same ch as last dc worked, skip next 3 ch, work 2nd half-closed dc in next ch, yo, complete cluster, ch 5; rep from * across to last ch, ch 2, tr in last ch already holding last dc made, turn.

Row 2: Ch 1, sc in first tr, skip next ch-2 space, *7 dc in next ch-5 loop, sc in next ch-5 loop; rep from * across, ending with last sc in 4th ch of turning ch, turn.

Row 3: Ch 6 (counts as tr, ch 2), work 1 cluster of 2 dc, working first half-closed dc in first sc, skip next 2 dc, work 2nd half-closed dc in next dc, complete cluster, ch 5, skip next dc, *work 1 cluster of 2 dc, working first half-closed dc in next dc, skip

next 2 dc, work 2nd half-closed dc in next sc, complete cluster**, ch 5, work 1 cluster of 2 dc, working first half-closed dc in same sc as last dc worked, skip next 2 dc, work 2nd half-closed dc in next dc, complete cluster, ch 5, skip next dc; rep from * across, ending last rep at **, ch 2, tr in last sc already holding last dc made, turn.

Rep Rows 2-3 for pattern.

150

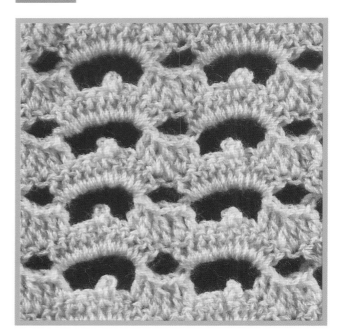

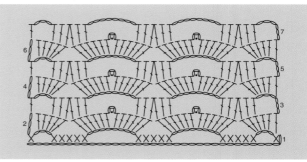

Picot: Ch 3, sl st in 3rd ch from hook.

Chain multiples of 11 plus 1.

Row 1: Sc in 2nd ch from hook, ch 3, skip next 2 ch, sc in each of next 5 ch, *ch 8, skip next 6 ch, sc in each of next 5 ch; rep from * across to within last 3 ch, ch 3, skip next 2 ch, sc in last ch, turn.

Row 2: Ch 3 (counts as dc), 5 dc in next ch-3 loop, (6 dc, picot, 6 dc) in each ch-8 loop across to last ch-8 loop, 5 dc in next ch-3 loop, dc in last sc, turn.

Row 3: Ch 6 (counts as dc, ch 3), skip first 3 dc, *dc in each of next 2 dc, work 1 cluster of 2 dc across next 2 dc, dc in each of next 2 dc**, ch 8, skip next 6 dc; rep from * across, ending last rep at **, ch 3, skip next 2 dc, dc in 3rd ch of turning ch, turn.

Row 4: Ch 3 (counts as dc), 5 dc in next ch-3 loop, (6 dc, picot, 6 dc) in each ch-8 loop across to last ch-8 loop, 5 dc in next ch-3 loop of turning ch, dc in 3rd ch of turning ch, turn.

Rep Rows 3-4 for pattern.

151

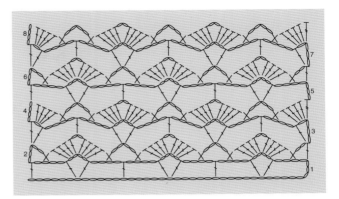

Chain multiples of 12 plus 7.

Row 1: (Dc, ch 4, dc) in 13th ch from hook, ch 4, skip next 5 ch, dc in next ch, *ch 4, skip next 5 ch, (dc, ch 4, dc) in next ch, ch 4, skip next 5 ch, dc in next ch; rep from * across, turn.

Row 2: Ch 5 (counts as dc, ch 2), sc in next ch-4 loop, *(4 dc, ch 2, 4 dc) in next ch-4 loop, sc in next ch-4 loop**, ch 4, sc in next ch-4 loop; rep from * across, ending last rep at **, ch 2, dc in next ch of turning ch, turn.

Row 3: Ch 4 (counts as dc, ch 1), dc in first dc, skip next ch-2 space, *ch 4, dc in next ch-2 space, ch 4**, (dc, ch 4, dc) in next ch-4 loop; rep from * across, ending last rep at **, (dc, ch 1, dc) in 3rd ch of turning ch, turn.

Row 4: Ch 4 (counts as tr), 4 dc in next ch-1 space, *sc in next ch-4 loop, ch 4, sc in next ch-4 loop**, (4 dc, ch 2, 4 dc) in next ch-4 loop, rep from * across, ending last rep at **, 4 dc in next ch-1 space of turning ch, tr in 3rd ch of turning ch, turn.

Row 5: Ch 7 (counts as dc, ch 4), (dc, ch 4, dc) in next ch-4 loop, ch 4**, dc in next ch-2 space, ch 4; rep from * across, ending last rep at **, dc in 3rd ch of turning ch, turn.

Rep Rows 2-5 for pattern.

.11.
Shells & Chains

152

Chain multiples of 3 plus 2.

Row 1: Sc in 2nd ch from hook, *ch 3, skip next 2 ch, sc in next ch; rep from * across, turn.

Row 2: Ch 3 (counts as dc), dc in first sc, *sc in next ch-3 loop, 3 dc in next sc; rep from * across, ending with 2 dc in last ch, turn.

Row 3: Ch 1, sc in first dc, *ch 3, skip next 3 sts, sc in next dc; rep from * across, ending with last sc in 3rd ch of turning ch, turn.

Rep Rows 2-3 for pattern.

153

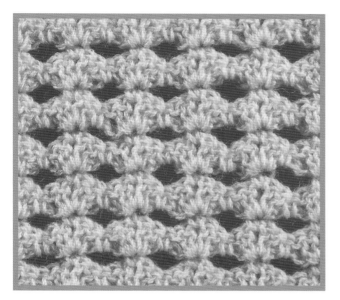

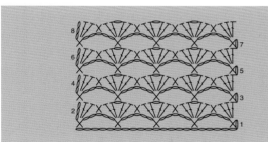

Chain multiples of 5 plus 2.

Row 1: Sc in 2nd ch from hook, *ch 5, skip next 4 ch, sc in next ch; rep from * across, turn.

Row 2: Ch 3 (counts as dc), 2 dc in first sc, *sc in next ch-5 loop, (2 dc, ch 1, 2 dc) in next sc; rep from * across, ending with 3 dc in last sc, turn.

Row 3: Ch 1, sc in first dc, ch 5, (sc, ch 5) in each ch-1 space across within last 6 sts, skip next 5 sts, sc in 3rd ch of turning ch, turn.

Rep Rows 2-3 for pattern.

154

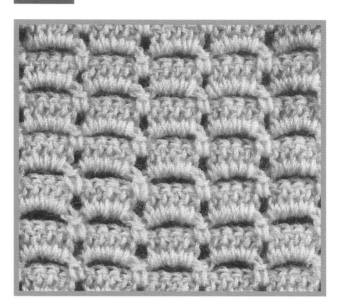

Chain multiples of 4 plus 2.

Row 1: Sc in 2nd ch from hook, *ch 5, skip next 3 ch, sc in next ch; rep from * across, turn.

Row 2: Ch 4 (counts as tr), 5 dc in each ch-5 loop across, tr in last sc, turn.

Row 3: Ch 1, sc in first tr, *ch 5, skip next 5 dc, sc bet last skipped and next dc; rep from * across, ending with last sc in 4th ch of turning ch, turn.

Rep Rows 2-3 for pattern.

155

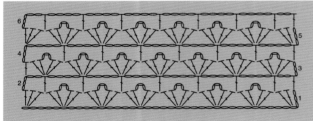

Chain multiples of 5 plus 4.

Row 1: 2 dc in 4th ch from hook, *skip next 4 ch, (2 dc, ch 3, 2 dc) in next ch; rep from * across, ending with 3 dc in last ch, turn.

Row 2: Ch 5 (counts as dc, ch 2), skip first 3 dc, dc bet last skipped and next dc, *ch 4, skip next 4 dc, dc bet last skipped and next dc; rep from * across to within last 3 sts, ch 2, skip next 2 dc, dc in 3rd ch of turning ch, turn.

Row 3: Ch 3 (counts as dc), (2 dc, ch 3, 2 dc) in each dc across, ending with dc in 3rd ch of turning ch, turn.

Row 4: Ch 7 (counts as dc, ch 4), skip first 5 dc, *dc bet last skipped and next dc, ch 4, skip next 4 dc; rep from * across to turning ch, dc in 3rd ch of turning ch, turn.

Row 5: Ch 3 (counts as dc), 2 dc in first dc, (2 dc, ch 2, 2 dc) in each dc across, ending with 3 dc in 3rd ch of turning ch, turn.

Rep Rows 2-5 for pattern.

156

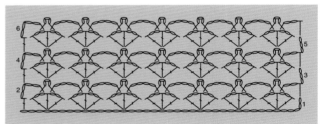

Chain multiples of 5 plus 4.

Row 1: (Dc, ch 2, dc, ch 2, dc) in 6th ch from hook, *skip next 4 ch, (dc, ch 2, dc, ch 2, dc) in next ch; rep from * across to within last 3 ch, skip next 2 ch, dc in last ch, turn.

Row 2: Ch 4 (counts as hdc, ch 2), *sc in next ch-2 space, ch 3, sc in next ch-2 space**, ch 4; rep from * across, ending last rep at **, ch 2, hdc in top of turning ch, turn.

Row 3: Ch 3 (counts as dc), skip next ch-2 space, (dc, ch 2, dc, ch 2, dc) in next ch-3 loop, *skip next ch-4 loop, (dc, ch 2, dc, ch 2, dc) in next ch-3 loop; rep from * across to last ch-3 loop, skip next 2 ch of turning ch, dc in 2nd ch of turning ch, turn.

Rep Rows 2-3 for pattern.

157

Chain multiples of 5 plus 4.

Row 1: (2 dc, ch 1, 2 dc) in 6th ch from hook, *skip next 4 ch, (2 dc, ch 1, 2 dc) in next ch; rep from * across to within last 3 ch, skip next 2 ch, dc in last ch, turn.

Row 2: Ch 1, sc in first dc, sc in next dc, *ch 2, (sc, ch 3, sc) in next ch-1 space, ch 2**, skip next 2 dc, sc bet last skipped and next dc; rep from * across, ending last rep at **, skip next dc, sc in next dc, sc in top of turning ch, turn.

Row 3: Ch 3 (counts as dc), skip next ch-2 space, *(2 dc, ch 1, 2 dc) in next ch-3 loop**, skip next 2 ch-2 spaces; rep from * across, ending last rep at **, skip next ch-2 space, dc in last sc, turn.

Rep Rows 2-3 for pattern.

158

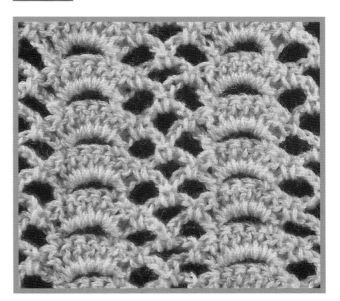

Chain multiples of 12 plus 1.

Row 1: Sc in 7th ch from hook, *ch 5, skip next 3 ch, sc in next ch; rep from * across to within last 2 ch, ch 2, skip next ch, dc in last ch, turn.

Row 2: Ch 1, sc in first dc, skip next ch-2 space, *7 dc in next ch-5 loop**, sc in next ch-5 loop, ch 5, sc in next ch-5 loop; rep from * across, ending last rep at **, skip next 2 ch of turning ch, sc in next ch of turning ch, turn.

Row 3: Ch 5 (counts as dc, ch 2), skip first sc, skip next dc, *sc in next dc, ch 5, skip next 3 dc, sc in next dc**, ch 5, sc in next ch-5 loop, ch 5, skip next dc; rep from * across, ending last rep at **, ch 2, skip next dc, dc in last sc, turn.

Rep Rows 2-3 for pattern.

159

Chain multiples of 16 plus 5.

Row 1: Sc in 7th ch from hook, *ch 5, skip next 3 ch, sc in next ch; rep from * across to within last 2 ch, ch 2, skip next ch, dc in last ch, turn.

Row 2: Ch 1, sc in first dc, ch 5, skip next ch-2 space, sc in next ch-5 loop, *8 dc in next ch-5 loop**, (sc, ch 5) in each of next 2 ch-5 loops, sc in next ch-5 loop; rep from * across, ending last rep at **, sc in next ch-5 loop, ch 5, skip next 2 ch of turning ch, sc in next ch of turning ch, turn.

Row 3: Ch 5 (counts as dc, ch 2), sc in next ch-5 loop, ch 4, *skip next dc, dc in each of next 6 dc, ch 4, sc in next ch-5 loop**, ch 5, sc in next ch-5 loop, ch 4; rep from * across, ending last rep at **, ch 2, skip next dc, dc in last sc, turn.

Row 4: Ch 1, sc in first dc, *ch 5, sc in next ch-4 loop, ch 3, skip next dc, dc in each of next 4 dc, ch 3, sc in next ch-4 loop, ch 5, sc in next ch-5 loop; rep from * across, ending with last sc in 3rd ch of turning ch, turn.

Row 5: Ch 5 (counts as dc, ch 2), sc in next ch-5 loop, ch 5, sc in next ch-3 loop, *ch 3, skip next dc, dc in each of next 2 dc, ch 3, sc in next ch-3 loop**, (ch 5, sc) in each of next 3 loops; rep from * across, ending last rep at **, ch 5, sc in next ch-5 loop, ch 2, dc in last sc, turn.

Row 6: Ch 3 (counts as dc), 3 dc in next ch-2 space, *sc in next ch-5 loop, ch 5, skip next ch-3 loop, sc bet next 2 dc, ch 5, skip next ch-3 loop, sc in next ch-5 loop**, 8 dc in next ch-5 loop; rep from * across, ending last rep at **, 3 dc in next ch-2 space of turning ch, dc in 3rd ch of turning ch, turn.

Row 7: Ch 3 (counts as dc), skip first dc, dc in each of next 2 dc, *ch 4, sc in next ch-5 loop, ch 5, sc in next ch-5 loop, ch 4**, skip next dc, dc in each of next 6 dc; rep from * across, ending last rep at **, skip next dc, dc in each of next 2 dc, dc in 3rd ch of turning ch, turn.

Row 8: Ch 3 (counts as dc), skip first dc, dc in next dc, *ch 3, (sc, ch 5) in each of next 2 loops, sc in next ch-3 loop, ch 3, skip next dc**, dc in each of next 4 dc; rep from * across, ending last rep at **, dc in next dc, dc in 3rd ch of turning ch, turn.

Row 9: Ch 6 (counts as dc, ch 3), *(sc, ch 5) in each of next 3 loops, sc in next ch-3 loop, ch 3, skip next dc**, dc in each of next 2 dc, ch 3; rep from * across, ending last rep at **, dc in 3rd ch of turning ch, turn.

Rep Rows 2-9 for pattern.

160

Chain multiples of 6.

Row 1: Sc in 7th ch from hook, *ch 3, skip next 2 ch, sc in next ch, ch 5, skip next 2 ch, sc in next ch; rep from * across to within last 5 ch, ch 3, skip next 2 ch, sc in next ch, ch 2, skip next ch, dc in last ch, turn.

Row 2: Ch 1, sc in first dc, skip next ch-2 space, *ch 2, dc in next ch-3 loop, ch 2, sc in next ch-5 loop; rep from * across to last ch-5 loop, ch 2, dc in next ch-3 loop, ch 2, skip next 2 ch of turning ch, sc in next ch of turning ch, turn.

Row 3: Ch 5 (counts as dc, ch 2), sc in next ch-2 space, *ch 3, sc in next ch-2 space, ch 5, sc in next ch-2 space; rep from * across to within last ch-2 space, ch 3, sc in next ch-2 space, ch 2, dc in last sc, turn.

Row 4: Ch 1, sc in first dc, skip next ch-2 space, *5 dc in next ch-3 loop, sc in next ch-5 loop; rep from * across, ending with last sc in 3rd ch of turning ch, turn.

Row 5: Ch 5 (counts as dc, ch 2), skip first sc, skip next dc, *sc in next dc, ch 3, skip next dc, sc in next dc**, ch 5, skip next 3 sts; rep from * across, ending last rep at **, ch 2, skip next dc, dc in last sc, turn.

Rep Rows 2-5 for pattern.

161

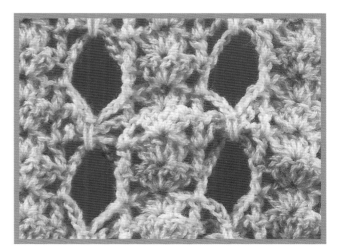

Chain multiples of 14 plus 4.

Row 1: 2 dc in 4th ch from hook, *skip next 2 ch, dc in next ch, ch 7, skip next 7 ch, dc in next ch, skip next 2 ch, 5 dc in next ch; rep from * across, ending with 3 dc in last ch, turn.

Row 2: Ch 3 (counts as dc), 2 dc in first dc, *skip next 2 dc, dc in next dc, ch 7, skip next ch-7 loop, dc in next dc, skip next 2 dc**, 5 dc in next dc, skip next 2 dc, dc in next dc; rep from * across, ending last rep at **, dc in 3rd ch of turning ch, turn.

Row 3: Ch 3 (counts as dc), 2 dc in first dc, *skip next 2 dc, dc in next dc, ch 3, sc over next 3 corresponding ch-7 loops in 3 rows below, ch 3, dc in next dc, skip next 2 dc**, 5 dc in next dc; rep from * across, ending last rep at **, dc in 3rd ch of turning ch, turn.

Row 4: Ch 3 (counts as dc), 2 dc in first dc, *skip next 2 dc, dc in next dc, ch 7, skip next 2 ch-3 loops, dc in next dc, skip next 2 dc**, 5 dc in next dc; rep from * across, ending last rep at **, 3 dc in 3rd ch of turning ch, turn.

Row 5: Rep Row 2.

Rep Rows 2-5 for pattern.

162

Chain multiples of 8 plus 2.

Row 1: Sc in 2nd ch from hook, *ch 5, skip next 3 ch, sc in next ch; rep from * across, turn.

Row 2: Ch 4 (counts as dc, ch 1), sc in next ch-5 loop, (ch 3, sc) in each ch-5 loop across to last ch-3 loop, ch 1, dc in last sc, turn.

Row 3: Ch 3 (counts as dc), 2 dc in first ch-1 space, sc in next ch-3 loop, *5 dc in next ch-3 loop, sc in next ch-3 loop; rep from * across to last ch-3 loop, 2 dc in ch-1 space of turning ch, dc in 3rd ch of turning ch, turn.

Row 4: Ch 4 (counts as dc, ch 1), skip first dc, (dc, ch 1) in each of next 2 dc, sc in next sc, ch 1, *(dc, ch 1) in each of next 5 dc, sc in next sc, ch 1; rep from * across to within last 3 sts, (dc, ch 1) in each of next 2 dc, dc in 3rd ch of turning ch, turn.

Row 5: Ch 5 (counts as dc, ch 2), skip next ch-1 space, sc in next dc, *ch 5, skip next 4 ch-1 spaces, sc in next dc, ch 5, skip next 2 ch-1 spaces, sc in next dc; rep from * across to within last 5 ch-1 spaces, ch 5, skip next 4 ch-1 spaces, sc in next dc, ch 2, skip next ch of turning ch, dc in 3rd ch of turning ch, turn.

Row 6: Ch 1, sc in first dc, ch 3, (sc, ch 3) in each ch-5 loop across to last ch-5 loop, sc in 3rd ch of turning ch, turn.

Row 7: Ch 3 (counts as dc), 4 dc in next ch-3 loop, *sc in next ch-3 loop, 5 dc in next ch-3 loop; rep from * across to within last ch-3 loop, sc in next ch-3 loop, ch 1, dc in last sc, turn.

Row 8: Ch 5 (counts as dc, ch 2), skip next ch-1 space, sc in next sc, ch 1, *(dc, ch 1) in each of next 5 dc, sc in next sc, ch 1; rep from * across to within last 5 sts, (dc, ch 1) in each of next 3 dc, dc in next dc, turn, leaving turning ch unworked.

Row 9: Ch 1, sc in first dc, ch 5, skip next 2 ch-1 spaces, sc in next dc, *ch 5, skip next 4 ch-1 spaces, sc in next dc, ch 5, skip next 2 ch-1 spaces, sc in next dc; rep from * across to within last 3 spaces, ch 5, skip next 2 ch-1 spaces, skip next 2 ch of turning ch, sc in 3rd ch of turning ch, turn.

Row 10: Ch 4 (counts as dc, ch 1), sc in next ch-5 loop, (ch 3, sc) in each ch-5 loop across to last ch-5 loop, ch 1, dc in last sc, turn.

Row 11: Ch 1, sc in first dc, skip next ch-1 space, *5 dc in next ch-3 loop, sc in next ch-3 loop; rep from * across, ending with last sc in 3rd ch of turning ch, turn.

Row 12: Ch 1, sc in first sc, *ch 1, (dc, ch 1) in each of next 5 dc, sc in next sc; rep from * across, turn.

Row 13: Ch 5 (counts as dc, ch 2), skip next 2 ch-1 spaces, *sc in next dc, ch 5, skip next 2 ch-1 spaces, sc in next dc**, ch 5, skip next 4 ch-1 spaces; rep from * across, ending last rep at **, ch 2, skip next 2 ch-1 spaces, dc in last sc, turn.

Row 14: Rep Row 6.

Row 15: Ch 4 (counts as dc, ch 1), *sc in next ch-3 loop, 5 dc in next ch-3 loop; rep from * across, ending with 4 dc in last ch-3 loop, turn.

Row 16: Ch 3 (counts as dc), dc in first dc, ch 1, (dc, ch 1) in each of next 3 dc, sc in next sc, *ch 1, (dc, ch 1) in each of next 5 dc, sc in next sc; rep from * across to turning ch, ch 2, dc in 3rd ch of turning ch, turn.

Row 17: Ch 1, sc in first dc, ch 5, skip next 3 spaces, *sc in next dc, ch 5, skip next 2 ch-1 spaces, sc in next dc**, ch 5, skip next 4 ch-1 spaces; rep from * across, ending last rep at **, turn, leaving turning ch unworked.

Rep Rows 2-17 for pattern.

Chain multiples of 12 plus 4.

Row 1: 2 dc in 4th ch from hook, *ch 3, skip next 3 ch, sc in next ch, ch 5, skip next 3 ch, sc in next ch, ch 3, skip next 3 ch, (2 dc, ch 1, 2 dc) in next ch; rep from * across, ending with 3 dc in last ch, turn.

Row 2: Ch 3 (counts as dc), 2 dc in first dc, *dc in next ch-3 loop, ch 3, sc in next ch-5 loop, ch 3, dc in next ch-3 loop**, (2 dc, ch 1, 2 dc) in next ch-1 space; rep from * across, ending last rep at **, skip next 2 dc, 3 dc in 3rd ch of turning ch, turn.

Row 3: Ch 3 (counts as dc), 2 dc in first dc, *ch 3, sc in next ch-3 loop, ch 5, sc in next ch-3 loop, ch 3**, (2 dc, ch 1, 2 dc) in next ch-1 space; rep from * across, ending last rep at **, skip next 3 dc, 3 dc in 3rd ch of turning ch, turn.

Rep Rows 2-3 for pattern.

Chain multiples of 12 plus 2.

Row 1: Sc in 2nd ch from hook, *ch 4, skip next 3 ch, sc in next ch; rep from * across, turn.

Row 2: Ch 5 (counts as dc, ch 2), *sc in next ch-4 loop, (3 dc, ch 3, 3 dc) in next ch-4 loop, sc in next ch-4 loop**, ch 4, sc in next ch-4 loop; rep from * across, ending last rep at **, ch 2, dc in last sc, turn.

Row 3: Ch 1, sc in first dc, *ch 4, skip next ch-2 space, (sc, ch 4, sc) in next ch-3 loop, ch 4, sc in next ch-4 loop; rep from * across, ending with last sc in 3rd ch of turning ch, turn.

Rep Rows 2-3 for pattern.

165

Chain multiples of 8 plus 3.

Row 1: Sc in 5th ch from hook, *ch 3, skip next 3 ch, sc in next ch; rep from * across to within last 2 ch, ch 1, skip next ch, hdc in last ch, turn.

Row 2: Ch 1, sc in first hdc, *ch 1 (dc, ch 1, dc, ch 1, dc, ch 1, dc) in next ch-3 loop, ch 1, sc in next ch-3 loop; rep from * across, ending with last sc in 3rd ch of turning ch, turn.

Row 3: Ch 4 (counts as dc, ch 1), skip next ch-1 space, *sc in next ch-1 space, ch 3, skip next ch-1 space, sc in next ch-1 space**, ch 3, skip next 2 ch-1 spaces; rep from * across, ending last rep at **, skip next ch-1 space, dc in last sc, turn.

Rep Rows 2-3 for pattern.

166

Chain multiples of 8 plus 2.

Row 1: Sc in 2nd ch from hook, *ch 5, skip next 3 ch, sc in next ch; rep from * across, turn.

Row 2: Ch 6 (counts as tr, ch 2), *sc in next ch-5 loop, (2 dc, ch 1, 2 dc) in next sc, sc in next ch-5 loop**, ch 5; rep from * across, ending last rep at **, ch 2, tr in last sc, turn.

Row 3: Ch 1, sc in first tr, skip next ch-2 space, *ch 5, sc in next ch-1 space, ch 5, sc in next ch-5 loop; rep from * across, ending with last sc in 4th ch of turning ch, turn.

Rep Rows 2-3 for pattern.

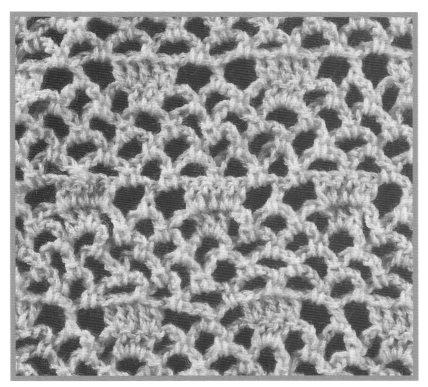

167

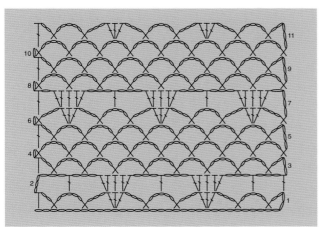

Chain multiples of 12.

Row 1: Sc in 6th ch from hook, *ch 5, skip next 3 ch, sc in next ch**, ch 3, skip next 3 ch, 3 dc in next ch, ch 3, skip next 3 ch, sc in next ch; rep from * across, ending last rep at **, ch 2, skip next ch, hdc in last ch, turn.

Row 2: Ch 6 (counts as dc, ch 3), skip next ch-2 space, dc in next ch-5 loop, ch 3, *skip next ch-3 loop, 2 dc in next dc, dc in next dc, 2 dc in next dc, ch 3, skip next ch-3 loop, dc in next ch-5 loop, ch 3; rep from * across to last ch-5 loop, skip next 2 ch of turning ch, dc in 3rd ch of turning ch, turn.

Row 3: Ch 4 (counts as hdc, ch 2), *(sc, ch 5) in each of next 2 ch-3 loops, skip next 2 dc, sc in next dc, ch 5; rep from * across to within last 2 ch-3 loops, sc in next ch-3 loop, ch 5, sc in next ch-3 loop of turning ch, ch 2, hdc in 3rd ch of turning ch, turn.

Row 4: Ch 1, sc in first hdc, (ch 5, sc) in each ch-5 loop across, ending with last sc in in 2nd ch of turning ch, turn.

Row 5: Ch 5 (counts as dc, ch 2), sc in next ch-5 loop, (ch 5, sc) in each ch-5 loop across to last ch-5 loop, ch 2, dc in 3rd ch of turning ch, turn.

Row 6: Ch 1, sc in first dc, *ch 3, 3 dc in next ch-5 loop, ch 3**, sc in next ch-5 loop, ch 5, sc in next ch-5 loop; rep from * across, ending last rep at **, sc in 3rd ch of turning ch, turn.

Row 7: Ch 4 (counts as dc, ch 1), skip next ch-3 loop, *2 dc in next dc, dc in next dc, 2 dc in next dc**, ch 3, skip next ch-3 loop, dc in next ch-5 loop, ch 3; rep from * across, ending last rep at **, ch 1, skip next ch-3 loop, dc in last sc, turn.

Row 8: Ch 1, sc in first dc, ch 5, *skip next 2 dc, sc in next dc, ch 5**, (sc, ch 5) in each of next 2 ch-3 loops; rep from * across, ending last rep at **, sc in 3rd ch of turning ch, turn.

Row 9: Rep Row 5.

Row 10: Ch 1, sc in first dc, (ch 5, sc) in each ch-5 loop across, ending with last sc in in 3rd ch of turning ch, turn.

Row 11: Ch 5 (counts as dc, ch 2), *sc in next ch-5 loop, ch 5, sc in next ch-5 loop**, ch 3, 3 dc in next ch-5 loop, ch 3; rep from * across, ending last rep at **, ch 2, dc in last sc, turn.

Rep Rows 2-11 for pattern.

168

Chain multiples of 6 plus 3.

Row 1: (2 dc, ch 2, 2 dc) in 6th ch from hook, *skip next 5 ch, (2 dc, ch 2, 2 dc) in next ch; rep from * across to within last 3 ch, skip next 2 ch, dc in last ch, turn.

Row 2: Ch 1, sc in first dc, *ch 3, dc in next ch-1 space, ch 3, skip next 2 dc, sc bet last skipped and next dc; rep from * across, ending with last sc in top of turning ch, turn.

Row 3: Ch 4 (counts as tr), skip next ch-3 loop, (2 dc, ch 2, 2 dc) in next dc, *skip next 2 ch-3 loops, (2 dc, ch 2, 2 dc) in next dc; rep from * across to within last ch-3 loop, skip next ch-3 loop, tr in last sc, turn.

Rep Rows 2-3 for pattern.

169

Chain multiples of 17 plus 7.

Row 1: Sc in 2nd ch from hook, *ch 5, skip next 4 ch, (sc in next ch, skip next 2 ch, [dc, ch 1, dc, ch 1, dc] in next ch, skip next 2 ch) twice, sc in next ch; rep from * across to within last 5 ch, ch 5, skip next 4 ch, sc in last ch, turn.

Row 2: Ch 5 (counts as dc, ch 2), sc in next ch-5 loop, *ch 5, skip next ch-1 space, sc in next dc, (dc, ch 1, dc, ch 1, dc) in next sc, skip next ch-1 space, sc in next dc, ch 5, skip next ch-1 space, sc in next ch-5 loop; rep from * across to last ch-5 loop, ch 2, dc in last sc, turn.

Row 3: Ch 1, sc in first dc, ch 5, sc in next ch-5 loop, *(dc, ch 1, dc, ch 1, dc) in next sc, skip next ch-1 space, sc in next dc, (dc, ch 1, dc, ch 1, dc) in next sc, sc in next ch-5 loop, ch 5, sc in next ch-5 loop; rep from * across, ending with last sc in 3rd ch of turning ch, turn.

Rep Rows 2-3 for pattern.

170

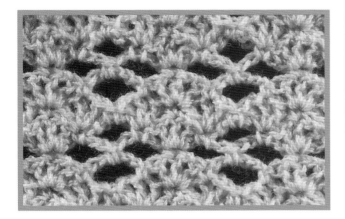

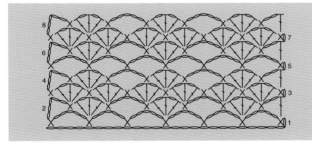

Chain multiples of 8 plus 2.

Row 1: Sc in 2nd ch from hook, *ch 5, skip next 3 ch, sc in next ch; rep from * across, turn.

Row 2: Ch 5 (counts as dc, ch 2), sc in next ch-5 loop, *(dc, ch 1, dc, ch 1, dc) in next sc, sc in next ch-5 loop**, ch 5, sc in next ch-5 loop; rep from * across, ending last rep at **, ch 2, dc in last sc, turn.

Row 3: Ch 1, sc in first dc, *(dc, ch 1, dc, ch 1, dc) in next sc, skip next ch-1 space, sc in next dc, (dc, ch 1, dc, ch 1, dc) in next sc, sc in next ch-5 loop; rep from * across, ending with last sc in 3rd ch of turning ch, turn.

Row 4: Ch 5, (counts as dc, ch 2), skip next ch-1 space, *sc in next dc, (dc, ch 1, dc, ch 1, dc) in next sc, skip next ch-1 space, sc in next dc**, ch 5, skip next 2 ch-1 spaces; rep from * across, ending last rep at **, ch 2, skip next ch-1 space, dc in last sc, turn.

Row 5: Ch 1, sc in first dc, *ch 5, skip next 2 spaces, *sc in next dc (center dc of shell), ch 5, skip next ch-1 space**, sc in next ch-5 loop, ch 5, skip next ch-1 space; rep from * across, ending last rep at **, sc in 3rd ch of turning ch, turn.

Rep Rows 2–5 for pattern.

171

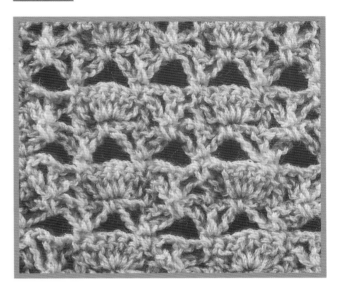

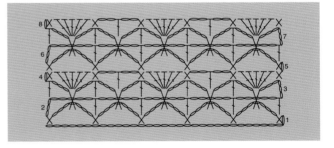

Chain multiples of 12 plus 8.

Row 1: Sc in 2nd ch from hook, *ch 7, skip next 5 ch, sc in next ch; rep from * across, turn.

Row 2: Ch 8 (counts as dc, ch 5), skip next ch-7 loop, dc in next sc, *ch 5, skip next ch-7 loop, dc in next sc; rep from * across, turn.

Row 3: Ch 6 (counts as dc, ch 3), *sc over next 2 corresponding loops in 2 rows below, ch 3**, dc in next dc, ch 3; rep from * across, ending last rep at **, dc in 3rd ch of turning ch, turn.

Row 4: Ch 1, sc in first dc, skip next ch-3 loop, 5 dc in next sc, *skip next ch-3 loop, sc in next dc, ch 2, skip next ch-3 loop, dc in next sc, ch 2, skip next ch-3 loop, sc in next dc, skip next ch-3 loop, 5 dc in next sc; rep from * across to last sc, skip next 3 ch of turning ch, sc in 3rd ch of turning ch, turn.

Row 5: Ch 1, sc in first sc, *ch 7, skip next 5 sts, sc in next sc; rep from * across, turn.

Rep Rows 2–5 for pattern.

.12.
Shells—Staggered

172

Chain multiples of 8 plus 2.

Row 1: Sc in 2nd ch from hook, *ch 4, skip next 3 ch, (sc, ch 3, 2 dc) in next ch, skip next 3 ch, sc in next ch; rep from * across, turn.

Row 2: Ch 5 (counts as dc, ch 2), *(sc, ch 3, 2 dc) in next ch-3 loop, sc in next ch-4 loop**, ch 4; rep from * across, ending last rep at **, ch 2, dc in last sc, turn.

Row 3: Ch 1, sc in first dc, *ch 4, (sc, ch 3, 2 dc) in next ch-3 loop, sc in next ch-4 loop; rep from * across, ending with last sc in 3rd ch of turning ch, turn.

Rep Rows 2-3 for pattern.

173

Chain multiples of 7 plus 2.

Row 1: 2 dc in 5th ch from hook, *ch 2, skip next 3 ch, sc in next ch**, ch 2, skip next 2 ch, (tr, 2 dc) in next ch; rep from * across, ending last rep at **, turn.

Row 2: Ch 4 (counts as tr), 2 dc in first sc, ch 2, skip next ch-2 space, *sc in next ch-2 space, ch 2, (tr, 2 dc) in next sc, ch 2, skip next ch-2 space; rep from * across to within last 3 sts, skip next 2 dc, sc in 4th ch of turning ch, turn.

Rep Row 2 for pattern.

174

Chain multiples of 14 plus 6.

Row 1: (Sc, ch 3, 3 dc) in 9th ch from hook, *skip next 3 ch, dc in next ch, skip next 3 ch, (3 dc, ch 3, sc) in next ch, ch 3, skip next 2 ch, dc in next ch**, ch 3, skip next 2 ch, (sc, ch 3, 3 dc) in next ch; rep from * across, ending last rep at **, turn.

Row 2: Ch 1, sc in first dc, ch 3, skip next ch-3 loop, *sc in next ch-3 loop, ch 3, skip next 3 dc, sc in next dc, ch 3, sc in next ch-3 loop, ch 3**, skip next ch-3 loop, sc in next dc, ch 3; rep from * across, ending last rep at **, skip next 3 ch of turning ch, sc in next ch of turning ch, turn.

Row 3: Ch 6 (counts as dc, ch 3), *skip next ch-3 loop, (sc, ch 3, 3 dc) in next sc, skip next ch-3 loop, dc in next sc, skip next ch-3 loop, (3 dc, ch 3, sc) in next sc, ch 3, skip next ch-3 loop, dc in next sc**, ch 3; rep from * across, ending last rep at **, turn.

Rep Rows 2-3 for pattern.

175

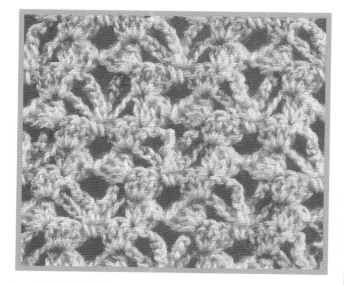

Chain multiples of 12 plus 4.

Row 1: 3 dc in 4th ch from hook, *skip next 5 ch, 4 dc in next ch, ch 4, skip next 2 ch, sc in next ch, ch 4, skip next 2 ch**, 4 dc in next ch; rep from * across, ending last rep at **, dc in last ch, turn.

Row 2: Ch 7 (counts as dc, ch 5), skip next ch-5 loop, *sc in next sc, ch 5, skip next ch-4 loop, 4 dc in next dc, skip next 6 dc**, 4 dc in next dc, ch 5, skip next ch-4 loop; rep from * across, ending last rep at **, 4 dc in 3rd ch of turning ch, turn.

Row 3: Ch 7 (counts as dc, ch 4), skip first 4 dc, *sc bet last skipped and next dc, ch 4, skip next 3 dc, 4 dc in next dc, skip next 2 ch-5 loops**, 4 dc in next dc, ch 4, skip next 3 dc; rep from * across, ending last rep at **, 4 dc in 3rd ch of turning ch, turn.

Row 4: Ch 3 (counts as dc), 3 dc in first dc, *skip next 6 dc, 4 dc in next dc, ch 5, skip next ch-4 loop, sc in next sc, ch 5, skip

next ch-4 loop**, 4 dc in next dc; rep from * across, ending last rep at **, dc in 3rd ch of turning ch, turn.

Row 5: Ch 3 (counts as dc), 3 dc in first dc, *skip next 2 ch-5 loops, 4 dc in next dc, ch 4, skip next 3 dc, sc bet last skipped and next dc, ch 4, skip next 3 dc**, 4 dc in next dc; rep from * across, ending last rep at **, dc in 3rd ch of turning ch, turn.

Rep Rows 2–5 for pattern.

176

Chain multiples of 4 plus 2.

Row 1: (Sc, ch 2, 4 dc) in 2nd ch from hook, *skip next 3 ch, (sc, ch 2, 4 dc) in next ch; rep from * across to within last 4 ch, skip next 3 ch, sc in last ch, turn.

Row 2: Ch 3 (counts as dc), 2 dc in first sc, *skip next 4 dc, (sc, ch 2, 4 dc) in next ch-2 space; rep from * across to within last ch-2 space, sc in last ch-2 space, turn.

Rep Row 2 for pattern.

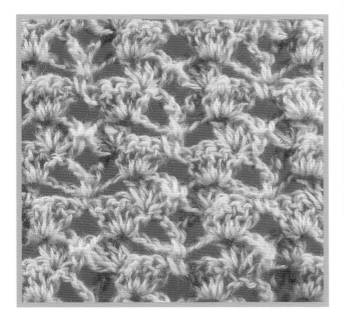

177

Chain multiples of 12 plus 2.

Row 1: Sc in 2nd ch from hook, *ch 3, skip next 2 ch, 5 dc in next ch, skip next 5 ch, 5 dc in next ch, ch 3, skip next 2 ch, sc in next ch; rep from * across, turn.

Row 2: Ch 1, sc in first sc, *ch 3, skip next ch-3 loop, 5 dc in next dc, skip next 8 dc, 5 dc in next dc, ch 3, skip next ch-3 loop, sc in next sc; rep from * across, turn.

Row 3: Ch 3 (counts as dc), skip next ch-3 loop, *5 dc in next dc, ch 3, skip next 4 dc, sc bet last skipped and next dc, ch 3, skip next 4 dc, 5 dc in next dc**, skip next 2 ch-3 loops; rep from * across, ending last rep at **, skip next ch-3 loop, dc in last sc, turn.

Row 4: Ch 3 (counts as dc), skip first 5 dc, *5 dc in next dc, ch 3, skip next ch-3 loop, sc in next sc, ch 3, skip next ch-3 loop, 5 dc in next dc**, skip next 8 dc; rep from * across, ending last rep at **, skip next 4 dc, dc in 3rd ch of turning ch, turn.

Row 5: Ch 1, sc in first dc, ch 3, skip first 5 dc, *5 dc in next dc, skip next 2 ch-3 loops, 5 dc in next dc, ch 3, skip next 4 dc**, sc bet last skipped and next dc, ch 3, skip next 4 dc; rep from * across, ending last rep at **, sc in 3rd ch of turning ch, turn.

Rep Rows 2-5 for pattern.

178

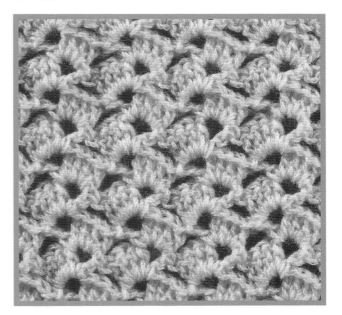

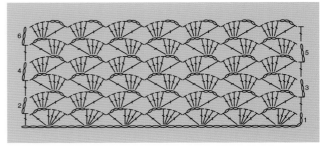

Chain multiples of 5 plus 4.

Row 1: (4 dc, ch 3, dc) in 6th ch from hook, *skip next 4 ch, (4 dc, ch 3, dc) in next ch; rep from * across to within last 3 ch, skip next 2 ch, dc in last ch, turn.

Row 2: Ch 3 (counts as dc), (4 dc, ch 3, dc) in each ch-3 loop across to last ch-3 loop, skip next 4 dc, dc in top of turning ch, turn.

Rep Row 2 for pattern

179

Chain multiples of 8 plus 4.

Row 1: Dc in 4th ch from hook, *skip next 3 ch, (4 dc, ch 3, dc) in next ch, skip next 3 ch**, (dc, ch 1, dc) in next ch; rep from * across, ending last rep at **, 2 dc in last ch, turn.

Row 2: Ch 3 (counts as dc), dc in first dc, *(4 dc, ch 3, dc) in next ch-3 loop**, (dc, ch 1, dc) in next ch-1 space; rep from * across, ending last rep at **, skip next 5 dc, 2 dc in 3rd ch of turning ch, turn.

Rep Row 2 for pattern.

.13.
Shells—Small Lace Patterns

180

Chain multiples of 8 plus 4.

Row 1: 2 dc in 4th ch from hook, *skip next 3 ch, (sc, ch 3, sc) in next ch, skip next 3 ch**, (2 dc, ch 2, 2 dc) in next ch; rep from * across, ending last rep at **, 3 dc in last ch, turn.

Row 2: Ch 3 (counts as hdc, ch 1), sc in first dc, *(2 dc, ch 2, 2 dc) in next ch-3 loop**, (sc, ch 3, sc) in next ch-2 space; rep from * across, ending last rep at **, skip next 3 sts, (sc, ch 1, hdc) in 3rd ch of turning ch, turn.

Row 3: Ch 3 (counts as dc), 2 dc in first hdc, *(sc, ch 3, sc) in next ch-2 space**, (2 dc, ch 2, 2 dc) in next ch-3 loop; rep from * across, ending last rep at **, skip next 3 sts, 3 dc in 2nd ch of turning ch, turn.

Rep Rows 2-3 for pattern.

181

Chain multiples of 8 plus 2

Row 1: Sc in 2nd ch from hook, *ch 2, skip next 3 ch, 5 dc in next ch, ch 2, skip next 3 ch, sc in next ch; rep from * across, turn.

Row 2: Ch 5 (counts as dc, ch 2), skip next ch-2 space, *sc in next dc, ch 3, sc in next dc, ch 3, skip next dc, sc in next dc, ch 3, sc in next dc**, ch 5, skip next 2 ch-2 spaces; rep from * across, ending last rep at **, ch 2, skip next ch-2 space, dc in last sc, turn.

Row 3: Ch 3 (counts as dc), 2 dc in first dc, skip next ch-2 space, *ch 2, skip next ch-3 loop, sc in next ch-3 loop, ch 2, skip next ch-3 loop**, 5 dc in next ch-5 loop; rep from * across, ending last rep at **, skip next 2 ch of turning ch, 3 dc in next ch of turning ch, turn.

Row 4: Ch 4 (counts as dc, ch 1), skip first dc, sc in next dc, ch 3, sc in next dc, *ch 5, skip next 2 ch-2 spaces, sc in next dc, ch 3, sc in next dc**, ch 3, skip next dc, sc in next dc, ch 3, sc

in next dc; rep from * across, ending last rep at **, ch 1, dc in 3rd ch of turning ch, turn.

Row 5: Ch 1, sc in first dc, *ch 2, skip next ch-3 loop, 5 dc in next ch-5 loop, ch 2, skip next ch-3 loop, sc in next ch-3 loop; rep from * across, ending with last sc in 3rd ch of turning ch, turn

Rep Rows 2-5 for pattern.

182

Chain multiples of 12 plus 6.

Row 1: Dc in 6th ch from hook, *skip next 3 ch, sc in each of next 5 ch, skip next 3 ch**, (dc, ch 2, dc, ch 2, dc) in next ch; rep from * across, ending last rep at **, (dc, ch 2, dc) in last ch, turn.

Row 2: Ch 3 (counts as dc), *4 dc in next ch-2 space, skip next sc, sc in each of next 3 sc, 4 dc in next ch-2 space, dc in next dc;

rep from * across, ending with last dc in 3rd ch of turning ch, turn.

Row 3: Ch 1, sc in each of first 3 dc, *skip next 3 sts, (dc, ch 2, dc, ch 2, dc) in next sc, skip next 3 sts**, sc in each of next 5 dc; rep from * across, ending last rep at **, sc in each of next 2 dc, sc in 3rd ch of turning ch, turn.

Row 4: Ch 1, sc in each of first 2 sc, *4 dc in next ch-2 space, dc in next dc, 4 dc in next ch-2 space, skip next 2 sts**, sc in each of next 3 sc; rep from * across, ending last rep at **, sc in each of last 2 sc, turn.

Row 5: Ch 5 (counts as dc, ch 2), dc in first sc, *skip next 3 sts, sc in each of next 5 dc, skip next 3 sts**, (dc, ch 2, dc, ch 2, dc) in next sc; rep from * across, ending last rep at **, (dc, ch 2, dc) in last sc, turn

Rep Rows 2-5 for pattern.

183

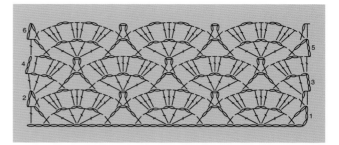

Chain multiples of 12 plus 5.

Row 1: Sc in 7th ch from hook, *skip next 3 ch, (dc, ch 2, dc, ch 2, dc, ch 2, dc) in next ch, skip next 3 ch, sc in next ch**, ch 5, skip next 3 ch, sc in next ch; rep from * across, ending last rep at **, ch 2, skip next ch, dc in last ch, turn.

Row 2: Ch 3 (counts as hdc, ch 1), sc in next ch-2 space, *(3 dc, ch 2) in each of next 2 ch-2 spaces, 3 dc in next ch-2 space**, (sc, ch 3, sc) in next ch-5 loop; rep from * across, ending last rep at **, sc in ch-2 space of turning ch, ch 1, hdc in 3rd ch of turning ch, turn.

Row 3: Ch 4 (counts as dc, ch 1), (dc, ch 2, dc) in next ch-1 space, *sc in next ch-2 space, ch 5, sc in next ch-2 space**, (dc, ch 2, dc, ch 2, dc, ch 2, dc) in next ch-3 loop; rep from * across, ending last rep at **, (dc, ch 2, dc) in ch-1 space of turning ch, ch 1, dc in 2nd ch of turning ch, turn.

Row 4: Ch 3 (counts as dc), dc in next ch-1 space, ch 2, 3 dc in next ch-2 space, *(sc, ch 3, sc) in next ch-5 loop**, (3 dc, ch 2) in each of next 2 ch-2 space, 3 dc in next ch-2 space; rep from * across, ending last rep at **, 3 dc in next ch-2 space, ch 2, dc in ch-1 space of turning ch, dc in 3rd ch of turning ch, turn.

Row 5: Ch 5 (counts as dc, ch 2), sc in next ch-2 space, *(dc, ch 2, dc, ch 2, dc, ch 2, dc) in next ch-3 loop, sc in next ch-2 space**, ch 5, sc in next ch-2 space; rep from * across, ending last rep at **, ch 2, dc in 3rd ch of turning ch, turn

Rep Rows 2-5 for pattern.

184

Chain multiples of 9 plus 5.

Row 1: Sc in 6th ch from hook, *skip next 2 ch, 5 dc in next ch, skip next 2 ch, sc in next ch**, ch 3, skip next 2 ch, sc in next ch; rep from * across, ending last rep at **, ch 1, skip next ch, dc in last ch, turn.

Row 2: Ch 1, sc in first dc, *skip next sc, dc in each of next 2 dc, ch 3, sc in next dc, ch 3, dc in each of next 2 dc**, sc in next ch-3 loop; rep from * across, ending last rep at **, skip first ch of turning ch, sc in next ch of turning ch, turn.

Row 3: Ch 3 (counts as dc), 2 dc in first sc, *sc in next ch-3 loop, ch 3, sc in next ch-3 loop, skip next 2 dc**, 5 dc in next sc; rep from * across, ending last rep at **, 3 dc in last sc, turn.

Row 4: Ch 1, sc in first dc, *ch 3, dc in each of next 2 dc, sc in next ch-3 loop, skip next sc, dc in each of next 2 dc, ch 3, sc in next dc; rep from * across, ending with last sc in 3rd ch of turning ch, turn.

Row 5: Ch 4 (counts as dc, ch 1), sc in next ch-3 loop, *skip next 2 dc, 5 dc in next sc, sc in next ch-3 loop**, ch 3, sc in next ch-3 loop; rep from * across, ending last rep at **, ch 1, dc in last sc, turn

Rep Rows 2-5 for pattern.

185

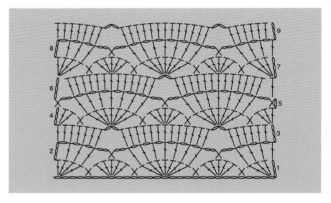

Chain multiples of 14 plus 4.

Row 1: 3 dc in 4th ch from hook, *skip next 3 ch, sc in next ch, skip next 2 ch, 5 dc in next ch, skip next 2 ch, sc in next ch, skip next 3 ch**, 7 dc in next ch; rep from * across, ending last rep at **, 4 dc in last ch, turn.

Row 2: Ch 4 (counts as dc, ch 1), skip first dc, (dc, ch 1) in each of next 2 dc, dc in next dc, *ch 2, skip next 3 sts, sc in next dc, ch 2, skip next 3 sts**, (dc, ch 1) in each of next 6 dc, dc in next dc; rep from * across, ending last rep at **, (dc, ch 1) in each of next 3 dc, dc in 3rd ch of turning ch, turn.

Row 3: Ch 3 (counts as dc), (dc in next ch-1 space, dc in next dc) 3 times, *ch 2, skip next 2 ch-2 spaces**, dc in next dc, (dc in next ch-1 space, dc in next dc) 6 times; rep from * across, ending last rep at **, (dc in next dc, dc in next ch-1 space) 3 times, dc in 3rd ch of turning ch, turn.

Row 4: Ch 3 (counts as dc), 2 dc in first dc, skip next 2 dc, *sc in next dc, 7 dc in next ch-2 space, skip next 3 dc, sc in next dc, skip next 2 dc**, 5 dc in next dc, skip next 2 dc; rep from * across, ending last rep at **, 3 dc in 3rd ch of turning ch, turn.

Row 5: Ch 1, sc in first dc, *ch 2, skip next 3 sts, (dc, ch 1) in each of next 6 dc, dc in next dc, ch 2, skip next 3 sts, sc in next dc; rep from * across, ending with last sc in 3rd ch of turning ch, turn.

Row 6: Ch 3 (counts as dc), skip next ch-2 space, *dc in next dc, (dc in next ch-1 space, dc in next dc) 6 times**, ch 2, skip next 2 ch-2 spaces; rep from * across, ending last rep at **, skip next ch-2 space, dc in last sc, turn.

Row 7: Ch 3 (counts as dc), 3 dc in first dc, *skip next 3 dc, sc in next dc, skip next 2 dc, 5 dc in next dc, skip next 2 dc, sc in next dc**, 7 dc in next ch-2 space; rep from * across, ending last rep at **, skip next 3 dc, 4 dc in 3rd ch of turning ch, turn.

Rep Rows 2-7 for pattern.

186

Chain multiples of 10 plus 3.

Row 1: Dc in 4th ch from hook, dc in next ch, *skip next 2 ch, (dc, ch 3, dc) in next ch, skip next 2 ch**, dc in each of next 5 ch; rep from * across, ending last rep at **, dc in each of last 3 ch, turn.

Row 2: Ch 3 (counts as dc), skip first 2 dc, dc in next dc, *ch 2, 5 dc in next ch-3 loop, ch 2, skip next dc**, 2-dc cluster working first half-closed dc in next dc, skip next 3 dc, work 2nd half-closed dc in next dc, yo, complete 2-dc cluster, ch 2; rep from * across, ending last rep at **, 2-dc cluster working first half-closed dc in next dc, skip next dc, work 2nd half-closed dc in 3rd ch of turning ch, yo, complete 2-dc cluster, turn.

Row 3: Ch 4 (counts as dc, ch 1), dc in first cluster, *skip next ch-2 space, dc in each of next 5 dc, skip next ch-2 space**, (dc, ch 3, dc) in next cluster; rep from * across, ending last rep at **, skip next dc, (dc, ch 1, dc) in 3rd ch of turning ch, turn.

Row 4: Ch 3 (counts as dc), 2 dc in next ch-1 space, *ch 2, skip next dc, 2-dc cluster working first half-closed dc in next dc, skip next 3 dc, work 2nd half-closed dc in next dc, yo, complete 2-dc cluster, ch 2**, 5 dc in next ch-3 loop; rep from * across, ending last rep at **, 2 dc in ch-1 space of turning ch, dc in 3rd ch of turning ch, turn.

Row 5: Ch 3 (counts as dc), skip first dc, dc in each of next 2 dc, *skip next ch-2 space, (dc, ch 3, dc) in next cluster, skip next ch-2 space**, dc in each of next 5 dc; rep from * across, ending last rep at **, dc in each of next 2 dc, dc in 3rd ch of turning ch, turn.

Rep Rows 2-5 for pattern.

187

Chain multiples of 10 plus 2.

Row 1: Sc in 2nd ch from hook, sc in next ch, *ch 1, skip next 3 ch, (dc, ch 3, dc) in next ch, ch 1, skip next 3 ch, sc in each of next 3 ch; rep from * across, ending with sc in each of last 2 ch, turn.

Row 2: Ch 3 (counts as dc), skip next ch-1 space, *dc in next dc, ch 1, 5 dc in next ch-3 loop, ch 1, dc in next dc**, skip next 5 sts; rep from * across, ending last rep at **, skip next sc, dc in last sc, turn.

Row 3: Ch 4 (counts as dc, ch 1), dc in first dc, *ch 1, skip next 3 sts, sc in each of next 3 dc, ch 1, skip next 3 sts**, (dc, ch 3, dc) bet last skipped and next dc; rep from * across, ending last rep at **, (dc, ch 1, dc) in 3rd ch of turning ch, turn.

Row 4: Ch 3 (counts as dc), 2 dc in next ch-1 space, ch 1, *dc in next dc, skip next 5 sts, dc in next dc, ch 1**, 5 dc in next ch-3 loop, ch 1; rep from * across, ending last rep at **, 2 dc in ch-1 space of turning ch, dc in 3rd ch of turning ch, turn.

Row 5: Ch 1, sc in first 2 dc, *ch 1, skip next 3 sts, (dc, ch 3, dc) bet last skipped and next dc, ch 1, skip next 3 sts**, sc in each of next 3 dc; rep from * across, ending last rep at **, sc in next dc, sc in 3rd ch of turning ch, turn.

Rep Rows 2-5 for pattern.

188

Chain multiples of 10 plus 2

Row 1: Sc in 2nd ch from hook, sc in next ch, *ch 3, skip next 3 ch, (dc, ch 2, dc) in next ch, ch 3, skip next 3 ch, sc in each of next 3 ch; rep from * across, ending with sc in each of last 2 ch, turn.

Row 2: Ch 1, sc in first sc, *ch 4, skip next ch-3 loop, 5 dc in next ch-2 space, ch 4, skip next sc, sc in next sc; rep from * across, turn.

Row 3: Ch 7 (counts as tr, ch 3), skip next ch-4 loop, *sc in each of next 5 dc**, ch 7, skip next 2 ch-4 loops; rep from * across, ending last rep at **, ch 3, skip next ch-4 loop, tr in last sc, turn.

Row 4: Ch 4 (counts as dc, ch 1), dc in first tr, *ch 3, skip next sc, sc in each of next 3 sc, ch 3**, (dc, ch 2, dc) in center ch of next ch-7 loop; rep from * across, ending last rep at **, skip first 3 ch of turning ch, 2 dc in 4th ch of turning ch, turn.

Row 5: Ch 3 (counts as dc), 2 dc in first dc, *ch 4, skip next sc, sc in next sc, ch 4, skip next ch-3 loop**, 5 dc in next ch-2 space; rep from * across, ending last rep at **, 2 dc in ch-1 space of turning ch, dc in 3rd ch of turning ch, turn.

Row 6: Ch 1, sc in each of first 3 dc, *ch 7, skip next 2 ch-4 loops**, sc in each of next 5 dc; rep from * across, ending last rep at **, sc in each of next 2 dc, sc in 3rd ch of turning ch, turn.

Row 7: Ch 1, sc in each of first 2 sc, *ch 3, (dc, ch 2, dc) in center ch of next ch-7 loop, ch 3, skip next sc**, sc in each of next 3 sc; rep from * across, ending last rep at **, sc in each of last 2 sc, turn.

Rep Rows 2-7 for pattern.

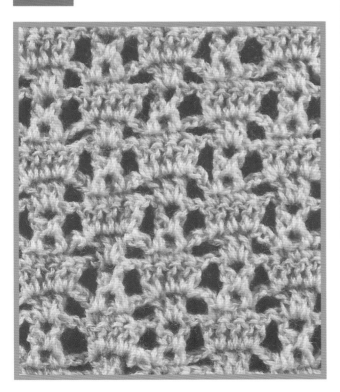

189

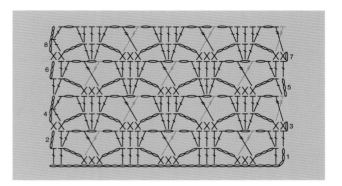

Chain multiples of 10 plus 3.

Row 1: Dc in 4th ch from hook, *ch 3, skip next 2 ch, sc in each of next 3 ch, ch 3, skip next 2 ch, dc in each of next 3 ch; rep from * across, ending with dc in each of last 2 ch, turn.

Row 2: Ch 3, skip first dc, *2 dc in next dc, ch 1, skip next ch-3 loop, skip next 2 sc, tr in next sc, ch 1, working over last tr made, skip 1 sc to the right of last tr worked, tr in next sc to the right (crossed tr made), ch 1, skip next ch-3 loop, 2 dc in next dc, dc in next dc; rep from * across, ending with last dc in 3rd ch of turning ch, turn.

Row 3: Ch 1, sc in each of first 2 dc, *ch 3, skip next ch-1 space, 3 dc in next ch-1 space, ch 3, skip next 3 sts**, sc in each of next 3 dc; rep from * across, ending last rep at **, sc in next dc, sc in 3rd ch of turning ch, turn.

Row 4: Ch 2, skip first sc, dc in next sc, ch 3, dc in last dc made (counts as first crossed tr), *ch 1, skip next ch-3 loop, 2 dc in next dc, dc in next dc, 2 dc in next dc, ch 1**, skip next ch-3 loop, skip next 2 sc, tr in next sc, ch 1, working over last tr made, skip 1 sc to the right of last tr worked, tr in next sc to the right (crossed tr made), ch 1, skip next ch-3 loop; rep from * across, ending last rep at **, skip next sc, tr in next sc, working over last tr made, tr in next sc to the right (crossed tr made), turn.

Row 5: Ch 3 (counts as dc), dc in first dc, *ch 3, skip next 3 sts, sc in each of next 3 dc, ch 3, skip next ch-1 space**, 3 dc in next ch-1 space; rep from * across, ending last rep at **, 2 dc in 3rd ch of turning ch, turn.

Rep Rows 2-5 for pattern.

each of next 5 dc; rep from * across, ending last rep at **, dc in each of next 2 dc, dc in 3rd ch of turning ch, turn.

Row 4: Ch 6 (counts as dc, ch 3), *sc in next ch-3 loop, 5 dc in next sc, sc in next ch-3 loop, ch 3, skip next 2 dc**, dc in next dc, ch 3; rep from * across, ending last rep at **, dc in 3rd ch of turning ch, turn.

Row 5: Ch 3 (counts as dc), *2 dc in next ch-3 loop, ch 3, skip next sc, skip next 2 dc, sc in next dc, ch 3, 2 dc in next ch-3 loop, dc in next dc; rep from * across, ending with last dc in 3rd ch of turning ch, turn.

Rep Rows 2–5 for pattern.

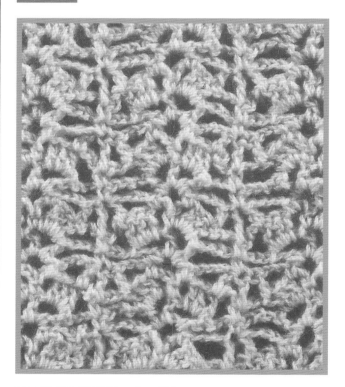

Chain multiples of 10 plus 3.

Row 1: 2 dc in 4th ch from hook, *ch 3, skip next 3 ch, sc in next ch, ch 3, skip next 3 ch, 2 dc in next ch**, 2 dc in next ch; rep from * across, ending last rep at **, turn.

Row 2: Ch 3 (counts as dc), skip first dc, dc in each of next 2 dc, *2 dc in next ch-3 loop, ch 1, 2 dc in next ch-3 loop**, dc in each of next 5 dc; rep from * across, ending last rep at **, dc in each of next 2 dc, dc in 3rd ch of turning ch, turn.

Row 3: Ch 3 (counts as dc), skip first dc, dc in each of next 2 dc, *ch 3, sc in next ch-1 space, ch 3, skip next 2 dc**, dc in

Chain multiples of 10 plus 2.

Row 1: Sc in 2nd ch from hook, *ch 3, skip next 4 ch, (dc, ch 3, dc, ch 3, dc) in next ch, ch 3, skip next 4 ch, sc in next ch; rep from * across, turn.

Row 2: Ch 1, sc in first sc, *ch 3, skip next ch-3 loop, 3 dc in next ch-3 loop, ch 3, sc in next dc, ch 3, 3 dc in next ch-3 loop, ch 3, skip next ch-3 loop, sc in next sc; rep from * across, turn.

Row 3: Ch 3 (counts as dc), *skip next ch-3 loop, dc in next dc, ch 3, sc in next ch-3 loop, ch 4, sc in next ch-3 loop, ch 3, skip next 2 dc, dc in next dc, skip next ch-3 loop, dc in next sc; rep from * across, turn.

Row 4: Ch 1, sc in first dc, *ch 3, skip next ch-3 loop, (dc, ch 3, dc, ch 3, dc) in next ch-4 loop, ch 3, skip next dc, sc in next dc; rep from * across, ending with last sc in 3rd ch of turning ch, turn.

Rep Rows 2-4 for pattern.

192

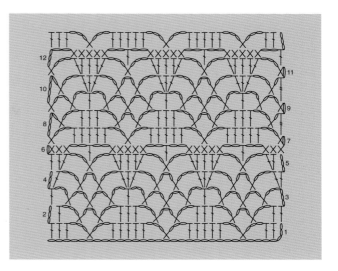

Chain multiples of 10 plus 3.

Row 1: Dc in 4th ch from hook, dc in next ch, *ch 3, skip next 2 ch, sc in next ch, ch 3, skip next 2 ch, dc in each of next 5 ch; rep from * across, ending with dc in each of last 3 ch, turn.

Row 2: Ch 3 (counts as dc), skip first dc, dc in next dc, *ch 3, (sc, ch 3) in each of next 2 ch-3 loops, skip next dc**, dc in each of next 3 dc; rep from * across, ending last rep at **, dc in next dc, dc in 3rd ch of turning ch, turn.

Row 3: Ch 6 (counts as dc, ch 3), *(sc, ch 3) in each of next 3 ch-3 loops, skip next dc**, dc in next dc, ch 3; rep from * across, ending last rep at **, dc in 3rd ch of turning ch, turn.

Row 4: Ch 3 (counts as dc), dc in first dc, *ch 3, skip next ch-3 loop, (sc, ch 3) in each of next 2 ch-3 loops, skip next ch-3 loop**, 3 dc in next dc; rep from * across, ending last rep at **, 2 dc in 3rd ch of turning ch, turn.

Row 5: Ch 3 (counts as dc), skip first dc, *2 dc in next dc, ch 3, skip next ch-3 loop, sc in next ch-3 loop, ch 3, skip next ch-3 loop, 2 dc in next dc, dc in next dc; rep from * across, ending with last dc in 3rd ch of turning ch, turn.

Row 6: Ch 1, sc in first 3 dc, *ch 2, skip next ch-3 loop, dc in next sc, ch 2, skip next ch-3 loop**, sc in each of next 5 dc; rep from * across, ending last rep at **, sc in each of next 2 dc, sc in 3rd ch of turning ch, turn.

Row 7: Ch 1, sc in first sc, *ch 3, 2 dc in next ch-2 space, dc in next dc, 2 dc in next ch-2 space, ch 3, skip next 2 sc, sc in next sc; rep from * across, turn.

Row 8: Ch 5 (counts as tr, ch 1), sc in next ch-3 loop, ch 3, *skip next dc, dc in each of next 3 dc, ch 3**, (sc, ch 3) in each of next 2 ch-3 loops; rep from * across, ending last rep at **, sc in next ch-3 loop, ch 1, tr in last sc, turn.

Row 9: Ch 1, sc in first dc, ch 3, sc in next ch-3 loop, ch 3, *skip next dc, dc in next dc, ch 3**, (sc, ch 3) in each of next 3 ch-3 loops; rep from * across, ending last rep at **, sc in next ch-3 loop, ch 3, sc in 4th ch of turning ch, turn.

Row 10: Ch 5 (counts as tr, ch 1), sc in next ch-3 loop, ch 3, skip next ch-3 loop, *3 dc in next dc, ch 3, skip next ch-3 loop**, (sc, ch 3) in each of next 2 ch-3 loops; rep from * across, ending last rep at **, sc in next ch-3 loop, ch 1, tr in last sc, turn.

Row 11: Ch 1, sc in first tr, ch 3, skip next ch-3 loop, *2 dc in next dc, dc in next dc, 2 dc in next dc, ch 3, skip next ch-3 loop**, sc in next ch-3 loop, ch 3, skip next ch-3 loop; rep from * across, ending last rep at **, sc in 4th ch of turning ch, turn.

Row 12: Ch 5 (counts as dc, ch 2), skip next ch-3 loop, *sc in each of next 5 dc, ch 2, skip next ch-3 loop, dc in next sc**, ch 2, skip next ch-3 loop; rep from * across, ending last rep at **, turn.

Row 13: Ch 3 (counts as dc), *2 dc in next ch-2 space, ch 3, skip next 2 sc, sc in next sc, ch 3, 2 dc in next ch-2 space, dc in next dc; rep from * across, ending with last dc in 3rd ch of turning ch, turn.

Rep Rows 2-13 for pattern.

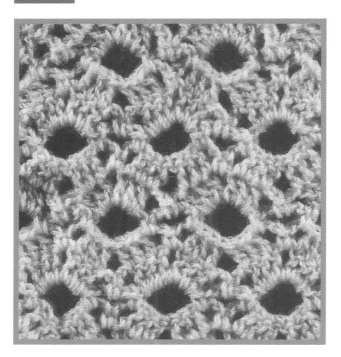

193

Chain multiples of 10 plus 5.

Row 1: Sc in 7th ch from hook, *ch 5, skip next 4 ch, sc in next ch; rep from * across to within last 3 ch, ch 2, skip next 2 ch, hdc in last ch, turn.

Row 2: Ch 3 (counts as dc), 3 dc in next ch-2 space, *ch 2, sc in next ch-5 loop, ch 2**, (3 dc, ch 2, 3 dc) in next ch-5 loop; rep from * across, ending last rep at **, 3 dc in next ch-2 space of turning ch, dc in 4th ch of turning ch, turn.

Row 3: Ch 1, sc in first dc, *ch 3, dc in each of next 3 dc, skip next 2 ch-2 spaces, dc in each of next 3 dc, ch 3, sc in next ch-2 space; rep from * across, ending with last sc in 3rd ch of turning ch, turn.

Row 4: Ch 5 (counts as dc, ch 2), sc in next ch-3 loop, (ch 5, sc) in each ch-3 loop across to last ch-3 loop, ch 2, dc in last sc, turn.

Row 5: Ch 1, sc in first dc, *ch 2, (3 dc, ch 2, 3 dc) in next ch-5 loop, ch 2, sc in next ch-5 loop; rep from * across, ending with last sc in 3rd ch of turning ch, turn.

Row 6: Ch 3 (counts as dc), skip next ch-2 space, *dc in each of next 3 dc, ch 3, sc in next ch-2 space, ch 3, dc in each of next 3 dc**, skip next 2 ch-2 spaces; rep from * across, ending last rep at **, skip next ch-2 space, dc in last sc, turn.

Row 7: Ch 5 (counts as dc, ch 2), sc in next ch-3 loop, (ch 5, sc) in each ch-3 loop across to last ch-3 loop, ch 2, dc in 3rd ch of turning ch, turn.

Rep Rows 2-7 for pattern.

194

Chain multiples of 18 plus 3.

Row 1: Dc in 4th ch from hook, dc in each of next 3 ch, *ch 2, skip next 4 ch, (dc, ch 1, dc, ch 1, dc, ch 1, dc) in next ch, ch 2, skip next 4 ch, dc in each of next 9 ch; rep from * across, ending with dc in each of last 5 ch, turn.

Row 2: Ch 3 (counts as dc), skip first dc, dc in each of next 4 dc, *ch 2, skip next ch-2 space, (sc in next ch-1 space, ch 3, sc in next dc) 3 times, ch 2, skip next ch-2 space**, dc in each of next 9 dc; rep from * across, ending last rep at **, dc in each of next 4 dc, dc in 3rd ch of turning ch, turn.

Row 3: Ch 3 (counts as dc), skip first dc, dc in each of next 4 dc, *ch 2, skip next 2 spaces, (dc, ch 1, dc, ch 1, dc, ch 1, dc) in next (center) ch-3 loop, ch 2, skip next 2 spaces**, dc in each of next 9 dc; rep from * across, ending last rep at **, dc in each of next 4 dc, dc in 3rd ch of turning ch, turn.

Row 4: Rep Row 2.

Row 5: Ch 3 (counts as dc), (dc, ch 1, dc) in first dc, *ch 2, skip next 2 dc, dc in each of next 2 dc, dc in next ch-2 space, dc in each of next 3 ch-3 loops, dc in next ch-2 space, dc in each of next 2 dc, ch 2, skip next 2 dc**, (dc, ch 1, dc, ch 1, dc, ch 1, dc) in next dc; rep from * across, ending last rep at **, (dc, ch 1, 2 dc) in 3rd ch of turning ch, turn.

Row 6: Ch 3 (counts as hdc, ch 1), skip first dc, sc in next dc, sc in next ch-1 space, ch 3, sc in next dc, *ch 2, skip next ch-2 space, dc in each of next 9 dc, ch 2, skip next ch-2 space**, (sc in next ch-1 space, ch 3, sc in next dc) 3 times, ch 2, skip next ch-2 space; rep from * across, ending last rep at **, sc in next ch-1 space, ch 3, sc in next dc, (sc, ch 1, hdc) in 3rd ch of turning ch, turn.

Row 7: Ch 3 (counts as dc), (dc, ch 1, dc) in first hdc, *ch 2, skip next 2 spaces, dc in each of next 9 dc, ch 2, skip next 2 spaces**, (dc, ch 1, dc, ch 1, dc, ch 1, dc) in next (center) ch-3 loop, ch 2, skip next 2 spaces; rep from * across, ending last rep at **, (dc, ch 1, 2 dc) in 2nd ch of turning ch, turn.

Row 8: Rep Row 6.

Row 9: Ch 3 (counts as dc), skip next ch-1 space, dc in next ch-3 loop, dc in next ch-2 space, *dc in each of next 2 dc, ch 2, skip next 2 dc, (dc, ch 1, dc, ch 1, dc, ch 1, dc) in next dc, ch 2, skip next 2 dc, dc in each of next 2 dc, dc in next ch-2 space**, dc in each of next 3 ch-3 loops, dc in next ch-2 space; rep from * across, ending last rep at **, dc in next ch-3 loop, dc in 2nd ch of turning ch, turn.

Rep Rows 2-9 for pattern.

195

Chain multiples of 21 plus 4.

Row 1: 3 dc in 5th ch from hook, *(skip next 2 ch, 3 dc in next ch) twice, *ch 13, skip next 5 ch, 3 dc in next ch**, (skip next 2 ch, 3 dc in next ch) 5 times; rep from * across, ending last rep at **, (skip next 2 ch, 3 dc in next ch) twice, skip next ch, dc in last ch, turn.

Row 2: Ch 3 (counts as dc), dc in first dc, (skip next 3 dc, 3 dc bet last skipped and next dc) twice, *ch 6, sc in next ch-13 loop, ch 6**, (skip next 3 dc, 3 dc bet last skipped and next dc) 5 times; rep from * across, ending last rep at **, (skip next 3 dc, 3 dc bet last skipped and next dc) twice, skip next 3 dc, 2 dc in top of turning ch, turn.

Row 3: Ch 3 (counts as dc), skip first 2 dc, 3 dc bet last skipped and next dc, skip next 3 dc, 3 dc bet last skipped and next dc, *ch 6, sc in next ch-6 loop, sc in next sc, sc in next ch-6 loop, ch 6**, (skip next 3 dc, 3 dc bet last skipped and next dc) 4 times; rep from * across, ending last rep at **, (skip next 3 dc, 3 dc bet last skipped and next dc) twice, skip next dc, dc in 3rd ch of turning ch, turn.

Row 4: Ch 3 (counts as dc), dc in first dc, skip next 3 dc, 3 dc bet last skipped and next dc, *ch 6, sc in next ch-6 loop, sc in each of next 3 sc, sc in next ch-6 loop, ch 6**, (skip next 3 dc, 3 dc bet last skipped and next dc) 3 times; rep from * across, ending last rep at **, skip next 3 dc, 3 dc bet last skipped and next dc, skip next 3 dc, 2 dc in 3rd ch of turning ch, turn.

Row 5: Ch 3 (counts as dc), skip first 2 dc, 3 dc bet last skipped and next dc, *ch 6, sc in next ch-6 loop, sc in each of next 5 sc, sc in next ch-6 loop, ch 6**, (skip next 3 dc, 3 dc bet last skipped and next dc) twice; rep from * across, ending last rep at **, skip next 3 dc, 3 dc bet last skipped and next dc, skip next dc, dc in 3rd ch of turning ch, turn.

Row 6: Ch 3 (counts as dc), dc in first dc, *ch 6, sc in next ch-6 loop, sc in each of next 7 sc, sc in next ch-6 loop, skip next 3 dc**, 3 dc bet last skipped and next dc; rep from * across, ending last rep at **, 2 dc in 3rd ch of turning ch, turn.

Row 7: Ch 3 (counts as dc), *3 dc in next ch-6 loop, ch 6, skip next sc, sc in each of next 7 sc, ch 6, 3 dc in next ch-6 loop; rep from * across to last ch-6 loop, skip next dc, dc in 3rd ch of turning ch, turn.

Row 8: Ch 3 (counts as dc), dc in first dc, *3 dc in next ch-6 loop, ch 6, skip next sc, sc in each of next 5 sc, ch 6, 3 dc in next ch-6 loop**, skip next 3 dc, 3 dc bet last skipped and next dc; rep from * across, ending last rep at **, skip next 3 dc, 2 dc in 3rd ch of turning ch, turn.

Row 9: Ch 3 (counts as dc), skip first 2 dc, 3 dc bet last skipped and next dc, *3 dc in next ch-6 loop, ch 6, skip next sc, sc in each of next 3 sc, ch 6, 3 dc in next ch-6 loop**, (skip next 3 dc, 3 dc bet last skipped and next dc) twice; rep from * across, ending last rep at **, skip next 3 dc, 3 dc bet last skipped and next dc, skip next dc, dc in 3rd ch of turning ch, turn.

Row 10: Ch 3 (counts as dc), dc in first dc, skip next 3 dc, 3 dc bet last skipped and next dc, 3 dc in next ch-6 loop, *ch 6, skip next sc, sc in next sc, ch 6, 3 dc in next ch-6 loop**, (skip next 3 dc, 3 dc bet last skipped and next dc) 3 times, 3 dc in next ch-6 loop; rep from * across, ending last rep at **, skip next 3 dc, 3 dc bet last skipped and next dc, skip next 3 dc, 2 dc in 3rd ch of turning ch, turn.

Row 11: Ch 3 (counts as dc), skip first 2 dc, (3 dc bet last skipped and next dc, skip next 3 dc) twice, *3 dc in next ch-6 loop, ch 13, 3 dc in next ch-6 loop**, (skip next 3 dc, 3 dc bet last skipped and next dc) 4 times; rep from * across, ending last rep at **, (skip next 3 dc, 3 dc bet last skipped and next dc) twice, skip next 3 dc, dc in 3rd ch of turning ch, turn.

Rep Rows 2-11 for pattern.

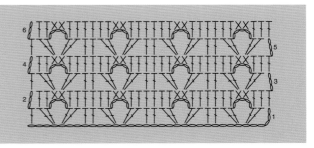

Chain multiples of 8 plus 2.

Row 1: 2 dc in 6th ch from hook, ch 5, 2 dc in next ch, skip next 2 ch, *dc in each of next 2 ch, skip next 2 ch, 2 dc in next ch, ch 5, 2 dc in next ch, skip next 2 dc; rep from * across to within last ch, dc in last ch, turn.

Row 2: Ch 3 (counts as dc), skip first dc, dc in each of next 2 dc, *2 sc in next ch-5 loop**, dc in each of next 6 dc; rep from * across, ending last rep at **, dc in each of next 2 dc, dc in 3rd ch of turning ch, turn.

Row 3: Ch 3 (counts as dc), skip first 3 dc, *2 dc in next sc, ch 5, 2 dc in next sc, skip next 2 dc**, dc in each of next 2 dc, skip next 2 dc; rep from * across, ending last rep at **, dc in 3rd ch of turning ch, turn.

Rep Rows 2-3 for pattern.

.14.
Fantail Shells

197

Chain multiples of 6 plus 2

Row 1: Sc in 2nd ch from hook, *skip next 2 ch, (dc, ch 1, dc, ch 1, dc, ch 1, dc, ch 1, dc) in next ch, skip next 2 ch, sc in next ch; rep from * across, turn.

Row 2: Ch 5 (counts as dc, ch 2), *skip next ch-1 space, sc in next ch-1 space, ch 1, sc in next ch-1 space, ch 2, skip next ch-1 space, dc in next sc**, ch 2; rep from * across, ending last rep at **, turn.

Row 3: Ch 1, sc in first dc, *skip next ch-2 space, (dc, ch 1, dc, ch 1, dc, ch 1, dc, ch 1, dc) in next ch-1 space, skip next ch-2 space, sc in next dc; rep from * across, ending with last sc in 3rd ch of turning ch, turn.

Rep Rows 2-3 for pattern.

198

199

Chain multiples of 8 plus 2.

Row 1: Sc in 2nd ch from hook, *skip next 3 ch, 9 dc in next ch, skip next ch 3, sc in next ch; rep from * across, turn.

Row 2: Ch 3 (counts as dc), dc in first sc, *ch 2, skip next 4 dc, sc in next dc, ch 2, skip next 4 dc**, (dc, ch 1, dc) in next sc; rep from * across, ending last rep at **, 2 dc in last sc, turn.

Row 3: Ch 3 (counts as dc), 4 dc in first dc, *skip next ch-2 space, sc in next sc, skip next ch-2 space**, 9 dc in next ch-1 space; rep from * across, ending last rep at **, 5 dc in 3rd ch of turning ch, turn.

Row 4: Ch 1, sc in first dc, *ch 2, skip next 4 dc, (dc, ch 1, dc) in next sc, ch 2, skip next 4 dc, sc in next dc; rep from * across, ending with last sc in 3rd ch of turning ch, turn.

Row 5: Ch 1, sc in first sc, *skip next ch-2 space, 9 dc in next ch-1 space, skip next ch-2 space, sc in next sc; rep from * across, turn.

Rep Rows 2-5 for pattern.

Chain multiples of 10 plus 2.

Row 1: Sc in 2nd ch from hook, *skip next 4 ch, 12 dc in next ch, skip next ch 4, sc in next ch; rep from * across, turn.

Row 2: Ch 7 (counts as dc, ch 4), skip first sc, *skip next 6 dc, sc bet last skipped and next dc, skip next 6 dc, 2 dc in next sc**, ch 4; rep from * across, ending last rep at **, turn.

Row 3: Ch 1, sc bet first 2 dc, *skip next ch-4 loop, 12 dc in next sc, skip next ch-4 loop, sc bet next 2 dc; rep from * across, ending with last sc in 3rd ch of turning ch, turn.

Rep Rows 2-3 for pattern.

200

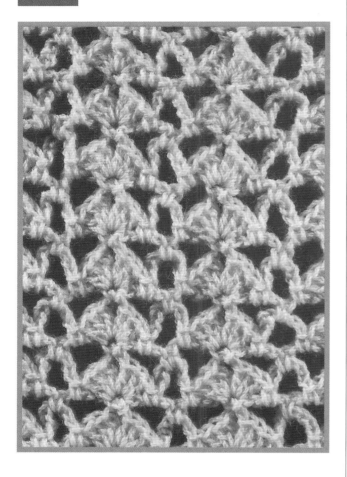

Chain multiples of 10 plus 5.

Row 1: 3 dc in 5th ch from hook, *skip next 3 ch, sc in next ch, ch 7, skip next ch, sc in next ch, skip next 3 ch**, (3 dc, ch 3, 3 dc) in next ch; rep from * across, ending last rep at **, (3 dc, ch 1, dc) in last ch, turn.

Row 2: Ch 1, sc in first dc, *ch 4, sc in next ch-5 loop, ch 4, sc in next ch-3 loop; rep from * across, ending with last sc in 3rd ch of turning ch, turn.

Row 3: Ch 4 (counts as dc, ch 1), 3 dc in first sc, *sc in next ch-4 loop, ch 7, sc in next ch-4 loop**, (3 dc, ch 3, 3 dc) in next sc; rep from * across, ending last rep at **, (3 dc, ch 1, dc) in last sc, turn.

Rep Rows 2-3 for pattern.

.15.
Shells—Treble Crochet

201

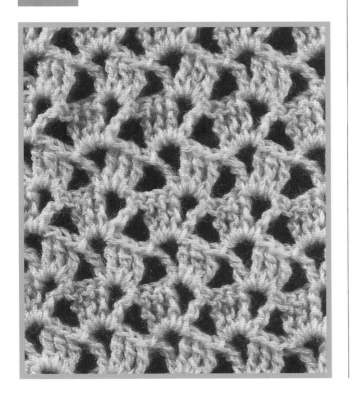

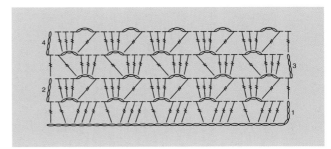

Chain multiples of 6 plus 5.

Row 1: Tr in 6th ch from hook, tr in each of next 2 ch, ch 3, tr in next ch, *skip next 2 ch, tr in each of next 3 ch, ch 3, tr in next ch; rep from * across to within last 2 ch, skip next ch, tr in last ch, turn.

Row 2: Ch 4 (counts as tr), (3 tr, ch 3, tr) in each ch-3 loop across to last ch-3 loop, skip next 3 tr, tr in top of turning ch, turn.

Rep Row 2 for pattern.

202

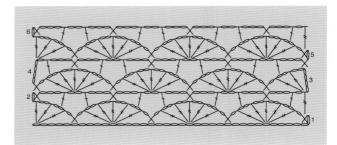

Chain multiples of 10 plus 7.

Row 1: Sc in 2nd ch from hook, *ch 1, skip next 4 ch, (tr, ch 2, tr, ch 2, tr, ch 2, tr, ch 2, tr) in next ch, ch 1, skip next 4 ch, sc in next ch; rep from * across to within last 5 ch, skip next 4 ch, (tr, ch 2, tr, ch 2, tr) in last ch, turn.

Row 2: Ch 1, sc in first tr, *ch 3, skip next ch-2 space, dc in next ch-2 space**, ch 2, skip next 2 ch-1 spaces, dc in next ch-2 space, ch 3, skip next ch-2 space, sc in next tr; rep from * across, ending last rep at **, ch 1, skip next ch-1 space, tr in last sc, turn.

Row 3: Ch 6 (counts as tr, ch 2), (tr, ch 2, tr) in first tr, ch 1, skip next ch-3 loop, sc in next sc, *ch 1, skip next ch-3 loop, (tr, ch 2, tr, ch 2, tr, ch 2, tr) in next ch-2 space, ch 1, skip next ch-3 loop, sc in next sc; rep from * across, turn.

Row 4: Ch 5 (counts as tr, ch 1), skip next ch-1 space, *dc in next ch-2 space, ch 3, skip next ch-2 space, sc in next tr, ch 3, skip next ch-2 space, dc in next ch-2 space, ch 2, skip next 2 ch-1 spaces; rep from * across to within last 2 ch-2 spaces, dc in next ch-2 space, ch 3, skip next 2 ch of turning ch, sc in 4th ch of turning ch, turn.

Row 5: Ch 1, sc in first sc, *ch 1, skip next ch-3 loop, (tr, ch 2, tr, ch 2, tr, ch 2, tr) in next ch-2 space, ch 1, skip next ch-3 loop, sc in next sc; rep from * across to within last ch-3 loop, ch 1, skip next ch-3 loop, (tr, ch 2, tr, ch 2, tr) in 4th ch of turning ch, turn.

Rep Rows 2-5 for pattern.

.16.
Shells—Large Lace Patterns

Chain multiples of 12 plus 2.

Row 1: Sc in 2nd ch from hook, *ch 3, skip next 5 ch, (dc, ch 2, dc, ch 2, dc, ch 2, dc, ch 2, dc) in next ch, ch 3, skip next 5 ch, sc in next ch; rep from * across, turn.

Row 2: Ch 3 (counts as dc), 2 dc in first sc, *ch 1, skip next ch-3 loop, (sc, ch 3) in each of next 3 ch-1 spaces, sc in next ch-1 space, ch 1, skip next ch-3 loop**, (2 dc, ch 1, 2 dc) in next sc; rep from * across, ending last rep at **, 3 dc in last sc, turn.

Row 3: Ch 3 (counts as dc), 2 dc in first dc, *ch 2, skip next ch-1 space, (sc, ch 3) in each of next 2 ch-3 loops, sc in next ch-3 loop, ch 2, skip next ch-1 space**, (2 dc, ch 1, 2 dc) in next ch-1 space; rep from * across, ending last rep at **, skip next 2 dc, 3 dc in 3rd ch of turning ch, turn.

Row 4: Ch 3 (counts as dc), 2 dc in first dc, *ch 3, skip next ch-2 space, (sc, ch 3) in each of next 2 ch-3 loops, skip next ch-2 space**, (2 dc, ch 1, 2 dc) in next ch-1 space; rep from * across, ending last rep at **, skip next 2 dc, 3 dc in 3rd ch of turning ch, turn.

Row 5: Ch 1, sc in first dc, *ch 3, skip next ch-3 loop, (dc, ch 2, dc, ch 2, dc, ch 2, dc, ch 2, dc) in next ch-3 loop, ch 3, skip next ch-3 loop, sc in next ch-1 space; rep from * across, ending with last sc in 3rd ch of turning ch, turn.

Rep Rows 2-5 for pattern.

Chain multiples of 14 plus 4.

Row 1: Dc in 4th ch from hook, *ch 2, skip next 2 ch, sc in next ch, skip next 3 ch, (dc, ch 1, dc, ch 1, dc, ch 1, dc, ch 1, dc) in next ch, skip next 3 ch, sc in next ch, ch 2, skip next 2 ch**, (dc, ch 1, dc) in next ch; rep from * across, ending last rep at **, 2 dc in last ch, turn.

Row 2: Ch 3 (counts as hdc, ch 1), sc in first dc, *ch 3, skip next ch-2 space, (sc, ch 3, sc) in each of next 4 ch-1 spaces, ch 3, skip next ch-2 space**, (sc, ch 3, sc) in next ch-1 space; rep from * across, ending last rep at **, (sc, ch 1, hdc) in 3rd ch of turning ch, turn.

Row 3: Ch 3 (counts as dc), dc in first hdc, *ch 3, skip next 2 ch-3 loops, sc in next ch-3 loop, ch 3, sc in next ch-3 loop, ch 3, skip next 2 ch-3 loops**, (dc, ch 1, dc) in next ch-3 loop; rep from * across, ending last rep at **, 2 dc in 2nd ch of turning ch, turn.

Row 4: Ch 3 (counts as hdc, ch 1), sc in first dc, *ch 2, skip next ch-3 loop, (dc, ch 1, dc, ch 1, dc, ch 1, dc, ch 1, dc) in next ch-3 loop, ch 2, skip next ch-3 loop**, (sc, ch 3, sc) in next ch-1 space; rep from * across, ending last rep at **, skip next dc, (sc, ch 1, hdc) in 3rd ch of turning ch, turn.

Row 5: Ch 3 (counts as dc), dc in first hdc, *ch 3, skip next ch-2 space, (sc, ch 3, sc) in each of next 4 ch-1 spaces, ch 3, skip next ch-2 space**, (dc, ch 1, dc) in next ch-3 loop; rep from * across, ending last rep at **, 2 dc in 2nd ch of turning ch, turn.

Row 6: Ch 3 (counts as hdc, ch 1), sc in first dc, *ch 3, skip next 2 ch-3 loops, sc in next ch-3 loop, ch 3, sc in next ch-3 loop, ch 3, skip next 2 ch-3 loops**, (sc, ch 3, sc) in next ch-1 space; rep from * across, ending last rep at **, skip next dc, (sc, ch 1, hdc) in 3rd ch of turning ch, turn.

Row 7: Ch 3 (counts as dc), dc in first hdc, *ch 2, skip next ch-3 loop, (dc, ch 1, dc, ch 1, dc, ch 1, dc, ch 1, dc) in next ch-3 loop, ch 2, skip next ch-3 loop**, (dc, ch 1, dc) in next ch-3 loop; rep from * across, ending last rep at **, 2 dc in 2nd ch of turning ch, turn.

Rep Rows 2-7 for pattern.

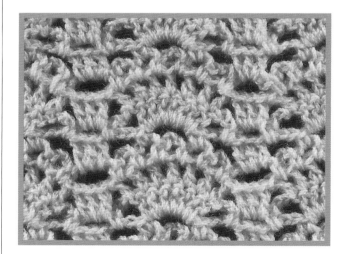

Chain multiples of 14 plus 3.

Row 1: Dc in 4th ch from hook, *ch 3, skip next 3 ch, sc in next ch, ch 4, skip next 3 ch, sc in next ch, ch 3, skip next 3 ch, dc in each of next 3 ch; rep from * across, ending with dc in each of last 2 ch, turn.

Row 2: Ch 1, sc in each of first 2 dc, *ch 3, skip next ch-3 loop, 7 dc in next ch-4 loop, ch 3, skip next ch-3 loop, sc in next dc**, ch 3, skip next dc, sc in next dc; rep from * across, ending last rep at **, sc in 3rd ch of turning ch, turn.

Row 3: Ch 3 (counts as dc), skip first sc, dc in next sc, *skip next ch-3 loop, (dc, ch 1) in each of next 6 dc, dc in next dc, skip next ch-3 loop**, 3 dc in next ch-3 loop; rep from * across, ending last rep at **, dc in each of last 2 sc, turn.

Row 4: Ch 4 (counts as hdc, ch 2), skip first 3 dc, *(sc, ch 3) in each of next 5 ch-1 spaces, sc in next ch-1 space**, ch 4, skip next 5 dc; rep from * across, ending last rep at **, ch 2, skip next 2 dc, hdc in 3rd ch of turning ch, turn.

Row 5: Ch 3 (counts as dc), dc in first hdc, *ch 3, skip next 2 spaces, sc in next ch-3 loop, ch 4, skip next ch-3 loop, sc in next ch-3 loop, ch 3, skip next ch-3 loop**, 3 dc in next ch-4 loop; rep from * across, ending last rep at **, 2 dc in 2nd ch of turning ch, turn.

Rep Rows 2-5 for pattern.

206

Chain multiples of 10 plus 5.

Row 1: Sc in 8th ch from hook, *ch 5, skip next 3 ch, sc in next ch**, ch 6, skip next 5 ch, sc in next ch; rep from * across, ending last rep at **, ch 2, skip next 2 ch, dc in last ch, turn.

Row 2: Ch 1, sc in first dc, skip next ch-2 space, *11 dc in next ch-5 loop**, sc in next ch-6 loop; rep from * across, ending last rep at **, skip next 2 ch of turning ch, sc in next ch of turning ch, turn.

Row 3: Ch 4 (counts as tr), skip first sc, skip next 2 dc, *(dc, ch 1) in each of next 6 dc, dc in next dc**, skip next 5 sts; rep from * across, ending last rep at **, skip next 2 dc, tr in last sc, turn.

Row 4: Ch 1, sc in first tr, *ch 1, (sc, ch 3) in each of next 5 ch-1 spaces, sc in next ch-1 space, ch 1, sc bet next 2 dc; rep from * across, ending with last sc in 4th ch of turning ch, turn.

Row 5: Ch 6 (counts as tr, ch 2), skip next 2 spaces, *sc in next ch-3 loop, ch 5, skip next ch-3 loop, sc in next ch-3 loop**, ch 6, skip next 4 spaces; rep from * across, ending last rep at **, ch 2, skip next 2 spaces, tr in last sc, turn.

Rep Rows 2-5 for pattern.

207

Chain multiples of 9 plus 2.

Row 1: Sc in 2nd ch from hook, *ch 3, skip next 3 ch, sc in next ch, ch 7, sc in next ch, ch 3, skip next 3 ch, sc in next ch; rep from * across, turn.

Row 2: Ch 1, sc in first sc, *skip next ch-3 loop, 13 dc in next ch-7 loop, skip next ch-3 loop, sc in next sc; rep from * across, turn.

Row 3: Ch 4 (counts as tr), skip first sc, skip next 5 dc, *(dc in next dc, ch 3) twice, dc in next dc**, skip next 11 sts; rep from * across, ending last rep at **, skip next 5 dc, tr in last sc, turn.

Row 4: Ch 3 (counts as dc), *3 dc in next ch-3 loop, ch 3, 3 dc in next ch-3 loop; rep from * across to last ch-3 loop, dc in 4th ch of turning ch, turn.

Row 5: Ch 6 (counts as dc, ch 3), skip first dc, *skip next 3 dc, (sc, ch 7, sc) in next ch-3 loop, ch 3, skip next 3 dc, dc bet last skipped and next dc; rep from * across, ending with last dc in 3rd ch of turning ch, turn.

Rep Rows 2-5 for pattern.

208

Chain multiples of 12 plus 2.

Row 1: Sc in 2nd ch from hook, *ch 5, skip next 3 ch, sc in next ch; rep from * across, turn.

Row 2: Ch 5 (counts as dc, ch 2), *sc in next ch-5 loop, 8 dc in next ch-5 loop, sc in next ch-5 loop**, ch 5; rep from * across, ending last rep at **, ch 2, dc in last sc, turn.

Row 3: Ch 1, sc in first dc, *skip next sc, (dc, ch 3) in each of next 7 dc, dc in next dc, sc in next ch-5 loop; rep from * across, ending with last sc in 3rd ch of turning ch, turn.

Row 4: Ch 8 (counts as dc, ch 5), *skip next 2 ch-3 loops, sc in next ch-3 loop, ch 5, skip next ch-3 loop, sc in next ch-3 loop, ch 5, skip next 2 ch-3 loops, skip next dc, dc in next sc; rep from * across, turn.

Rep Rows 2-4 for pattern.

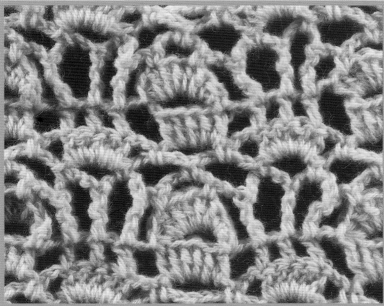

Chain multiples of 14 plus 4.

Row 1: Dc in 6th ch from hook, *ch 2, skip next 2 ch, dc in each of next 5 ch, ch 7, turn, skip next 5 dc, sl st in next ch-2 space, turn, (sc, hdc, 5 dc, hdc, sc) in next ch-7 loop, sl st in last ch of ch-7 loop, ch 2, skip next 2 ch, dc in next ch, ch 1, skip next ch, dc in next dc**, ch 1, skip next ch, dc in next dc; rep from * across, ending last rep at **, turn.

Row 2: Ch 9 (counts as tr, ch 5), skip next ch-1 space, tr in next dc, *ch 2, skip next ch-2 space, skip next 2 sts, sc in next dc, ch 5, skip next 3 dc, sc in next dc, ch 2, skip next ch-2 space, tr in next dc, ch 5**, tr in next dc, ch 5, tr in next dc; rep from * across, ending last rep at **, tr in 4th ch of turning ch, turn.

Row 3: Ch 6 (counts as tr, ch 2), sc in next ch-5 loop, *(ch 5, skip next ch-2 space, sc in next ch-5 loop) twice**, ch 5, sc in next ch-5 loop; rep from * across, ending last rep at **, ch 2, tr in 4th ch of turning ch, turn.

Row 4: Ch 3 (counts as dc), 2 dc in next ch-2 space, *ch 2, sc in next ch-5 loop, ch 5, sc in next ch-5 loop, ch 2**, 5 dc in next ch-5 loop; rep from * across, ending last rep at **, 2 dc in next ch-2 space of turning ch, dc in 4th ch of turning ch, turn.

Row 5: Ch 4 (counts as dc, ch 1), skip first 2 dc, dc in next dc, *ch 2, skip next ch-2 space, 5 dc in next ch-5 loop, ch 7, turn, skip next 5 dc, sl st in next ch-2 space, turn, (sc, hdc, 5 dc, hdc, sc) in next ch-7 loop, sl st in last ch of ch-7 loop, ch 2, skip next ch-2 space, dc in next dc, ch 1, skip next dc**, dc in next dc, ch 1, skip next dc, dc in next dc; rep from * across, ending last rep at **, dc in 3rd ch of turning ch, turn.

Rep Rows 2-5 for pattern.

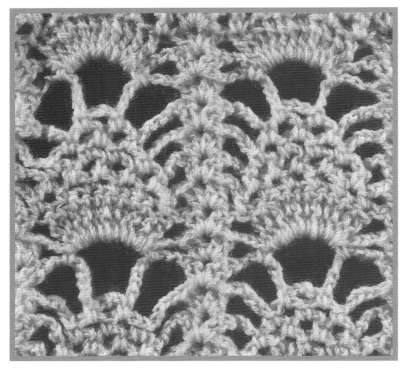

Chain multiples of 15 plus 4.

Row 1: 2 dc in 4th ch from hook, *ch 7, skip next 5 ch, sc in next ch, ch 3, skip next 2 ch, sc in next ch, ch 7, skip next 5 ch**, (2 dc, ch 1, 2 dc) in next ch; rep from * across, ending last rep at **, 3 dc in last ch, turn.

Row 2: Ch 3 (counts as dc), 2 dc in first dc, *ch 3, sc in next ch-7 loop, ch 5, skip next ch-3 loop, sc in next ch-7 loop, ch 3**, (2 dc, ch 1, 2 dc) in next ch-1 space; rep from * across, ending last rep at **, skip next 2 dc, 3 dc in 3rd ch of turning ch, turn.

Row 3: Ch 3 (counts as dc), 2 dc in first dc, *skip next ch-3 loop, 11 tr in next ch-5 loop, skip next ch-3 loop**, (2 dc, ch 1, 2 dc) in next ch-1 space; rep from * across, ending last rep at **, skip next 2 dc, 3 dc in 3rd ch of turning ch, turn.

Row 4: Ch 3 (counts as dc), 2 dc in first dc, *ch 2, skip next 2 dc, (sc in next tr, ch 3, skip next tr) 5 times, sc in next tr, ch 2**, (2 dc, ch 1, 2 dc) in next ch-1 space; rep from * across, ending last rep at **, skip next 2 dc, 3 dc in 3rd ch of turning ch, turn.

Row 5: Ch 3 (counts as dc), 2 dc in first dc, *ch 3, skip next ch-2 space, (sc, ch 3) in each of next 5 ch-3 loops, skip next ch-2 space**, (2 dc, ch 1, 2 dc) in next ch-1 space; rep from * across, ending last rep at **, skip next 2 dc, 3 dc in 3rd ch of turning ch, turn.

Row 6: Ch 3 (counts as dc), 2 dc in first dc, *ch 3, skip next ch-3 loop, (sc, ch 3) in each of next 4 ch-3 loops, skip next ch-3 loop**, (2 dc, ch 1, 2 dc) in next ch-1 space; rep from * across, ending last rep at **, skip next 2 dc, 3 dc in 3rd ch of turning ch, turn.

Row 7: Ch 3 (counts as dc), 2 dc in first dc, *ch 3, skip next ch-3 loop, (sc, ch 3) in each of next 3 ch-3 loops, skip next ch-3 loop**, (2 dc, ch 1, 2 dc) in next ch-1 space; rep from * across, ending last rep at **, skip next 2 dc, 3 dc in 3rd ch of turning ch, turn.

Row 8: Ch 3 (counts as dc), 2 dc in first dc, *ch 7, skip next ch-3 loop, sc in next ch-3 loop, ch 3, sc in next ch-3 loop, ch 7, skip next ch-3 loop**, (2 dc, ch 1, 2 dc) in next ch-1 space; rep from * across, ending last rep at **, skip next 2 dc, 3 dc in 3rd ch of turning ch, turn.

Rep Rows 2-8 for pattern.

.17.
Clusters

211

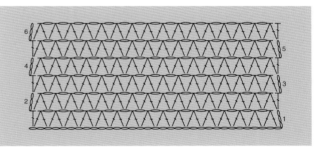

Chain multiples of 2.

Row 1: Work 2-dc cluster working first half-closed dc in 4th ch from hook, skip next ch, work 2nd half-closed dc in next ch, yo, complete 2-dc cluster, *ch 1, work 2-dc cluster working first half-closed dc in same ch holding last dc of last cluster, skip next ch, work 2nd half-closed dc in next ch, yo, complete 2-dc cluster; rep from * across to last ch, dc in last ch already holding last dc of last cluster, turn.

Row 2: Ch 3 (counts as dc), work 2-dc cluster working first half-closed dc in first dc, skip next cluster, work 2nd half-closed dc in next ch-1 space, yo, complete 2-dc cluster, *ch 1, work 2-dc cluster working first half-closed dc in same ch-1 space holding last dc of last cluster, skip next cluster, work 2nd half-closed dc in next ch-1 space, yo, complete 2-dc cluster; rep from * across to turning ch, dc in 3rd ch of turning ch already holding last dc of last cluster, turn.

Rep Row 2 for pattern.

212

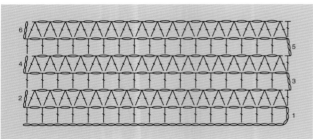

Chain multiples of 2.

Row 1: Dc in 6th ch from hook, *ch 1, skip next ch, dc in next ch; rep from * across, turn.

Row 2: Ch 3 (counts as dc), work 2-dc cluster working first half-closed dc in first dc, skip next ch-1 space, work 2nd half-closed dc in next dc, yo, complete 2-dc cluster, *ch 1, work 2-dc cluster across next 2 dc; rep from * across to turning ch, dc in 4th ch of turning ch already holding last dc of last cluster, turn.

Row 3: Ch 4 (counts as dc, ch 1), (dc, ch 1) in each ch-1 space across, dc in 3rd ch of turning ch, turn.

Rep Row 2-3 for pattern.

213

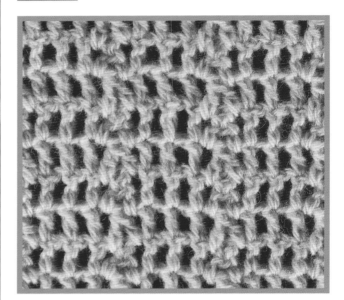

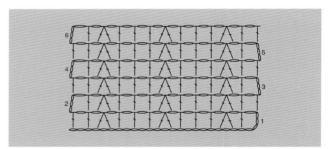

Chain multiples of 8 plus 4.

Row 1: Dc in 6th ch from hook, *ch 1, work 2-dc cluster working first half-closed dc in next ch, skip next ch, work 2nd half-closed dc in next ch, yo, complete 2-dc cluster, ch 1, dc in next ch, ch 1, skip next ch, dc in next ch**, ch 1, skip next ch, dc in next ch; rep from * across, ending last rep at **, turn.

Row 2: Ch 4 (counts as dc, ch 1), skip next ch-1 space, dc in next dc, ch 1, *work 2-dc cluster across next 2 ch-1 spaces, ch 1**, (dc, ch 1) in each of next 3 dc; rep from * across, ending last rep at **, dc in next dc, ch 1, skip next ch of turning ch, dc in next ch of turning ch, turn.

Rep Row 2 for pattern.

214

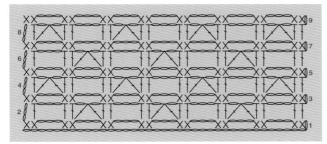

Chain multiples of 10 plus 8.

Row 1: Sc in 2nd ch from hook, sc in next ch, *ch 3, skip next 3 ch, sc in each of next 2 ch; rep from * across, turn.

Row 2: Ch 3 (counts as dc), skip first sc, dc in next sc, ch 3, skip next ch-3 loop, dc in each of next 2 sc, *ch 1, work 2-dc cluster working first half-closed dc in same sc already holding last dc, skip next ch-3 loop, work 2nd half-closed dc in next sc, yo, complete 2-dc cluster, ch 1, dc in same sc holding last dc of last cluster, dc in next sc, ch 3, skip next ch-3 loop, dc in each of next 2 sc; rep from * across, turn.

Row 3: Ch 1, sc in each of first 2 dc, *ch 3, skip next 3 sts, sc in each of next 2 dc; rep from * across, ending with last sc in 3rd ch of turning ch, turn.

Row 4: Ch 3 (counts as dc), skip first sc, dc in next sc, *ch 1, work 2-dc cluster working first half-closed dc in same sc already holding last dc, skip next ch-3 loop, work 2nd half-closed dc in next sc, yo, complete 2-dc cluster, ch 1, dc in same sc holding last dc of last cluster, dc in next sc**, ch 3, skip next ch-3 loop, dc in each of next 2 sc; rep from * across, ending last rep at **, turn.

Row 5: Rep Row 3.

Rep Rows 2-5 for pattern.

215

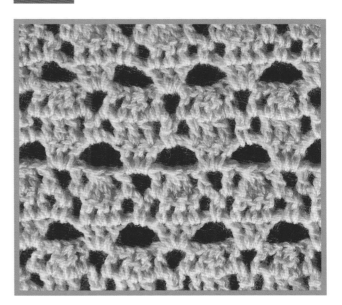

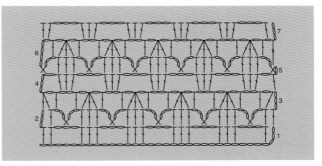

Chain multiples of 6 plus 3.

Row 1: Dc in 4th ch from hook, *ch 3, skip next 3 ch, dc in each of next 3 ch; rep from * across, ending with dc in each of last 2 ch, turn.

Row 2: Ch 3 (counts as dc), skip first dc, dc in next dc, *ch 3, sc in next ch-3 loop, ch 3**, dc in each of next 3 dc; rep from * across, ending last rep at **, dc in next dc, dc in 3rd ch of turning ch, turn.

Row 3: Ch 3 (counts as dc), skip first dc, dc in next dc, *ch 1, dc in next ch-3 loop, ch 2, dc in next ch-3 loop, ch 1**, work 3-dc cluster across next 3 dc; rep from * across, ending last rep at **, work 2-dc cluster across next dc and top of turning ch, turn.

Row 4: Ch 4 (counts as dc, ch 1), skip next ch-1 space, 3 dc in next ch-2 space, *ch 3, skip next 2 ch-1 spaces, 3 dc in next ch-2 space; rep from * across to last ch-2 space, ch 1, skip next ch-1 space, skip next dc, dc in 3rd ch of turning ch, turn.

Row 5: Ch 1, sc in first dc, *ch 3, skip next ch-1 space, dc in each of next 3 dc, ch 3, sc in next ch-3 loop; rep from * across, ending with last sc in 3rd ch of turning ch, turn.

Row 6: Ch 5 (counts as tr, ch 1), *dc in next ch-3 loop, ch 1, work 3-dc cluster across next 3 dc, ch 1, dc in next ch-3 loop**, ch 2; rep from * across, ending last rep at **, ch 1, tr in last sc, turn.

Row 7: Ch 3 (counts as dc), dc in next ch-1 space, *ch 3, skip next 2 ch-1 spaces**, 3 dc in next ch-2 space; rep from * across, ending last rep at **, dc in ch-1 space of turning ch, dc in 4th ch of turning ch, turn.

Rep Rows 2-7 for pattern.

216

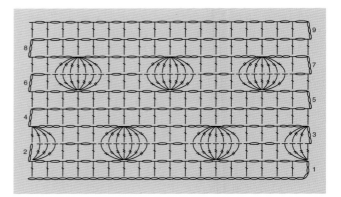

Chain multiples of 12 plus 4.

Row 1: Dc in 6th ch from hook, *ch 1, skip next ch, dc in next ch; rep from * across, turn.

Row 2: Ch 3 (counts as dc), 3 tr in first dc, *skip next 2 ch-1 spaces, (dc, ch 1) in each of next 2 dc, dc in next dc, skip next 2 ch-1 spaces**, 7 tr in next dc; rep from * across, ending last rep at **, 4 tr in next ch of turning ch, turn.

Row 3: Ch 3 (counts as dc), skip first tr, 3-tr cluster worked across next 3 tr, *ch 3, (dc, ch 1) in each of next 2 dc, dc in next dc, ch 3**, 7-tr cluster worked across next 7 tr, ch 3; rep from * across, ending last rep at **, 4-tr cluster worked across last 4 sts, turn.

Row 4: Ch 4 (counts as dc, ch 1), *dc in next ch-3 loop, ch 1, (dc, ch 1) in each of next 3 dc, dc in next ch-3 loop, ch 1**, dc in next cluster, ch 1; rep from * across, ending last rep at **, dc in 3rd ch of turning ch, turn.

Row 5: Ch 4 (counts as dc, ch 1), skip first dc, (dc, ch 1) in each dc across to turning ch, dc in 3rd ch of turning ch, turn.

Row 6: Ch 4 (counts as dc, ch 1), skip next ch-1 space, dc in next dc, *skip next 2 ch-1 spaces, 7 tr in next dc, skip next 2 ch-1 spaces**, (dc, ch 1) in each of next 2 dc, dc in next dc; rep from * across, ending last rep at **, dc in next dc, ch 1, dc in 3rd ch of turning ch, turn.

Row 7: Ch 4 (counts as dc, ch 1), skip first dc, dc in next dc, *ch 3, 7-tr cluster worked across next 7 tr, ch 3**, (dc, ch 1) in each of next 2 dc, dc in next dc; rep from * across, ending last rep at **, dc in next dc, ch 1, dc in 3rd ch of turning ch, turn.

Row 8: Ch 4 (counts as dc, ch 1), skip next ch-1 space, dc in next dc, ch 1, *dc in next ch-3 loop, ch 1, dc in next cluster, ch 1, dc in next ch-3 loop, ch 1**, (dc, ch 1) in each of next 3 dc; rep from * across, ending last rep at **, dc in next dc, ch 1, dc in 3rd ch of turning ch, turn.

Row 9: Rep Row 5.

Rep Rows 2-9 for pattern.

217

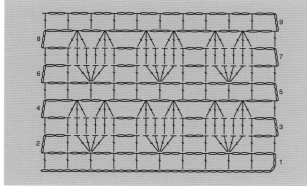

Chain multiples of 9 plus 8.

Row 1: Dc in 8th ch from hook, *ch 2, skip next 2 ch, dc in next ch; rep from * across, turn.

Row 2: Ch 5 (counts as dc, ch 2), skip next ch-2 space, *dc in next dc, skip next ch-2 space, 4 dc in next dc, skip next ch-2 space, dc in next dc, ch 2, skip next ch-2 space; rep from * across to turning ch, dc in next ch of turning ch, turn.

Row 3: Ch 5 (counts as dc, ch 2), skip next ch-2 space, *dc in each of next 6 dc, ch 2, skip next ch-2 space; rep from * across to turning ch, dc in 3rd ch of turning ch, turn.

Row 4: Ch 5 (counts as dc, ch 2), skip next ch-2 space, *3-dc cluster worked across next 3 dc, ch 2, 3-dc worked across next 3 dc**, ch 3, skip next ch-2 space; rep from * across, ending last rep at **, ch 2, dc in 3rd ch of turning ch, turn.

Row 5: Ch 5 (counts as dc, ch 2), dc in next ch-2 space, ch 2, *dc in next ch-2 space, ch 2**, (dc, ch 2, dc) in next ch-3 loop, ch 2; rep from * across, ending last rep at **, dc in next ch-2 space of turning ch, ch 2, dc in 3rd ch of turning ch, turn.

Rep Rows 2-5 for pattern.

218

Chain multiples of 10 plus 2.

Row 1: Sc in 2nd ch from hook, sc in next ch, *ch 3, skip next 4 ch, dc in next ch, ch 1, working over dc just made, skip 1 ch to the right of last dc worked, dc in next ch to the right (crossed dc made), ch 3, skip next 2 unworked ch, sc in next ch**, ch 1, skip next ch, sc in next ch; rep from * across, ending last rep at **, sc in last ch, turn.

Row 2: Ch 3 (counts as dc), 2 dc in first sc, *ch 3, skip next ch-3 loop, sc in next ch-1 space, ch 3, skip next ch-3 loop**, 5 dc in next ch-1 space; rep from * across, ending last rep at **, skip next sc, 3 dc in last sc, turn.

Row 3: Ch 3 (counts as dc), skip first dc, work 2-dc cluster across next 2 dc, *ch 4, sc in next ch-3 loop, ch 1, sc in next ch-3 loop, ch 4**, work 5-dc cluster across next 5 dc; rep from * across, ending last rep at **, work 3-dc cluster across last 3 sts, turn.

Row 4: Ch 1, sc in first cluster, sc in first ch of next ch-4 loop, *ch 3, skip next sc, dc in next sc, ch 1, working over last dc made, dc in last skipped sc (crossed dc made), ch 3, skip next 3 ch, sc in last ch of ch-4 loop**, ch 1, sc in first ch of next ch-4 loop; rep from * across, ending last rep at **, sc in 3rd ch of turning ch, turn.

Rep Rows 2-4 for pattern.

219

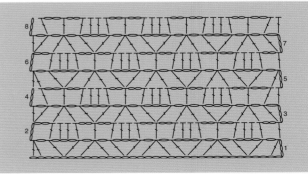

Chain multiples of 8 plus 4.

Row 1: Dc in 5th ch from hook, *ch 1, skip next 2 ch, (dc, ch 3, dc) in next ch, ch 1**, skip next ch, work 2-dc cluster working first half-closed dc in next ch, skip next 3 ch, work 2nd half closed dc in next ch, yo, complete 2-dc cluster; rep from * across, ending last rep at **, skip next 2 ch, work 2 dc cluster across last 2 ch, turn.

Row 2: Ch 5 (counts as dc, ch 2), skip next ch-1 space, *dc in next dc, 2 dc in next ch-3 loop, dc in next dc, ch 2, skip next ch-1 space**, dc in next cluster, ch 2, skip next ch-1 space; rep from * across, ending last rep at **, dc in top of turning ch, turn.

Row 3: Ch 4 (counts as dc, ch 1), dc in first dc, *ch 1, skip next ch-2 space, work 2-dc cluster working first half-closed dc in next dc, skip next 2 dc, work 2nd half-closed dc in next dc, yo, complete 2-dc cluster, ch 1, skip next ch-2 space**, (dc, ch 3, dc) in next dc; rep from * across, ending last rep at **, (dc, ch 1, dc) in 3rd ch of turning ch, turn.

Row 4: Ch 3 (counts as dc), skip next ch-1 space, *dc in next dc, ch 2, skip next ch-1 space, dc in next cluster, ch 2, skip next ch-1 space, dc in next dc**, 2 dc in next ch-3 loop; rep from * across, ending last rep at **, dc in 3rd ch of turning ch, turn.

Row 5: Ch 3 (counts as dc), skip first dc, dc in next dc, *ch 1, skip next ch-2 space, (dc, ch 3, dc) in next dc, ch 1, skip next ch-2 space**, work 2-dc cluster working first half-closed dc in next dc, skip next 2 dc, work 2nd half-closed dc in next dc, yo, complete 2-dc cluster; rep from * across, ending last rep at **, work 2-dc cluster across last 2 sts, turn.

Rep Rows 2-5 for pattern.

Chain multiples of 7 plus 1.

Row 1: Sc in 2nd ch from hook, *skip next 2 ch, 6 dc in next ch, skip next 2 ch**, sc in each of next 2 ch; rep from * across, ending last rep at **, sc in last ch, turn.

Row 2: Ch 5 (counts as dc, ch 2), skip first 3 sts, *sc in each of next 2 dc, ch 2, skip next 2 dc**, dc in each of next 2 sc, ch 2, skip next 2 dc; rep from * across, ending last rep at **, dc in last sc, turn.

Row 3: Ch 5 (counts as dc, ch 2), skip next ch-2 space, *work 2-dc cluster across next 2 sc, ch 2, skip next ch-2 space**, dc in each of next 2 dc, ch 2, skip next ch-2 space; rep from * across, ending last rep at **, dc in 3rd ch of turning ch, turn.

Row 4: Ch 1, sc in first dc, *2 sc in next ch-2 space, sc in next cluster, 2 sc in next ch-2 space**, sc in each of next 2 dc; rep from * across, ending last rep at **, sc in 3rd ch of turning ch, turn.

Row 5: Ch 1, sc in first sc, *skip next 2 sc, 6 dc in next sc, skip next 2 sc**, sc in each of next 2 sc; rep from * across, ending last rep at **, sc in last sc, turn.

Rep Rows 2-5 for pattern.

220

221

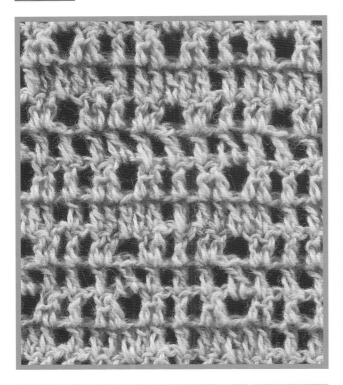

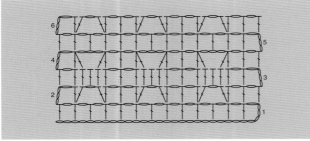

Chain multiples of 8 plus 6.

Row 1: Dc in 6th ch from hook, *ch 1, skip next ch, dc in next ch; rep from * across, turn.

Row 2: Ch 4 (counts as dc, ch 1), skip next ch-1 space, *2 dc in next dc, ch 1, skip next 2 ch-1 spaces, 2 dc in next dc, ch 1, skip next ch-1 space, dc in next dc, ch 1, skip next ch-1 space; rep from * across, dc in next ch of turning ch, turn.

Row 3: Ch 4 (counts as dc, ch 1), skip next ch-1 space, *dc in next dc, ch 1, skip next ch-1 space, dc in each of next 2 dc, dc in next ch-1 space, dc in each of next 2 dc, ch 1, skip next ch-1 space; rep from * across to turning ch, dc in 3rd ch of turning ch, turn.

Row 4: Ch 4 (counts as dc, ch 1), skip next ch-1 space, *2-dc cluster worked across next 2 dc, ch 3, skip next dc, 2-dc cluster across next 2 dc, ch 1, skip next ch-1 space, dc in next dc, ch 1, skip next ch-1 space; rep from * across to turning ch, dc in 3rd ch of turning ch, turn.

Row 5: Ch 4 (counts as dc, ch 1), skip next ch-1 space, *dc in next dc, ch 1, skip next ch-1 space, dc in next cluster, ch 1, dc in next ch-3 loop, ch 1, dc in next cluster, ch 1; rep from * across to turning ch, dc in 3rd ch of turning ch, turn.

Rep Rows 2-5 for pattern.

222

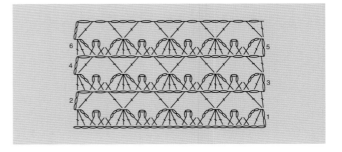

Chain multiples of 6 plus 3.

Row 1: Dc in 4th ch from hook, *ch 3, sc in each of next 2 ch, ch 3, sc in next ch, ch 2**, 3-dc cluster worked across next 3 ch; rep from * across, ending last rep at **, 2-dc cluster worked across last 2 ch, turn.

Row 2: Ch 4 (counts as dc, ch 1), dc in first cluster, *ch 1, skip next 3 spaces**, (dc, ch 3, dc) in next cluster; rep from * across, ending last rep at **, skip next dc, (dc, ch 1, dc) in 3rd ch of turning ch, turn.

Row 3: Ch 2 (counts as dc), dc in next ch-1 space, *ch 3, sc in next dc, sc in next ch-1 space, ch 3, sc in next dc, ch 2**, work 3-dc cluster in next ch-3 loop; rep from * across, ending last rep at **, work half-closed dc in ch-1 space of turning ch, work half-closed dc in 3rd ch of turning ch, yo, complete 2-dc cluster, turn.

Rep Rows 2-3 for pattern.

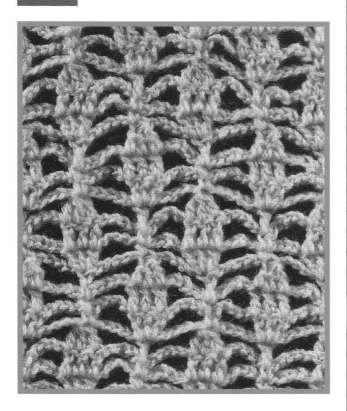

223

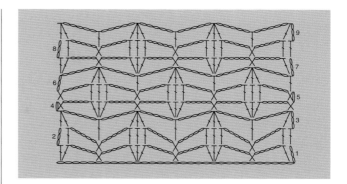

Chain multiples of 10 plus 4.

Row 1: Dc in 4th ch from hook, *ch 5, skip next 4 ch, sc in next ch, ch 5, skip next 4 ch**, 3 dc in next ch; rep from * across, ending last rep at **, 2 dc in last ch, turn.

Row 2: Ch 3 (counts as dc), skip first dc, dc in next dc, *ch 5, skip next ch-5 loop, sc in next sc, ch 5, skip next ch-5 loop**, dc in each of next 3 dc; rep from * across, ending last rep at **, dc in next dc, dc in 3rd ch of turning ch, turn.

Row 3: Ch 3 (counts as dc), skip first dc, dc in next dc, *ch 5, skip next ch-5 loop, dc in next sc, ch 5, skip next ch-5 loop**, 3-dc cluster worked across next 3 dc; rep from * across, ending last rep at **, 2-dc cluster worked across last 2 sts, turn.

Row 4: Ch 1, sc in first cluster, *ch 5, skip next ch-5 loop, 3 dc in next dc, ch 5, skip next ch-5 loop, sc in next cluster; rep from * across, ending with last sc in 3rd ch of turning ch, turn.

Row 5: Ch 1, sc in first sc, *ch 5, skip next ch-5 loop, dc in each of next 3 dc, ch 5, skip next ch-5 loop, sc in next sc; rep from * across, turn.

Row 6: Ch 8 (counts as dc, ch 5), *skip next ch-5 loop, 3-dc cluster worked across next 3 dc, ch 5, skip next ch-5 loop, dc in next sc**, ch 5; rep from * across, ending last rep at **, turn.

Row 7: Ch 3 (counts as dc), dc in first dc, *ch 5, skip next ch-5 loop, sc in next cluster, ch 5, skip next ch-5 loop**, 3 dc in next dc; rep from * across, ending last rep at **, 2 dc in 3rd ch of turning ch, turn.

Rep Rows 2-7 for pattern.

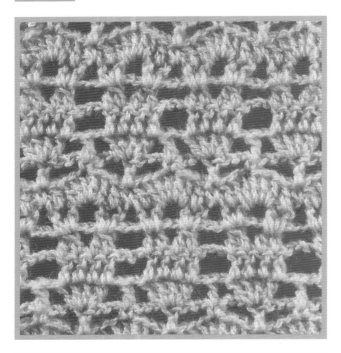

224

Chain multiples of 8 plus 4.

Row 1: 4 dc in 8th ch from hook, *ch 1, skip next 3 ch, dc in next ch**, ch 1, skip next 3 ch, 4 dc in next ch; rep from * across, ending last rep at **, turn.

Row 2: Ch 4 (counts as dc, ch 1), skip next ch-1 space, *dc in each of next 4 dc**, ch 3, skip next 2 ch-1 spaces; rep from * across, ending last rep at **, ch 1, skip next ch of turning ch, dc in next ch of turning ch, turn.

Row 3: Ch 4 (counts as dc, ch 1), skip next ch-1 space, *2-dc cluster worked across next 2 ch, ch 2, 2-dc cluster worked across next 2 dc**, ch 3, skip next ch-3 loop; rep from * across, ending last rep at **, ch 1, dc in 3rd ch of turning ch, turn.

Row 4: Ch 3 (counts as dc), skip next ch-1 space, *(dc, ch 1, dc) in next cluster, ch 2, skip next ch-2 space, (dc, ch 1, dc) in next cluster**, ch 1, skip next ch-3 loop; rep from * across, ending last rep at **, dc in 3rd ch of turning ch, turn.

Row 5: Ch 1, sc in first dc, *dc in next ch-1 space, 5 dc in next ch-2 space, dc in next ch-1 space, sc in next ch-1 space; rep from * across, ending with last sc in 3rd ch of turning ch, turn.

Row 6: Ch 6 (counts as dc, ch 3), skip first 4 sts, *sc in next dc, ch 3, skip next 3 dc, dc in next sc**, ch 3, skip next 3 dc; rep from * across, ending last rep at **, turn.

Row 7: Ch 3 (counts as dc), dc in first dc, *ch 1, skip next ch-3 loop, dc in next sc, ch 1, skip next ch-3 loop**, 4 dc in next dc; rep from * across, ending last rep at **, 2 dc in 3rd ch of turning ch, turn.

Row 8: Ch 3 (counts as dc), skip first dc, dc in next dc, *ch 3, skip next 2 ch-1 spaces**, dc in each of next 4 dc; rep from * across, ending last rep at **, dc in next dc, dc in 3rd ch of turning ch, turn.

Row 9: Ch 3 (counts as dc), 2-dc cluster worked across first 2 dc, *ch 3, skip next ch-3 loop**, 2-dc cluster worked across next 2 dc, ch 2, 2-dc worked across next 2 dc; rep from * across, ending last rep at **, 2-dc cluster worked across last 2 sts, dc in 3rd ch of turning ch already holding last dc of last cluster, turn.

Row 10: Ch 3 (counts as dc), skip first dc, *(dc, ch 1, dc) in next cluster, ch 1, skip next ch-3 loop, (dc, ch 1, dc) in next cluster**, ch 2, skip next ch-2 space; rep from * across, ending last rep at **, dc in 3rd ch of turning ch, turn.

Row 11: Ch 3 (counts as dc), 2 dc in first dc, *dc in next ch-1 space, sc in next ch-1 space, dc in next ch-1 space**, 5 dc in next ch-2 space; rep from * across, ending last rep at **, 3 dc in 3rd ch of turning ch, turn.

Row 12: Ch 1, sc in first dc, *ch 3, skip next 3 dc, dc in next sc, ch 3, skip next 3 dc, sc in next dc; rep from * across, ending with last sc in 3rd ch of turning ch, turn.

Row 13: Ch 4 (counts as dc, ch 1), *skip next ch-3 loop, 4 dc in next dc, ch 1, skip next ch-3 loop, dc in next sc**, ch 1; rep from * across, ending last rep at **, turn.

Rep Rows 2–13 for pattern.

225

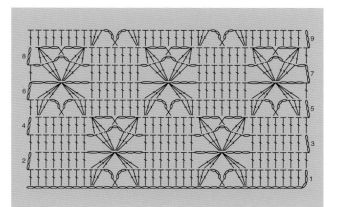

Chain multiples of 14 plus 11.

Row 1: Dc in 4th ch from hook, dc in each of next 6 ch, *3 dc in next ch, ch 3, skip next 2 ch, sc in next ch, ch 3, skip next 2 ch, 3 dc in next ch, dc in each of next 7 ch; rep from * across to within last ch, dc in last ch, turn.

Row 2: Ch 3 (counts as dc), skip first dc, *dc in each of next 7 dc**, ch 2, 6-dc cluster worked across next 6 dc, skipping 2 ch-3 loops bet, ch 3; rep from * across, ending last rep at **, dc in 3rd ch of turning ch, turn.

Row 3: Ch 3 (counts as dc), skip first dc, *dc in each of next 7 dc**, ch 1, skip next ch-3 loop, (3 dc, ch 3, 3 dc) in next cluster, ch 1, skip next ch-2 space; rep from * across, ending last rep at **, dc in 3rd ch of turning ch, turn.

Row 4: Ch 3 (counts as dc), skip first dc, *dc in each of next 7 dc**, skip next ch-1 space, 3-dc cluster worked across next 3 dc, ch 2, sc in next ch-3 loop, ch 2, 3-dc cluster worked across next 3 dc, skip next ch-1 space; rep from * across, ending last rep at **, dc in 3rd ch of turning ch, turn.

Row 5: Ch 3 (counts as dc), skip first dc, *3 dc in next dc, ch 3, skip next 2 dc, sc in next dc, ch 3, skip next 2 dc, 3 dc in next dc**, dc in next cluster, 2 dc in next ch-2 space, dc in next sc, 2 dc in next ch-2 space, dc in next cluster; rep from * across, ending last rep at **, dc in 3rd ch of turning ch, turn.

Row 6: Ch 5 (counts as dc, ch 2), skip first dc, *6-dc cluster worked across next 6 dc, skipping 2 ch-3 loops bet, ch 3**, dc in each of next 7 dc, ch 2; rep from * across, ending last rep at **, dc in 3rd ch of turning ch, turn.

Row 7: Ch 4 (counts as dc, ch 1), *skip next ch-3 loop, (3 dc, ch 3, 3 dc) in next cluster, ch 1, skip next ch-2 space**, dc in each of next 7 dc, ch 1; rep from * across, ending last rep at **, dc in 3rd ch of turning ch, turn.

Row 8: Ch 3 (counts as dc), *skip next ch-1 space, 3-dc cluster worked across next 3 dc, ch 2, sc in next ch-3 loop, ch 2, 3-dc cluster worked across next 3 dc, skip next ch-1 space**, dc in each of next 7 dc; rep from * across, ending last rep at **, dc in 3rd ch of turning ch, turn.

Row 9: Ch 3 (counts as dc), skip first dc, *dc in next cluster, 2 dc in next ch-2 space, dc in next sc, 2 dc in next ch-2 space, dc in next cluster**, 3 dc in next dc, ch 3, skip next 2 dc, sc in next dc, ch 3, skip next 2 dc, 3 dc in next dc; rep from * across, ending last rep at **, dc in 3rd ch of turning ch, turn.

Rep Rows 2-9 for pattern.

226

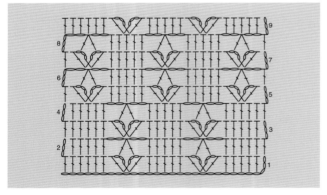

Chain multiples of 10 plus 9.

Row 1: Dc in 4th ch from hook, dc in each of next 4 ch, *skip next 2 ch, (dc, ch 3, sc, ch 3, dc) in next ch, skip next 2 ch, dc in each of next 5 ch; rep from * across to within last ch, dc in last ch, turn.

Row 2: Ch 3 (counts as dc), skip first dc, *dc in each of next 5 dc**, ch 2, 2-dc cluster worked across next 2 ch-3 loops, ch 2, skip next dc; rep from * across, ending last rep at **, dc in 3rd ch of turning ch, turn.

Row 3: Ch 3 (counts as dc), skip first dc, *dc in each of next 5 dc**, skip next ch-2 space, (dc, ch 3, sc, ch 3, dc) in next cluster, skip next ch-2 space; rep from * across, ending last rep at **, dc in 3rd ch of turning ch, turn.

Row 4: Rep Row 2.

Row 5: Ch 3 (counts as dc), skip first 3 dc, *(dc, ch 3, sc, ch 3, dc) in next dc, skip next 2 dc**, 2 dc in next ch-2 space, dc in next cluster, 2 dc in next ch-2 space, skip next 2 dc; rep from * across, ending last rep at **, dc in 3rd ch of turning ch, turn.

Row 6: Ch 5 (counts as dc, ch 2), skip first 2 dc, *2-dc cluster worked across next 2 ch-3 loops, ch 2, skip next dc**, dc in each of next 5 dc, ch 2, skip next dc; rep from * across, ending last rep at **, dc in 3rd ch of turning ch, turn.

Row 7: Ch 3 (counts as dc), *skip next ch-2 space, (dc, ch 3, sc, ch 3, dc) in next cluster, skip next ch-2 space**, dc in each of next 5 dc; rep from * across, ending last rep at **, dc in 3rd ch of turning ch, turn.

Row 8: Rep Rows 6.

Row 9: Ch 3 (counts as dc), skip first dc, *2 dc in next ch-2 space, dc in next cluster, 2 dc in next ch-2 space**, skip next 2 dc, (dc, ch 3, sc, ch 3, dc) in next dc, skip next 2 dc; rep from * across, ending last rep at **, dc in 3rd ch of turning ch, turn.

Rep Rows 2-9 for pattern.

.18.
Clusters—Inverted Shells

227

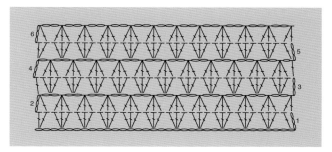

Chain multiples of 3 plus 1.

Row 1: Dc in 4th ch from hook, skip next 2 ch, *3 dc in next ch, skip next 2 ch; rep from * across to within last ch, 2 dc in last ch, turn.

Row 2: Ch 3 (counts as dc), skip first dc, dc in next dc, ch 2, *3-dc cluster worked across next 3 dc, ch 2; rep from * across to within last 2 sts, 2-dc cluster worked across last 2 sts, turn.

Row 3: Ch 3 (counts as dc), 3 dc in each ch-2 space across, dc in 3rd ch of turning ch, turn.

Row 4: Ch 4 (counts as dc, ch 1), 3-dc cluster worked across next 3 dc, *ch 2, 3-dc cluster worked across next 3 dc; rep from * across to turning ch, ch 1, dc in 3rd ch of turning ch, turn.

Row 5: Ch 3 (counts as dc), dc in first dc, skip next ch-1 space, 3 dc in eacch ch-2 space across, 2 dc in 3rd ch of turning ch, turn.

Rep Rows 2-5 for pattern.

228

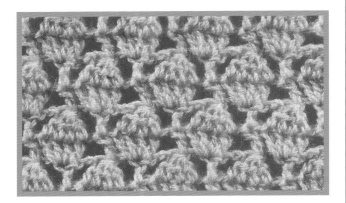

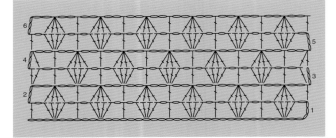

Chain multiples of 6 plus 4.

Row 1: 4 dc in 7th ch from hook, *ch 1, skip next 2 ch, dc in next ch**, ch 1, skip next 2 ch, 4 dc in next ch; rep from * across, ending last rep at **, turn.

Row 2: Ch 5 (counts as dc, ch 2), skip next ch-1 space, *4-dc cluster worked across next 4 dc, ch 2, skip next ch-1 space**, dc in next dc, ch 2, skip next ch-1 space; rep from * across, ending last rep at **, dc in next ch of turning ch, turn.

Row 3: Ch 3 (counts as dc), dc in first dc, *ch 1, skip next ch-2 space, dc in next cluster, ch 1, skip next ch-2 space**, 4 dc in next dc; rep from * across, ending last rep at **, 2 dc in 3rd ch of turning ch, turn.

Row 4: Ch 3 (counts as dc), skip first dc, dc in next dc, *ch 2, skip next ch-1 space, dc in next dc, ch 2, skip next ch-1 space**, 4-dc cluster worked across next 4 dc; rep from * across, ending last rep at **, 2-dc cluster worked across last 2 sts, turn.

Row 5: Ch 4 (counts as dc, ch 1), *skip next ch-2 space, 4 dc in next dc, ch 1, skip next ch-2 space**, dc in next cluster, ch 1; rep from * across, ending last rep at **, skip next dc, dc in 3rd ch of turning ch, turn.

Rep Rows 2-5 for pattern.

229

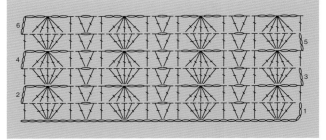

Chain multiples of 10 plus 9.

Row 1: 5 dc in 6th ch from hook, skip next 2 ch, dc in next ch, *skip next ch, (dc, ch 1, dc) in next ch, skip next ch, dc in next ch, skip next 2 ch, 5 dc in next ch, skip next 2 ch, dc in next ch; rep from * across, turn.

Row 2: Ch 5 (counts as dc, ch 2), skip first dc, *5-dc cluster worked across next 5 dc, ch 2**, dc in next dc, (dc, ch 1, dc) in next ch-1 space, skip next dc, dc in next dc, ch 2; rep from * across, ending last rep at **, dc in top of turning ch, turn.

Row 3: Ch 3 (counts as dc), skip next ch-2 space, *5 dc in next cluster, skip next ch-2 space**, dc in next dc, (dc, ch 1, dc) in next ch-1 space, skip next dc, dc in next dc, skip next ch-2 space; rep from * across, ending last rep at **, dc in 3rd ch of turning ch, turn.

Rep Rows 2-3 for pattern.

230

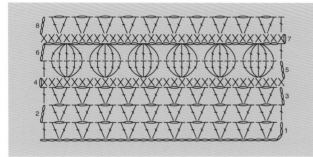

Chain multiples of 15 plus 4.

Row 1: (Dc, ch 1, dc) in 5th ch from hook, *skip next 2 ch, (dc, ch 1, dc) in next ch; rep from * across to within last 2 ch, skip next ch, dc in last ch, turn.

Row 2: Ch 3 (counts as dc), (dc, ch 1, dc) in each ch-1 space across to last ch-1 space, skip next dc, dc in 4th ch of turning ch, turn.

Row 3: Ch 3 (counts as dc), (dc, ch 1, dc) in each ch-1 space across to last ch-1 space, skip next dc, dc in 3rd ch of turning ch, turn.

Row 4: Ch 1, sc in each dc and ch-1 space across, ending with last sc in 3rd ch of turning, turn.

Row 5: Ch 3 (counts as dc), skip first 3 sc, 5 dc in next sc, *skip next 4 sc, 5 dc in next sc; rep from * across to within last 3 sc, skip next 2 sc, dc in last sc, turn.

Row 6: Ch 5 (counts as dc, ch 2), skip first dc, 5-dc cluster worked across next 5 dc, *ch 4, 5-dc cluster worked across next 5 dc; rep from * across to turning ch, ch 2, dc in 3rd ch of turning ch, turn.

Row 7: Ch 1, sc in first dc, 2 sc in next ch-2 space, sc in next cluster, *4 sc in next ch-4 loop, sc in next cluster; rep from * across to turning ch, 2 sc in ch-2 space of turning ch, sc in 3rd ch of turning ch, turn.

Row 8: Ch 3 (counts as dc), skip first 2 sc, (dc, ch 1, dc) in next sc, *skip next 2 sc, (dc, ch 1, dc) in next sc; rep from * across to within last 2 sc, skip next sc, dc in last sc, turn.

Rep Rows 2-8 for pattern.

231

Chain multiples of 12 plus 4.

Row 1: Dc in 4th ch from hook, *skip next 5 ch, (4 dc, ch 3, 4 dc) in next ch, skip next 5 ch**, (dc, ch 1, dc) in next ch; rep from * across, ending last rep at **, 2 dc in last ch, turn.

Row 2: Ch 3 (counts as dc), dc in first dc, *ch 5, 8-dc cluster worked across next 8 dc, skipping ch-3 loop, ch 3**, (dc, ch 1, dc) in next ch-1 space; rep from * across, ending last rep at **, skip next dc, 2 dc in 3rd ch of turning ch, turn.

Row 3: Ch 3 (counts as dc), dc in first dc, skip next ch-3 loop, (4 dc, ch 3, 4 dc) in next cluster, skip next ch-5 loop**, (dc, ch 1, dc) in next ch-1 space; rep from * across, ending last rep at **, skip next dc, 2 dc in 3rd ch of turning ch, turn.

Rep Rows 2-3 for pattern.

232

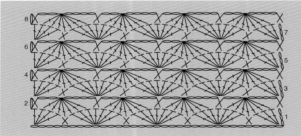

Chain multiples of 8 plus 4.

Row 1: 3 dc in 4th ch from hook, skip next 3 ch, sc in next ch, skip next 3 ch, *7 dc in next ch, skip next 3 ch, sc in next ch, skip next 3 ch; rep from * across to within last ch, 4 dc in last ch, turn.

Row 2: Ch 1, sc in first dc, *ch 2, 7-dc cluster worked across next 7 sts, ch 4, sc in next dc; rep from * across, ending with last sc in 3rd ch of turning ch, turn.

Row 3: Ch 3 (counts as dc), 3 dc in first dc, *skip next ch-4 loop, sc in next cluster, skip next ch-2 space**, 7 dc in next sc; rep from * across, ending last rep at **, 4 dc in last sc, turn.

Rep Rows 2-3 for pattern.

233

Chain multiples of 8 plus 2.

Row 1: Sc in 2nd ch from hook, *skip next 3 ch, 7 dc in next ch, skip next 3 ch, sc in next ch; rep from * across, turn.

Row 2: Ch 3 (counts as dc), skip first sc, work 1 cluster of 3 FPdc worked around the posts of next 3 dc, *ch 4, sc in next dc, ch 2**, work 1 cluster of 6 FPdc worked around the posts of next 6 dc, skipping sc bet; rep from * across, ending last rep at **, work 1 cluster of 3 FPdc worked around the posts of next 3 dc, dc in 3rd ch of turning ch, turn.

Row 3: Ch 3 (counts as dc), 3 dc in first cluster, *skip next ch-2 space, sc in next sc, skip next ch-4 loop**, 7 dc in next cluster; rep from * across, ending last rep at **, 4 dc in 3rd ch of turning ch, turn.

Row 4: Ch 1, sc in first dc, *ch 3, skip next 3 dc, dc in next sc, ch 3, skip next 3 dc, sc in next dc; rep from * across, ending with last sc in 3rd ch of turning ch, turn.

Row 5: Ch 1, sc in first sc, *skip next ch-3 loop, 7 dc in next dc, skip next ch-3 loop, sc in next sc; rep from * across, turn.

Rep Rows 2-5 for pattern.

234

Chain multiples of 12 plus 4.

Row 1: Dc in 4th ch from hook, *ch 1, skip next 5 ch, (4 dc, ch 2, 4 dc) in next ch, ch 1, skip next 5 ch**, (dc, ch 1, dc) in next ch; rep from * across, ending last rep at **, 2 dc in last ch, turn.

Row 2: Ch 3 (counts as dc), dc in first dc, *ch 1, skip next ch-1 space, 4-dc cluster worked across next 4 dc, ch 4, sc in next ch-2 space, ch 3, 4-dc cluster worked across next 4 dc, ch 1, skip next ch-1 space**, (dc, ch 1, dc) in next ch-1 space; rep from * across, ending last rep at **, skip next dc, 2 dc in 3rd ch of turning ch, turn.

Row 3: Ch 3 (counts as dc), 4 dc in first dc, *ch 1, skip next ch-1 space and ch-3 loop, (dc, ch 1, dc) in next sc, ch 1, skip next ch-4 loop and next ch-1 space**, (4 dc, ch 2, 4 dc) in next ch-1 space; rep from * across, ending last rep at **, skip next dc, 5 dc in 3rd ch of turning ch, turn.

Row 4: Ch 1, sc in first dc, *ch 3, 4-dc cluster worked across next 4 dc, ch 1, skip next ch-1 space, (dc, ch 1, dc) in next ch-1 space, ch 1, skip next ch-1 space, 4-dc cluster worked across next 4 dc, ch 4, sc in next ch-2 space; rep from * across, ending with last sc in 3rd ch of turning ch, turn.

Row 5: Ch 3 (counts as dc), dc in first sc, *ch 1, skip next ch-4 loop and ch-1 space, (4 dc, ch 2, 4 dc) in next ch-1 space, ch 1, skip next ch-1 space and ch-3 loop**, (dc, ch 1, dc) in next ch-1 space; rep from * across, ending last rep at **, 2 dc in last sc, turn.

Rep Rows 2-5 for pattern.

235

Chain multiples of 12 plus 4.

Row 1: Dc in 4th ch from hook, *ch 3, skip next 5 ch, 5 dc in next ch, ch 3, skip next 5 ch, 2-dc cluster worked across next 2 ch; rep from * across, turn.

Row 2: Ch 1, sc in first cluster, *ch 3, skip next ch-3 loop, dc in each of next 2 dc, (dc, ch 3, dc) in next dc, dc in each of next 2 dc, ch 3, skip next ch-3 loop, sc in next cluster; rep from * across, ending with last sc in 3rd ch of turning ch, turn.

Row 3: Ch 4 (counts as tr), skip next ch-3 loop, *3-dc cluster worked across next 3 dc, ch 3, (sc, ch 5, sc) in next ch-3 loop, ch 3, 3-dc cluster worked across next 3 dc**, skip next 2 ch-3 loops; rep from * across, ending last rep at **, skip next ch-3 loop, tr in last sc, turn.

Row 4: Ch 3 (counts as dc), skip first dc, dc in next cluster, *ch 3, skip next ch-3 loop, 5 dc in next ch-5 loop, ch 3, skip next ch-3 loop, 2-dc cluster worked across next 2 clusters; rep from * across, ending with last 2-dc cluster worked across last cluster and 3rd ch of turning ch, turn.

Rep Rows 2-4 for pattern.

236

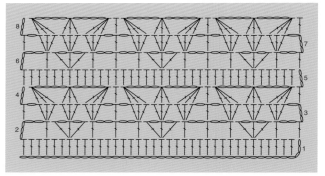

Chain multiples of 12 plus 3.

Row 1: Dc in 4th ch from hook, dc in each ch across, turn.

Row 2: Ch 5 (counts as dc, ch 2), skip first 3 dc, *dc in next dc, skip next 2 dc, (dc, ch 1, dc, ch 1, dc) in next dc, skip next 2 dc**, (dc in next dc, ch 2, skip next 2 dc) twice; rep from * across, ending last rep at **, dc in next dc, ch 2, skip next 2 dc, dc in 3rd ch of turning ch, turn.

Row 3: Ch 4 (counts as dc, ch 1), *(skip next 2 sts, 3 dc in next dc) 3 times, ch 1, skip next ch-2 space**, dc in next dc, ch 1; rep from * across, ending last rep at **, dc in 3rd ch of turning ch, turn.

Row 4: Ch 3 (counts as dc), skip next ch-1 space, *(3-dc cluster worked across next 3 dc, ch 4) twice, 3-dc cluster worked across next 3 dc, skip next ch-1 space, dc in next dc; rep from * across, ending with last dc in 3rd ch of turning ch, turn.

Row 5: Ch 3 (counts as dc), skip first dc, *(dc in next cluster, 4 dc in next ch-4 loop) twice, dc in each of next 2 sts; rep from * across, ending with last dc in 3rd ch of turning ch, turn.

Rep Rows 2-4 for pattern.

237

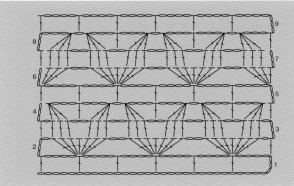

Chain multiples of 10 plus 7.

Row 1: Dc in 12th ch from hook, *ch 4, skip next 4 ch, dc in next ch; rep from * across, turn.

Row 2: Ch 4 (counts as dc, ch 1), *skip next ch-4 loop, 7 dc in next dc**, ch 2, skip next 2 ch-4 loops; rep from * across, ending last rep at **, ch 1, skip next 4 ch of turning ch, dc in next ch of turning ch, turn.

Row 3: Ch 4 (counts as dc, ch 1), skip next ch-1 space, *dc in each of next 3 dc, ch 2, skip next dc, dc in each of next 3 dc**, ch 2, skip next ch-2 space; rep from * across, ending last rep at **, ch 1, dc in 3rd ch of turning ch, turn.

Row 4: Ch 3 (counts as dc), skip next ch-1 space, *3-dc cluster worked across next 3 dc, ch 3, dc in next ch-2 space, ch 3, 3-dc cluster worked across next 3 dc**, ch 1, skip next ch-2 space; rep from * across, ending last rep at **, dc in 3rd ch of turning ch, turn.

Row 5: Ch 7 (counts as dc, ch 4), skip next ch-3 loop, *dc in next dc, ch 4, skip next ch-3 loop**, dc in next ch-1 space, ch 4, skip next ch-3 loop; rep from * across, ending last rep at **, dc in 3rd ch of turning ch, turn.

Row 6: Ch 3 (counts as dc), 3 dc in first dc, *ch 2, skip next 2 ch-4 loops**, 7 dc in next dc; rep from * across, ending last rep at **, 4 dc in 3rd ch of turning ch, turn.

Row 7: Ch 3 (counts as dc), skip first dc, dc in each of next 3 dc, *ch 2, skip next ch-2 space, dc in each of next 3 dc**, ch 2, skip next dc, dc in each of next 3 dc; rep from * across, ending last rep at **, dc in 3rd ch of turning ch, turn.

Row 8: Ch 6 (counts as dc, ch 3), skip first dc, *3-dc cluster worked across next 3 dc, ch 1, skip next ch-2 space, 3-dc cluster worked across next 3 dc, ch 3**, dc in next ch-2 space, ch 3; rep from * across, ending last rep at **, dc in 3rd ch of turning ch, turn.

Row 9: Ch 7 (counts as dc, ch 4), skip next ch-3 loop, *dc in next ch-1 space, ch 4, skip next ch-3 loop**, dc in next dc, ch 4, skip next ch-3 loop; rep from * across, ending last rep at **, dc in 3rd ch of turning ch, turn.

Rep Rows 2-9 for pattern.

238

Chain multiples of 8 plus 3.

Row 1: (3 dc, ch 3, 3 dc) in 7th ch from hook, *skip next 3 ch, dc in next ch**, skip next 3 ch, (3 dc, ch 3, 3 dc) in next ch; rep from * across, ending last rep at **, turn.

Row 2: Ch 3 (counts as dc), *(3 dc, ch 3, 3 dc) in next ch-3 loop, skip next 3 dc, dc in next dc; rep from * across, ending with last dc in top of turning ch, turn.

Row 3: Ch 3 (counts as dc), skip first dc, 3-dc cluster worked across next 3 dc, *ch 3, sc in next ch-3 loop, ch 3**, work 6-dc cluster working first 3 half-closed dc in next 3 dc, skip next dc, work next 3 half-closed dc in next 3 dc, yo, complete 6-dc cluster; rep from * across, ending last rep at **, 4-dc cluster worked across last 4 sts, turn.

Row 4: Ch 3 (counts as dc), *skip next ch-3 loop, (3 dc, ch 3, 3 dc) in next sc, skip next ch-3 loop, dc in next cluster; rep from * across, ending with last dc in 3rd ch of turning ch, turn.

Rep Rows 2-4 for pattern.

239

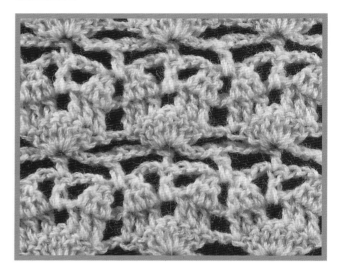

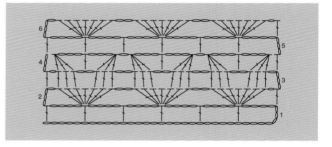

Chain multiples of 10 plus 7.

Row 1: Dc in 12th ch from hook, *ch 4, skip next 4 ch, dc in next ch; rep from * across, turn.

Row 2: Ch 4 (counts as dc, ch 1), skip next ch-4 loop, *7 dc in next dc**, ch 2, skip next 2 ch-4 loops; rep from * across, ending last rep at **, ch 1, skip next 4 ch of turning ch, dc next ch of turning ch, turn.

Row 3: Ch 4 (counts as dc, ch 1), skip next ch-1 space, *dc in each of next 3 dc, ch 2, skip next dc, dc in each of next 3 dc**, ch 2, skip next ch-2 space; rep from * across, ending last rep at **, ch 1, dc in 3rd ch of turning ch, turn.

Row 4: Ch 3 (counts as dc), skip next ch-1 space, *3-dc cluster worked across next 3 dc, ch 3, dc in next ch-2 space, ch 3, 3-dc cluster worked across next 3 dc**, ch 1, skip next ch-2 space; rep from * across, ending last rep at **, dc in 3rd ch of turning ch, turn.

Row 5: Ch 7 (counts as dc, ch 4), *skip next ch-3 loop, dc in next dc, ch 4, skip next ch-3 loop, dc in next ch-1 space; rep from * across, ending with last dc in 3rd ch of turning ch, turn.

Rep Rows 2-5 for pattern.

.19.
Wraparound Stitches

240

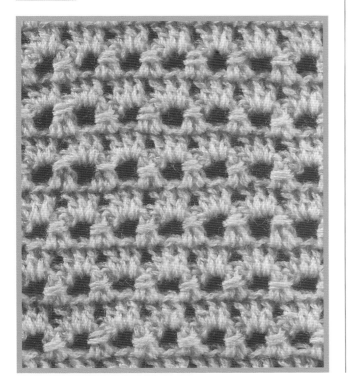

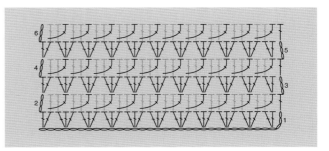

Chain multiples of 3 plus 1.

Row 1: 2 dc in 4th ch from hook, *skip next 2 ch, 3 dc in next ch; rep from * across, ending with 2 dc in last ch, turn.

Row 2: Ch 3 (counts as dc), skip first dc, *dc in each of next 2 dc, dc around the posts of last 2 dc made, skip next dc; rep from * across to turning ch, dc in 3rd ch of turning ch, turn.

Row 3: Ch 3 (counts as dc), skip first dc, 2 dc in next dc, skip next 2 dc, *3 dc in next dc, skip next 2 dc; rep from * across to turning ch, 2 dc in 3rd ch of turning ch, turn.

Rep Rows 2-3 for pattern.

241

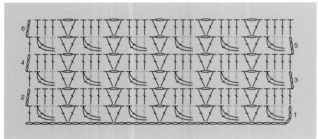

Chain multiples of 6 plus 1.

Row 1: Dc in 4th ch from hook, dc in next ch, 2-dc cluster worked around the posts of last 2 dc made, *skip next 2 ch, (dc, ch 1, dc) in next ch, skip next ch, dc in each of next 2 ch, 2-dc cluster worked around the posts of last 2 dc made; rep from * across to within last 2 ch, skip next ch, dc in last ch, turn.

Row 2: Ch 3 (counts as dc), skip first dc, dc in each of next 3 sts, *(dc, ch 1, dc) in next ch-1 space, skip next dc, dc in each of next 3 dc; rep from * across to turning ch, dc in 3rd ch of turning ch, turn.

Row 3: Ch 3 (counts as dc), skip first dc, *dc in each of next 2 dc, 2-dc cluster worked around the posts of last 2 dc made**, (dc, ch 1, dc) in next ch-1 space, skip next dc; rep from * across, ending last rep at **, skip next dc, dc in 3rd ch of turning ch, turn.

Rep Rows 2-3 for pattern.

242

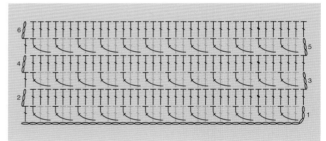

Chain multiples of 3 plus 1.

Row 1: Dc in 4th ch from hook, dc in next ch, dc around the posts of last 2 dc made, skip next ch, *dc in each of next 2 ch, dc around the posts of last 2 dc made, skip next ch; rep from * across to within last ch, dc in last ch, turn.

Row 2: Ch 3 (counts as dc), skip first dc, dc in each dc across to turning ch, dc in 3rd ch of turning ch, turn.

Row 3: Ch 3 (counts as dc), skip first dc, *dc in each of next 2 dc, dc around the posts of last 2 dc made, skip next dc; rep from * across to turning ch, dc in 3rd ch of turning ch, turn.

Rep Rows 2-3 for pattern.

243

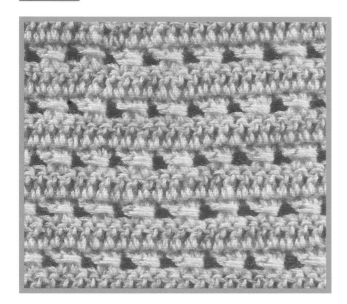

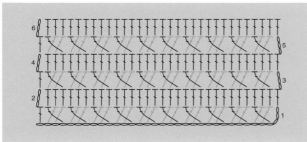

Chain multiples of 3 plus 1.

Row 1: Dc in 5th ch from hook, dc in next ch, working over last 2 dc made, dc in ch to the right of last 2 dc made, *skip next ch, dc in each of next 2 ch, working over last 2 dc made, dc in last skipped ch; rep from * across to within last ch, dc in last ch, turn.

Row 2: Ch 3 (counts as dc), skip first dc, dc in each dc across to turning ch, dc in 3rd ch of turning ch, turn.

Row 3: Ch 3 (counts as dc), skip first dc, *skip next dc, dc in each of next 2 dc, working over last 2 dc made, dc in last skipped dc; rep from * across to turning ch, dc in 3rd ch of turning ch, turn.

Rep Rows 2-3 for pattern.

244

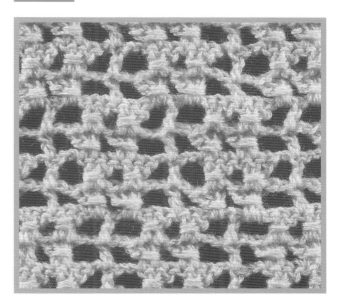

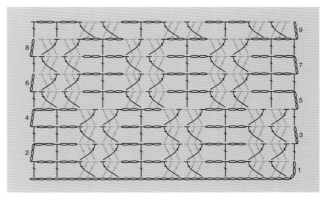

Chain multiples of 11 plus 4.

Row 1: Dc in 5th ch from hook, dc in next ch, working over last 2 dc made, dc in ch to the right of last 2 dc made, *skip next ch, dc in each of next 2 ch, working over last 2 dc made, dc in last skipped ch, ch 2, skip next 2 ch, dc in next ch, ch 2**, skip next 3 ch, dc in each of next 2 ch, working over last 2 dc made, dc in last skipped ch; rep from * across, ending last rep at **, skip next 2 ch, dc in last ch, turn.

Row 2: Ch 5 (counts as dc, ch 2), *skip next ch-2 space, dc in next dc, ch 2, (skip next dc, dc in each of next 2 dc, working over last 2 dc made, dc in last skipped dc) twice**, ch 2; rep from * across, ending last rep at **, dc in 3rd ch of turning ch, turn.

Row 3: Ch 3 (counts as dc), skip first dc, *(skip next dc, dc in each of next 2 dc, working over last 2 dc made, dc in last skipped dc) twice, ch 2, skip next ch-2 space, dc in next dc, ch 2, skip next ch-2 space; rep from * across to turning ch, dc in 3rd ch of turning ch, turn.

Row 4: Rep Row 2.

Row 5: Ch 5 (counts as dc, ch 2), skip first dc, *skip next 2 dc, dc in next dc, ch 2, skip next 3 dc, (dc in each of next 2 ch, working over last 2 dc made, dc in last skipped dc) twice**, ch 2; rep from * across, ending last rep at **, dc in 3rd ch of turning ch, turn.

Row 6: Rep Row 3.

Rows 7-8: Rep Rows 2-3.

Row 9: Ch 3 (counts as dc), *(skip first ch of next ch-2 space, dc in next ch, dc in next dc, working over last 2 dc made, dc in last skipped ch) twice, ch 2, skip next 2 dc, dc in next dc, ch 2, skip next 2 dc; rep from * across to turning ch, dc in 3rd ch of turning ch, turn.

Rep Rows 2-9 for pattern.

245

Chain multiples of 6 plus 5.

Row 1: Dc in 8th ch from hook, *ch 2, 3-dc cluster working first half-closed dc around the post of last dc made, 2nd half-closed dc in ch at base of same dc, skip nexr ch, work 3rd half-closed dc in next ch, yo, complete 3-dc cluster, ch 2, skip next 2 ch, dc in next ch; rep from * across, turn.

Row 2: Ch 1, sc in first st, *ch 2, skip next ch-2 space, sc in next st; rep from * across, ending with last sc in next ch of turning ch, turn.

Row 3: Ch 5 (counts as dc, ch 2), skip next ch-2 space, 3-dc cluster working first half-closed dc around the post of turning ch, 2nd half-closed dc in sc at base of turning ch, and 3rd half-closed dc in next sc, yo, complete 3-dc cluster, *ch 2, skip next ch-2 space, dc in next sc**, 3-dc cluster working first half-closed dc around the post of last dc made, 2nd half-closed dc in sc at base of same dc, and 3rd half-closed dc in next sc, yo, complete 3-dc cluster; rep from * across, ending last rep at **, turn.

Row 4: Rep Row 2.

Row 5: Ch 5 (counts as dc, ch 2), *skip next ch-2 space, dc in next sc, ch 2, skip next ch-2 space, 3-dc cluster working first half-closed dc around the post of last dc made, 2nd half-closed dc in sc at base of same dc, and 3rd half-closed dc in next sc, yo, complete 3-dc cluster; rep from * across, turn.

Rep Rows 2-5 for pattern.

246

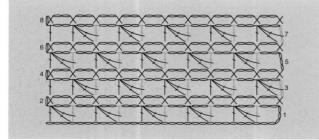

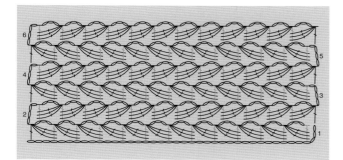

Chain multiples of 3 plus 1.

Row 1: Dc in 4th ch from hook, *ch 3, skip next 2 ch, 4-dc cluster working first 3 half closed dc around the post of last dc made and 4th half-closed dc in next ch, yo, complete 4-dc cluster; rep from * across, turn.

Row 2: Ch 4 (counts as dc, ch 1), dc in next ch-3 loop, *ch 3, 4-dc cluster working first 3 half closed dc around the post of last dc made and 4th half-closed dc in next ch-3 loop, yo, complete 4-dc cluster; rep from * across, ending in 3rd ch of turning ch, turn.

Rep Row 2 for pattern.

247

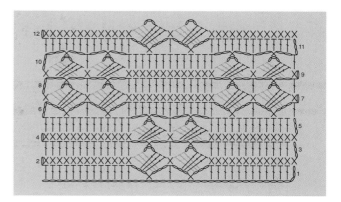

Chain multiples of 24 plus 15.

Row 1: Dc in 4th ch from hook, dc in each of next 11 ch, *(ch 3, skip next 2 ch, sc in next ch, ch 3, skip next 2 ch, dc in next ch) twice, dc in each of next 12 ch; rep from * across, turn.

Row 2: Ch 1, sc in first 13 dc, *(skip next loop, 3 dc in next loop, ch 3, working over last 3 dc made, work 3 dc in last skipped loop, sc in next dc) twice, sc in each of next 12 dc; rep from * across, ending with last sc in 3rd ch of turning ch, turn.

Row 3: Ch 3 (counts as dc), skip first sc, dc in each of next 12 sc, *(ch 2, sc in next ch-3 loop, ch 2, skip next 3 dc, dc in next sc) twice, dc in each of next 12 sc; rep from * across, turn.

Rows 4-5: Rep Rows 2-3.

Row 6: Ch 6 (counts as dc, ch 3), skip first 3 dc, sc in next dc, ch 3, skip next 2 dc, dc in next dc, ch 3, skip next 2 dc, sc in next dc, ch 3, skip next 2 dc, *dc in next dc, (2 dc in next ch-2 space, dc in next sc, 2 dc in next ch-2 space, dc in next dc) twice, (ch 3, skip next 2 dc, sc in next dc, ch 3, skip next 2 dc, dc in next dc) twice; rep from * across, ending with last dc in 3rd ch of turning ch, turn.

Row 7: Ch 1, sc in first dc, (skip next loop, 3 dc in next loop, ch 3, working over last 3 dc made, work 3 dc in last skipped loop, sc in next dc) twice, *sc in each of next 12 dc, (skip next loop, 3 dc in next loop, ch 3, working over last 3 dc made, work 3 dc in last skipped loop, sc in next dc) twice; rep from * across, ending with last sc in 3rd ch of turning ch, turn.

Row 8: Ch 5 (counts as dc, ch 2), sc in next ch-3 loop, ch 2, skip next 3 dc, dc in next sc, ch 2, sc in next ch-3 loop, ch 2, skip next 3 dc, *dc in each of next 13 sc, (ch 2, sc in next ch-3 loop, ch 2, skip next 3 dc, dc in next sc) twice; rep from * across, turn.

Rows 9-10: Rep Rows 7-8.

Row 11: Ch 3 (counts as dc), (2 dc in next ch-2 space, dc in next sc, 2 dc in next ch-2 space, dc in next dc) twice, *(ch 3, skip next 2 dc, sc in next dc, ch 3, skip next 2 dc, dc in next dc) twice, (2 dc in next ch-2 space, dc in next sc, 2 dc in next ch-2 space, dc in next dc) twice; rep from * across, ending with last dc in 3rd ch of turning ch, turn.

Rep Rows 2-11 for pattern.

.20.
Staggered Squares

248

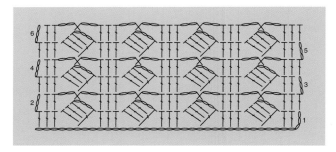

Chain multiples of 8 plus 5.

Row 1: Dc in 4th ch from hook, dc in next ch, *skip next 2 ch, dc in next ch, ch 3, 3 dc around the post of last dc made, skip next 2 ch, dc in each of next 3 ch; rep from * across, turn.

Row 2: Ch 3 (counts as dc), skip first dc, dc in each of next 2 dc, *ch 2, sc in next ch-3 loop, ch 2, skip next dc, dc in each of next 3 dc; rep from * across, ending with last dc in 3rd ch of turning ch, turn.

Row 3: Ch 3 (counts as dc), skip first dc, dc in each of next 2 dc, *skip next ch-2 space, dc in next sc, ch 3, 3 dc around the post of last dc made, skip next ch-2 space, dc in each of next 3 dc; rep from * across, ending with last dc in 3rd ch of turning ch, turn.

Rep Rows 2-3 for pattern.

249

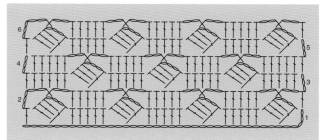

Chain multiples of 10 plus 9.

Row 1: Dc in 6th ch from hook, ch 3, ch 3, 3 dc around the post of last dc made, skip next 2 ch, *dc in each of next 5 ch, skip next 2 ch, dc in next ch, ch 3, 3 around the post of last dc made, skip next 2 ch; rep from * across to last ch, dc in last ch, turn.

Row 2: Ch 5 (counts as dc, ch 2), sc in next ch-3 loop, ch 2, skip next dc, *dc in each of next 5 dc, ch 2, sc in next ch-3 loop, ch 2, skip next dc; rep from * across to turning ch, dc in 5th ch of turning ch, turn.

Row 3: Ch 3 (counts as dc), 2 dc in next ch-2 space, dc in next sc, 2 dc in next ch-2 space, *skip next 2 dc, dc in next dc, ch 3, 3 dc around the post of last dc made, skip next 2 dc, 2 dc in next ch-2 space, dc in next sc, 2 dc in next ch-2 space; rep from * across to ch-2 space of turning ch, dc in 3rd ch of turning ch, turn.

Row 4: Ch 3 (counts as dc), skip first dc, dc in each of next 5 dc, *ch 2, sc in next ch-3 loop, ch 2, skip next dc, dc in each of next 5 dc; rep from * across to turning ch, dc in 3rd ch of turning ch, turn.

Row 5: Ch 3 (counts as dc), skip first 3 dc, dc in next dc, ch 3, 3 dc around the post of last dc made, skip next 2 dc, *2 dc in next ch-2 space, dc in next sc, 2 dc in next ch-2 space, skip next 2 dc, dc in next dc, ch 3, 3 dc around the post of last dc made, skip next 2 dc; rep from * across to turning ch, dc in 3rd ch of turning ch, turn.

Rep Rows 2-5 for pattern.

250

Chain multiples of 4 plus 2.

Row 1: Sc in 2nd ch from hook, *ch 5, skip next 3 ch, sc in next ch; rep from * across, turn.

Row 2: Ch 4 (counts as dc, ch 1), sc in next ch-5 loop, (ch 3, sc) in each ch-5 loop across to last ch-5 loop, ch 1, dc in last sc, turn.

Row 3: Ch 3 (counts as dc), 2 dc in first dc, (sc, ch 3, 2 dc) in each sc across to within last sc, sc in last sc, 2-dc cluster working first half-closed dc in same sc holding last sc, and 2nd half-closed dc in 3rd ch of turning ch, yo, complete 2-dc cluster, turn.

Row 4: Ch 1, sc in first cluster, ch 2, 2 dc in next ch-2 space, (sc, ch 2, 2 dc) in each ch-2 space across to last ch-2 space, sc in 3rd ch of turning ch, turn.

Row 5: Ch 5 (counts as dc, ch 2), sc in next ch-2 space, (ch 5, sc) in each ch-2 space across to last ch-2 space, ch 2, dc in last sc, turn.

Row 6: Ch 1, sc in first dc, (ch 5, sc) in each ch-5 loop across, ending with last sc in 3rd ch of turning ch, turn.

Rep Rows 2-6 for pattern.

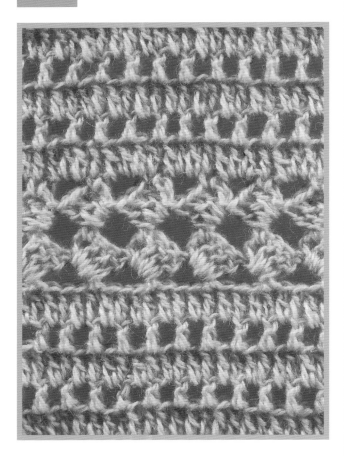

251

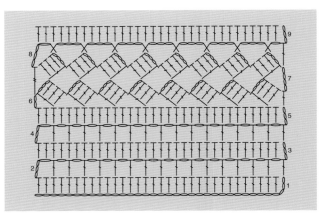

Chain multiples of 4 plus 3.

Row 1: Dc in 4th ch from hook, dc in each ch across, turn.

Row 2: Ch 4 (counts as dc, ch 1), skip first 2 dc, *dc in next dc, ch 1, skip next dc; rep from * across to turning ch, dc in 3rd ch of turning ch, turn.

Row 3: Ch 3 (counts as dc), *dc in next ch-1 space, dc in next dc; rep from * across, ending with last dc in 3rd ch of turning ch, turn.

Rows 4-5: Rep Rows 2-3.

Row 6: Ch 2, skip first 2 dc, dc in next dc, ch 3, 3 dc around the post of last dc made, *skip next 3 dc, dc in next dc, ch 3, 3 dc around the post of last dc made; rep from * across to within last 2 sts, skip next dc, dc in 3rd ch of turning ch, turn.

Row 7: Ch 4 (counts as tr), *skip next 4 dc, dc in top of next ch-3 loop, ch 3, 3 dc around the post of last dc made; rep from * across to turning ch, tr in 2nd ch of turning ch, turn.

Row 8: Ch 4 (counts as dc, ch 1), *skip next 4 dc, sc in top of next ch-3 loop**, ch 3; rep from * across, ending last rep at **, ch 1, dc in 4th ch of turning ch, turn.

Row 9: Ch 3 (counts as dc), dc in next ch-1 space, *dc in next sc, 3 dc in next ch-3 loop; rep from * across to last ch-3 loop, dc in next sc, dc in ch-1 space of turning ch, dc in 3rd ch of turning ch, turn.

Rep Rows 2-9 for pattern.

252

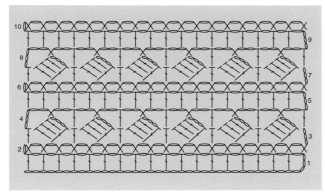

Chain multiples of 6 plus 4.

Row 1: Dc in 6th ch from hook, *ch 1, skip next ch, dc in next ch; rep from * across, turn.

Row 2: Ch 1, sc in first dc, *ch 1, skip next ch-1 space, sc in next dc; rep from * across, ending with last dc in next ch of turning ch, turn.

Row 3: Ch 3 (counts as dc), skip next ch-1 space, *dc in next ch-1 space, ch 3, 3 dc around the post of last dc made, skip next ch-1 space, dc in next sc**, skip next ch-1 space; rep from * across, ending last rep at **, turn.

Row 4: Ch 5 (counts as dc, ch 2), skip first 4 dc, *sc in top of next ch-3 loop, ch 2, skip next dc**, dc in next dc, ch 2, skip next 3 dc; rep from * across, ending last rep at **, dc in 3rd ch of turning ch, turn.

Row 5: Ch 4 (counts as dc, ch 1), *(dc, ch 1) in each of next 2 ch-2 spaces**, dc in next dc, ch 1; rep from * across, ending last rep at **, dc in 3rd ch of turning ch, turn.

Rep Rows 2-5 for pattern.

253

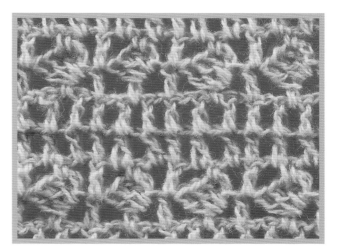

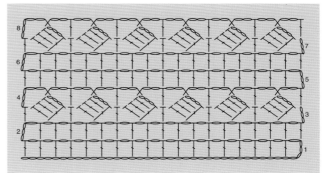

Chain multiples of 6 plus 4.

Row 1: Dc in 6th ch from hook, *ch 1, skip next ch, dc in next ch; rep from * across, turn.

Row 2: Ch 4 (counts as dc, ch 1), skip next ch-1 space, dc in next dc, *ch 1, skip next ch-1 space, dc in next dc; rep from * across, ending with last dc in next ch of turning ch, turn.

Row 3: Ch 3 (counts as dc), skip next ch-1 space, *dc in next ch-1 space, ch 3, 3 dc around the post of last dc made, skip next ch-1 space**, dc in next dc, ch 1, skip next ch-1 space; rep from * across, ending last rep at **, dc in 3rd ch of turning ch, turn.

Row 4: Ch 5 (counts as dc, ch 2), skip first 4 dc, *sc in top of next ch-3 loop, ch 2, skip next dc**, dc in next dc, ch 2, skip next 3 dc; rep from * across, ending last rep at **, dc in 3rd ch of turning ch, turn.

Row 5: Ch 4 (counts as dc, ch 1), *(dc, ch 1) in each of next 2 ch-2 spaces**, dc in next dc, ch 1; rep from * across, ending last rep at **, dc in 3rd ch of turning ch, turn.

Rep Rows 2-5 for pattern.

254

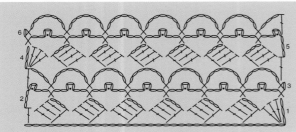

Picot: Ch 3, sl st in 3rd ch from hook.

Chain multiples of 5 plus 2.

Row 1: 3 dc in 4th ch from hook, *skip next 4 ch, dc in next ch, ch 3, 3 dc around the post of last dc made; rep from * across to within last 3 ch, skip next 2 ch, dc in last ch, turn.

Row 2: Ch 3 (counts as dc), picot, ch 2, skip first 4 dc, *sc in top of next ch-3 loop, ch 2, picot, ch 2, skip next 4 dc; rep from * across to turning ch, sc in 3rd ch of turning ch, turn.

Row 3: Ch 1, sc in first sc, (ch 7, sc) in each sc across to last sc, ch 3, skip next picot, dc in 3rd ch of turning ch, turn.

Row 4: Ch 3 (counts as dc), 3 dc in first dc, *dc in next ch-7 loop, ch 3, 3 dc around the post of last dc made; rep from * across to last ch-7 loop, dc in last sc, turn.

Rep Rows 2-4 for pattern.

255

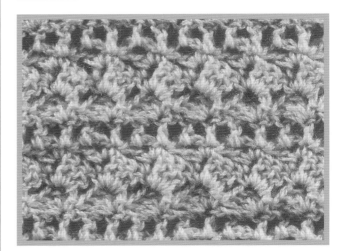

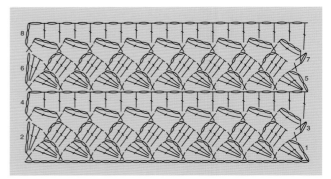

Chain multiples of 4.

Row 1: 3 dc in 4th ch from hook, skip next 3 ch, *sc in next ch, ch 3, 3 dc in last sc made, skip next 3 ch; rep from * across to within last ch, sc in last ch, turn.

Row 2: Ch 3 (counts as dc), 2 dc in first sc, (sc, ch 3, 3 dc) in each ch-3 loop across to turning ch, sc in 3rd ch of turning ch, turn.

Row 3: Ch 1, sc in first sc, ch 3, dc in last sc made, *sc in top of next ch-3 loop, ch 3, dc in last sc made; rep from * across to last ch-3 loop, skip next 3 sts, sc in 3rd ch of turning ch, turn.

Row 4: Ch 4 (counts as dc, ch 1), dc in next ch-3 loop, ch 1, *dc in next sc, ch 1, dc in next ch-3 loop, ch 1; rep from * across to within last sc, dc in last sc, turn.

Row 5: Ch 3 (counts as dc), 3 dc in first dc, skip next 2 ch-1 spaces, *sc in next dc, ch 3, 3 dc in last sc made, skip next 2 ch-1 spaces; rep from * across to turning ch, sc in 3rd ch of turning ch, turn.

Rep Rows 2-5 for pattern.

256

Chain multiples of 10 plus 4.

Row 1: Dc in 4th ch from hook, *ch 3, skip next 4 ch, (sc, ch 3, 3 dc) in next ch, skip next 4 ch**, (dc, ch 1, dc) in next ch; rep from * across, ending last rep at **, 2 dc in last ch, turn.

Row 2: Ch 3 (counts as dc), dc in first dc, *ch 3, (sc, ch 3, 3 dc) in next ch-3 loop, skip next ch-3 loop**, (dc, ch 1, dc) in next ch-1 space; rep from * across, ending last rep at **, 2 dc in 3rd ch of turning ch, turn.

Rep Row 2 for pattern.

257

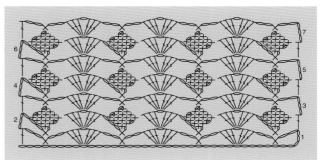

Chain multiples of 10 plus 1.

Row 1: Sc in 8th ch from hook, *ch 2, skip next 4 ch, (3 dc, ch 1, 3 dc) in next ch, ch 2, skip next 4 ch, sc in next ch; rep from * across to within last 3 ch, ch 2, skip next 2 ch, dc in last ch, turn.

Row 2: Ch 6 (counts as dc, ch 3), skip next ch-2 space, *sc in next sc, turn, ch 1, 4 sc in next ch-3 loop, (turn, ch 1, sc in each of next 4 sc) 3 times forming a sc-square, skip next ch-2 space**, (3 dc, ch 1, 3 dc) in next ch-1 space, ch 3, skip next ch-2 space; rep from * across, ending last rep at **, dc in next ch of turning ch, turn.

Row 3: Ch 5 (counts as dc, ch 2), *sc in top corner of next sc-square, ch 2**, (3 dc, ch 1, 3 dc) in next ch-1 space, ch 2; rep from * across, ending last rep at **, dc in 3rd ch of turning ch, turn.

Rep Rows 2-3 for pattern.

258

Chain multiples of 12 plus 4.

Row 1: 2 dc in 4th ch from hook, *ch 8, skip next 11 ch**, (2 dc, ch 1, 2 dc) in next ch; rep from * across, ending last rep at **, 3 dc in last ch, turn.

Row 2: Ch 3 (counts as dc), 2 dc in first dc, *ch 4, sc over 2 loops in last 2 rows, ch 4**, (2 dc, ch 1, 2 dc) in next ch-1 space; rep from * across, ending last rep at **, skip next 2 dc, 3 dc in next ch of turning ch, turn.

Row 3: Ch 3 (counts as dc), 2 dc in first dc, *ch 5, skip next ch-4 loop, sc in next sc, ch 3, turn, 5 dc in next ch-5 loop, ch 3, turn, skip first dc, dc in each of next 5 sts forming a dc-square, skip next ch-4 loop**, (2 dc, ch 1, 2 dc) in next ch-1 space; rep from * across, ending last rep at **, skip next 2 dc, 3 dc in 3rd ch of turning ch, turn.

Row 4: Ch 3 (counts as dc), 2 dc in first dc, *ch 8, skip next dc-square**, (2 dc, ch 1, 2 dc) in next ch-1 space; rep from * across, ending last rep at **, skip next 2 dc, 3 dc in 3rd ch of turning ch, turn.

Row 5: Ch 3 (counts as dc), 2 dc in first dc, *ch 8, skip next ch-8 loop**, (2 dc, ch 1, 2 dc) in next ch-1 space; rep from * across, ending last rep at **, skip next 2 dc, 3 dc in 3rd ch of turning ch, turn.

Row 6: Ch 3 (counts as dc), 2 dc in first dc, *ch 5, working over 2 loops in last 2 rows, sc in top of next dc-square 3 rows below, ch 3, turn, 5 dc in next ch-5 loop, ch 3, turn, skip first dc, dc in each of next 5 sts forming a dc-square**, (2 dc, ch 1, 2 dc) in next ch-1 space; rep from * across, ending last rep at **, skip next 2 dc, 3 dc in 3rd ch of turning ch, turn.

Rep Rows 4-6 for pattern.

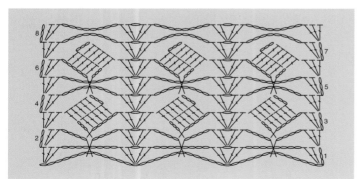

259

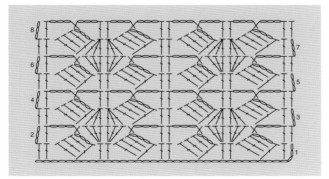

Chain multiples of 8 plus 4.

Row 1: Dc in 4th ch from hook, *skip next 2 ch, dc in next ch, ch 3, 3 dc around the post of last dc made, skip next 3 ch, dc in each of next 2 ch; rep from * across, turn.

Row 2: Ch 3 (counts as dc), skip in first dc, dc in next dc, *ch 3, sc in top of next ch-3 loop, skip next dc, 3 dc in each of next 2 dc, sc in top of next ch-3 loop, ch 3, skip next dc, dc in each of next 2 dc; rep from * across, ending with last dc in 3rd ch of turning ch, turn.

Row 3: Ch 3 (counts as dc), skip in first dc, dc in next dc, *skip next ch-3 loop, dc in next sc, ch 3, 3 dc around the post of last dc made, (3-dc cluster worked across next 3 dc) twice, dc in next sc, ch 3, 3 dc around the post of last dc made, skip next ch-3 loop, dc in each of next 2 dc; rep from * across, ending with last dc in 3rd ch of turning ch, turn.

Row 4: Ch 3 (counts as dc), skip in first dc, dc in next dc, *ch 3, sc in top of next ch-3 loop, ch 3, skip next dc, dc in each of next 2 clusters, ch 3, sc in top of next ch-3 loop, ch 3, skip next dc, dc in each of next 2 dc; rep from * across, ending with last dc in 3rd ch of turning ch, turn.

Row 5: Ch 3 (counts as dc), skip in first dc, dc in next dc, *skip next ch-3 loop, dc in next sc, ch 3, 3 dc around the post of last dc made, skip next ch-3 loop, dc in each of next 2 dc; rep from * across, ending with last dc in 3rd ch of turning ch, turn.

Rep Rows 2-5 for pattern.

.21.
Y-Stitches

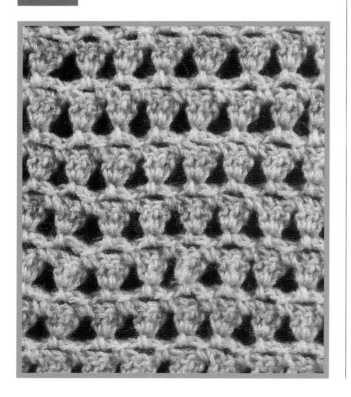

260

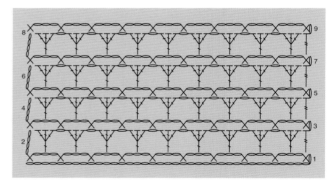

Y-st: *Tr in next st, 2 dc in center of last tr made.*

Chain multiples of 4 plus 2.

Row 1: Sc in 2nd ch from hook, *ch 3, skip next 3 ch, sc in next ch; rep from * across, turn.

Row 2: Ch 4 (counts as tr), (Y-st, ch 1) in each ch-3 loop across to within last ch-3 loop, Y-st in last ch-3 loop, tr in last sc, turn.

Row 3: Ch 1, sc in first tr, (ch 3, sc) in each ch-1 space across, ending with last sc in 4th ch of turning ch, turn.

Rep Rows 2-3 for pattern.

261

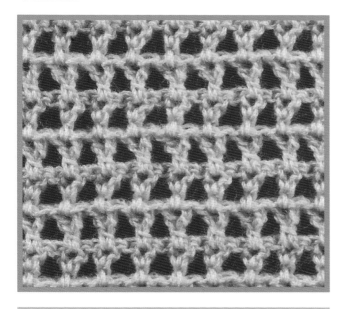

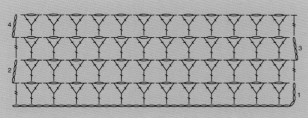

Y-st: Tr in next st, ch 1, dc in center of last tr made.

Chain multiples of 3 plus 2.

Row 1: Y-st in 6th ch from hook, *skip next 2 ch, Y-st in next ch; rep from * across to within last 2 ch, skip next ch, tr in last ch, turn.

Row 2: Ch 4 (counts as tr), Y-st in each ch-1 space of each Y-st across to last ch-1 space, tr in top of turning ch, turn.

Rep Row 2 for pattern.

262

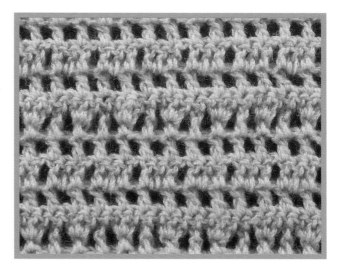

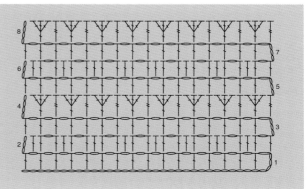

Y-st: Tr in next st, 2 dc in center of last tr made.

Chain multiples of 4.

Row 1: Dc in 6th ch from hook, *ch 1, skip next ch, dc in next ch; rep from * across, turn.

Row 2: Ch 3 (counts as dc), *dc in next ch-1 space, dc in next dc, ch 1, skip next ch-1 space, dc in next dc; rep from * across, ending with last dc in next ch of turning ch, turn.

Row 3: Ch 4 (counts as dc, ch 1), skip first 2 sts, *dc in next dc, ch 1, skip next st; rep from * across to turning ch, dc in 3rd ch of turning ch, turn.

Row 4: Ch 4 (counts as tr), *skip next ch-1 space, Y-st in next dc, skip next ch-1 space, tr in next dc; rep from * across, ending with last tr in 3rd ch of turning ch, turn.

Row 5: Rep Row 3.

Rep Rows 2-5 for pattern.

.22.

X-Stitches & Crossed Stitches

263

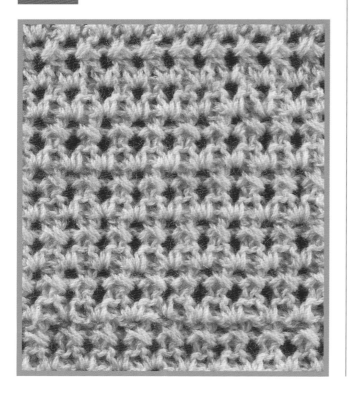

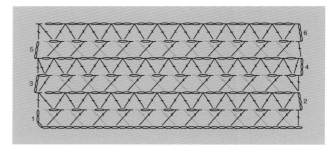

Chain multiples of 3 plus 1.

Row 1: (WS): Dc in 6th ch from hook, ch 1, working over last dc made, skip next ch to the right, dc in next ch to the right (crossed dc made), *skip next 2 ch, dc in next ch, ch 1, working over last dc made, dc in first skipped ch (crossed dc made); rep from * across to within last ch, dc in last ch, turn.

Row 2: Ch 3 (counts as dc), dc in next ch-1 space, *ch 2, work 2-dc cluster, working first half-closed dc in ch-1 space holding last dc, and 2nd half-closed dc in next ch-1 space, complete 2-dc cluster; rep from * across, ending with last half-closed dc in 3rd ch of turning ch, turn.

Row 3: Ch 4 (counts as dc, ch 1), dc in first cluster, skip next ch-2 space, dc in next ch-2 space, ch 1, working behind last dc made, dc in last skipped ch-2 space (crossed dc made), *dc in next ch-2 space, ch 1, working behind last dc made, dc in last ch-2 space holding previous dc (crossed dc made); rep from * across to last ch-2 space, skip next dc, (dc, ch 1, dc) in 3rd ch of turning ch, turn.

Row 4: Ch 3 (counts as dc), dc in next ch-1 space, ch 1, *work 2-dc cluster, working first half-closed dc in ch-1 space holding last dc, and 2nd half-closed dc in next ch-1 space, complete 2-dc cluster**, ch 2; rep from * across, ending last rep at **, ch 1, 2-dc cluster worked across ch-1 space of turning ch and in 3rd ch of turning ch, turn.

Row 5: Ch 3 (counts as dc, ch 1), skip next space, dc in next space, ch 1, working over last dc made, dc in last skipped space (crossed dc made), *dc in next space, ch 1, working over last dc made, dc in last space holding previous dc (crossed dc made); rep from * across to last space, dc in 3rd ch of turning ch, turn.

Rep Rows 2-5 for pattern.

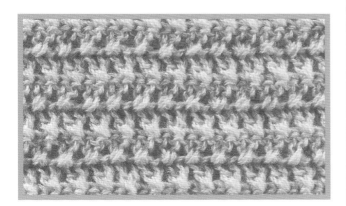

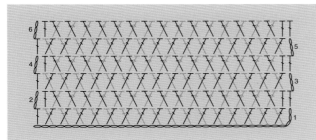

Chain multiples of 2.

Row 1: Dc in 5th ch from hook, working behind last dc made, dc in next ch to the right (crossed dc made), *skip next ch, dc in next ch, working behind last dc made, dc in next ch to the right (crossed dc made); rep from * across to within last ch, dc in last ch, turn.

Row 2: Ch 3 (counts as dc), dc in next dc, *skip next dc, dc in next dc, working behind last dc made, dc in last skipped dc

(crossed dc made); rep from * across to within last 2 sts, dc in next dc, dc in 3rd ch of turning ch, turn.

Row 3: Ch 3 (counts as dc), skip first dc, *skip next dc, dc in next dc, working behind last dc made, dc in last skipped dc (crossed dc made); rep from * across to turning ch, dc in 3rd ch of turning ch, turn.

Rep Rows 2-3 for pattern.

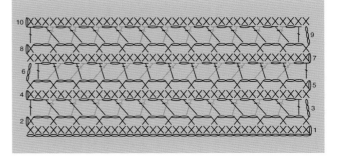

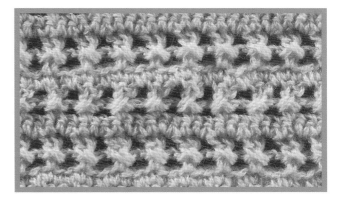

Chain multiples of 3 plus 2.

Row 1: Sc in 2nd ch from hook, sc in each ch across, turn.

Row 2: Ch 1, sc in first sc, *ch 2, skip next 2 sc, sc in next sc; rep from * across, turn.

Row 3: Ch 3 (counts as dc), dc in next ch-2 space, ch 1, *dc in next space, working behind last dc made, dc in last space holding previous dc (crossed dc made), ch 1; rep from * across to within last sc, dc in last sc, turn.

Row 4: Ch 1, sc in first dc, *sc in next ch-1 space, dc in each of next 2 dc; rep from * across, ending with last sc in 3rd ch of turning ch, turn.

Rep Rows 2-4 for pattern.

266

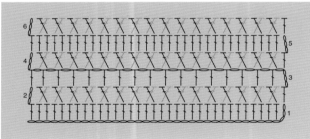

Chain multiples of 2.

Row 1: Dc in 4th ch from hook, dc in each ch across, turn.

Row 2: Ch 3 (counts as dc), skip first dc, *skip next dc, dc in next dc, working behind last dc made, dc in last skipped dc (crossed dc made); rep from * across to turning ch, dc in 3rd ch of turning ch, turn.

Row 3: Ch 4 (counts as dc, ch 1), skip first dc, *(dc, ch 1) bet 2 dc of next crossed dc, skip next 2 dc; rep from * across to turning ch, dc in 3rd ch of turning ch, turn.

Row 4: Ch 3 (counts as dc), skip first dc, *skip next ch-1 space, dc in next ch-1 space, working behind last dc made, dc in last skipped ch-1 space (crossed dc made); rep from * across to turning ch, dc in 3rd ch of turning ch, turn.

Row 5: Ch 3 (counts as dc), skip first dc, dc in each dc across, ending with last dc in 3rd ch of turning ch, turn.

Rep Rows 2-5 for pattern.

267

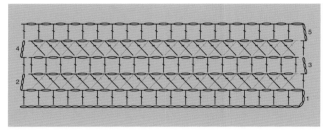

Chain multiples of 2.

Row 1: Dc in 6th ch from hook, *ch 1, skip next ch, dc in next ch; rep from * across, turn.

Row 2: Ch 3 (counts as dc), skip next ch-1 space, dc in next ch-1 space, *ch 1, 2-dc cluster, working behind last dc made, work first half-closed dc in last skipped ch-1 space, skip next ch-1 space, work 2nd half closed dc in next ch-1 space, complete cluster, ch 1; rep from * across to turning ch, working behind last dc made, dc in last skipped ch-1 space, dc in 3rd ch of turning ch, turn.

Row 3: Ch 3 (counts as dc), skip first dc, dc in next dc, *ch 1, skip next ch-1 space, dc in next st; rep from * across to turning ch, dc in 3rd ch of turning ch, turn.

Row 4: Ch 3 (counts as dc), skip first dc, *skip next dc, dc in next dc, ch 1, 2-dc cluster, working behind last dc made, work first half-closed dc in last skipped dc, skip next 2 ch-1 spaces, work 2nd half closed dc in next dc, complete cluster, ch 1; rep from * across to turning ch, working behind last dc made, dc in last skipped dc, dc in 3rd ch of turning ch, turn.

Row 5: Ch 4 (counts as dc, ch 1), skip first dc, (dc, ch 1) in each ch-1 space across, dc in 3rd ch of turning ch, turn.

Rep Rows 2-5 for pattern.

268

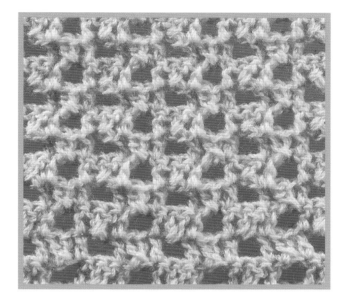

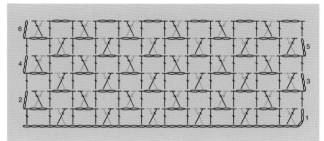

Chain multiples of 6 plus 3.

Row 1: Dc in 5th ch from hook, working behind last dc made, dc in last skipped ch (crossed dc made), *dc in next ch, ch 2, skip next 2 ch, dc in next ch**, skip next ch, dc in next ch, working behind last dc made, dc in last skipped ch (crossed dc made), dc in next ch; rep from * across, ending last rep at **, turn.

Row 2: Ch 3 (counts as dc), *skip next ch, dc in next ch, working behind last dc made, dc in last skipped ch (crossed dc made), dc in next dc, ch 2, skip next 2 dc, dc in next dc; rep from * across, ending with last dc in 3rd ch of turning ch, turn.

Rep Row 2 for pattern.

269

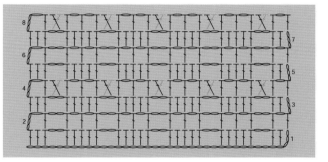

Chain multiples of 7 plus 3.

Row 1: Dc in 4th ch from hook, dc in next ch, *ch 2, skip next 2 ch**, dc in each of next 5 ch; rep from * across, ending last rep at **, dc in last 3 ch, turn.

Row 2: Ch 4 (counts as dc, ch 1), skip first 2 dc, dc in next dc, ch 2, skip next ch-2 space, *(dc in next dc, ch 1, skip next dc) twice, dc in next dc, ch 2, skip next ch-2 space; rep from * across to within last 3 sts, dc in next dc, ch 1, skip next dc, dc in 3rd ch of turning ch, turn.

Row 3: Ch 3 (counts as dc), dc in next ch-1 space, dc in next dc, *ch 2, skip next 2 sts**, (dc in next dc, dc in next ch-1 space) twice, dc in next dc; rep from * across, ending last rep at **, dc in next dc, dc in next ch-1 space of turning ch, dc in 3rd ch of turning ch, turn.

Row 4: Ch 4 (counts as dc, ch 1), skip first 2 dc, dc in next dc, *skip next ch, dc in next ch, working behind last dc made, dc in last skipped ch (crossed dc made)**, (dc in next dc, ch 1, skip next dc) twice, dc in next dc; rep from * across, ending last rep at **, dc in next dc, ch 1, skip next dc, dc in 3rd ch of turning ch, turn.

Row 5: Rep Row 3.

Rep Rows 2-5 for pattern.

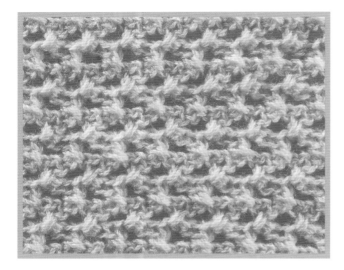

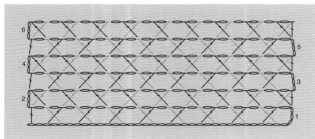

Chain multiples of 4 plus 2.

Row 1: Dc in 8th ch from hook, ch 1, working behind last dc made, skip next ch to the right, dc in next ch to the right (crossed dc made), ch 1, *skip next 3 ch, dc in next ch, working behind last dc made, skip next ch to the right, dc in next ch to the right (crossed dc made), ch 1; rep from * across to within last 2 ch, skip next ch, dc in last ch, turn.

Row 2: Ch 3 (counts as dc), skip first dc, skip next ch-1 space, *dc in next dc, ch 1, working behind last dc made, dc in last skipped dc (crossed dc made), ch 1, skip next 2 ch-1 spaces; rep from * across to turning ch, dc in 3rd ch of turning ch, ch 1, work 2-dc cluster, working behind last dc made, work first half-closed dc in last skipped dc, work 2nd half-closed dc in 3rd ch of turning ch, turn.

Row 3: Ch 4 (counts as dc, ch 1), *skip next 2 ch-2 space, dc in next dc, ch 1, working behind last dc made, dc in last skipped dc (crossed dc made), ch 1; rep from * across to within last ch-1 space, skip next dc, dc in 3rd ch of turning ch, turn.

Rep Rows 2-3 for pattern.

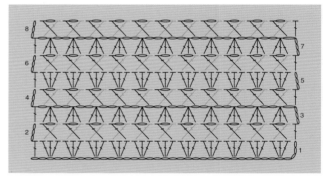

Chain multiples of 3 plus 1.

Row 1: 3 dc in 5th ch from hook, *skip next 2 ch, 3 dc in next ch; rep from * across to within last 2 ch, skip next ch, dc in last ch, turn.

Row 2: Ch 3 (counts as dc), skip first dc, *skip next 2 dc, dc in next dc, ch 1, working behind last dc made, dc in first of last 2 skipped dc (crossed dc made); rep from * across to turning ch, dc in top of turning ch, turn.

Row 3: Ch 4 (counts as dc, ch 1), skip first dc, *work 3-dc cluster across next 3 sts**, ch 2; rep from * across, ending last rep at **, ch 1, dc in 3rd ch of turning ch, turn.

Row 4: Ch 3 (counts as dc), skip first dc, *skip next ch and cluster, dc in next ch, ch 1, working behind last dc made, dc in last skipped ch (crossed dc made); rep from * across to turning ch, dc in 3rd ch of turning ch, turn.

Row 5: Ch 3 (counts as dc), 3 dc in each ch-1 space across to last ch-1 space, dc in 3rd ch of turning ch, turn.

Rep Rows 2-5 for pattern.

272

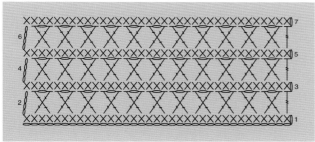

X-stitch (X-st): Yo twice, insert hook in next st, yo, draw yarn through st, yo, draw yarn through 2 loops on hook (3 loops on hook), skip next st, yo, insert hook in next st, yo, draw yarn through st, (yo, draw yarn through 2 loops on hook) 4 times (inverted Y made), ch 1, yo, insert hook through 2 strands at the center of cluster just made, yo, draw yarn through st, (yo, draw yarn through 2 loops on hook) twice.

Chain multiples of 3.

Row 1: Sc in 2nd ch from hook, sc in each ch across, turn.

Row 2: Ch 4 (counts as tr), skip first sc, *X-st worked across next 3 sts; rep from * across to last sc, tr in last sc, turn.

Row 3: Ch 1, sc in each tr and ch-1 space across, ending with sc in 4th ch of turning ch, turn.

Rep Rows 2-3 for pattern.

273

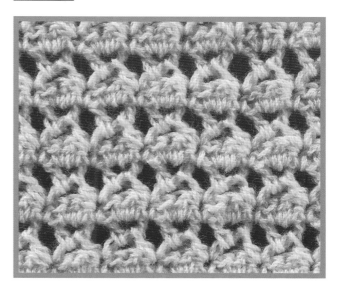

X-stitch (X-st): Yo twice, insert hook in next st, yo, draw yarn through st, yo, draw yarn through 2 loops on hook (3 loops on hook), skip designated number of sts, yo, insert hook in next st, yo, draw yarn through st, (yo, draw yarn through 2 loops on hook) 4 times (inverted Y made), ch 2, yo, insert hook through 2 strands at the center of cluster just made, yo, draw yarn through st, (yo, draw yarn through 2 loops on hook) twice.

Chain multiples of 4 plus 1.

Row 1: Starting in 5th ch from hook, work X-st across next 4 ch (skipping 2 ch at base), *work X-st across next 4 ch (skipping 2 ch at base); rep from * across to within last ch, tr in last ch, turn.

Row 2: Ch 1, sc in first tr, *(hdc, dc, hdc) in next ch-2 space, sc bet next 2 tr; rep from * across, ending with last sc in top of turning ch, turn.

Row 3: Ch 4 (counts as tr), *work X-st across next 5 sts (skipping 3 sts at base); rep from * across to last sc, tr in last sc already holding last leg of X-st, turn.

Rep Rows 2-3 for pattern.

274

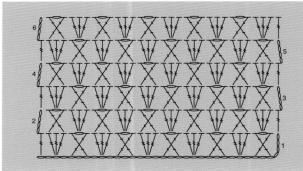

X-stitch (X-st): Yo twice, insert hook in next st, yo, draw yarn
through st, yo, draw yarn through 2 loops on hook (3 loops on
hook), skip next st, yo, insert hook in next st, yo, draw yarn
through st, (yo, draw yarn through 2 loops on hook) 4 times
(inverted Y made), ch 1, yo, insert hook through 2 strands at the
center of cluster just made, yo, draw yarn through st, (yo, draw
yarn through 2 loops on hook) twice.

Chain multiples of 6 plus 5.

Row 1: Starting in 5th ch from hook work X-st across next 3 ch,
*skip next ch, 3 tr in next ch**, skip next ch, work X-st across
next 3 ch; rep from * across, ending last rep at **, skip next ch,
tr in last ch, turn.

Row 2: Ch 4 (counts as tr), skip first tr, *work X-st across next 3
sts, 3 tr in next ch–1 space, skip next dc; rep from * across to
last ch–1 space, tr in top of turning ch, turn.

Rep Row 2 for pattern.

275

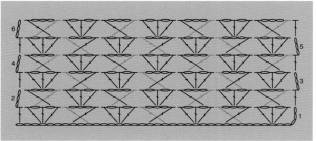

Chain multiples of 10 plus 9.

Row 1: (Dc, ch 1, dc, ch 1, dc) in 6th ch from hook, *skip next
5 ch, dc in next ch, ch 3, working behind last dc made, skip next
ch to the right, dc in next ch to the right (crossed dc made), skip
next 3 ch, (dc, ch 1, dc, ch 1, dc) in next ch; rep from * across
to within last 3 ch, skip next 2 ch, dc in last ch, turn.

Row 2: Ch 3 (counts as dc), *skip next ch-1 space, dc in next ch-1 space, ch 3, working behind last dc made, dc in last skipped ch-1 space (crossed dc made)**, (dc, ch 1, dc, ch 1, dc) in next ch-3 loop; rep from * across, ending last rep at **, dc in top of turning ch, turn.

Row 3: Ch 3 (counts as dc), *(dc, ch 1, dc, ch 1, dc) in next ch-3 loop**, skip next ch-1 space, dc in next ch-1 space, ch 3, working behind last dc made, dc in last skipped ch-1 space (crossed dc made); rep from * across, ending last rep at **, dc in 3rd ch of turning ch, turn.

Rep Rows 2-3 for pattern.

276

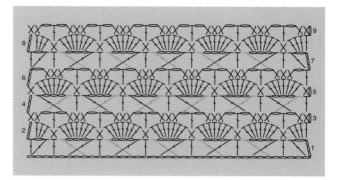

Chain multiples of 6 plus 5.

Row 1: Dc in 5th ch from hook, skip next 2 ch, dc in next ch, *skip next 3 ch, dc in next ch, ch 3, working behind last dc made, skip next ch to the right, dc in next ch to the right (crossed dc made), skip next ch, dc in next ch; rep from * across to within last 3 ch, skip next 2 ch, (dc, ch 1, dc) in last ch, turn.

Row 2: Ch 3 (counts as dc), 3 dc in next ch-1 space, skip next dc, sc in next dc, *7 dc in next ch-3 loop, skip next dc, sc in next dc; rep from * across to turning ch, 3 dc in next ch-1 space of turning ch, dc in 3rd ch of turning ch, turn.

Row 3: Ch 1, sc in each of first 2 dc, *ch 1, skip next 2 dc, dc in next sc, ch 1, skip next 2 dc**, sc in each of next 3 dc; rep from * across, ending last rep at **, sc in next dc, sc in 3rd ch of turning ch, turn.

Row 4: Ch 3 (counts as dc), *skip next ch-1 space, dc in next ch-1 space, ch 3, working behind last dc made, dc in last skipped ch-1 space (crossed dc made), skip next sc, dc in next sc; rep from * across, turn.

Row 5: Ch 1, sc in first dc, *7 dc in next ch-3 loop, skip next dc, sc in next dc; rep from * across, ending with last sc in 3rd ch of turning ch, turn.

Rpw 6: Ch 4 (counts as dc, ch 1), skip first 3 sts, *sc in each of next 3 dc, ch 1, skip next 2 dc, dc in next sc**, ch 1, skip next 2 dc; rep from * across, ending last rep at **, turn.

Row 7: Ch 4 (counts as dc, ch 1), dc in first dc, skip next sc, dc in next sc, *skip next ch-1 space, dc in next ch-1 space, ch 3, working behind last dc made, dc in last skipped ch-1 space (crossed dc made), skip next sc, dc in next sc; rep from * across to turning ch, skip next ch-1 space of turning ch, (dc, ch 1 dc) in 3rd ch of turning ch, turn.

Rep Rows 2-7 for pattern.

277

Chain multiples of 6 plus 2.

Row 1: Sc in 2nd ch from hook, *ch 1, skip next 2 ch, (2 dc, ch 1, 2 dc) in next ch, ch 1, skip next 2 ch, sc in next ch; rep from * across, turn.

Row 2: Ch 5 (counts as dc, ch 2), skip next ch-1 space, sc in next ch-1 space, *ch 2, skip next ch-1 space, dc in next ch-1 space, ch 1, working behind last dc, made, dc in last skipped ch-1 space (crossed dc made), ch 2, sc in next ch-1 space; rep from * across to within last ch-1 space, ch 2, skip next ch-1 space, dc in last sc, turn.

Row 3: Ch 1, sc in first dc, *ch 1, skip next ch-2 space, (2 dc, ch 1, 2 dc) in next sc, ch 1, skip next ch-2 space, sc in next ch-1 space; rep from * across, ending with last sc in 3rd ch of turning ch, turn.

Rep Rows 2-3 for pattern.

278

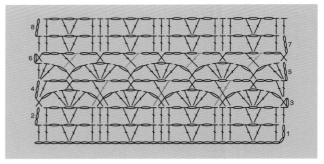

Chain multiples of 8 plus 3.

Row 1: Dc in 4th ch from hook, *ch 1, skip next 2 ch, (dc, ch 1, dc) in next ch, ch 1, skip next 2 ch**, dc in each of next 3 ch; rep from * across, ending last rep at **, dc in each of last 2 ch, turn.

Row 2: Ch 3 (counts as dc), skip first dc, dc in next dc, *ch 1, skip next ch-1 space, (dc, ch 1, dc) in next ch-1 space, ch 1, skip next ch-1 space**, dc in each of next 3 dc; rep from * across, ending last rep at **, dc in next dc, dc in 3rd ch of turning ch, turn.

Row 3: Ch 1, sc in first dc, *ch 1, skip next ch-1 space, (2 dc, ch 1, 2 dc) in next ch-1 space, ch 1, skip next ch-1 space, skip next dc, sc in next dc; rep from * across, ending with last sc in 3rd ch of turning ch, turn.

Row 4: Ch 3 (counts as dc), dc in first sc, *ch 2, skip next ch-1 space, sc in next ch-1 space, ch 2**, working behind sts in last row, skip next 2 dc 2 rows below, dc in next dc 2 rows below, ch

1, working behind last dc made and sts in row below, dc in first of 2 skipped dc 2 rows below (crossed dc made); rep from * across, ending last rep at **, skip next ch-1 space, 2 dc in last sc, turn.

Row 5: Ch 3 (counts as dc), 2 dc in first dc, *ch 1, skip next ch-2 space, sc in next sc, ch 1**, skip next ch-2 space, (2 dc, ch 1, 2 dc) in next ch-1 space; rep from * across, ending last rep at **, skip next dc, 3 dc in 3rd ch of turning ch, turn.

Row 6: Ch 1, sc in first dc, *ch 2, skip next ch-1 space, dc in next ch-1 space, ch 1, working behind last dc made, dc in last skipped ch-1 space, ch 2, sc in next ch-1 space; rep from * across, ending with last sc in 3rd ch of turning ch, turn.

Row 7: Ch 3 (counts as dc), *dc in next ch-2 space, ch 1, (dc, ch 1, dc) in next ch-1 space, ch 1, dc in next ch-2 space, dc in next sc; rep from * across, turn.

Rep Rows 2-7 for pattern.

279

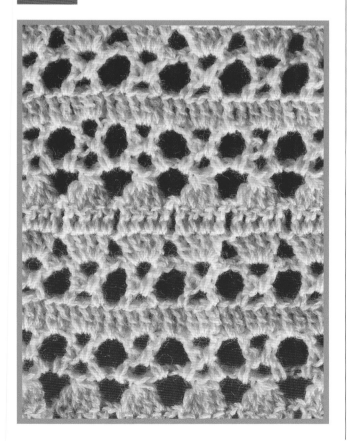

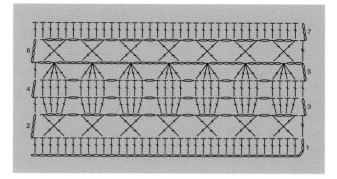

X-stitch (X-st): Yo twice, insert hook in next st, yo, draw yarn through st, yo, draw yarn through 2 loops on hook (3 loops on hook), skip designated number of sts, yo, insert hook in next st, yo, draw yarn through st, (yo, draw yarn through 2 loops on hook) 4 times (inverted Y made), ch 2, yo, insert hook through 2 strands at the center of cluster just made, yo, draw yarn through st, (yo, draw yarn through 2 loops on hook) twice.

Chain multiples of 5 plus 3.

Row 1: Dc in 4th ch from hook, dc in each ch across, turn.

Row 2: Ch 4 (counts as tr), skip first dc, *work X-st across next 4 dc (skipping 2 dc at base)**, ch 1, skip next dc; rep from * across, ending last rep at **, tr in 3rd ch of turning ch, turn.

Row 3: Ch 3 (counts as dc), *4 dc in next ch-2 space**, ch 1, skip next ch-1 space; rep from * across, ending last rep at **, dc in 4th ch of turning ch, turn.

Row 4: Ch 3 (counts as dc), skip first dc, *dc in each of next 4 dc**, ch 1, skip next ch-1 space; rep from * across, ending last rep at **, dc in 3rd ch of turning ch, turn.

Row 5: Ch 5 (counts as dc, ch 2), skip first dc, *4-dc cluster worked across next 4 dc**, ch 5, skip next ch-1 space; rep from * across, ending last rep at **, ch 2, dc in 3rd ch of turning ch, turn.

Row 6: Ch 4 (counts as tr), starting in next ch-2 space, work X-st across next 2 spaces (skipping cluster at base), *ch 1, work X-st in same loop as last st worked and next loop; rep from * across to turning ch, tr in 3rd ch of turning ch, turn.

Row 7: Ch 3 (counts as dc), skip first tr, *dc in next tr, 2 dc in next ch-2 space, dc in next tr**, dc in next ch-1 space; rep from * across, ending last rep at **, dc in 4th ch of turning ch, turn.

Rep Rows 2-7 for pattern.

.23.
Picots

280

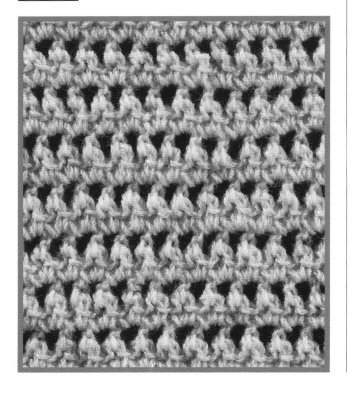

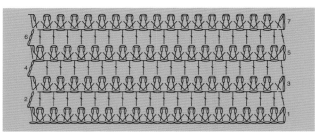

Chain multiples of 2.

Row 1: (Sc, ch 3, sc) in 5th ch from hook, *skip next ch, (sc, ch 3, sc) in next ch; rep from * across to within last ch, ch 1, hdc in last ch, turn.

Row 2: Ch 3 (counts as dc), skip next ch-1 space, dc in next ch-3 loop, (ch 1, dc) in each ch-3 loop across to last ch-3 loop, skip next ch of turning ch, dc in next ch of turning ch, turn.

Row 3: Ch 3 (counts as hdc, ch 1), sc in first dc, (sc, ch 3, sc) in each ch-1 space across to last ch-1 space, ch 1, hdc in 3rd ch of turning ch, turn.

Row 4: Ch 4 (counts as dc, ch 1), skip next ch-1 space, (dc, ch 1) in each ch-3 loop across to last ch-3 loop, dc in 2nd ch of turning ch, turn.

Row 5: Ch 3 (counts as hdc, ch 1), (sc, ch 3, sc) in each ch-1 space across to ch-1 space of turning ch, ch 1, hdc in 3rd ch of turning ch, turn.

Rep Rows 2-5 for pattern.

281

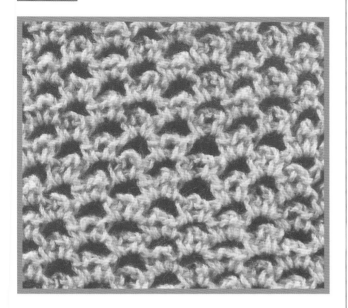

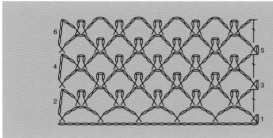

Chain multiples of 5 plus 2.

Row 1: Sc in 2nd ch from hook, *ch 5, skip next 4 ch, sc in next ch; rep from * across, turn.

Row 2: Ch 5 (counts as dc, ch 2), (sc, ch 3, sc) in next ch-5 loop, (ch 5, sc, ch 3, sc) in each ch-5 loop across to last ch-5 loop, ch 2, dc in last sc, turn.

Row 3: Ch 1, sc in first dc, ch 5, (sc, ch 3, sc, ch 5) in each ch-5 loop across to last ch-5 loop, sc in 3rd ch of turning ch, turn.

Rep Rows 2-3 for pattern.

282

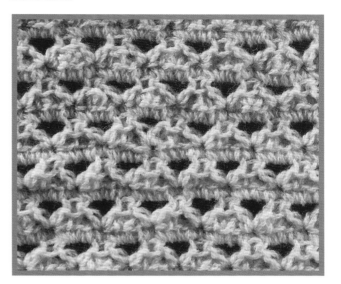

Chain multiples of 4.

Row 1: Sc in 2nd ch from hook, ch 3, sl st in 3rd ch from hook (picot), *sc in each of next 4 ch, picot; rep from * across to within last 2 ch, sc in each of last 2 ch, turn.

Row 2: Ch 4 (counts as dc, ch 1), work 2-dc cluster, working first half-closed dc in first sc, skip next 3 sc, work 2nd half-closed dc in next sc, complete 2-dc cluster, *ch 3, work 2-dc cluster, working first half-closed dc in same sc as last dc of last cluster, skip next 3 sc, work 2nd half-closed dc in next sc, complete 2-dc cluster; rep from * across to within last 2 sc, ch 3, work 2-dc cluster, working first half-closed dc in same sc as last dc of last cluster, skip next sc, work 2nd half-closed dc in last sc, complete 2-dc cluster, turn.

Row 3: Ch 1, sc in first cluster, *(2 sc, picot, sc) in next ch-3 loop, sc in next cluster; rep from * across to turning ch, sc in ch-1 space of turning ch, sc in 3rd ch of turning ch, turn.

Row 4: Ch 3 (counts as dc), skip first 2 sc, dc in next sc, *ch 3, work 2-dc cluster, working first half-closed dc in same sc as last dc worked, skip next 3 sc, work 2nd half-closed dc in next sc, complete 2-dc cluster; rep from * across to last sc, ch 1, dc in last sc, turn.

Row 5: Ch 1, sc in first dc, picot, sc in next ch-1 space, *sc in next cluster, (2 sc, picot, sc) in next ch-3 loop; rep from * across to last ch-3 loop, skip next dc, sc in 3rd ch of turning ch, turn.

Rep Rows 2-5 for pattern.

Row 3: Ch 3 (counts as dc), picot, ch 3, skip first 2 dc, sc bet last skipped and next dc, *ch 3, skip next dc, dc in next dc, picot, ch 3, skip next dc, sc bet last skipped and next dc; rep from * across to within last 2 sts, ch 3, skip next dc, dc in 3rd ch of turning ch, turn.

Rep Rows 2-3 for pattern.

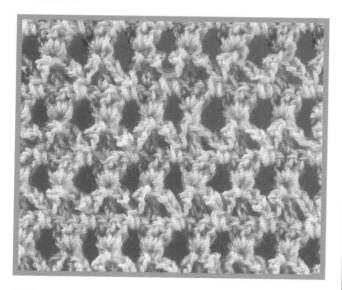

Chain multiples of 4 plus 3.

Row 1: Ch 3, sl st in 3rd ch from hook (picot), ch 3, sc in 5th ch before picot, ch 3, skip next ch, dc in next ch, *picot, ch 3, skip next ch, sc in next ch, ch 3, skip next ch, dc in next ch; rep from * across, turn.

Row 2: Ch 3 (counts as dc), dc in first dc, skip next 2 ch-3 loops, 3 dc in next picot; rep from * across, ending with 2 dc in last picot, turn.

Chain multiples of 7 plus 1.

Row 1: Sc in 2nd ch from hook, *skip next 2 ch, 5 dc in next ch, skip next 2 ch, sc in next ch**, ch 3, sc in next ch; rep from * across, ending last rep at **, turn.

Row 2: Ch 6 (counts as dc, ch 3), skip first 3 sts, *(sc, ch 3, sc) in next dc (center dc of shell), ch 3**, skip next 3 sts, dc in next ch-3 loop, skip next 3 sts; rep from * across, ending last rep at **, skip next 2 dc, dc in last sc, turn.

Row 3: Ch 1, sc in first sc, *skip next ch-3 loop, 5 dc in next ch-3 loop, skip next ch-3 loop**, (sc, ch 3, sc) in next dc; rep from * across, ending last rep at **, sc in 3rd ch of turning ch, turn.

Rep Rows 2-3 for pattern.

285

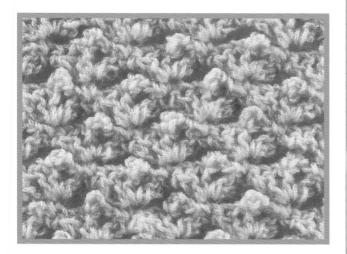

Chain multiples of 6 plus 2.

Row 1: Sc in 2nd ch from hook, *ch 7, skip next 5 ch, sc in next ch; rep from * across, turn.

Row 2: Ch 4 (counts as dc, ch 1), dc in first sc, sc in next ch-7 loop, *(dc, ch 1, dc, ch 3, sl st in 3rd ch from hook [picot], ch 1, dc) in next sc (shell), sc in next ch-7 loop; rep from * across to last ch-7 loop, (dc, ch 1, dc) in last sc, turn.

Row 3: Ch 6 (counts as dc, ch 3), skip first 3 sts, sc in next sc, *ch 7, skip next shell, sc in next sc; rep from * across to within last 3 sts, skip next dc, dc in 3rd ch of turning ch, turn.

Row 4: Ch 1, sc in first dc, skip next ch-3 loop, *(dc, ch 1, dc, picot, ch 1, dc) in next sc (shell), sc in next ch-7 loop; rep from * across, ending with last sc in 3rd ch of turning ch, turn.

Row 5: Ch 1, sc in first sc, *ch 7, skip next shell, sc in next sc; rep from * across, turn.

Rep Rows 2-5 for pattern.

286

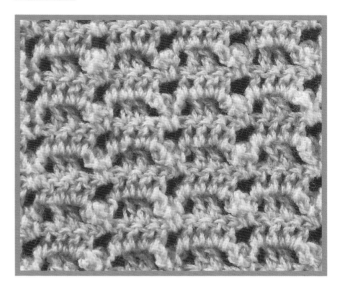

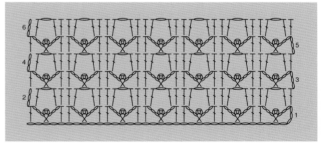

Chain multiples of 5.

Row 1: Sc in 8th ch from hook, ch 3, sl st in 3rd ch from hook (picot), ch 3, skip next ch, *dc in each of next 2 ch, ch 3, skip next ch, sc in next ch, picot, ch 3, skip next ch; rep from * across to last ch, dc in last ch, turn.

Row 2: Ch 3 (counts as dc), *dc in next ch-3 loop, ch 1, dc in next ch-3 loop**, dc in each of next 2 dc; rep from * across, ending last rep at **, dc in 3rd ch of turning ch, turn.

Row 3: Ch 6 (counts as dc, ch 3), skip first 2 dc, *sc in next ch-1 space, picot, ch 3, skip next dc**, dc in each of next 2 dc, ch 3, skip next dc; rep from * across, ending last rep at **, dc in 3rd ch of turning ch, turn.

Rep Rows 2-3 for pattern.

287

Chain multiples of 8 plus 6.

Row 1: Sc in 2nd ch from hook, *ch 1, skip next 3 ch, (dc, ch 1, dc, ch 1, dc) in next ch, ch 1, skip next 3 ch, (sc, ch 3, sc) in next ch; rep from * across to within last 4 ch, ch 1, skip next 3 ch, (dc, ch 1, dc) in last ch, turn.

Row 2: Ch 1, sc in first sc, *ch 1, skip next 2 ch-1 space, (dc, ch 1, dc, ch 1, dc) in next ch-3 loop, ch 1, skip next 2 ch-1 space, (sc, ch 3, sc) in next dc; rep from * across to within last 2 ch-1 spaces, ch 1, skip next 2 ch-1 spaces, (dc, ch 1, dc) in last sc, turn.

Rep Row 2 for pattern.

288

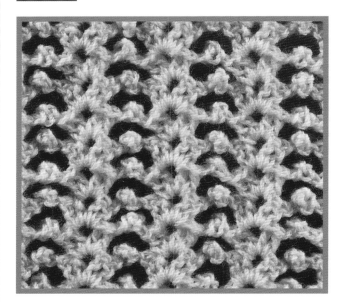

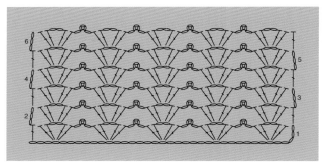

Chain multiples of 7 plus 2.

Row 1: (2 dc, ch 2, 2 dc) in 6th ch from hook, *ch 1, ch 3 more, sl st in 3rd ch from hook (picot), ch 1, skip next 6 ch, (2 dc, ch 2, 2 dc) in next ch; rep from * across to within last 3 ch, skip next 2 ch, dc in last ch, turn.

Row 2: Ch 3 (counts as dc), skip first 3 dc, (2 dc, ch 2, 2 dc) in next ch-2 space, *ch 1, picot, ch 1, (2 dc, ch 2, 2 dc) in next ch-2 space; rep from * across to last ch-2 space, skip next 2 dc, dc in top of turning ch, turn.

Rep Row 2 for pattern.

289

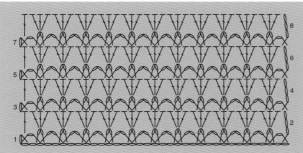

Chain multiples of 3.

Row 1: Sc in 2nd ch from hook, ch 1, skip next ch, (sc, ch 2, sc) in next ch, *ch 2, skip next 2 ch, (sc, ch 2, sc) in next ch; rep from * across to within last 2 ch, ch 1, skip next ch, sc in last ch, turn.

Row 2: Ch 3 (counts as dc), skip next ch-1 space, 3 dc in next ch-2 space, *skip next ch-2 spaces, 3 dc in next ch-2 space; rep from * across to last ch-2 space, skip next ch-1 space, dc in last sc, turn.

Row 3: Ch 1, sc in first dc, ch 1, skip next dc, (sc, ch 2, sc) in next dc, *ch 2, skip next 2 dc, (sc, ch 2, sc) in next dc; rep from * across to within last 2 sts, ch 1, skip next dc, sc in 3rd ch of turning ch, turn.

Rep Rows 2-3 for pattern.

290

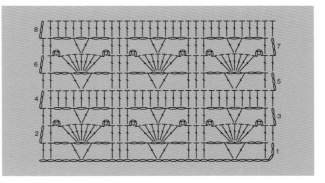

Chain multiples of 10 plus 3.

Row 1: Dc in 4th ch from hook, *ch 2, skip next 3 ch, (dc, ch 2, dc) in next ch, ch 2, skip next 3 ch**, dc in each of next 3 ch; rep from * across, ending last rep at **, dc in each of last 2 ch, turn.

Row 2: Ch 3 (counts as dc), skip first dc, dc in next dc, *ch 3, sl st in 3rd ch from hook (picot), skip next ch-2 space, 7 dc in next ch-2 space, picot, skip next ch-2 space**, dc in each of next 3 dc; rep from * across, ending last rep at **, dc in next dc, dc in 3rd ch of turning ch, turn.

Row 3: Ch 3 (counts as dc), skip first dc, dc in next dc, *ch 2, skip next 3 dc, (dc, ch 1, dc) in next dc, ch 2, skip next picot**, dc in each of next 3 dc; rep from * across, ending last rep at **, dc in next dc, dc in 3rd ch of turning ch, turn.

Row 4: Ch 3 (counts as dc), skip first dc, dc in next dc, *2 dc in next ch-2 space, dc in next dc, dc in next ch-1 space, dc in next dc, 2 dc in next ch-2 space**, dc in each of next 3 dc; rep from * across, ending last rep at **, dc in next dc, dc in 3rd ch of turning ch, turn.

Row 5: Ch 3 (counts as dc), skip first dc, dc in next dc, *ch 2, skip next 3 dc, (dc, ch 2, dc) in next dc, ch 2, skip next 3 dc**, dc in each of next 3 dc; rep from * across, ending last rep at **, dc in next dc, dc in 3rd ch of turning ch, turn.

Rep Rows 2-5 for pattern.

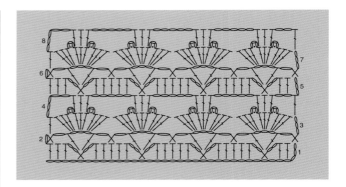

291

Chain multiples of 8 plus 3.

Row 1: Dc in 4th ch from hook, dc in next ch, *ch 2, skip next ch, sc in next ch, ch 2, skip next ch**, dc in each of next 5 ch; rep from * across, ending last rep at **, dc in each of last 3 ch, turn.

Row 2: Ch 1, sc in first dc, *ch 1, skip next ch-2 space, (dc, ch 3, dc) in next sc, ch 1, skip next 2 dc, sc in next dc; rep from * across, ending with last sc in 3rd ch of turning ch, turn.

Row 3: Ch 3 (counts as dc), skip next ch-1 space, *(3 dc, ch 3, sl st in 3rd ch from hook [picot], 3 dc, picot, 3 dc) in next ch-3 loop**, skip next 2 ch-1 spaces; rep from * across, ending last rep at **, skip next ch-1 space, dc in last sc, turn.

Row 4: Ch 5 (counts as dc, ch 2), skip next picot, dc in each of next 3 dc, *ch 5, skip next 2 picots, dc in each of next 3 dc; rep from * across to within last picot, ch 2, skip next 3 dc, dc in 3rd ch of turning ch, turn.

Row 5: Ch 3 (counts as dc), 2 dc in next ch-2 space, *ch 2, skip next dc, sc in next dc, ch 2**, 5 dc in next ch-5 loop; rep from * across, ending last rep at **, 2 dc in next ch-2 space of turning ch, dc in 3rd ch of turning ch, turn.

Rep Rows 2-5 for pattern

292

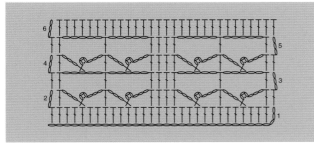

Chain multiples of 15 plus 2.

Row 1: Dc in 4th ch from hook, dc in each ch across, turn.

Row 2: Ch 3 (counts as dc), skip in first dc, dc in next dc, *(ch 3, skip next 2 sts, sc in next st, ch 3, sl st in 3rd ch from hook [picot], ch 3, skip next 2 sts, dc in next dc) twice**, dc in each of next 3 dc; rep from * across, ending last rep at **, dc in 3rd ch of turning ch, turn.

Row 3: Ch 3 (counts as dc), skip first dc, dc in next dc, *(ch 5, skip next 2 ch-3 loops, dc in next dc) twice**, dc in each of next 3 dc; rep from * across, ending last rep at **, dc in 3rd ch of turning ch, turn.

Rows 4-5: Rep Rows 2-3.

Row 6: Ch 3 (counts as dc), skip first dc, dc in next dc, *(5 dc in next ch-5 loop, dc in next dc) twice**, dc in each of next 3 dc; rep from * across, ending last rep at **, dc in 3rd ch of turning ch, turn.

Rep Rows 2-6 for pattern.

293

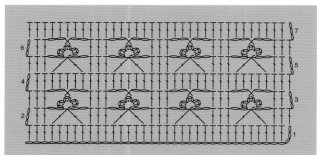

Chain multiples of 8 plus 5.

Row 1: Dc in 4th ch from hook, dc in each ch across, turn.

Row 2: Ch 3 (counts as dc), skip in first dc, dc in each of next 2 dc, *ch 2, work 2-dc cluster, working first half-closed dc in next dc, skip next 3 dc, work 2nd half-closed dc in next dc, complete 2-dc cluster, (ch 3, sl st in 3rd ch from hook [picot]) 3 times, sl st in last cluster made, ch 2, dc in each of next 3 dc; rep from * across, ending with last dc in 3rd ch of turning ch, turn.

Row 3: Ch 3 (counts as dc), skip first dc, dc in each of next 2 dc, *ch 2, skip next picot, sc in next picot, ch 2, skip next ch-2 space, dc in each of next 3 dc; rep from * across, ending with last dc in 3rd ch of turning ch, turn.

Row 4: Ch 3 (counts as dc), skip first dc, dc in each of next 2 dc, *2 dc in next ch-2 space, dc in next sc, 2 dc in next ch-2 space, dc in each of next 3 dc; rep from * ending with last dc in 3rd ch of turning ch, turn.

Rep Rows 2-4 for pattern.

294

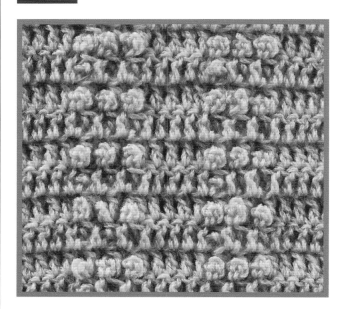

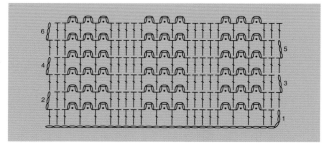

Chain multiples of 10 plus 3.

Row 1: Dc in 4th ch from hook, dc in next ch, *(ch 3, sl st in 3rd ch from hook [picot], skip next ch, dc in next ch) 3 times**, dc in each of next 4 ch; rep from * across, ending last rep at **, dc in each of last 2 ch, turn.

Row 2: Ch 3 (counts as dc), skip in first dc, dc in each of next 2 dc, (picot, dc in next dc) 3 times**, dc in each of next 4 dc; rep from * across, ending last rep at **, dc in next dc, dc in 3rd ch of turning ch, turn.

Rep Row 2 for pattern.

295

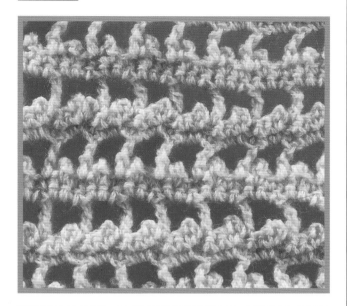

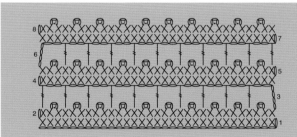

Chain multiples of 3 plus 2.

Row 1: Sc in 2nd ch from hook, sc in each ch across, turn.

Row 2: Ch 1, sc in first 2 sc, *ch 3, sl st in 3rd ch from hook (picot)**, sc in each of next 3 sc; rep from * across, ending last rep at **, sc in each of last 2 sc, turn.

Row 3: Ch 6 (counts as tr, ch 2), skip first sc, *skip next (sc, picot, sc), tr in next sc**, ch 2; rep from * across, ending last rep at **, turn.

Row 4: Ch 1, sc in first tr, *2 sc in next ch-2 space, sc in next tr; rep from * across, ending with last sc in 4th ch of turning ch, turn.

Rep Rows 2-4 for pattern.

296

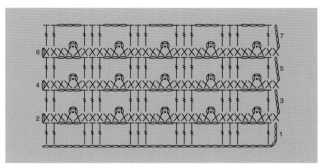

Chain multiples of 6 plus 4.

Row 1: Tr in 5th ch from hook, *ch 3, skip next 3 ch, tr in each of next 3 ch; rep from * across, ending with tr in each of last 2 ch, turn.

Row 2: Ch 1, sc in first 2 tr, *(2 sc, ch 3, sl st in 3rd ch from hook [picot], sc) in next ch-3 loop**, sc in each of next 3 tr; rep from * across, ending last rep at **, sc in next tr, sc in 4th ch of turning ch, turn.

Row 3: Ch 4 (counts as tr), skip first sc, tr in next sc, *ch 3, skip next (sc, picot, 2 sc)**, tr in each of next 3 sc; rep from * across, ending last rep at **, tr in each of last 2 sc, turn.

Rep Rows 2-3 for pattern.

297

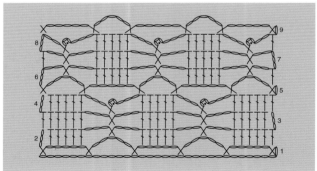

Chain multiples of 12 plus 8.

Row 1: Sc in 2nd ch from hook, *ch 5, skip next 5 ch, sc in next ch; rep from * across, turn.

Row 2: Ch 3 (counts as dc), 5 dc in next ch-5 loop, *ch 3, sc in next ch-5 loop, ch 3, 5 dc in next ch-5 loop; rep from * across to last ch-5 loop, dc in last sc, turn.

Row 3: Ch 3 (counts as dc), skip first dc, dc in each of next 5 dc, *ch 3, skip next ch-3 loop, sc in next sc, ch 3, skip next ch-3 loop, dc in each of next 5 dc; rep from * across to turning ch, dc in 3rd ch of turning ch, turn.

Row 4: Ch 3 (counts as dc), skip first dc, dc in each of next 5 dc, *ch 3, skip next ch-3 loop, sc in next sc, ch 3, sl st in 3rd ch from hook (picot), ch 3, skip next ch-3 loop, dc in each of next 5 dc; rep from * across to turning ch, dc in 3rd ch of turning ch, turn.

Row 5: Ch 1, sc in first dc, ch 5, skip next 4 dc, sc in next dc, *ch 5, skip next 2 ch-3 loops, sc in next dc, ch 5, skip next 3 dc,

sc in next dc; rep from * across, ending with last sc in 3rd ch of turning ch, turn.

Row 6: Ch 5 (counts as dc, ch 2), sc in next ch-5 loop, ch 3, *5 dc in next ch-5 loop, ch 3, sc in next ch-5 loop**, ch 3; rep from * across, ending last rep at **, ch 2, dc in last sc, turn.

Row 7: Ch 5 (counts as dc, ch 2), skip next ch-2 space, sc in next sc, ch 3, *dc in each of next 5 dc, ch 3, skip next ch-3 loop, sc in next sc**, ch 3, skip next ch-3 loop; rep from * across, ending last rep at **, ch 2, dc in 3rd ch of turning ch, turn.

Row 8: Ch 5 (counts as dc, ch 2), skip next ch-2 space, sc in next sc, picot, *ch 3, skip next ch-3 loop, dc in each of next 5 dc, ch 3, skip next ch-3 loop, sc in next sc, picot; rep from * across to turning ch, ch 2, dc in 3rd ch of turning ch, turn.

Row 9: Ch 1, sc in first dc, *ch 5, skip next 2 ch-3 loops, *sc in next dc, ch 5, skip next 3 dc, sc in next dc; rep from * across to within last 2 loops, ch 5, skip next ch-3 loop and picot, sc in 3rd ch of turning ch, turn.

Rep Rows 2-9 for pattern.

298

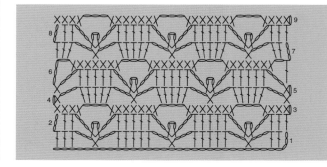

Chain multiples of 10 plus 3.

Row 1: Dc in 4th ch from hook, dc in next ch, *ch 3, skip next 2 ch, sc in next ch, ch 3, skip next 2 ch, dc in each of next 5 ch; rep from * across, ending with dc in each of last 3 ch, turn.

Row 2: Ch 3 (counts as dc), skip first dc, dc in each of next 2 dc, *ch 3, skip next ch-3 loop, (sc, ch 3, sc) in next sc, ch 3, skip next ch-3 loop**, dc in each of next 5 dc; rep from * across, ending last rep at **, dc in each of next 2 dc, dc in 3rd ch of turning ch, turn.

Row 3: Ch 1, sc in first 3 dc, *sc in next ch-3 loop, ch 3, skip next ch-3 loop, sc in next ch-3 loop**, sc in each of next 5 dc; rep from * across, ending last rep at **, sc in each of next 2 dc, sc in 3rd ch of turning ch, turn.

Row 4: Ch 1, sc in first sc, *ch 3, skip next 3 sc, 5 dc in next ch-3 loop, ch 3, skip next 3 sc, sc in next sc; rep from * across, turn.

Row 5: Ch 1, sc in first sc, *ch 3, skip next ch-3 loop, dc in each of next 5 dc, ch 3, skip next ch-3 loop**, (sc, ch 3, sc) in next sc; rep from * across, ending last rep at **, sc in last sc, turn.

Row 6: Ch 4 (counts as dc, ch 1), *sc in next ch-3 loop, sc in each of next 5 dc, sc in next ch-3 loop**, ch 3; rep from * across, ending last rep at **, ch 1, dc in last sc, turn.

Row 7: Ch 3 (counts as dc), 2 dc in next ch-1 space, *ch 3, skip next 3 sc, sc in next sc, ch 3, skip next 3 sc**, 5 dc in next ch-3 loop; rep from * across, ending last rep at **, 2 dc in next ch-1 space of turning ch, dc in 3rd ch of turning ch, turn.

Rep Rows 2-7 for pattern.

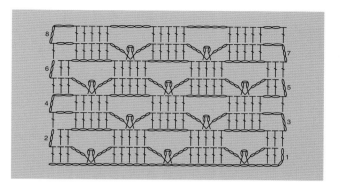

Chain multiples of 10 plus 3.

Row 1: Dc in 4th ch from hook, dc in next ch, *ch 3, skip next 2 ch, (sc, ch 3, sc) in next ch, ch 3, skip next 2 ch, dc in each of next 5 ch; rep from * across, ending with dc in each of last 3 ch, turn.

Row 2: Ch 3 (counts as dc), skip first dc, dc in each of next 2 dc, *ch 5, skip next 3 ch-3 loops**, dc in each of next 5 dc; rep from * across, ending last rep at **, dc in each of next 2 dc, dc in 3rd ch of turning ch, turn.

Row 3: Ch 5 (counts as dc, ch 2), skip first 3 dc, *5 dc in next ch-5 loop**, ch 3, skip next 2 dc, (sc, ch 3, sc) in next dc, ch 3, skip next 2 dc; rep from * across, ending last rep at **, ch 2, skip next 2 dc, dc in 3rd ch of turning ch, turn.

Row 4: Ch 5 (counts as dc, ch 2), skip next ch-2 space, *dc in each of next 5 dc**, ch 5, skip next 3 ch-3 loops; rep from * across, ending last rep at **, ch 2, dc in 3rd ch of turning ch, turn.

Row 5: Ch 3 (counts as dc), 2 dc in next ch-2 space, *ch 3, skip next 2 dc, (sc, ch 3, sc) in next dc, ch 3, skip next 2 dc**, 5 dc in next ch-5 loop; rep from * across, ending last rep at **, 2 dc in ch-2 space of turning ch, dc in 3rd ch of turning ch, turn.

Rep Rows 2-5 for pattern.

299

300

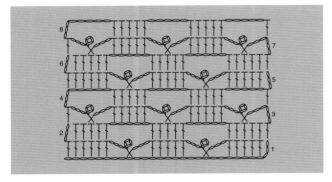

Chain multiples of 10 plus 9.

Row 1: Dc in 4th ch from hook, dc in each of next 4 ch, *ch 3, skip next 2 ch, sc in next ch, ch 4, drop loop from hook, insert hook in first of 4 ch, pick up dropped loop (picot), ch 3, skip next 2 ch, dc in each of next 5 ch; rep from * across to last ch, dc in last ch, turn.

Row 2: Ch 3 (counts as dc), skip first dc, dc in each of next 5 dc, *ch 5, skip next 3 loops, dc in each of next 5 dc; rep from * across to turning ch, dc in 3rd ch of turning ch, turn.

Row 3: Ch 6 (counts as dc, ch 3), skip first 3 dc, *sc in next dc, picot, ch 3, skip next 2 dc**, 5 dc in next ch-5 loop, ch 3, skip next 2 dc; rep from * across, ending last rep at **, dc in 3rd ch of turning ch, turn.

Row 4: Ch 8 (counts as dc, ch 5), skip next 3 loops, *dc in each of next 5 dc, ch 5, skip next 3 loops; rep from * across to turning ch, dc in 3rd ch of turning ch, turn.

Row 5: Ch 3 (counts as dc), *5 dc in next ch-5 loop**, ch 3, skip next 2 dc, sc in next dc, picot, ch 3, skip next 2 dc; rep from * across, ending last rep at **, dc in 3rd ch of turning ch, turn.

Rep Rows 2-5 for pattern.

301

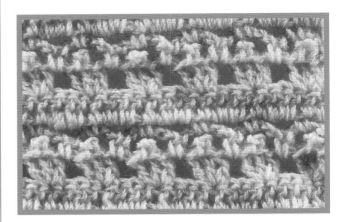

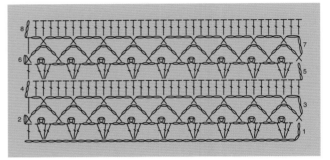

Chain multiples of 4 plus 3.

Row 1: (2 dc, ch 3, sl st in 3rd ch from hook [picot], dc) in 5th ch from hook (shell), *ch 2, skip next 3 ch, (2 dc, picot, dc) in next ch (shell); rep from * across to within last 2 ch, skip next ch, dc in last ch, turn.

Row 2: Ch 1, sc in first dc, *ch 5, skip next shell, sc in next ch-2 space; rep from * across, ending with last sc in top of turning ch, turn.

Row 3: Ch 3 (counts as hdc, ch 1), sc in next ch-5 loop, (ch 5, sc) in each ch-5 loop across to last ch-5 loop, ch 1, hdc in last sc, turn.

Row 4: Ch 3 (counts as dc), dc in next ch-1 space, dc in next sc, *3 dc in next ch-3 loop, dc in next sc; rep from * across to turning ch, dc in ch-1 space of turning ch, dc in 2nd ch of turning ch, turn.

Row 5: Ch 3 (counts as dc), skip first 2 dc, *(2 dc, picot, dc) in next dc (shell)**, ch 2, skip next 3 dc; rep from * across, ending last rep at **, skip next dc, dc in 3rd ch of turning ch, turn.

Rep Rows 2-5 for pattern.

302

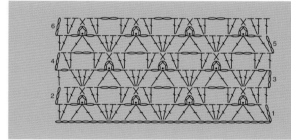

Chain multiples of 7 plus 4.

Row 1: Dc in 4th ch from hook, *ch 1, skip next ch, work 2-dc cluster, working first half-closed dc in next ch, skip next 2 ch, work 2nd half-closed dc in next ch, 2-dc complete cluster, ch 4, sl st in 4th ch from hook (picot), ch 1, skip next ch**, 4 dc in next ch; rep from * across, ending last rep at **, 2 dc in last ch, turn.

Row 2: Ch 3 (counts as dc), skip first dc, *2 dc in next dc, skip next ch-1 space, sc in next picot, skip next ch-1 space, 2 dc in next dc**, ch 2, skip next 2 dc; rep from * across, ending last rep at **, dc in 3rd ch of turning ch, turn.

Row 3: Ch 3 (counts as dc), skip first dc, dc in next dc, ch 1, skip next dc, *4 dc in next sc, ch 1**, skip next dc, work 2-dc cluster, working first half-closed dc in next dc, skip next ch-2 space, work 2nd half-closed dc in next dc, complete 2-dc cluster, picot, ch 1, skip next dc; rep from * across, ending last rep at **, skip next 2 dc, dc in 3rd ch of turning ch, turn.

Row 4: Ch 3 (counts as dc), skip first dc, *2 dc in next dc, ch 2, skip next 2 dc, 2 dc in next dc, skip next ch-1 space**, sc in next picot, skip next ch-1 space; rep from * across, ending last rep at **, skip next dc, dc in 3rd ch of turning ch, turn.

Row 5: Ch 3 (counts as dc), dc in first dc, *ch 1, skip next dc, work 2-dc cluster, working first half-closed dc in next dc, skip next ch-2 space, work 2nd half-closed dc in next dc, complete cluster, picot, ch 1, skip next dc**, 4 dc in next sc; rep from * across, ending last rep at **, 2 dc in 3rd ch of turning ch, turn.

Rep Rows 2-5 for pattern.

303

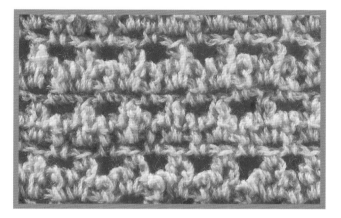

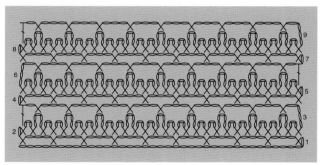

Chain multiples of 4 plus 2.

Row 1: Sc in 2nd ch from hook, *ch 3, skip next 3 ch, sc in next ch; rep from * across, turn.

Row 2: Ch 1, sc in first sc, *ch 3, (sc, ch 4, sc) in next ch-3 loop, ch 3, sc in next sc; rep from * across, turn.

Row 3: Ch 4 (counts as dc, ch 1), skip next ch-3 loop, sc in next ch-4 loop, *ch 3, skip next 2 ch-3 loops, sc in next ch-4 loop; rep from * across to last ch-4 loop, ch 1, skip next ch-3 loop, dc in last sc, turn.

Row 4: Ch 1, sc in first dc, (ch 3, sc) in each ch-3 loop across, ending with last sc in 3rd ch of turning ch, turn.

Rep Rows 2-4 for pattern.

304

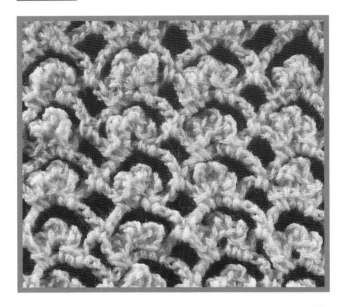

Chain multiples of 6 plus 5.

Row 1: Sc in 7th ch from hook, *ch 3, sl st in 3rd ch from hook (picot), work 2nd picot, sc in next ch, picot, sc in next ch**, ch 5, skip next 3 ch, sc in next ch; rep from * across, ending last rep at **, ch 2, skip next ch, dc in last ch, turn.

Row 2: Ch 1, sc in first dc, *ch 9, skip next 3 picots**, sc in next ch-5 loop; rep from * across, ending last rep at **, skip next 2 ch of turning ch, sc in next ch of turning ch, turn.

Row 3: Ch 5 (counts as dc, ch 2), *(sc, 2 picots, sc, picot, sc) in next ch-9 loop**, ch 5; rep from * across, ending last rep at **, ch 2, dc in last sc, turn.

Rep Rows 2-3 for pattern.

305

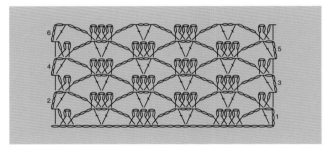

Chain multiples of 11.

Row 1: Dc in 5th ch from hook, ch 3, skip next 3 ch, *(sc, ch 3) in each of next 4 ch, skip next 3 ch, (dc, ch 2, dc) in next ch, ch 3, skip next 3 ch; rep from * across to within last 3 ch, sc in next ch, ch 3, sc in next ch, ch 1, hdc in last ch, turn.

Row 2: Ch 4 (counts as dc, ch 1), dc in first hdc, *ch 3, skip next 2 ch-3 loops, sc in next dc, ch 3**, (sc, ch 3, sc) in next ch-2 space, ch 3, sc in next dc, ch 3, skip next 2 ch-3 loops, (dc, ch 2, dc) in next ch-3 loop; rep from * across, ending last rep at **, sc in next ch-1 space of turning ch, ch 1, hdc in 3rd ch of turning ch, turn.

Rep Row 2 for pattern.

306

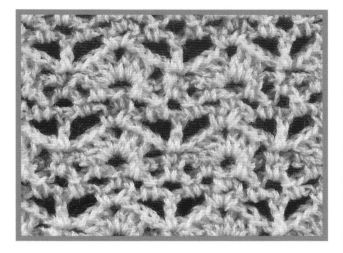

Chain multiples of 8 plus 2.

Row 1: Sc in 2nd ch from hook, *ch 1, skip next 3 ch, (3 dc, ch 2, 3 dc) in next ch, ch 1, skip next 3 ch, sc in next ch; rep from * across, turn.

Row 2: Ch 6 (counts as dc, ch 3), *skip next ch-1 space, (sc, ch 3, sc) in next ch-2 space, ch 3, skip next ch-1 space, dc in next sc**, ch 3; rep from * across, ending last rep at **, turn.

Row 3: Ch 3 (counts as hdc, ch 1), sc in next ch-3 loop, (ch 3, sc) in each ch-3 loop across to last ch-3 loop of turning ch, ch 1, hdc in 3rd ch of turning ch, turn.

Row 4: Ch 1, sc in first hdc, (ch 3, sc) in each ch-3 loop across, ending with last sc in 2nd ch of turning ch, turn.

Row 5: Ch 1, sc in first sc, *ch 1, skip next ch-3 loop, (3 dc, ch 2, 3 dc) in next ch-3 loop, ch 1, skip next ch-3 loop, sc in next sc; rep from * across, turn.

Rep Rows 2-5 for pattern.

307

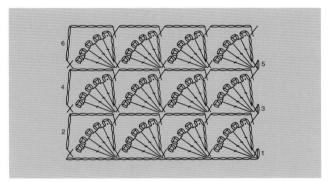

Chain multiples of 6 plus 2.

Row 1: (Sc, ch 3, ch 3 more, sl st in 3rd ch from hook [picot], [dc, picot] 4 times) in 2nd ch from hook, *skip next 5 ch, (sc, ch 3, picot, [dc, picot] 4 times) in next ch; rep from * across to within last 6 ch, skip next 5 ch, sc in last ch, turn.

Row 2: Ch 8 (counts as dc, ch 5), *skip next 5 picots, sc in top of next ch-3 loop; rep from * across, turn.

Row 3: Ch 1, (sc, ch 3, picot, [dc, picot] 4 times) in first sc, *skip next ch-5 loop, (sc, ch 3, picot, [dc, picot] 4 times) in next sc; rep from * across to turning ch, skip next 5 ch of turning ch, sc in next ch of turning ch, turn.

Rep Rows 2-3 for pattern.

308

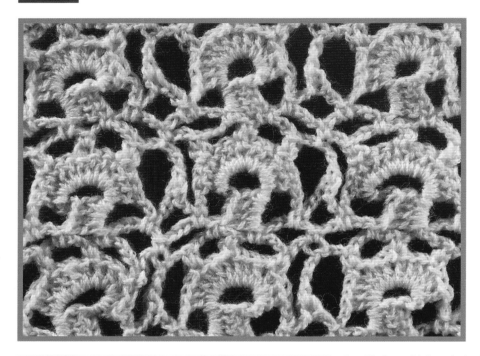

Chain multiples of 12 plus 2.

Row 1: Sc in 2nd ch from hook, *ch 5, skip next 3 ch, sc in next ch, ch 11, dc in 8th ch from hook, dc in each of next 3 ch, skip next 3 ch on foundation ch, sc in next ch, ch 5, skip next 3 ch, sc in next ch; rep from * across, turn.

Row 2: Ch 3 (counts as dc), ch 3 more, sl st in 3rd ch from hook (picot), ch 2, *sc in next ch-5 loop, ch 2, ([3 dc, picot] 3 times, 3 dc) in next ch-7 loop, ch 2, sc in next ch-5 loop**, ch 3, picot, ch 2; rep from * across, ending last rep at **, ch 2, picot, dc in last sc, turn.

Row 3: Ch 6 (counts as tr, ch 2), skip next 2 ch-2 spaces, *(sc, ch 5) in each of next 2 picots, sc in next picot, ch 2, skip next 2 ch-2 spaces, tr in next picot**, ch 2, skip next 2 spaces; rep from * across, ending last rep at **, turn.

Row 4: Ch 1, sc in first tr, skip next ch-2 space, *ch 5, sc in next ch-5 loop, ch 11, dc in 8th ch from hook, dc in each of next 3 ch, sc in next ch-5 loop, ch 5, skip next ch-2 space, sc in next tr; rep from * across, ending with last sc in 4th ch of turning ch, turn.

Rep Rows 2-4 for pattern.

.24.
Bobbles

309

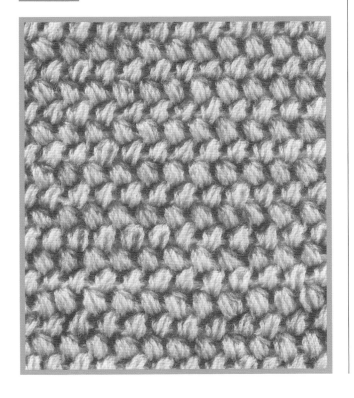

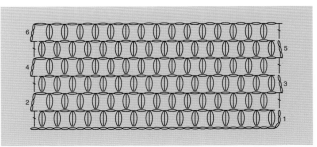

Bobble: *(Yo, insert hook in next st, yo, draw yarn through st and up to level of work) 3 times in same st, yo, draw yarn through 7 loops on hook.*

Chain multiples of 2 plus 1.

Row 1: Bobble in 4th ch from hook, *ch 1, skip next ch, bobble in next ch; rep from * across to within last ch, dc in last ch, turn.

Row 2: Ch 4 (counts as dc, ch 1), (bobble, ch 1) in each ch-1 space across to last ch-1 space, skip next bobble, dc in 3rd ch of turning ch, turn.

Row 3: Ch 3 (counts as dc), (bobble, ch 1) in each ch-1 space across to turning ch, bobble in ch-1 space of turning ch, dc in 3rd ch of turning ch, turn.

Rep Rows 2-3 for pattern.

310

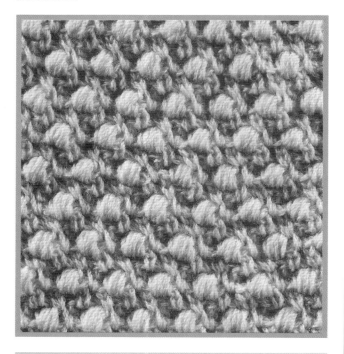

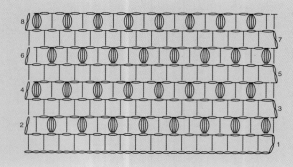

Bobble: *(Yo, insert hook in next st, yo, draw yarn through st and up to level of work) 5 times in same st, yo, draw yarn through 11 loops on hook.*

Chain multiples of 4 plus 3.

Row 1: Hdc in 5th ch from hook, *ch 1, skip next ch, hdc in next ch; rep from * across, turn.

Row 2: Ch 2 (counts as hdc), *hdc in next ch-1 space, ch 1, bobble in next ch-1 space**, ch 1; rep from * across, ending last rep at **, hdc in next ch of turning ch, turn.

Row 3: Ch 3 (counts as hdc, ch 1), (hdc, ch 1) in each ch-1 space across to turning ch, hdc in 2nd ch of turning ch, turn.

Row 4: Ch 2 (counts as hdc), *bobble in next ch-1 space, ch 1, hdc in next ch-1 space**, ch 1; rep from * across, ending last rep at **, hdc in 2nd ch of turning ch, turn.

Row 5: Rep Row 3.

Rep Rows 2-5 for pattern.

311

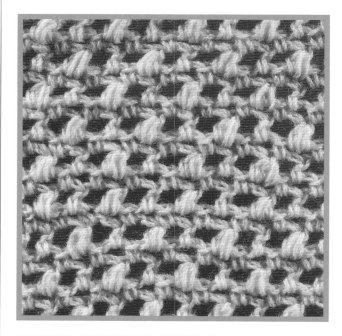

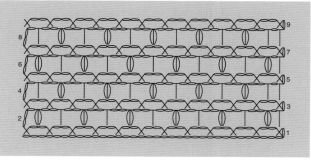

Bobble: *(Yo, insert hook in next st, yo, draw yarn through st and up to level of work) 3 times in same st, yo, draw yarn through 7 loops on hook.*

Chain multiples of 3 plus 2.

Row 1: Sc in 2nd ch from hook, *ch 2, skip next 2 ch, sc in next ch; rep from * across, turn.

Row 2: Ch 3 (counts as hdc, ch 1), bobble in next ch-2 space, *ch 2, hdc in next ch-2 space, ch 2, bobble in next ch-2 space; rep from * across to last ch-2 space, ch 1, hdc in last sc, turn.

Row 3: Ch 1, sc in first hdc, (ch 2, sc) in each ch-2 space across, ending with last sc in 2nd ch of turning ch, turn.

Row 4: Ch 3 (counts as hdc, ch 1), hdc in next ch-2 space, *ch 2, bobble in next ch-2 space, ch 2, hdc in next ch-2 space; rep from * across to last ch-2 space, ch 1, hdc in last sc, turn.

Row 5: Ch 1, sc in first hdc, skip next ch-1 space, (sc, ch 2) in each ch-2 space across to turning ch, sc in 2nd ch of turning ch, turn.

Rep Rows 2-5 for pattern.

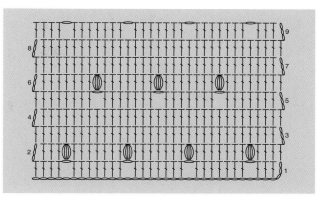

312

Bobble: (Yo, insert hook in next st, yo, draw yarn through st and up to level of work) 5 times in same st, yo, draw yarn through 11 loops on hook.

Chain multiples of 8 plus 3.

Row 1: Dc in 4th ch from hook, dc in each of next 2 ch, *ch 1, skip next ch, dc in each of next 7 ch; rep from * across to within last 5 ch, ch 1, skip next ch, dc in each of last 4 ch, turn.

Row 2: Ch 3 (counts as dc), skip first dc, dc in each of next 3 dc, *bobble in next ch-1 space, dc in each of next 7 dc; rep from * across to within last 5 sts, bobble in next ch-1 space, dc in each of next 3 dc, dc in 3rd ch of turning ch, turn.

Rows 3-4: Ch 3 (counts as dc), dc in each st across to turning ch, dc in 3rd ch of turning ch, turn.

Row 5: Ch 3 (counts as dc), skip first dc, *dc in each of next 7 dc**, ch 1, skip next dc; rep from * across, ending last rep at **, dc in 3rd ch of turning ch, turn.

Row 6: Ch 3 (counts as dc), skip first dc, *dc in each of next 7 dc**, bobble in next ch-1 space; rep from * across, ending last rep at **, dc in 3rd ch of turning ch, turn.

Rows 7-8: Rep Rows 3-4.

Row 9: Ch 3 (counts as dc), skip first dc, dc in each of next 3 dc, *ch 1, skip next dc**, dc in each of next 7 dc; rep from * across, ending last rep at **, dc in each of next 3 dc, dc in 3rd ch of turning ch, turn.

Rep Rows 2-9 for pattern.

313

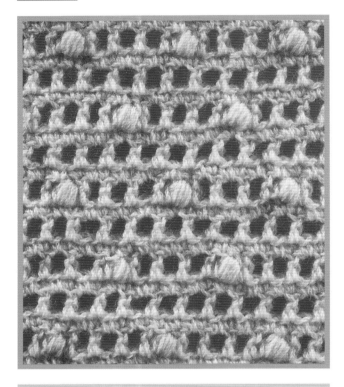

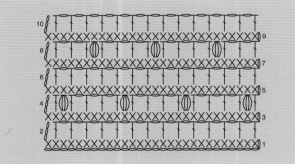

Bobble: (Yo, insert hook in next st, yo, draw yarn through st and up to level of work) 4 times in same st, yo, draw yarn through 9 loops on hook.

Chain multiples of 8 plus 5.

Row 1: Sc in 2nd ch from hook, sc in each ch across, turn.

Row 2: Ch 3 (counts as dc), skip first sc, dc in next sc, *ch 1, skip next sc, dc in next sc; rep from * across, turn.

Row 3: Ch 1, sc in each st and space across, sc in 3rd ch of turning ch, turn.

Row 4: Ch 3 (counts as dc), skip first sc, dc in next sc, *bobble in next sc, dc in next sc** (ch 1, skip next sc, dc in next sc) 3 times; rep from * across, ending last rep at **, turn.

Row 5: Rep Row 3.

Rows 6-7: Rep Rows 2-3.

Row 8: Ch 3 (counts as dc), skip first sc, dc in next sc, (ch 1, skip next sc, dc in next sc) twice, *bobble in next sc, dc in next sc** (ch 1, skip next sc, dc in next sc) 3 times; rep from * across, ending last rep at **, (ch 1, skip next sc, dc in next sc) twice, turn.

Row 9: Rep Row 3.

Rep Rows 2-9 for pattern.

314

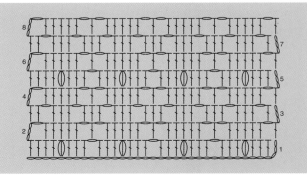

Bobble: *(Yo, insert hook in next st, yo, draw yarn through st and up to level of work) 3 times in same st, yo, draw yarn through 7 loops on hook.*

Chain multiples of 8 plus 3.

Row 1: Dc in 4th ch from hook, dc in each of next 2 ch, *bobble in next ch, dc in each of next 3 ch**, ch 1, skip next ch, dc in each of next 3 ch; rep from * across, ending last rep at **, dc in last ch, turn.

Row 2: Ch 4 (counts as dc, ch 1), skip first 2 dc, *dc in each of next 5 sts, ch 1, skip next dc**, dc in next ch-1 space, ch 1, skip next dc; rep from * across, ending last rep at **, dc in 3rd ch of turning ch, turn.

Row 3: Ch 3 (counts as dc), dc in next ch-1 space, *ch 1, skip next dc, dc in each of next 3 dc, ch 1, skip next dc, dc in next ch-1 space**, dc in next dc, dc in next ch-1 space; rep from * across, ending last rep at **, dc in 3rd ch of turning ch, turn.

Row 4: Ch 4 (counts as dc, ch 1), skip first 2 dc, *dc in next ch-1 space, dc in each of next 3 dc, dc in next ch-1 space, ch 1, skip next dc**, dc in next dc, ch 1, skip next dc; rep from * across, ending last rep at **, dc in 3rd ch of turning ch, turn.

Row 5: Ch 3 (counts as dc), *dc in next ch-1 space, dc in each of next 2 dc, bobble in next dc, dc in each of next 2 dc, dc in next ch-1 space**, ch 1; rep from * across, ending last rep at **, dc in 3rd ch of turning ch, turn.

Rep Rows 2-5 for pattern.

315

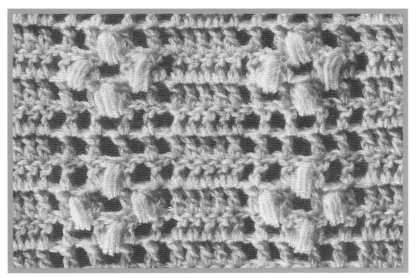

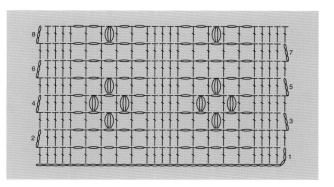

Bobble: *(Yo, insert hook in next st, yo, draw yarn through st and up to level of work) 4 times in same st, yo, draw yarn through 9 loops on hook.*

Chain multiples of 14 plus 7.

Row 1: Dc in 4th ch from hook, dc in each of next 3 ch, *(ch 1, skip next ch, dc in next ch) 5 times, dc in each of next 4 ch; rep from * across, turn.

Row 2: Ch 3 (counts as dc), skip first dc, dc in each of next 4 dc, *(ch 1, skip next st, dc in next dc) 5 times, dc in each of next 4 dc; rep from * across, ending with last dc in 3rd ch of turning ch, turn.

Row 3: Ch 3 (counts as dc), skip first dc, dc in each of next 4 dc, *(ch 1, dc) in each of next 2 dc, bobble in next ch-1 space, dc in next dc, (ch 1, dc) in each of next 2 dc, dc in each of next 4 dc; rep from * across, ending with last dc in 3rd ch of turning ch, turn.

Row 4: Ch 3 (counts as dc), skip first dc, dc in each of next 4 dc, *ch 1, dc in next dc, (bobble in next ch-1 space, dc in next dc, ch 1, skip next st, dc in next dc) twice, dc in each of next 4 dc; rep from * across, ending with last dc in 3rd ch of turning ch, turn.

Row 5: Rep Row 3.

Row 6: Rep Row 2.

Rep Rows 2-6 for pattern.

316

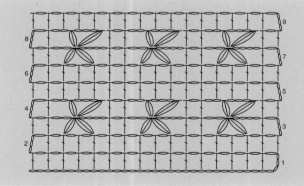

Chain multiples of 10 plus 6.

Row 1: Dc in 6th ch from hook, *ch 1, skip next ch, dc in next ch; rep from * across, turn.

Row 2: Ch 4 (counts as dc, ch 1), skip first ch-1 space, (dc, ch 1) in each dc across, skip next ch of turning ch, dc in next ch of turning ch, turn.

Row 3: Ch 4 (counts as dc, ch 1), skip first ch-1 space, dc in next dc, *ch 4, skip next ch-1 space, work cluster across next 5 sts, ch 2, skip next ch-1 space, dc in next dc, ch 1, dc in next dc; rep from * across, ending with last dc in 3rd ch of turning ch, turn.

Row 4: Ch 4 (counts as dc, ch 1), skip first ch-1 space, dc in next dc, *ch 2, (bobble, ch 3, bobble) in next cluster, skip next ch-4 loop, dc in next dc, ch 1, dc in next dc; rep from * across, ending with last dc in 3rd ch of turning ch, turn.

Row 5: Ch 4 (counts as dc, ch 1), skip first ch-1 space, dc in next dc, *ch 1, (dc, ch 1, dc) in next ch-3 loop, ch 1, dc in next ch-2 space, ch 1, dc in next dc, ch 1, dc in next dc; rep from * across, ending with last dc in 3rd ch of turning ch, turn.

Rep Rows 2-5 for pattern.

317

Bobble: *(Yo, insert hook in next st, yo, draw yarn through st and up to level of work) 3 times in same st, yo, draw yarn through 7 loops on hook.*

Cluster: *(Yo, insert hook in next st, yo, draw yarn through st and up to level of work) 3 times in next dc, skip next 2 ch-2 spaces, (yo, insert hook in next st, yo, draw yarn through st and up to level of work) 3 times in next dc, yo, draw yarn through 13 loops on hook.*

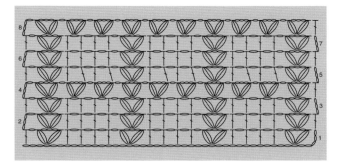

Bobble: (Yo, insert hook in next st, yo, draw yarn through st and up to level of work) 3 times in same st, yo, draw yarn through 7 loops on hook.

Chain multiples of 12 plus 9.

Row 1: (Bobble, ch 3, bobble) in 6th ch from hook, *ch 1, skip next 2 ch, dc in next ch**, (ch 1, skip next ch, dc in next ch) 3 times, skip next 2 ch, (bobble, ch 3, bobble) in next ch; rep from * across, ending last rep at **, turn.

Row 2: Ch 4 (counts as dc, ch 1), skip first ch-1 space, (bobble, ch 3, bobble) in next ch-3 loop, skip next bobble**, (dc, ch 1) in each of next 4 dc; rep from * across, ending last rep at **, dc in top of turning ch, turn.

Row 3: Ch 3 (counts as dc), *(bobble, ch 3, bobble) in next ch-3 loop**, skip next ch-1 space, (ch 1, dc) in each of next 4 dc; rep from * across, ending last rep at **, ch 1, dc in 3rd ch of turning ch, turn.

Row 4: Ch 4 (counts as dc, ch 1), skip first ch-1 space, *(bobble, ch 3, bobble) in next ch-3 loop**, ch 1, ([bobble, ch 3, bobble] in next ch-1 space, ch 1, skip next ch-1 space) twice; rep from * across, ending last rep at **, skip next bobble, dc in 3rd ch of turning ch, turn.

Row 5: Ch 3 (counts as dc), *(bobble, ch 3, bobble) in next ch-3 loop**, skip next ch-1 space, (ch 1, dc) in each of next 4 bobbles, skip next ch-1 space; rep from * across, ending last rep at **, ch 1, dc in 3rd ch of turning ch, turn.

Rep Rows 2-5 for pattern.

318

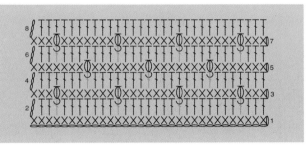

Front post bobble (FPbobble): (Yo, insert hook from front to back to front again around the post of next st, yo, draw yarn through st and up to level of work) 3 times around the post of same st, yo, draw yarn through 7 loops on hook.

Chain multiples of 8.

Row 1: Sc in 2nd ch from hook, sc in each ch across, turn.

Row 2: Ch 3 (counts as dc), skip first sc, dc in each st across, turn.

Row 3: Ch 1, sc in each of first 3 dc, *FPbobble around the post of next dc**, sc in each of next 7 dc; rep from * across, ending last rep at **, sc in each of next 2 dc, sc in 3rd ch of turning ch, turn.

Row 4: Rep Row 2.

Row 5: Ch 1, sc in each of first 7 dc, *FPbobble around the post of next dc, sc in each of next 7 dc; rep from * across, ending with last sc in 3rd ch of turning ch, turn.

Rep Rows 2-5 for pattern.

319

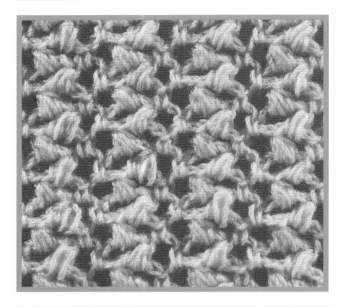

Bobble: *(Yo, insert hook in next st, yo, draw yarn through st and up to level of work) 3 times in same st, yo, draw yarn through 7 loops on hook.*

Chain multiples of 6 plus 2.

Row 1: Sc in 2nd ch from hook, *ch 3, skip next 2 ch, bobble in next ch, ch 3, skip next 2 ch, sc in next ch; rep from * across, turn.

Row 2: Ch 5 (counts as dc, ch 2), *sc in next ch-3 loop, ch 3, bobble in next ch-3 loop**, ch 3; rep from * across, ending last rep at **, dc in last sc, turn.

Row 3: Ch 1, sc in first dc, *ch 3, bobble in next ch-3 loop, ch 3, sc in next ch-3 loop; rep from * across, ending with last sc in 3rd ch of turning ch, turn.

Rep Rows 2-3 for pattern.

320

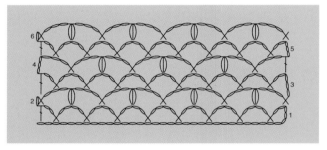

Bobble: *(Yo, insert hook in next st, yo, draw yarn through st and up to level of work) 3 times in same st, yo, draw yarn through 7 loops on hook.*

Chain multiples of 8 plus 5.

Row 1: Sc in 7th ch from hook, *ch 4, skip next 3 ch, sc in next ch; rep from * across to within last 2 ch, ch 2, skip next ch, dc in last ch, turn.

Row 2: Ch 1, sc in first dc, skip next ch-2 space, *ch 3, bobble in next ch-4 loop, ch 3**, sc in next ch-4 loop; rep from * across, ending last rep at **, skip next 2 ch of turning ch, sc in next ch of turning ch, turn.

Row 3: Ch 5 (counts as dc, ch 2), sc in next ch-3 loop, (ch 4, sc) in each ch-3 loop across to last ch-3 loop, ch 2, dc in last sc, turn.

Row 4: Ch 6 (counts as dc, ch 3), skip next ch-2 space, *sc in next ch-4 loop, ch 3**, bobble in next ch-4 loop, ch 3; rep from * across, ending last rep at **, dc in 3rd ch of turning ch, turn.

Row 5: Ch 5 (counts as dc, ch 2), sc in next ch-3 loop, (ch 4, sc) in each ch-3 loop across to last ch-3 loop of turning ch, ch 2, dc in 3rd ch of turning ch, turn.

Rep Rows 2-5 for pattern.

321

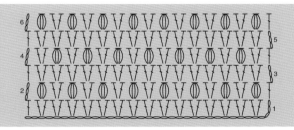

Bobble: *(Yo, insert hook in next st, yo, draw yarn through st and up to level of work) 4 times in same st, yo, draw yarn through 9 loops on hook.*

Chain multiples of 4 plus 3.

Row 1: 2 dc in 5th ch from hook, *skip next ch, 2 dc in next ch; rep from * across to within last 2 ch, skip next ch, dc in last ch, turn.

Row 2: Ch 3 (counts as dc), skip first 2 dc, *bobble bet last skipped and next dc**, skip next 2 dc, 2 dc bet last skipped and next dc, skip next 2 dc; rep from * across, ending last rep at **, skip next dc, dc in top of turning ch, turn.

Row 3: Ch 3 (counts as dc), skip first dc, *2 dc in next bobble**, skip next dc, 2 dc bet last skipped and next dc, skip next dc; rep from * across, ending last rep at **, dc in 3rd ch of turning ch, turn.

Row 4: Ch 3 (counts as dc), skip first 2 dc, *2 dc bet last skipped and next dc**, skip next 2 dc, bobble bet last skipped and next dc, skip next 2 dc; rep from * across, ending last rep at **, skip next dc, dc in 3rd ch of turning ch, turn.

Row 5: Ch 3 (counts as dc), skip first 2 dc, *2 dc bet last skipped and next dc**, 2 dc in next bobble, skip next dc; rep from * across, ending last rep at **, skip next dc, dc in 3rd ch of turning ch, turn.

Rep Rows 2-5 for pattern.

322

Bobble: *(Yo, insert hook in next st, yo, draw yarn through st and up to level of work) 3 times in same st, yo, draw yarn through 7 loops on hook.*

Chain multiples of 6 plus 2.

Row 1: Sc in 2nd ch from hook, *ch 3, skip next 2 ch, (dc, ch 1, dc) in next ch, ch 3, skip next 2 ch, sc in next ch; rep from * across, turn.

Row 2: Ch 6 (counts as dc, ch 3), skip next ch-3 loop, *sc in next ch-1 space, ch 3, skip next ch-3 loop, bobble in next sc**, ch 3, skip next ch-3 loop; rep from * across, ending last rep at **, turn.

Row 3: Ch 1, sc in first bobble, *ch 3, skip next ch-3 loop, (dc, ch 1, dc) in next sc, ch 3, skip next ch-3 loop, sc in next bobble; rep from * across, ending with last sc in 3rd ch of turning ch, turn.

Rep Rows 2-3 for pattern.

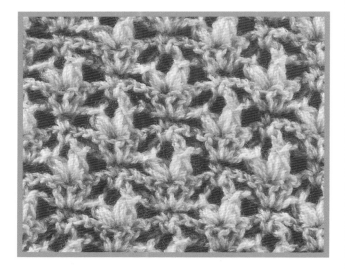

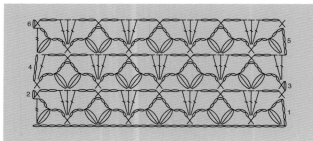

Bobble: (Yo, insert hook in next st, yo, draw yarn through st and up to level of work) 3 times in same st, yo, draw yarn through 7 loops on hook.

Chain multiples of 8 plus 7.

Row 1: Bobble in 7th ch from hook, *ch 3, skip next 3 ch, sc in next ch, ch 3, skip next 3 ch**, (bobble, ch 5, bobble) in next ch; rep from * across, ending last rep at **, (bobble, ch 2, tr) in last ch, turn.

Row 2: Ch 1, sc in first tr, skip next ch-2 space, *ch 2, skip next ch-3 loop, 3 dc in next sc, ch 2, skip next ch-3 loop, sc in next ch-5 loop; rep from * across, ending with last sc in 4th ch of turning ch, turn.

Row 3: Ch 1, sc in first sc, *ch 3, skip next ch-2 space, skip next dc, (bobble, ch 5, bobble) in next dc, ch 3, skip next ch-2 space, sc in next sc; rep from * across, turn.

Row 4: Ch 3 (counts as dc), dc in first sc, *ch 2, skip next ch-3 loop, sc in next ch-5 loop, ch 2, skip next ch-3 loop**, 3 dc in next sc; rep from * across, ending last rep at **, 2 dc in last sc, turn.

Row 5: Ch 6 (counts as tr, ch 2), bobble in first dc, *ch 3, skip next ch-2 space, sc in next sc, ch 3, skip next ch-2 space, skip next dc**, (bobble, ch 5, bobble) in next dc; rep from * across, ending last rep at **, (bobble, ch 2, tr) in 4th ch of turning ch, turn.

Rep Rows 2-5 for pattern.

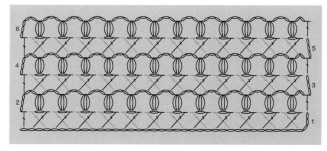

Bobble: (Yo, insert hook in next st, yo, draw yarn through st and up to level of work) 4 times in same st, yo, draw yarn through 9 loops on hook.

Chain multiples of 3 plus 1.

Row 1: Dc in 6th ch from hook, ch 1, working over last dc made, skip next ch to the right, dc in next ch to the right (crossed dc made), *skip next 2 ch, dc in next ch, ch 1, working over last dc made, dc in first skipped ch; rep from * across to within last ch, dc in last ch, turn.

Row 2: Ch 5 (counts as dc, ch 2), bobble in next ch-1 space, (ch 3, bobble) in each ch-1 space across to last ch-1 space, ch 2, dc in top of turning ch, turn.

Row 3: Ch 3 (counts as dc), skip next ch-2 space, dc in next ch-3 loop, ch 1, working over last dc made, dc in last skipped ch-2 space, *dc in next ch-3 loop, ch 1, working over last dc made, dc in last ch-3 loop (crossed dc made); rep from * across to turning ch, dc in 3rd ch of turning ch, turn.

Rep Rows 2-3 for pattern.

325

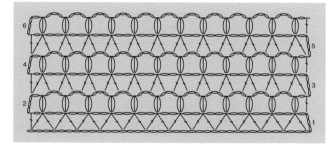

Bobble: (Yo, insert hook in next st, yo, draw yarn through st and up to level of work) 3 times in same st, yo, draw yarn through 7 loops on hook.

2-Dc Cluster: : (Yo, insert hook in next st, yo, draw yarn through st, yo, draw yarn through 2 loops on hook) twice in designated sts, yo, draw yarn through 3 loops on hook.

Chain multiples of 3 plus 1.

Row 1: Work 2-dc cluster, with first half-closed dc in 5th ch from hook, skip next 2 ch, work 2nd half closed dc in next ch, yo, complete cluster, *ch 2, work 2-dc cluster, working first half-closed dc in same ch holding last dc, skip next 2 ch, work 2nd half-closed dc in next ch, yo, complete cluster; rep from * across to last ch, ch 1, dc in last ch, turn.

Row 2: Ch 4 (counts as dc, ch 1), skip next ch-1 space, bobble in next cluster, *ch 3, skip next ch-2 space, bobble in next cluster; rep from * across to turning ch, ch1, dc in 3rd ch of turning ch, turn.

Row 3: Ch 4 (counts as dc, ch 1), work 2-dc cluster, working first half-closed dc in first dc, skip next ch-1 space, work 2nd half-closed dc in next ch-3 loop, yo, complete cluster, *ch 2, work 2-dc cluster, working first half-closed dc in same ch-3 loop holding last dc, work 2nd half-closed dc in next ch-3 loop, yo complete cluster; rep from * across, working last half-closed dc in 3rd ch of turning ch, ch 1, dc in 3rd ch of turning ch, turn.

Rep Rows 2-3 for pattern.

326

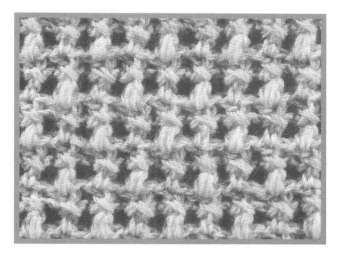

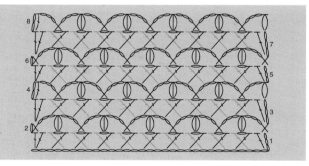

3-looped bobble: (Yo, insert hook in next st, yo, draw yarn through st and up to level of work) 3 times in same st, yo, draw yarn through 7 loops on hook.

2-looped bobble: (Yo, insert hook in next st, yo, draw yarn through st and up to level of work) twice in same st, yo, draw yarn through 5 loops on hook.

Chain multiples of 3 plus 1.

Row 1: Dc in 4th ch from hook, skip next 3 ch, *dc in next ch, ch 1, working over last dc, skip next ch to the right, dc in next ch to the right (crossed dc made), skip next 2 ch; rep from * across to within last 2 ch, skip next ch, 2 dc in last ch, turn.

Row 2: Ch 1, sc in first dc, *ch 3, bobble in next ch-1 space, ch 3, sc in next ch-1 space; rep from * across, ending with last sc in 3rd ch of turning ch, turn.

Row 3: Ch 3 (counts as dc), dc in first sc, skip next ch-3 loop, *dc in next ch-3 loop, ch 1, working over last dc, dc in next ch-3 loop to the right (crossed dc made); rep from * across to last ch-3 loop, 2 dc in last sc, turn.

Row 4: ch 3 (counts as dc), dc in first dc, *ch 3, sc in next ch-1 space, ch 3**, bobble in next ch-1 space; rep from * across, ending last rep at **, 2-looped bobble in 3rd ch of turning ch, turn.

Row 5: Ch 3 (counts as dc), dc in first bobble, skip next ch-3 loop, *dc in next ch-3 loop, ch 1, working over last dc, dc in next ch-3 loop to the right (crossed dc made); rep from * across to last ch-3 loop, skip next dc, 2 dc in 3rd ch of turning ch, turn.

Rep Rows 2-5 for pattern.

327

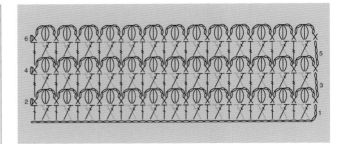

Bobble: (Yo, insert hook in next st, yo, draw yarn through st and up to level of work) 3 times in same st, yo, draw yarn through 7 loops on hook.

Chain multiples of 3.

Row 1: Dc in 5th ch from hook, working over last dc made, dc in next ch to the right (crossed dc made), *dc in next ch, skip next ch, dc in next ch, working over last dc, dc in last skipped ch (crossed dc made); rep from * across to within last ch, dc in last ch, turn.

Row 2: Ch 1, sc in first dc, *ch 2, skip next dc, bobble bet last skipped and next dc, ch 3, skip next dc, sc in next dc; rep from * across, ending with last sc in top of turning ch, turn.

Row 3: Ch 4 (counts as tr), *skip next ch-3 loop, dc in next ch-3 loop, working over last dc, dc in last skipped ch-3 loop (crossed dc made), tr in next sc; rep from * across, turn.

Rep Rows 2-3 for pattern.

328

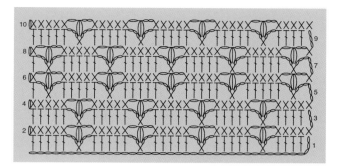

Bobble: (Yo, insert hook in next st, yo, draw yarn through st and up to level of work) 3 times in same st, yo, draw yarn through 7 loops on hook.

Chain multiples of 8 plus 7.

Row 1: Dc in 4th ch from hook, dc in each of next 3 ch, *ch 3, skip next ch, sc in next ch, ch 3, skip next ch, dc in each of next 5 ch; rep from * across, turn.

Row 2: Ch 1, sc in each of first 5 dc, *ch 1, skip next ch-3 loop, bobble in next sc, ch 2, skip next ch-3 loop, sc in each of next 5 dc; rep from * across, ending with last sc in 3rd ch of turning ch, turn.

Row 3: Ch 3 (counts as dc), skip first sc, dc in each of next 4 sc, *ch 3, skip next ch-2 space, sc in next bobble, ch 3, skip next ch-1 space, dc in each of next 5 sc; rep from * across, turn.

Row 4: Rep Row 2.

Row 5: Ch 6 (counts as dc, ch 3), skip first 2 sc, *sc in next sc, ch 3, skip next sc, dc in next sc**, dc in next ch-2 space, dc in next bobble, dc in next ch-1 space, dc in next sc, ch 3, skip next sc; rep from * across, ending last rep at **, turn.

Row 6: Ch 1, sc in first dc, *ch 1, skip next ch-3 loop, bobble in next sc, ch 2, skip next ch-3 loop**, sc in each of next 5 dc; rep from * across, ending last rep at **, sc in 3rd ch of turning ch, turn.

Row 7: Ch 6 (counts as dc, ch 3), skip next ch-2 space, *sc in next bobble, ch 3, skip next ch-1 space**, dc in each of next 5 sc, ch 3, skip next ch-2 space; rep from * across, ending last rep at **, dc in last sc, turn.

Row 8: Rep Row 6.

Row 9: Ch 3 (counts as dc), *dc in next ch-2 space, dc in next bobble, dc in next ch-1 space, dc in next sc**, ch 3, skip next sc, sc in next sc, ch 3, skip next sc, dc in next sc; rep from * across, ending last rep at **, turn.

Rep Rows 2-9 for pattern.

329

Bobble: (Yo, insert hook in next st, yo, draw yarn through st and up to level of work) 3 times in same st, yo, draw yarn through 7 loops on hook.

Chain multiples of 4 plus 2.

Row 1: Sc in 2nd ch from hook, *ch 4, bobble in last sc made, skip next 3 ch, sc in next ch; rep from * across, turn.

Row 2: Ch 3 (counts as dc), dc in first sc, *skip next ch-4 loop, 4 dc in next sc; rep from * across, ending with 3 dc in last sc, turn.

Row 3: Ch 1, sc in first dc, *ch 4, bobble in last sc made, skip next 3 dc, sc in next dc; rep from * across, turn.

Rep Rows 2-3 for pattern.

330

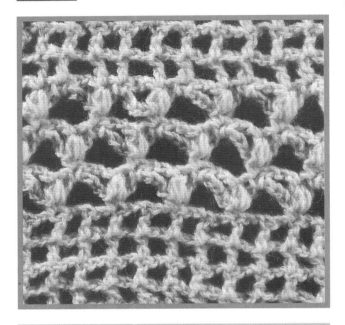

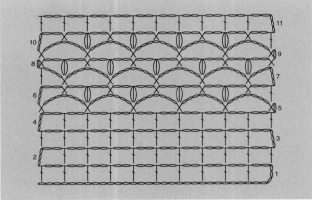

Row 6: Ch 5 (counts as dc, ch 2), *sc in next ch-7 loop, ch 2**, bobble in next sc, ch 2; rep from * across, ending last rep at **, dc in last sc, turn.

Row 7: Ch 6 (counts as dc, ch 3), skip next ch-2 space, sc in next sc, *ch 7, skip next 2 ch-2 spaces, sc in next sc; rep from * across to last sc, ch 3, dc in 3rd ch of turning ch, turn.

Row 8: Ch 1, sc in first dc, *ch 2, skip next ch-3 loop, bobble in next sc, ch 2, sc in next ch-7 loop; rep from * across, ending with last sc in 3rd ch of turning ch, turn.

Row 9: Ch 1, sc in first sc, *ch 7, skip next 2 ch-2 spaces, sc in next sc; rep from * across, turn.

Row 10: Rep Row 6.

Row 11: Ch 5 (counts as dc, ch 2), skip next ch-2 space, *dc in next sc, ch 2, skip next ch-2 space**, dc in next bobble, ch 2; rep from * across, ending last rep at **, dc in 3rd ch of turning ch, turn.

Rep Rows 2-11 for pattern.

331

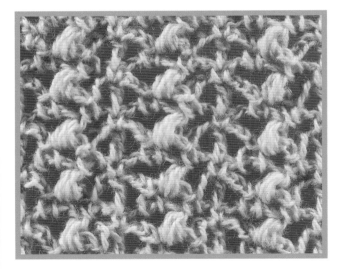

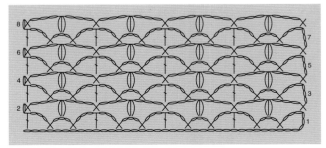

Bobble: (Yo, insert hook in next st, yo, draw yarn through st and up to level of work) 3 times in same st, yo, draw yarn through 7 loops on hook.

Chain multiples of 6 plus 5.

Row 1: Dc in 8th ch from hook, *ch 2, skip next 2 ch, dc in next ch; rep from * across, turn.

Rows 2-4: Ch 5 (counts as dc, ch 2), skip first ch-2 space, *dc in next dc, ch 2, skip next ch-2 space; rep from * across, dc in next ch of turning ch, turn.

Row 5: Ch 1, sc in first dc, *ch 7, skip next 2 ch-2 spaces, sc in next dc; rep from * across, ending with last sc in 3rd ch of turning ch, turn.

Bobble: (Yo, insert hook in next st, yo, draw yarn through st and up to level of work) 3 times in same st, yo, draw yarn through 7 loops on hook.

Chain multiples of 9 plus 6.

Row 1: Sc in 9th ch from hook, *ch 3, skip next 2 ch, sc in next ch, ch 3, skip next 2 ch, dc in next ch**, ch 3, skip next 2 ch, sc in next ch; rep from * across, ending last rep at **, turn.

Row 2: Ch 1, sc in first dc, *ch 3, skip next ch-3 loop, bobble in next ch-3 loop, ch 3, skip next ch-3 loop, sc in next dc; rep from * across, ending with last sc next ch of turning ch, turn.

Row 3: Ch 6 (counts as dc, ch 3), *sc in next ch-3 loop, ch 3, sc in next ch-3 loop, ch 3, dc in next sc**, ch 3; rep from * across, ending last rep at **, turn.

Rep Rows 2-3 for pattern.

332

3-looped bobble: (Yo, insert hook in next st, yo, draw yarn through st and up to level of work) 3 times in same st, yo, draw yarn through 7 loops on hook.

2-looped bobble: (Yo, insert hook in next st, yo, draw yarn through st and up to level of work) twice in same st, yo, draw yarn through 5 loops on hook.

Chain multiples of 8 plus 2.

Row 1: Sc in 2nd ch from hook, *ch 3, skip next 3 ch, (dc, ch 3, dc) in next ch, ch 3, skip next 3 ch, sc in next ch; rep from * across, turn.

Row 2: Ch 5 (counts as dc, ch 2), skip next ch-3 loop, *3-looped bobble in next dc, ch 2, 3-looped bobble in next ch-3 loop, ch 2, 3-looped bobble in next dc**, ch 3, skip next 2 ch-3 loops; rep from * across, ending last rep at **, ch 2, skip next ch-3 loop, dc in last sc, turn.

Row 3: Ch 4 (counts as dc, ch 1), *(3-looped bobble, ch 2, 3-looped bobble) in next ch-2 space, ch 2, (3-looped bobble, ch 2, 3-looped bobble) in next ch-2 space**, ch 2, skip next ch-3 loop; rep from * across, ending last rep at **, ch 1, dc in 3rd ch of turning ch, turn.

Row 4: Ch 4 (counts as dc, ch 1), skip next ch-1 space, (dc, ch 1) in each ch-2 space across to turning ch, dc in 3rd ch of turning ch, turn.

Row 5: Ch 4 (counts as dc, ch 1), dc in first dc, *ch 3, skip next 2 ch-1 spaces, sc in next dc, ch 3, skip next 2 ch-1 spaces**, (dc, ch 3, dc) in next dc; rep from * across, ending last rep at **, (dc, ch 1, dc) in 3rd ch of turning ch, turn.

Row 6: Ch 3 (counts as dc), dc in first dc, ch 2, skip next ch-1 space, 3-looped bobble in next dc, *ch 3, skip next 2 ch-3 loops, 3-looped bobble in next dc, ch 2**, 3-looped bobble in next ch-3 loop, ch 2, 3-looped bobble in next dc; rep from * across, ending last rep at **, 2-looped bobble in 3rd ch of turning ch, turn.

Row 7: Ch 4 (counts as dc, ch 1), (3-looped bobble, ch 2, 3-looped bobble) in next ch-2 space, ch 2, skip next ch-3 loop, (3-looped bobble, ch 2, 3-looped bobble) in next ch-2 space**, ch 2; rep from * across, ending last rep at **, ch 1, dc in 3rd ch of turning ch, turn.

Row 8: Rep Row 4.

Row 9: Ch 1, sc in first dc, *ch 3, skip next 2 ch-1 spaces, (dc, ch 3, dc) in next dc, ch 3, skip next 2 ch-1 spaces, sc in next dc; rep from * across, ending with last sc in 3rd ch of turning ch, turn.

Rep Rows 2-9 for pattern.

333

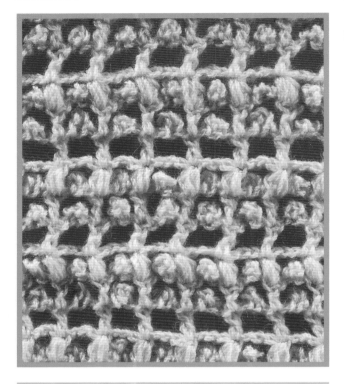

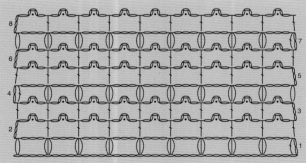

3-looped bobble: *(Yo, insert hook in next st, yo, draw yarn through st and up to level of work) 3 times in same st, yo, draw yarn through 7 loops on hook.*

2-looped bobble: *(Yo, insert hook in next st, yo, draw yarn through st and up to level of work) twice in same st, yo, draw yarn through 5 loops on hook.*

Chain multiples of 4 plus 3.

Row 1: Dc in 3rd ch from hook, *ch 3, skip next 3 ch, 3-looped bobble in next ch; rep from * across to within last 4 ch, ch 3, skip next 3 ch, 2-looped bobble in last ch, turn.

Row 2: Ch 4 (counts as dc, ch 1), ch 3 more, sl st in 3rd ch from hook (picot), ch 1, skip next ch-3 loop, *dc in next bobble, ch 1, picot, ch 1, skip next ch-3 loop; rep from * across to turning ch, dc in 2nd ch of turning ch, turn.

Row 3: Ch 4 (counts as dc, ch 1), picot, ch 1, skip next (ch1, picot, ch1) *dc in next dc, ch 1, picot, ch 1, skip next (ch 1, picot, ch 1); rep from * across to turning ch, dc in 3rd ch of turning ch, turn.

Row 4: Ch 2 (counts as dc), dc in first dc, *ch 3, skip next (ch 1, picot, ch 1), 3-looped bobble in next dc; rep from * across to last dc, ch 3, skip next (ch 1, picot, ch 1), 2-looped bobble in 3rd ch of turning ch, turn.

Rep Rows 2-4 for pattern.

334

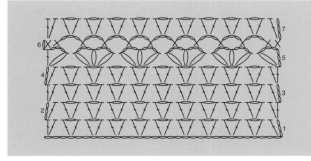

Bobble: (Yo, insert hook in next st, yo, draw yarn through st and up to level of work) twice in same st, yo, draw yarn through 5 loops on hook.

Chain multiples of 6 plus 4.

Row 1: Dc in 4th ch from hook, *skip next 2 ch, (dc, ch 1, dc) in next ch; rep from * across, ending with 2 dc in last ch, turn.

Rows 2-4: Ch 3 (counts as dc), dc in first st, (dc, ch 1, dc) in each ch-1 space across to last ch-1 space, 2 dc in 3rd ch of turning ch, turn.

Row 5: Ch 6 (counts as dc, ch 3), bobble in first dc, *skip next ch-1 space**, (bobble, ch 3, bobble, ch 3, bobble) in next ch-1 space; rep from * across, ending last rep at **, (bobble, ch 3, dc) in 3rd ch of turning ch, turn.

Row 6: Ch 1, sc in first dc, sc in next ch-3 loop, (ch 3, sc) in each ch-3 loop across to ch-3 loop of turning ch, sc in 3rd ch of turning ch, turn.

Row 7: Rep Row 2.

Rep Rows 2-7 for pattern.

335

Bobble: (Yo, insert hook in next st, yo, draw yarn through st and up to level of work) 3 times in same st, yo, draw yarn through 7 loops on hook.

Chain multiples of 10 plus 2.

Row 1: Sc in 2nd ch from hook, *ch 3, skip next 5 ch, dc in next ch, ch 5, working over last dc, skip next ch to the right, dc in next ch to the right (crossed dc made), ch 3, skip next 3 ch, sc in next ch; rep from * across, turn.

Row 2: Ch 3 (counts as dc), *skip next ch-3 loop, 11 dc in next ch-5 loop, skip next ch-3 loop**, bobble in next sc, ch 1, skip next ch-3 loop; rep from * across, ending last rep at **, dc in last sc, turn.

Row 3: Ch 2, skip first 2 dc, hdc in next dc, ch 4, hdc in last hdc made (counts as first crossed dc), *ch 3, skip next 3 dc, sc in next dc, ch 3**, skip next 8 sts, dc in next dc, ch 5, working over last dc made, skip 4 sts to the right, dc in next dc to the right (crossed dc made); rep from * across, ending last rep at **, skip next 5 dc, dc in 3rd ch of turning ch, ch 2, working over last dc made, skip 1 st to the right, dc in next dc to the right (crossed dc made), turn.

Row 4: Ch 3 (counts as dc), 5 dc in next ch-2 space, *skip next ch-3 loop, bobble in next sc, ch 1, skip next ch-3 loop**, 11 dc in next ch-5 loop; rep from * across, ending last rep at **, 5 dc in ch-2 space of turning ch, dc in 2nd ch of turning ch, turn.

Row 5: Ch 1, sc in first dc, ch 3, *skip next 8 sts, dc in next dc, ch 5, working over last dc made, skip 4 sts to the right, dc in next dc to the right (crossed dc made), ch 3, skip next 3 dc**, sc in next dc, ch 3; rep from * across, ending last rep at **, sc in 3rd ch of turning ch, turn.

Rep Rows 2-5 for pattern.

336

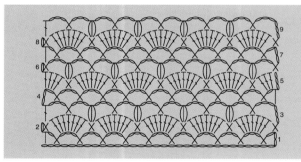

Bobble: (Yo, insert hook in next st, yo, draw yarn through st and up to level of work) 3 times in same st, yo, draw yarn through 7 loops on hook.

Chain multiples of 6 plus 4.

Row 1: Sc in 5th ch from hook, *ch 3, skip next 2 ch, sc in next ch; rep from * across to within last 2 ch, ch 1, skip next ch, hdc in last ch, turn.

Row 2: Ch 1, sc in first dc, skip next ch-1 space, *7 dc in next ch-3 loop, sc in next ch-3 loop; rep from * across, ending with last sc in 3rd ch of turning ch, turn.

Row 3: Ch 6 (counts as dc, ch 3), skip first 4 sts, sc in next dc, ch 3, skip next 3 dc**, bobble in next sc, skip next 3 dc; rep from * across, ending last rep at **, dc in last sc, turn.

Row 4: Ch 3 (counts as hdc, ch 1), sc in next ch-3 loop, (ch 3, sc) in each ch-3 loop across to ch-3 loop of turning ch, ch 1, hdc in 3rd ch of turning ch, turn.

Row 5: Ch 3 (counts as dc), 3 dc in next ch-1 space, *sc in next ch-3 loop**, 7 dc in next ch-3 loop; rep from * across, ending last rep at **, 3 dc in ch-1 space of turning ch, dc in 2nd ch of turning ch, turn.

Row 6: Ch 1, sc in first dc, *ch 3, skip next 3 dc, bobble in next sc, ch 3, skip next 3 dc, sc in next dc; rep from * across, ending with last sc in 3rd ch of turning ch, turn.

Row 7: Ch 3 (counts as hdc, ch 1), sc in next ch-3 loop, (ch 3, sc) in each ch-3 loop across to last ch-3 loop, ch 1, hdc in last sc, turn.

Rep Rows 2-7 for pattern.

337

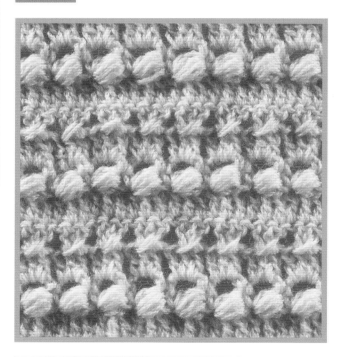

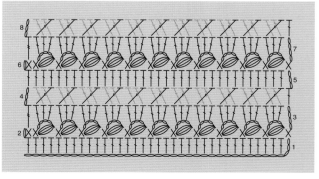

Bobble: *(Yo, insert hook in next st, yo, draw yarn through st and up to level of work) 4 times in same st, yo, draw yarn through 9 loops on hook.*

Chain multiples of 3 plus 1.

Row 1: Dc in 4th ch from hook, dc in each ch across, turn.

Row 2: Ch 1, sc in first dc, *sc in next dc, ch 4, bobble in last sc made, skip next 2 dc; rep from * across to turning ch, sc in 3rd ch of turning ch, turn.

Row 3: Ch 4 (counts as tr), 3 dc in each ch-4 loop across to last ch-4 loop, skip next sc, tr in last sc, turn.

Row 4: Ch 3 (counts as dc), skip first dc, *skip next dc, dc in each of next 2 dc, working over last 2 dc made, dc in last skipped dc; rep from * across to turning ch, dc in 3rd ch of turning ch, turn.

Row 5: Ch 3 (counts as dc), skip first dc, dc in each dc across, ending with dc in 3rd ch of turning ch, turn.

Rep Rows 2-5 for pattern.

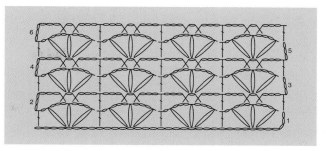

Bobble: *(Yo, insert hook in next st, yo, draw yarn through st and up to level of work) twice in same st, yo, draw yarn through 5 loops on hook.*

Chain multiples of 8 plus 3.

Row 1: (Bobble, ch 3, bobble, ch 3, bobble) in 7th ch from hook, *ch 1, skip next 3 ch, dc in next ch, skip next 3 ch, (bobble, ch 3, bobble, ch 3, bobble) in next ch; rep from * across to within last 4 ch, ch 1, skip next 3 ch, dc in last ch, turn.

Row 2: Ch 6 (counts as dc, ch 3), *skip next ch-1 space, sc in next ch-3 loop, ch 1, sc in next ch-3 loop, ch 3, skip next bobble**, dc in next dc, ch 3; rep from * across, ending last rep at **, dc in 3rd ch of turning ch, turn.

Row 3: Ch 3 (counts as dc), skip next ch-3 loop, (bobble, ch 3, bobble, ch 3, bobble) in next ch-1 space, ch 1, skip next ch-3 loop, dc in next dc; rep from * across, ending with last dc in 3rd ch of turning ch, turn.

Rep Rows 2-3 for pattern.

338

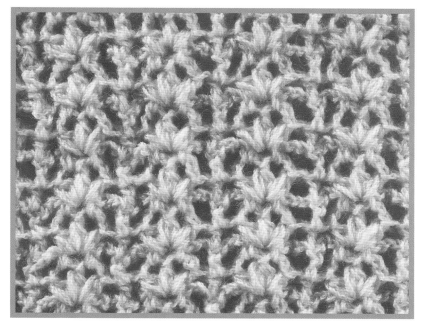

339

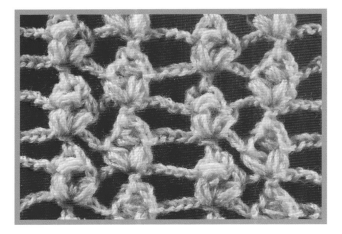

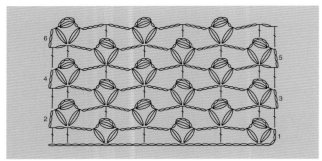

Bobble: (Yo, insert hook in next st, yo, draw yarn through st and up to level of work) 3 times in same st, yo, draw yarn through 7 loops on hook.

Chain multiples of 10 plus 2.

Row 1: (Bobble, ch 4, bobble in last bobble made, ch 1, bobble) in 5th ch from hook, *ch 4, skip next 4 ch, dc in next ch**, ch 4, skip next 4 ch, (bobble, ch 4, bobble in last bobble made, ch 1, bobble) in next ch; rep from * across, ending last rep at **, ch 1, skip next ch, dc in last ch, turn.

Row 2: Ch 3 (counts as dc), skip next ch-1 space, *(bobble, ch 4, bobble in last bobble made, ch 1, bobble) in next dc, ch 4, skip next ch-4 loop, skip next ch-1 space, dc in next ch-4 loop**, ch 4, skip next ch-4 loop; rep from * across, ending last rep at **, ch 1, dc in top of of turning ch, turn.

Row 3: Ch 3 (counts as dc), skip next ch-1 space, (bobble, ch 4, bobble in last bobble made, ch 1, bobble) in next dc, ch 4, skip next ch-4 loop, skip next ch-1 space, dc in next ch-4 loop**, ch 4, skip next ch-4 loop; rep from * across, ending last rep at **, ch 1, dc in 3rd ch of turning ch, turn.

Rep Rows 2-3 for pattern.

340

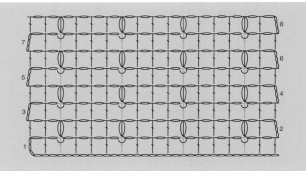

Front Post Bobble (FPbobble): (Yo, insert hook from front to back around the post of next st, yo, draw yarn through st and up to level of work) 3 times around the post of same st, yo, draw yarn through 7 loops on hook.

Chain multiples of 8 plus 4.

Row 1 (WS): Dc in 6th ch from hook, *ch 1, skip next ch, dc in next ch; rep from * across, turn.

Row 2: Ch 4 (counts as dc, ch 1), skip next ch-1 space, *dc in next dc, ch 1, skip next ch-1 space, FPbobble around the post of next dc**, (ch 1, dc) in each of next 2 dc, ch 1; rep from * across, ending last rep at **, ch 1, dc in next dc, ch 1, skip next ch of turning ch, dc in next ch of turning ch, turn.

Row 3: Ch 4 (counts as dc, ch 1), skip next ch-1 space, dc in next dc, *ch 1, skip next ch-1 space, dc in next st; rep from * across, ending with last dc in 3rd ch of turning ch, turn.

Rep Rows 2-3 for pattern.

.25.
Puff Stitches

341

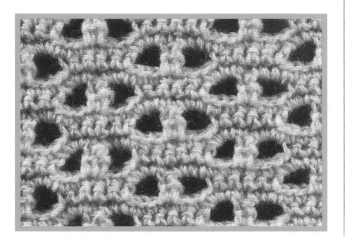

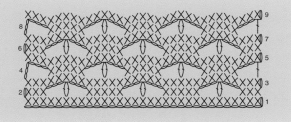

2-Dc Puff st: (Yo, insert hook in next st, yo, draw yarn through st, yo, draw yarn through 2 loops on hook) twice in same st, yo, draw yarn through 3 loops on hook.

Chain multiples of 10 plus 2.

Row 1: Sc in 2nd ch from hook, sc in each ch across, turn.

Row 2: Ch 1, sc in each of first 3 sc, *ch 3, skip next 2 sc, 2-dc puff st in next sc, ch 3**, skip next 2 sc, sc in each of next 5 sc; rep from * across, ending last rep at **, sc in each of last 3 sc, turn.

Row 3: Ch 1, sc in each of first 3 sc, *2 sc in next ch-3 loop, sc in next puff st, 2 sc in next ch-3 loop**, sc in each of next 5 sc; rep from * across, ending last rep at **, sc in each of last 3 sc, turn.

Row 4: Ch 6 (counts as dc, ch 3), skip first 3 sc, *sc in each of next 5 sc, ch 3, skip next 2 sc**, 2-dc puff st in next sc, ch 3, skip next 2 sc; rep from * across, ending last rep at **, dc in last sc, turn.

Row 5: Ch 1, sc in first dc, *2 sc in next ch-3 loop, sc in each of next 5 sc, 2 sc in next ch-3 loop, sc in next puff st; rep from * across, ending with last sc in 3rd ch of turning ch, turn.

Rep Rows 2-5 for pattern.

342

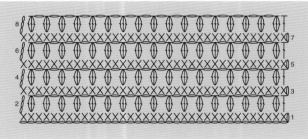

3-Dc Puff st: (Yo, insert hook in next st, yo, draw yarn through st, yo, draw yarn through 2 loops on hook) 3 times in same st, yo, draw yarn through 4 loops on hook.

Chain multiples of 2.

Row 1: Sc in 2nd ch from hook, sc in each ch across, turn.

Row 2: Ch 3 (counts as dc), skip first sc, 3-dc puff st in next sc, *ch 1, skip next sc, 3-dc puff st in next sc; rep from * across to within last sc, dc in last sc, turn.

Row 3: Ch 1, sc in first dc, sc in next puff st, *sc in next ch-1 space, sc in next puff st; rep from * across to turning ch, sc in 3rd ch of turning ch, turn.

Rep Rows 2-3 for pattern.

343

2-Dc Puff st: (Yo, insert hook in next st, yo, draw yarn through st, yo, draw yarn through 2 loops on hook) twice in same st, yo, draw yarn through 3 loops on hook.

Chain multiples of 4 plus 2.

Row 1: Sc in 2nd ch from hook, *ch 2, skip next ch, 2-dc puff st in next ch, ch 2, skip next ch, sc in next ch; rep from * across, turn.

Row 2: Ch 5 (counts as dc, ch 2), skip next ch-2 space, sc in next puff st, *ch 5, skip next 2 ch-2 spaces, sc in next puff st; rep from * across to within last ch-2 space, ch 2, skip next ch-2 space, dc in last sc, turn.

Row 3: Ch 1, sc in first dc, ch 2, skip next ch-2 space, *2-dc puff st in next sc, ch 2**, sc in next ch-5 loop, ch 2; rep from * across, ending last rep at **, sc in 3rd ch of turning ch, turn.

Rep Rows 2-3 for pattern.

344

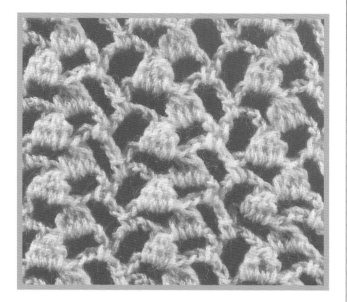

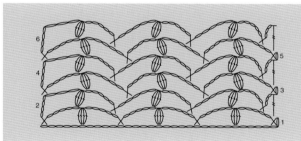

4-Dc Puff st: (Yo, insert hook in next st, yo, draw yarn through st, yo, draw yarn through 2 loops on hook) 4 times in same st, yo, draw yarn through 5 loops on hook.

Chain multiples of 10 plus 2.

Row 1: Sc in 2nd ch from hook, *ch 5, skip next 4 ch, 4-dc puff st in next ch, ch 5, skip next 4 ch, sc in next ch; rep from * across, turn.

Row 2: Ch 7 (counts as tr, ch 3), *skip next 4 ch of next ch-5 loop, 4-dc puff st in next ch, ch 5, sc in next ch-5 loop; rep from * across to last ch-5 loop, ch 3, tr in last sc, turn.

Row 3: Ch 1, sc in first tr, skip next ch-3 loop, *ch 5, skip next 4 ch of next ch-5 loop, 4-dc puff st in next ch, ch 5, sc in next ch-5 loop; rep from * across, ending with last sc in 4th ch of turning ch, turn.

Rep Rows 2-3 for pattern.

345

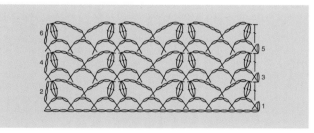

3-Dc Puff st: (Yo, insert hook in next st, yo, draw yarn through st, yo, draw yarn through 2 loops on hook) 3 times in same st, yo, draw yarn through 4 loops on hook.

Chain multiples of 9 plus 2.

Row 1: Sc in 2nd ch from hook, *ch 3, skip next 2 ch, sc in next ch; rep from * across, turn.

Row 2: Ch 3 (counts as dc), skip first sc, *3-dc puff st in next ch-3 loop, ch 5, sc in next ch-5 loop, ch 4, 3-dc puff st in next ch-3 loop; rep from * across to last ch-3 loop, dc in last sc, turn.

Row 3: Ch 1, sc in first dc, *ch 3, sc in next ch-4 loop, ch 3, sc in next ch-5 loop, ch 3, skip next puff st, sc between last skipped and next puff st; rep from * across, ending with last sc in 3rd ch of turning ch, turn.

Rep Rows 2-3 for pattern.

346

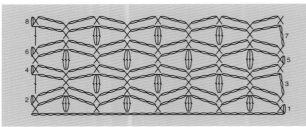

3-Dc Puff st: (Yo, insert hook in next st, yo, draw yarn through st, yo, draw yarn through 2 loops on hook) 3 times in same st, yo, draw yarn through 4 loops on hook.

Chain multiples of 8 plus 2.

Row 1: Sc in 2nd ch from hook, *ch 3, skip next 3 ch, 3-dc puff st in next ch, ch 3, skip next 3 ch, sc in next ch; rep from * across, turn.

Row 2: Ch 1, sc in first sc, *ch 3, skip next ch-3 loop, sc in next puff st, ch 3, skip next ch-3 loop, sc in next sc; rep from * across, turn.

Row 3: Ch 6 (counts as dc, ch 3), *skip next ch-3 loop, sc in next sc, ch 3, skip next ch-3 loop**, 3-dc puff st in next sc, ch 3; rep from * across, ending last rep at **, dc in last sc, turn.

Row 4: Ch 1, sc in first dc, *ch 3, skip next ch-3 loop, sc in next sc, ch 3, skip next ch-3 loop, sc in next puff st; rep from * across, ending with last sc in 3rd ch of turning ch, turn.

Row 5: Ch 1, sc in first dc, *ch 3, skip next ch-3 loop, 3-dc puff st in next sc, ch 3, skip next ch-3 loop, sc in next sc; rep from * across, turn.

Rep Rows 2-5 for pattern.

347

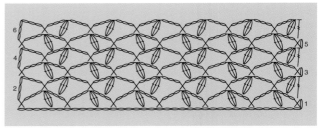

3-Dc Puff st: (Yo, insert hook in next st, yo, draw yarn through st, yo, draw yarn through 2 loops on hook) 3 times in same st, yo, draw yarn through 4 loops on hook.

Chain multiples of 6 plus 2.

Row 1: Sc in 2nd ch from hook, *ch 3, skip next ch, 3-dc puff st in next ch, ch 3, skip next 3 ch, sc in next ch; rep from * across, turn.

Row 2: Ch 6 (counts as dc, ch 3), skip next ch-3 loop, *sc in next puff st, ch 3, 3-dc puff st in next ch-3 loop**, ch 3; rep from * across, ending last rep at **, tr in last sc, turn.

Row 3: Ch 1, sc in first tr, *ch 3, 3-dc puff st in next ch-3 loop, ch 3, skip next ch-3 loop, sc in next puff st; rep from * across, ending with last sc in 3rd ch of turning ch, turn.

Rep Rows 2-3 for pattern.

348

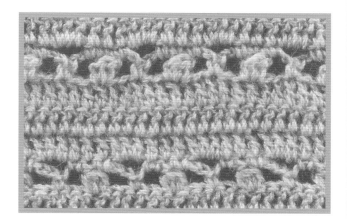

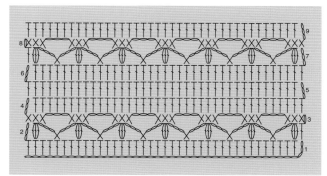

3-Dc Puff st: *(Yo, insert hook in next st, yo, draw yarn through st, yo, draw yarn through 2 loops on hook) 3 times in same st, yo, draw yarn through 4 loops on hook.*

Chain multiples of 6 plus 5.

Row 1: Dc in 4th ch from hook, dc in each ch across, turn.

Row 2: Ch 3 (counts as dc), skip first dc, 3-dc puff st in next dc, *ch 3, skip next 2 dc, sc in next dc, ch 3, skip next 2 dc, 3-dc puff st in next dc; rep from * across to turning ch, dc in 3rd ch of turning ch, turn.

Row 3: Ch 1, sc in first dc, sc in next puff st, *sc in next ch of ch-3 loop, ch 3, skip first 2 ch of next ch-3 loop, sc in next ch, sc in next puff st; rep from * across to turning ch, sc in 3rd ch of turning ch, turn.

Row 4: Ch 3 (counts as dc), skip first sc, dc in each of next 2 sc, *3 dc in next ch-3 loop, dc in each of next 3 sc; rep from * across, turn.

Rows 5-6: Ch 3 (counts as dc), skip first dc, dc in each dc across, ending with dc in 3rd ch of turning ch, turn.

Rep Rows 2-6 for pattern.

349

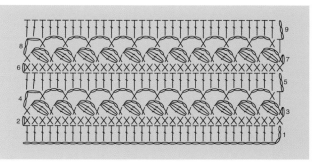

3-Dc Puff st: *(Yo, insert hook in next st, yo, draw yarn through st, yo, draw yarn through 2 loops on hook) 3 times in same st, yo, draw yarn through 4 loops on hook.*

Chain multiples of 3.

Row 1: Dc in 4th ch from hook, dc in each ch across, turn.

Row 2: Ch 1, sc in first dc, sc in each dc across, ending with last sc in 3rd ch of turning ch, turn.

Row 3: Ch 1, (sc, ch 3, 3-dc puff st) in first sc, *skip next 2 sc**, (sc, ch 3, 3-dc puff st) in next sc; rep from * across, ending last rep at **, sc in last sc, turn.

Row 4: Ch 3 (counts as hdc, ch 1), skip next puff st, sc in next ch-3 loop, (ch 3, sc) in each ch-3 loop across to last ch-3 loop, hdc in last sc, turn.

Row 5: Ch 3 (counts as dc), skip first dc, *dc in next sc, 2 dc in next ch-3 loop; rep from * across to turning ch, dc in ch-1 space of turning ch, dc in 3rd ch of turning ch, turn.

Rep Rows 2-5 for pattern.

350

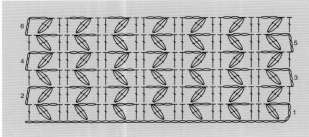

3-Dc Puff st: (Yo, insert hook in next st, yo, draw yarn through st, yo, draw yarn through 2 loops on hook) 3 times in same st, yo, draw yarn through 4 loops on hook.

Chain multiples of 5 plus 4.

Row 1: 3-dc puff st in 6th ch from hook, *skip next 2 ch, dc in each of next 2 ch, ch 2, 3-dc puff st in next ch; rep from * across to within last 3 ch, skip next 2 ch, dc in last ch, turn.

Row 2: Ch 5 (counts as dc, ch 2), skip first dc, 3-dc puff st in next puff st, *skip next ch-2 space, dc in each of next 2 dc, ch 2, 3-dc puff st in next puff st; rep from * across to turning ch, skip next 2 ch of turning ch, dc in next ch of turning ch, turn.

Rep Row 2 for pattern.

351

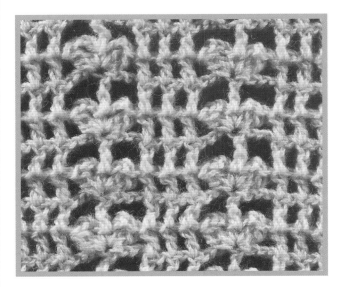

2-Dc Puff st: (Yo, insert hook in next st, yo, draw yarn through st, yo, draw yarn through 2 loops on hook) twice in same st, yo, draw yarn through 3 loops on hook.

Chain multiples of 12 plus 4.

Row 1: Dc in 6th ch from hook, *skip next 3 ch, (2-dc puff st, ch 3, sc, ch 2, 2-dc puff st) in next ch, skip next 3 ch**, (dc, ch 1, skip next ch) twice, dc in next ch; rep from * across, ending last rep at **, dc in next ch, ch 1, skip next ch, dc in last ch, turn.

Row 2: Ch 4 (counts as dc, ch 1), skip next ch-1 space, dc in next dc, *ch 3, skip next ch-2 space, tr in next sc, ch 3, skip next ch-3 loop, skip next puff st**, (dc, ch 1) in each of next 2 dc, dc in next dc; rep from * across, ending last rep at **, dc in next dc, ch 1, dc in 3rd ch of turning ch, turn.

Row 3: Ch 4 (counts as dc, ch 1), skip next ch-1 space, dc in next dc, skip next ch-3 loop, (2-dc puff st, ch 3, sc, ch 2, 2-dc puff st) in next tr, skip next ch-3 loop**, (dc, ch 1) in each of next 2 dc, dc in next dc; rep from * across, ending last rep at **, dc in next dc, ch 1, dc in 3rd ch of turning ch, turn.

Rep Rows 2-3 for pattern.

352

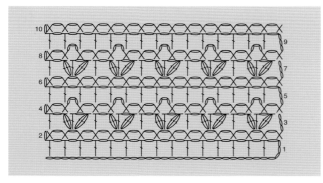

3-Dc Puff st: (Yo, insert hook in next st, yo, draw yarn through st, yo, draw yarn through 2 loops on hook) 3 times in same st, yo, draw yarn through 4 loops on hook.

Chain multiples of 6 plus 4.

Row 1: Dc in 6th ch from hook, *ch 1, skip next ch, dc in next ch; rep from * across, turn.

Row 2: Ch 1, sc in first dc, ch 1, (sc, ch 1) in each dc across to last dc, skip next ch of turning ch, sc in next ch, turn.

Row 3: Ch 3 (counts as dc), skip next ch-1 space, (3-dc puff st, ch 1, dc, 3-dc puff st) in next ch-1 space, ch 1, skip next ch-1 space, dc in next sc; rep from * across, turn.

Row 4: Ch 1, sc in first dc, *ch 1, skip next ch-1 space, sc in next puff st, ch 3, skip next dc, sc in next ch-1 space, ch 1, skip next puff st, sc in next dc; rep from * across, ending with last sc in 3rd ch of turning ch, turn.

Row 5: Ch 4 (counts as dc, ch 1), skip next ch-1 space, dc in next sc, (ch 1, dc) in each sc across, turn.

Rep Rows 2-5 for pattern.

353

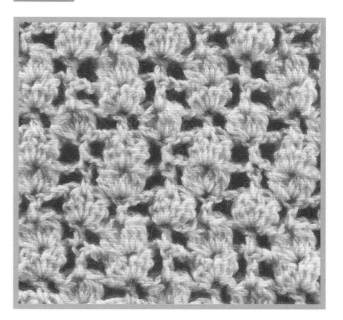

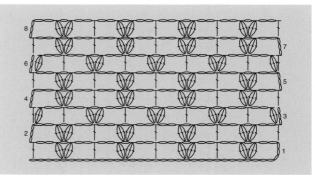

3-Dc Puff st: (Yo, insert hook in next st, yo, draw yarn through st, yo, draw yarn through 2 loops on hook) 3 times in same st, yo, draw yarn through 4 loops on hook.

Chain multiples of 8 plus 5.

Row 1: (3-dc puff st, ch 1, 3-dc puff st) in 9th ch from hook, *ch 2, skip next 3 ch, dc in next ch**, ch 2, skip next 3 ch, (3-dc puff st, ch 1, 3-dc puff st) in next ch; rep from * across, ending last rep at **, turn.

Row 2: Ch 5 (counts as dc, ch 2), skip next ch-2 space, *(3-dc puff st, ch 1, 3-dc puff st) in next ch-1 space, ch 2, skip next ch-2 space**, dc in next dc, ch 2, skip next ch-2 space; rep from * across, ending last rep at **, dc in next ch of turning ch, turn.

Row 3: Ch 3 (counts as dc), 3-dc puff st in first dc, *ch 2, skip next ch-2 space, dc in next ch-1 space, ch 2, skip next ch-2 space**, (3-dc puff st, ch 1, dc, 3-dc puff st) in next dc; rep from * across, ending last rep at **, (3-dc puff st, dc) in 3rd ch of turning ch, turn.

Row 4: Ch 5 (counts as dc, ch 2), skip next ch-2 space, *(3-dc puff st, ch 1, 3-dc puff st) in next dc, ch 2, skip next ch-2 space**, dc in next ch-1 space, ch 2, skip next ch-2 space; rep from * across, ending last rep at **, dc in 3rd ch of turning ch, turn.

Rep Rows 2-4 for pattern.

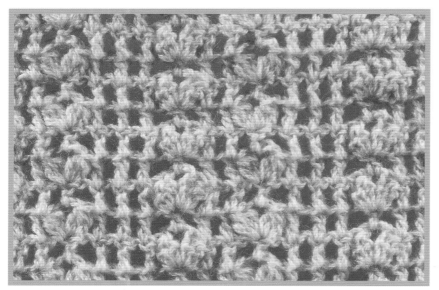

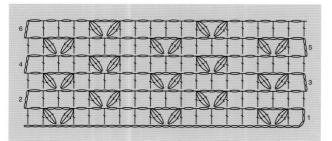

4-Dc Cluster: (Yo, insert hook in next st, yo, draw yarn through st, yo, draw yarn through 2 loops on hook) 4 times in designated sts, yo, draw yarn through 5 loops on hook.

Chain multiples of 14 plus 12.

Row 1: Skip first 5 ch, *work 4-dc cluster, working first half-closed dc in next ch, skip next ch, work next 3 half-closed dc in next ch, yo, complete 4-dc cluster, *ch 3, work 4-dc cluster, working first 3 half-closed dc in same ch holding last 3 dc of last cluster, skip next ch, work 4th half-closed dc in next ch, yo, complete 4-dc cluster**, (ch 1, skip next ch, dc in next ch) 4 times, ch 1, skip next ch; rep from * across, ending last rep at **, ch 1, skip next ch, dc in last ch, turn.

Row 2: Ch 4 (counts as dc, ch 1), skip next ch-1 space, *dc in next cluster, ch 1, dc in next ch-3 loop, ch 1, dc in next cluster, ch 1**, work 4-dc cluster, working first half-closed dc in next dc, skip next ch-1 space, work next 3 half-closed dc in next dc, yo, complete 4-dc cluster, ch 3, work 4-dc cluster, working first 3 half-closed dc in same dc holding last 3 dc of last cluster, skip next ch-1 space, work 4th half-closed dc in next dc, yo, complete 4-dc cluster, ch 1, skip next ch-1 space, dc in next dc, ch 1, skip next ch-1 space; rep from * across, ending last rep at **, skip next ch of turning ch, dc in next ch of turning ch, turn.

Row 3: Ch 4 (counts as dc, ch 1), skip next ch-1 space, *work 4-dc cluster, working first half-closed dc in next dc, skip next ch-1 space, work next 3 half-closed dc in next dc, yo, complete 4-dc cluster, ch 3, work 4-dc cluster, working first 3 half-closed dc in same dc holding last 3 dc of last cluster, skip next ch-1 space, work 4th half-closed dc in next dc, yo, complete 4-dc cluster, ch 1**, skip next ch-1 space, dc in next dc, ch 1, skip next ch-1 space, dc in next cluster, ch 1, dc in next ch-3 loop, ch 1, dc in next cluster, ch 1; rep from * across, ending last rep at **, skip next ch of turning ch, dc in next ch of turning ch, turn.

Rep Rows 2-3 for pattern.

355

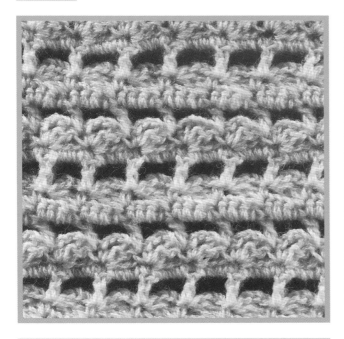

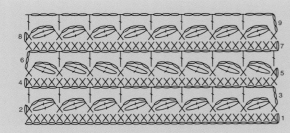

2-Dc Puff st: *(Yo, insert hook in next st, yo, draw yarn through st, yo, draw yarn through 2 loops on hook) twice in same st, yo, draw yarn through 3 loops on hook.*

Chain multiples of 4 plus 2.

Row 1: Sc in 2nd ch from hook, sc in each ch across, turn.

Row 2: Ch 1, sc in first sc, *ch 3, 2-dc puff st in last sc made, skip next 3 sc, sc in next sc; rep from * across, turn.

Row 3: Ch 6 (counts as dc, ch 3), *skip next ch-3 loop, dc in next sc; rep from * across, turn.

Row 4: Ch 1, sc in first dc, *3 sc in next ch-3 loop, sc in next dc; rep from * across, ending with last sc in 3rd ch of turning ch, turn.

Rep Rows 2-4 for pattern.

356

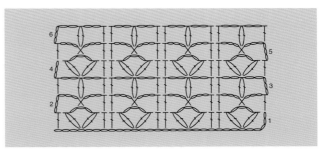

2-Dc Puff st: *(Yo, insert hook in next st, yo, draw yarn through st, yo, draw yarn through 2 loops on hook) twice in same st, yo, draw yarn through 3 loops on hook.*

Chain multiples of 7 plus 2.

Row 1: (2-dc puff st, ch 3, 2-dc puff st) in 6th ch from hook, skip next 2 ch, *dc in each of next 2 ch, skip next 2 ch, (2-dc puff st, ch 3, 2-dc puff st) in next ch, skip next 2 ch; rep from * across to within last ch, dc in last ch, turn.

Row 2: Ch 6 (counts as dc, ch 3), *sc in next ch-3 loop, ch 3, skip next puff st**, dc in each of next 2 dc, ch 3; rep from * across, ending last rep at **, dc in top of turning ch, turn.

Row 3: Ch 5 (counts as dc, ch 2), skip next ch-3 loop, *2-dc puff st in next sc, ch 2, skip next ch-3 loop**, dc in each of next 2 dc, ch 2, skip next ch-3 loop; rep from * across, ending last rep at **, dc in 3rd ch of turning ch, turn.

Row 4: Ch 3 (counts as dc), *skip next ch-2 space, (2-dc puff st, ch 3, 2-dc puff st) in next puff st, skip next ch-2 space**, dc in each of next 2 dc; rep from * across, ending last rep at **, dc in 3rd ch of turning ch, turn.

Rep Rows 2-4 for pattern.

357

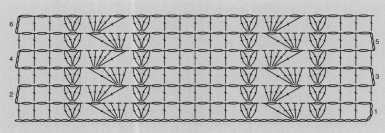

2-Dc Puff st: *(Yo, insert hook in next st, yo, draw yarn through st, yo, draw yarn through 2 loops on hook) twice in same st, yo, draw yarn through 3 loops on hook.*

Chain multiples of 23 plus 4.

Row 1: Dc in 6th ch from hook, ch 1, skip next ch, *dc in next ch, ch 1, skip next 2 ch, (2-dc puff st, ch 1, 2-dc puff st) in next ch, skip next 2 ch, (4 dc, ch 1, dc) in next ch, skip next 5 ch, (2-dc puff st, ch 3, 2-dc puff st) in next ch, ch 1, skip next 2 ch**, (dc in next ch, ch 1, skip next ch) 4 times; rep from * across, ending last rep at **, (dc in next ch, ch 1, skip next ch) twice, dc in last ch, turn.

Row 2: Ch 4 (counts as dc, ch 1), skip next ch-1 space, (dc, ch 1) in each of next 2 dc, *skip next ch-1 space, (2-dc puff st, ch 3, 2-dc puff st) in next ch-1 space, (4 dc, ch 1, dc) in next ch-1 space, skip next 4 dc, skip next puff st, (2-dc puff st, ch 3, 2-dc puff st) in next ch-1 space, ch 1, skip next ch-1 space**, (dc, ch 1) in each of next 5 dc; rep from * across, ending last rep at **, (dc, ch 1) in each of next 2 dc, skip next ch of turning ch, dc in next ch of turning ch, turn.

Rep Row 2 for pattern.

358

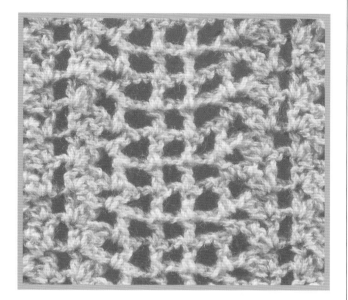

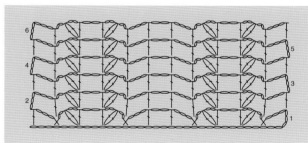

2-Dc Puff st: (Yo, insert hook in next st, yo, draw yarn through st, yo, draw yarn through 2 loops on hook) twice in same st, yo, draw yarn through 3 loops on hook.

Chain multiples of 18 plus 3.

Row 1: Sc in 9th ch from hook, *ch 2, skip next 2 ch, (2-dc puff st, ch 2, dc) in next ch, ch 2, skip next 2 ch, (dc, ch 2, 2-dc puff st) in next ch, ch 2, skip next 2 ch, sc in next ch, ch 3, skip next 2 ch, dc in next ch**, ch 2, skip next 2 ch, dc in next ch; rep from * across, ending last rep at **, turn.

Row 2: Ch 6 (counts as dc, ch 3), skip next ch-3 loop, *dc in next sc, ch 2, skip next 2 ch-2 spaces, (2-dc puff st, ch 2, dc) in next dc, ch 2, skip next ch-2 space, (dc, ch 2, 2-dc puff st) in next dc, ch 2, skip next 2 ch-2 spaces, dc in next sc, ch 3**, skip next ch-3 loop, dc in next dc, ch 2, skip next ch-2 space, dc in next dc, ch 3, skip next ch-3 loop; rep from * across, ending last rep at **, skip next 3 ch of turning ch, dc in next ch, turn.

Rep Row 2 for pattern.

359

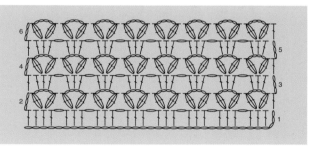

3-Dc Puff st: (Yo, insert hook in next st, yo, draw yarn through st, yo, draw yarn through 2 loops on hook) 3 times in same st, yo, draw yarn through 4 loops on hook.

Chain multiples of 4 plus 3.

Row 1: Dc in 4th ch from hook, dc in each of next 2 ch, *ch 1, skip next ch, dc in each of next 3 ch; rep from * across to within last ch, dc in last ch, turn.

Row 2: Ch 3 (counts as dc), skip first 2 dc, (3-dc puff st, ch 4, 3-dc puff st) in next dc, *skip next 3 sts, (3-dc puff st, ch 4, 3-dc puff st) in next dc; rep from * across to within last 2 sts, skip next dc, dc in 3rd ch of turning ch, turn.

Row 3: Ch 3 (counts as dc), 3 dc in next ch-4 loop, (ch 1, 3 dc) in each ch-4 loop across to last ch-4 loop, dc in 3rd ch of turning ch, turn.

Rep Rows 2-3 for pattern.

360

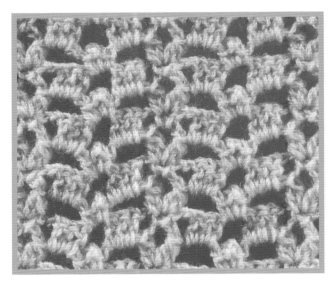

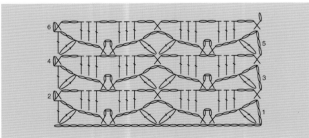

2-Dc Puff st: (Yo, insert hook in next st, yo, draw yarn through st, yo, draw yarn through 2 loops on hook) twice in same st, yo, draw yarn through 3 loops on hook.

Chain multiples of 13 plus 6.

Row 1: 2-dc puff st in 6th ch from hook, *ch 3, skip next 5 ch, sc in next ch, ch 3, sc in next ch, ch 3, skip next 5 ch**, (2-dc puff st, ch 5, 2-dc puff st) in next ch; rep from * across, ending last rep at **, (2-dc puff st, ch 2, dc) in last ch, turn.

Row 2: Ch 1, sc in first dc, *ch 2, skip next ch-2 space, 3 dc in next ch-3 loop, ch 2, 3 dc in next ch-3 loop, ch 2, sc in next ch-5 loop; rep from * across, ending with last sc in 3rd ch of turning ch, turn.

Row 3: Ch 5 (counts as dc, ch 2), 2-dc puff st in first sc, *ch 3, skip next ch-2 space, (sc, ch 3, sc) in next ch-2 space, ch 3, skip next ch-2 space**, (2-dc puff st, ch 5, 2-dc puff st) in next sc; rep from * across, ending last rep at **, (2-dc puff st, ch 2, dc) in last sc, turn.

Rep Rows 2-3 for pattern.

361

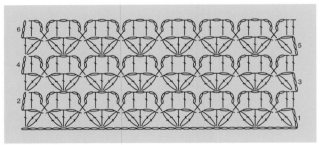

2-Dc Puff st: (Yo, insert hook in next st, yo, draw yarn through st, yo, draw yarn through 2 loops on hook) twice in same st, yo, draw yarn through 3 loops on hook.

Chain multiples of 5.

Row 1: 2-dc puff st in 5th ch from hook, *skip next 4 ch, (2-dc puff st, ch 1, dc, ch 1, 2-dc puff st) in next ch; rep from * across to within last 5 ch, skip next 4 ch, (2-dc puff st, ch 1, dc) in last ch, turn.

Row 2: Ch 3 (counts as dc), *dc in next ch-1 space, ch 3, sc between next 2 puff sts, ch 3, dc in next ch-1 space**, ch 1; rep from * across, ending last rep at **, dc in 3rd ch of turning ch, turn.

Row 3: Ch 4 (counts as dc, ch 1), 2-dc puff st in first dc, *skip next 2 ch-3 loops, (2-dc puff st, ch 1, dc, ch 1, 2-dc puff st) in next ch-1 space; rep from * across to last ch-1 space, skip next 2 ch-3 loops, skip next dc, (2-dc puff st, ch 1, dc) in 3rd ch of turning ch, turn.

Rep Rows 2-3 for pattern.

362

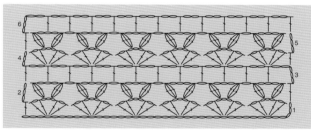

3-Dc Puff st: (Yo, insert hook in next st, yo, draw yarn through st, yo, draw yarn through 2 loops on hook) 3 times in same st, yo, draw yarn through 4 loops on hook.

Chain multiples of 6 plus 3.

Row 1: (Dc, ch 1, dc, ch 3, dc, ch 1, dc) in 6th ch from hook, *skip next 5 ch (dc, ch 1, dc, ch 3, dc, ch 1, dc) in next ch; rep from * across to within last 3 ch, skip next 2 ch, dc in last ch, turn.

Row 2: Ch 3 (counts as dc), skip next ch-1 space, *(3-dc puff st, ch 3, 3-dc puff st) in next ch-3 loop**, ch 1, skip next 2 ch-1 spaces; rep from * across, ending last rep at **, skip next ch-1 space, skip next dc, dc in 3rd ch of turning ch, turn.

Row 3: Ch 5 (counts as dc, ch 2), dc in next ch-3 loop, ch 2, *dc in next ch-1 space, ch 2, dc in next ch-3 loop, ch 2; rep from * across to last ch-3 loop, dc in 3rd ch of turning ch, turn.

Row 4: Ch 3 (counts as dc), skip next ch-2 space, *(dc, ch 1, dc, ch 3, dc, ch 1, dc) in next dc**, skip next 2 ch-2 spaces; rep from * across, ending last rep at **, skip next 2 ch of turning ch, dc in 3rd ch of turning ch, turn.

Rep Rows 2-4 for pattern.

363

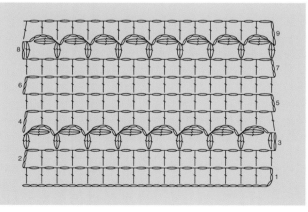

2-Dc Puff st: (Yo, insert hook in next st, yo, draw yarn through st, yo, draw yarn through 2 loops on hook) twice in same st, yo, draw yarn through 3 loops on hook.

6-Dc Cluster: (Yo, insert hook in next st, yo, draw yarn through st, yo, draw yarn through 2 loops on hook) 3 times in same st, (yo, insert hook in next st, yo, draw yarn through st, yo, draw yarn through 2 loops on hook) 3 times in next designated st, yo, draw yarn through 7 loops on hook.

Chain multiples of 4.

Row 1: Dc in 6th ch from hook, *ch 1, skip next ch, dc in next ch; rep from * across, turn.

Row 2: Ch 4 (counts as dc, ch 1), skip next ch-1 space, (dc, ch 1) in each dc across to turning ch, skip next ch of turning ch, dc in next ch of turning ch, turn.

Row 3: Ch 2 (counts as dc), 2-dc puff st in first dc, *ch 4, work 6-dc cluster, working first 3 half-closed dc in 4th ch from hook, skip next 2 ch-2 spaces, work next 3 half-closed dc in next dc, yo, complete 6-dc cluster; rep from * across, ending with last 3 half-closed dc in 3rd ch of turning ch, turn.

Row 4: Ch 4 (counts as dc, ch 1), *dc in next ch-4 loop, ch 1**, dc in next cluster, ch 1; rep from * across, ending last rep at **, dc in 3rd ch of turning ch, turn.

Rows 5-7: Rep Row 2.

Rep Rows 3-7 for pattern.

364

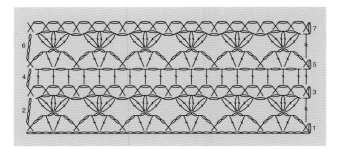

2-Dc Puff st: (Yo, insert hook in next st, yo, draw yarn through st, yo, draw yarn through 2 loops on hook) twice in same st, yo, draw yarn through 3 loops on hook.

Chain multiples of 6 plus 2.

Row 1: Sc in 2nd ch from hook, *ch 2, skip next 2 ch, (dc, ch 2, dc) in next ch, ch 2, skip next 2 ch, sc in next ch; rep from * across, turn.

Row 2: Ch 4 (counts as tr), skip next ch-2 space, *(2-dc puff st, ch 1, 2-dc puff st, ch 1, 2-dc puff st) in next ch-2 space**, ch 1, skip next 2 ch-2 space; rep from * across, ending last rep at **, skip next ch-2 space, tr in last sc, turn.

Row 3: Ch 1, sc in first tr, ch 1, (sc, ch 1) in each ch-1 space across to turning ch, sc in 4th ch of turning ch, turn.

Row 4: Ch 3 (counts as dc), dc in next ch-1 space, (ch 1, dc) in each ch-1 space across to last ch-1 space, dc in last sc, turn.

Row 5: Ch 1, sc in first dc, *ch 2, skip next ch-1 space, (dc, ch 2, dc) in next dc, ch 2, skip next ch-1 space, sc in next ch-1 space; rep from * across, ending with last sc in 3rd ch of turning ch, turn.

Rep Rows 2-5 for pattern.

365

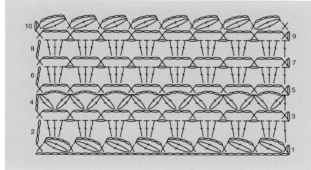

2-Dc Puff st: (Yo, insert hook in next st, yo, draw yarn through st, yo, draw yarn through 2 loops on hook) twice in same st, yo, draw yarn through 3 loops on hook.

3-Dc Cluster: (Yo, insert hook in next st, yo, draw yarn through st, yo, draw yarn through 2 loops on hook) twice in same space, yo, insert hook in next designated st, yo, draw yarn through st, yo, draw yarn through 2 loops on hook, yo, draw yarn through 4 loops on hook.

4-Dc Cluster: (Yo, insert hook in next st, yo, draw yarn through st, yo, draw yarn through 2 loops on hook) twice in same space, (yo, insert hook in next st, yo, draw yarn through st, yo, draw yarn through 2 loops on hook) twice in next designated space, yo, draw yarn through 5 loops on hook.

Chain multiples of 4 plus 2.

Row 1: (Sc, ch 4, 2-dc puff st) in 2nd ch from hook, *skip next 3 ch, (sc, ch 4, 2-dc puff st) in next ch; rep from * across, ending with sc in last ch, turn.

Row 2: Ch 3 (counts as dc), 3 dc in next loop, (ch 1, 3 dc) in each loop across to last ch-4 loop, dc in last sc, turn.

Row 3: Ch 1, sc in first dc, (ch 3, sc) in each ch-1 space across, ending with last sc in 3rd ch of turning ch, turn.

Row 4: Ch 3 (counts as dc), 2-dc puff st in next ch-3 loop, ch 3, *work 4-dc cluster, working first 2 half-closed dc in same ch-3 loop as last cluster, work next 2 half-closed dc in next ch-3 loop, yo, complete cluster, ch 4; rep from * across to last ch-3 loop, work 3-dc cluster, working first 2 half-closed dc in same ch-3 loop as last cluster, work next half-closed dc in last sc, yo, complete 3-dc cluster, turn.

Row 5: Ch 1, sc in first cluster, (ch 3, sc) in each cluster across, ending with last sc in 3rd ch of turning ch, turn.

Rows 6-9: Rep Rows 2-3 (twice).

Row 10: Ch 1, (sc, ch 4, 2-dc puff st) in first sc, *skip next ch-3 loop, (sc, ch 4, 2-dc puff st) in next sc; rep from * across, ending with sc in last sc, turn.

Rep Rows 2-10 for pattern.

366

3-Dc Puff st: (Yo, insert hook in next st, yo, draw yarn through st, yo, draw yarn through 2 loops on hook) 3 times in same st, yo, draw yarn through 4 loops on hook.

Chain multiples of 16 plus 8.

Row 1: Dc in 6th ch from hook, *ch 1, skip next ch, dc in next ch; rep from * across, turn.

Row 2: Ch 4 (counts as dc, ch 1), skip next ch-1 space, dc in next dc, ch 1, skip next ch-1 space, dc in next dc, *ch 5, skip next 3 ch-1 spaces, 3-dc puff st in next dc, ch 5, skip next 3 ch-1 spaces, (dc, ch 1) in each of next 2 dc**, dc in next dc; rep from * across, ending last rep at **, skip next ch of turning ch, dc in next ch of turning ch, turn.

Row 3: Ch 4 (counts as dc, ch 1), skip next ch-1 space, dc in next dc, ch 1, skip next ch-1 space, dc in next dc, *ch 4, skip first 4 ch of next ch-5 loop, sc in next ch, skip next puff st, sc in first ch of next ch-5 loop, ch 4, (dc, ch 1) in each of next 2 dc, dc in next dc; rep from * across, ending with last dc in 3rd ch of turning ch, turn.

Row 4: Ch 4 (counts as dc, ch 1), skip next ch-1 space, dc in next dc, ch 1, skip next ch-1 space, dc in next dc, *ch 4, skip first 3 ch of next ch-4 loop, sc in next ch, sc between next 2 sc, sc in first ch of next ch-4 loop, ch 4, (dc, ch 1) in each of next 2 dc, dc in next dc; rep from * across, ending with last dc in 3rd ch of turning ch, turn.

Row 5: Ch 4 (counts as dc, ch 1), skip next ch-1 space, dc in next dc, ch 1, skip next ch-1 space, dc in next dc, *ch 5, skip next ch-4 loop, skip next sc, 3-dc puff st in next sc, ch 5, skip next ch-4 loop, (dc, ch 1) in each of next 2 dc, dc in next dc; rep from * across, ending with last dc in 3rd ch of turning ch, turn.

Row 6: Ch 4 (counts as dc, ch 1), skip next ch-1 space, dc in next dc, ch 1, skip next ch-1 space, dc in next dc, ch 1, (dc, ch 1, dc, ch 1) in next ch-5 loop, dc in next puff st, ch 1, (dc, ch 1, dc, ch 1) in next ch-5 loop, (dc, ch 1) in each of next 2 dc, dc in next dc; rep from * across, ending with last dc in 3rd ch of turning ch, turn.

Rep Rows 2-6 for pattern.

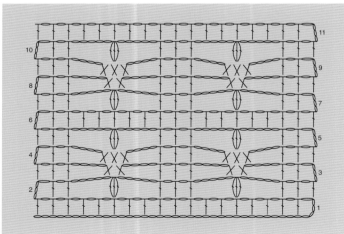

367

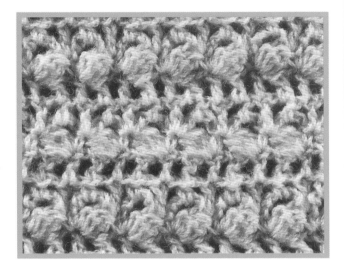

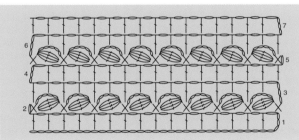

4-Dc Puff st: (Yo, insert hook in next st, yo, draw yarn through st, yo, draw yarn through 2 loops on hook) 4 times in same st, yo, draw yarn through 5 loops on hook

Chain multiples of 4.

Row 1: Dc in 6th ch from hook, *ch 1, skip next ch, dc in next ch; rep from * across, turn.

Row 2: Ch 1, sc in first dc, *ch 5, 4-dc puff st in last sc made, skip next 2 ch-1 spaces**, sc in next dc; rep from * across, ending last rep at **, skip next ch of turning ch, sc in next ch of turning ch, turn.

Row 3: Ch 4 (counts as dc, ch 1), *hdc in next ch-5 loop, ch 1, dc in next sc**, ch 1; rep from * across, ending last rep at **, turn.

Row 4: Ch 4 (counts as dc, ch 1), skip next ch-1 space, *dc in next hdc, ch 1, skip next ch-1 space**, dc in next dc, skip next ch-1 space; rep from * across, ending last rep at **, dc in 3rd ch of turning ch, turn.

Rep Rows 2-4 for pattern.

368

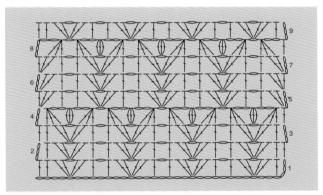

3-Dc Cluster: (Yo, insert hook in next st, yo, draw yarn through st, yo, draw yarn through 2 loops on hook) 3 times in designated sts, yo, draw yarn through 4 loops on hook.

3-Dc Puff st: (Yo, insert hook in next st, yo, draw yarn through st, yo, draw yarn through 2 loops on hook) 3 times in same st, yo, draw yarn through 4 loops on hook.

Chain multiples of 8 plus 3.

Row 1: Dc in 4th ch from hook, *skip next 2 ch (2 dc, ch 1, 2 dc) in next ch, skip next 2 ch, dc in next ch**, ch 1, skip next ch, dc in next ch; rep from * across, ending last rep at **, dc in last ch, turn.

Rows 2-3: Ch 3 (counts as dc), skip first dc, dc in next dc, *(2 dc, ch 1, 2 dc) in next ch-1 space, skip next 2 dc, dc in next dc**, ch 1, skip next ch-1 space, dc in next dc; rep from * across, ending last rep at **, dc in 3rd ch of turning ch, turn.

Row 4: Ch 3 (counts as dc), skip first dc, *3-dc cluster worked across next 3 dc, ch 2, work 3-dc puff st in next ch-1 space, ch 2, 3-dc cluster worked across next 3 dc**, ch 1, skip next ch-1

space; rep from * across, ending last rep at **, dc in 3rd ch of turning ch, turn.

Row 5: Ch 3 (counts as dc), 2 dc in first dc, *dc in next ch-2 space, ch 1, dc in next ch-2 space**, (2 dc, ch 1, 2 dc) in next ch-1 space; rep from * across, ending last rep at **, skip next cluster, 3 dc in 3rd ch of turning ch, turn.

Rows 6-7: Ch 3 (counts as dc), 2 dc in first dc, skip next 2 dc, *dc in next dc, ch 1, skip next ch-1 space, dc in next dc**, (2 dc, ch 1, 2 dc) in next ch-1 space, skip next 2 dc; rep from * across, ending last rep at **, skip next 2 dc, 3 dc in 3rd ch of turning ch, turn.

Row 8: Ch 5 (counts as dc, ch 2), skip first dc, *3-dc cluster worked across next 3 dc, ch 1, skip next ch-1 space, 3-dc cluster worked across next 3 dc, ch 2**, work 3-dc puff st in next ch-1 space, ch 2; rep from * across, ending last rep at **, dc in 3rd ch of turning ch, turn.

Row 9: Ch 3 (counts as dc), dc in next ch-2 space, *(2 dc, ch 1, 2 dc) in next ch-1 space, dc in next ch-2 space**, ch 1, dc in next ch-2 space; rep from * across, ending last rep at **, dc in 3rd ch of turning ch, turn.

Rep Rows 2-9 for pattern.

369

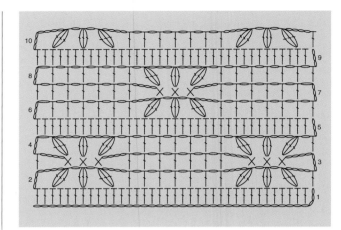

3-Dc Puff st: (Yo, insert hook in next st, yo, draw yarn through st, yo, draw yarn through 2 loops on hook) 3 times in same st, yo, draw yarn through 4 loops on hook

Chain multiples of 24 plus 15.

Row 1: Dc in 4th ch from hook, dc in each ch across, turn.

Row 2: Ch 7 (counts as dc, ch 4), skip first 2 dc, *3-dc puff st in next dc, (ch 1, skip next 3 dc, 3-dc puff st in next dc) twice, ch 4, skip next dc**, (dc in next dc, ch 1, skip next dc) 6 times, dc in next dc, ch 4, skip next dc; rep from * across, ending last rep at **, dc in 3rd ch of turning ch, turn.

Row 3: Ch 7 (counts as dc, ch 4), *sc in each of next 3 puff sts, ch 4, skip next ch-4 loop**, (dc, ch 1) in each of next 6 dc, dc in next dc, ch 4; rep from * across, ending last rep at **, dc in 3rd ch of turning ch, turn.

Row 4: Ch 4 (counts as dc, ch 1), skip next ch-4 loop, *(3-dc puff st, ch 3) in each of next 2 sc, 3-dc puff st in next sc, ch 1, skip next ch-4 loop**, (dc, ch 1) in each of next 6 dc, dc in next dc; rep from * across, ending last rep at **, dc in 3rd ch of turning ch, turn.

Row 5: Ch 3 (counts as dc), skip first dc, *dc in next ch-1 space, (dc in next puff st, 3 dc in next ch-3 loop) twice, dc in next puff st, dc in next ch-1 space**, (dc in next dc, dc in next ch-1 space) 6 times, dc in next dc; rep from * across, ending last rep at **, dc in 3rd ch of turning ch, turn.

Row 6: Ch 4 (counts as dc, ch 1), skip first 2 dc, (dc in next dc, ch 1, skip next dc) 5 times, dc in next dc, *ch 4, skip next dc, 3-dc puff st in next dc, (ch 1, skip next 3 dc, 3-dc puff st in next dc) twice, ch 4, skip next dc, (dc in next dc, ch 1, skip next dc) 6 times, dc in next dc; rep from * across, ending with last dc in 3rd ch of turning ch, turn.

Row 7: Ch 4 (counts as dc, ch 1), skip next ch-1 space, (dc in next dc, ch 1, skip next dc) 5 times, dc in next dc, *ch 4, skip next ch-4 loop, sc in each of next 3 puff sts, ch 4, skip next ch-4 loop, (dc in next dc, ch 1, skip next dc) 6 times, dc in next dc; rep from * across, ending with last dc in 3rd ch of turning ch, turn.

Row 8: Ch 4 (counts as dc, ch 1), skip next ch-1 space, (dc in next dc, ch 1, skip next ch-1 space) 5 times, dc in next dc, *ch 1, skip next ch-4 loop, (3-dc puff st, ch 3) in each of next 2 sc, 3-dc puff st in next sc, ch 1, skip next ch-4 loop, (dc in next dc, ch 1, skip next ch-1 space) 6 times, dc in next dc; rep from * across, ending with last dc in 3rd ch of turning ch, turn.

Row 9: Ch 3 (counts as dc), skip first dc, *(dc in next ch-1 space, dc in next dc) 6 times**, dc in next ch-1 space, (dc in next puff st, 3 dc in next ch-3 loop) twice, dc in next puff st, dc in next ch-1 space**; rep from * across, ending last rep at **, working last dc in 3rd ch of turning ch, turn.

Rep Rows 2-9 for pattern.

370

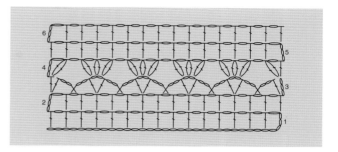

2-Dc Puff st: (Yo, insert hook in next st, yo, draw yarn through st, yo, draw yarn through 2 loops on hook) twice in same st, yo, draw yarn through 3 loops on hook.

Chain multiples of 6 plus 4.

Row 1: Dc in 6th ch from hook, *ch 1, skip next ch, dc in next ch; rep from * across, turn.

Row 2: Ch 4 (counts as dc, ch 1), skip next ch-1 space, (dc, ch 1) in each dc across to turning ch, skip next ch of turning ch, dc in next ch of turning ch, turn.

Row 3: Ch 3 (counts as dc), dc in first dc, *ch 2, skip next ch-1 space, sc in next ch-1 space, ch 2, skip next ch-1 space**, (dc, ch 2, dc) in next dc; rep from * across, ending last rep at **, 2 dc in 3rd ch of turning ch, turn.

Row 4: Ch 4 (counts as dc, ch 1), 2-dc puff st in first dc, ch 1, skip next 2 ch-2 spaces, *(2-dc, puff st, ch 1, 2-dc puff st, ch 1, 2-dc puff st) in next ch-2 space, ch 1, skip next 2 ch-2 spaces; rep from * across to within last 2 sts, skip next dc, (2-dc, ch 1, dc) in 3rd ch of turning ch, turn.

Row 5: Ch 4 (counts as dc, ch 1), skip next ch-1 space, *dc in next st, ch 1, skip next ch-1 space; rep from * across to turning ch, dc in 3rd ch of turning ch, turn.

Rep Rows 2-5 for pattern.

371

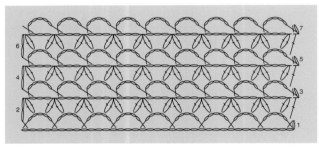

2-Dc Puff st: *(Yo, insert hook in next st, yo, draw yarn through st, yo, draw yarn through 2 loops on hook) twice in same st, yo, draw yarn through 3 loops on hook.*

4-Dc Cluster: *(Yo, insert hook in next st, yo, draw yarn through st, yo, draw yarn through 2 loops on hook) twice in same space, (yo, insert hook in next st, yo, draw yarn through st, yo, draw yarn through 2 loops on hook) twice in next designated space, yo, draw yarn through 5 loops on hook.*

Chain multiples of 4 plus 2.

Row 1: Sc in 2nd ch from hook, *ch 5, skip next 3 ch, sc in next ch; rep from * across, turn.

Row 2: Ch 2 (counts as dc), 2-dc puff st in next ch-5 loop, *ch 3, 4-dc cluster, working first 2 half-closed dc in same loop as last cluster, work next 2 half-closed dc in next loop, yo, complete cluster; rep from * across to last ch-5 loop, ch 3, 2-dc puff st in same loop as last cluster, dc in last sc, turn.

Row 3: Ch 1, sc in first dc, (ch 5, sc) in each ch-3 loop across, turn.

Rep Rows 2-3 for pattern.

372

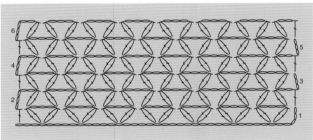

2-Dc Puff st: *(Yo, insert hook in next st, yo, draw yarn through st, yo, draw yarn through 2 loops on hook) twice in same st, yo, draw yarn through 3 loops on hook.*

Chain multiples of 5 plus 4.

Row 1: (2-dc puff st, ch 3, 2-dc puff st) in 6th ch from hook, *skip next 4 ch, (2-dc puff st, ch 3, 2-dc puff st) in next ch; rep from * across to within last 3 ch, skip next 2 ch, dc in last ch, turn.

Row 2: Ch 5 (counts as dc, ch 2), *2-dc puff st in next cluster, skip next ch-3 loop, 2-dc puff st, in next cluster**, ch 3; rep from * across, ending last rep at **, ch 2, dc in top of turning ch, turn.

Row 3: Ch 3 (counts as dc), skip next ch-2 space, *2-dc puff st in next cluster, ch 3, 2-dc puff st in next cluster**, skip next ch-3 loop; rep from * across, ending last rep at **, skip next 2 ch of turning ch, dc in 3rd ch of turning ch, turn.

Rep Rows 2-3 for pattern.

.26.
Puff Stitch Combinations

373

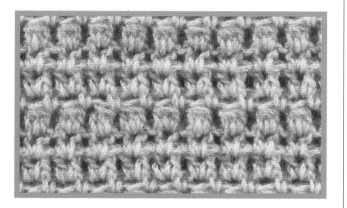

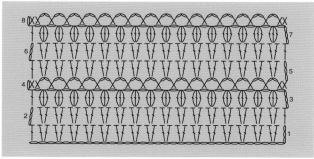

3-Dc Puff st: (Yo, insert hook in next st, yo, draw yarn through st, yo, draw yarn through 2 loops on hook) 3 times in same st, yo, draw yarn through 4 loops on hook

Chain multiples of 2.

Row 1: 2 dc in 5th ch from hook, *skip next ch, 2 dc in next ch; rep from * across to within last ch, dc in last ch, turn.

Row 2: Ch 3 (counts as dc), skip first 2 dc, *2 dc between last skipped and next dc**, skip next 2 dc; rep from * across, ending last rep at **, skip next dc, dc in top of turning ch, turn.

Row 3: Ch 4 (counts as dc, ch 1), skip first 2 dc, *3-dc puff st between last skipped and next dc, ch 1**, skip next 2 dc; rep from * across, ending last rep at **, skip next dc, dc in 3rd ch of turning ch, turn.

Row 4: Ch 1, sc in first dc, sc in next ch-1 space, (ch 2 sc) in each ch-1 space across, sc in 3rd ch of turning ch, turn.

Row 5: Ch 3 (counts as dc), 2 dc in each ch-2 space across to last ch-2 space, skip next sc, dc in last sc, turn.

Rep Rows 2-5 for pattern.

374

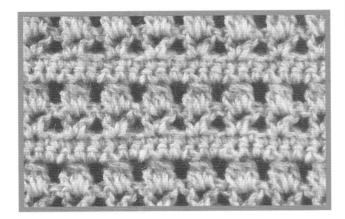

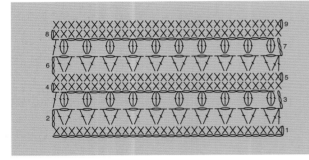

2-Dc Cluster: *(Yo, insert hook in next st, yo, draw yarn through st, yo, draw yarn through 2 loops on hook) twice, yo, draw yarn through 3 loops on hook.*

3-Dc Puff st: *(Yo, insert hook in next st, yo, draw yarn through st, yo, draw yarn through 2 loops on hook) 3 times in same st, yo, draw yarn through 4 loops on hook.*

Chain multiples of 3 plus 1.

Row 1: Sc in 2nd ch from hook, sc in each ch across, turn.

Row 2: Ch 3 (counts as dc), skip first sc, *(dc, ch 1, dc) in next sc, skip next 2 sc; rep from * across to within last 2 sc, dc in next sc, ch 1, work 2-dc cluster, working first half-closed dc in last sc worked, work 2nd half-closed dc in last sc, turn.

Row 3: Ch 3 (counts as dc), 3-dc puff st in next ch-1 space, (ch 2, 3-dc puff st) in each ch-1 space across, skip next dc, dc in 3rd ch of turning ch, turn.

Row 4: Ch 1, sc in first dc, sc in next cluster, *2 sc in next ch-2 space, sc in next cluster; rep from * across to turning ch, sc in 3rd ch of turning ch, turn.

Row 5: Ch 1, sc in each sc across, turn.

Rep Rows 2-5 for pattern.

375

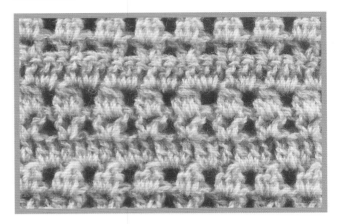

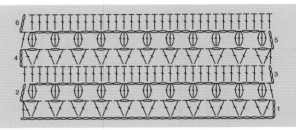

2-Dc Cluster: *(Yo, insert hook in next st, yo, draw yarn through st, yo, draw yarn through 2 loops on hook) twice, yo, draw yarn through 3 loops on hook.*

3-Dc Puff st: *(Yo, insert hook in next st, yo, draw yarn through st, yo, draw yarn through 2 loops on hook) 3 times in same st, yo, draw yarn through 4 loops on hook.*

Chain multiples of 3.

Row 1: (Dc, ch 1, dc) in 5th ch from hook, *skip next 2 ch, (dc, ch 1, dc) in next ch; rep from * across to within last 2 ch, dc in next ch, ch 1, 2-dc cluster, working first half-closed dc in last ch worked, work 2nd half-closed dc in last ch, turn.

Row 2: Ch 3 (counts as dc), 3-dc puff st in next ch-1 space, (ch 2, 3-dc puff st) in each ch-1 space across to within last 2 sts, skip next dc, dc in top of turning ch, turn.

Row 3: Ch 3 (counts as dc), skip first dc, dc in next cluster, *2 dc in next ch-2 space, dc in next cluster; rep from * across to turning ch, dc in 3rd ch of turning ch, turn.

Row 4: Ch 3 (counts as dc), skip first dc, *(dc, ch 1, dc) in next dc, skip next 2 dc; rep from * across to within last 2 sts, dc in next dc, 2-dc cluster, working first half-closed dc in last dc worked, work 2nd half-closed dc in 3rd ch of turning ch, turn.

Rep Rows 2-4 for pattern.

376

2-Dc Puff st: *(Yo, insert hook in next st, yo, draw yarn through st, yo, draw yarn through 2 loops on hook) twice in same st, yo, draw yarn through 3 loops on hook.*

Chain multiples of 6 plus 5.

Row 1: Dc in 5th ch from hook, *ch 1, skip next 2 ch, sc in next ch, ch 1, skip next 2 ch**, (dc, ch 1, dc, ch 1, dc) in next ch; rep from * across, ending last rep at **, (dc, ch 1, dc) in last ch, turn.

Row 2: Ch 1, sc in first dc, *ch 3, skip next 2 ch-1 spaces, 2-dc puff st in next sc, ch 3, skip next 2 ch-1 spaces, sc in next dc; rep from * across, ending with last sc in 3rd ch of turning ch, turn.

Row 3: Ch 4 (counts as dc, ch 1), dc in first sc, *ch 1, skip next ch-3 loop, sc in next puff st, ch 1, skip next ch-3 loop**, (dc, ch 1, dc, ch 1, dc) in next sc; rep from * across, ending last rep at **, (dc, ch 1, dc) in last sc, turn.

Rep Rows 2-3 for pattern.

377

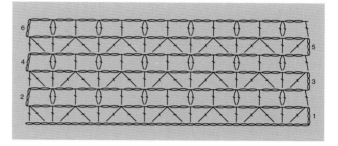

2-Dc Cluster: *(Yo, insert hook in next st, yo, draw yarn through st, yo, draw yarn through 2 loops on hook) twice, yo, draw yarn through 3 loops on hook.*

2-Dc Puff st: *(Yo, insert hook in next st, yo, draw yarn through st, yo, draw yarn through 2 loops on hook) twice, yo, draw yarn through 3 loops on hook.*

Chain multiples of 6 plus 4.

Row 1: Dc in 6th ch from hook, ch 2, *dc in next ch, ch 2**, work 2-dc cluster, working first half-closed dc in next ch, skip next 3 ch, work 2nd half-closed dc in next ch, yo, complete cluster, ch 2; rep from * across, ending last rep at **, work 2-dc cluster, working first half-closed dc in next ch, skip next ch, work 2nd half-closed dc in last ch, yo, complete cluster, turn.

Row 2: Ch 5 (counts as dc, ch 2), skip next ch-2 space, *2-dc puff st in next dc, ch 2, skip next ch-2 space**, dc in next cluster, ch 2, skip next ch-2 space; rep from * across, ending last rep at **, dc in top of turning ch, turn.

Row 3: Ch 3 (counts as dc), dc in next ch-2 space, *ch 2, dc in next puff st, ch 2**, 2-dc cluster worked across next 2 ch-2 spaces; rep from * across, ending last rep at **, work 2-dc cluster, working first half-closed dc in ch-2 space of turning ch, work 2nd half-closed dc in 3rd ch of turning ch, yo, complete cluster, turn.

Rep Rows 2-3 for pattern.

378

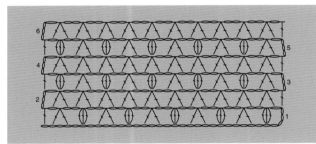

2-Dc Cluster: (Yo, insert hook in next st, yo, draw yarn through st, yo, draw yarn through 2 loops on hook) twice, yo, draw yarn through 3 loops on hook.

3-Dc Puff st: (Yo, insert hook in next st, yo, draw yarn through st, yo, draw yarn through 2 loops on hook) 3 times in same st, yo, draw yarn through 4 loops on hook.

Chain multiples of 6 plus 5.

Row 1: 3-dc puff st in 6th ch from hook, *skip next 2 ch, 2-dc cluster, working first half-closed dc in next ch, skip next ch, work 2nd half-closed dc in next ch, yo, complete cluster**, ch 2, skip next ch, 3-dc puff st in next ch; rep from * across, ending last rep at **, ch 1, dc in last ch, turn.

Row 2: Ch 4 (counts as dc, ch 1), 2-dc cluster worked across next 2 space, *ch 2, starting in same ch-2 space as last cluster worked, work 2-dc cluster across next 2 spaces; rep from * across to turning ch, ch 1, dc in next ch of turning ch, turn.

Row 3: Ch 4 (counts as dc, ch 1), *2-dc cluster worked across next 2 spaces, ch 2, 3-dc puff st in next cluster, ch 2; rep from * across to turning ch, dc in 3rd ch of turning ch, turn.

Rep Rows 2-3 for pattern.

379

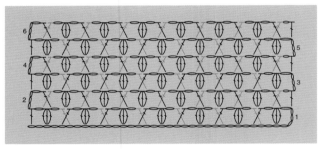

3-Dc Puff st: (Yo, insert hook in next st, yo, draw yarn through st, yo, draw yarn through 2 loops on hook) 3 times in same st, yo, draw yarn through 4 loops on hook.

Chain multiples of 5 plus 3.

Row 1: 3-dc puff st in 6th ch from hook, *ch 1, skip next 2 ch, dc in next ch, working behind last dc made, dc in last skipped ch (crossed dc made), ch 1, skip next ch, 3-dc puff st in next ch; rep from * across to within last 2 ch, ch 1, skip next ch, dc in last ch, turn.

Row 2: Ch 4 (counts as dc, ch 1), *skip next ch-1 space, dc in next ch-1 space, working behind last dc made, dc in last skipped ch-1 space (crossed dc made), ch 1**, 3-dc puff st between next 2 dc, ch 1; rep from * across, ending last rep at**, dc in next ch of turning ch, turn.

Row 3: Ch 4 (counts as dc, ch 1), skip next ch-1 space, *3-dc puff st between next 2 dc, ch 1, skip next ch-1 space**, dc in next ch-1 space, working behind last dc made, dc in last skipped ch-1 space (crossed dc made), ch 1; rep from * across, ending last rep at**, dc in 3rd ch of turning ch, turn.

Rep Rows 2-3 for pattern.

380

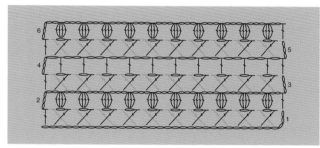

4-Dc Puff st: (Yo, insert hook in next st, yo, draw yarn through st, yo, draw yarn through 2 loops on hook) 4 times in same st, yo, draw yarn through 5 loops on hook

Chain multiples of 3 plus 1.

Row 1: Dc in 6th ch from hook, ch 1, skip 1 ch to the right, working behind last dc made, dc in next ch to the right (crossed dc made), *skip next 2 ch, dc in next ch, ch 1, working behind last dc made, dc in first skipped ch (crossed dc made); rep from * across to within last ch, dc in last ch, turn.

Row 2: Ch 5 (counts as dc, ch 2), *4-dc puff st in next ch-1 space**, ch 3; rep from * across, ending last rep at **, ch 2, dc in top of turning ch, turn.

Row 3: Ch 3 (counts as dc), *skip next space, dc in next space, ch 1, working behind last dc made, dc in last skipped space; rep from * across to turning ch, dc in 3rd ch of turning ch, turn.

Row 4: Ch 4 (counts as dc, ch 1), dc in next ch-1 space, (ch 2, dc) in each ch-1 space across to last ch-1 space, ch 1, dc in 3rd ch of turning ch, turn.

Row 5: Rep Row 3.

Rep Rows 2-5 for pattern.

381

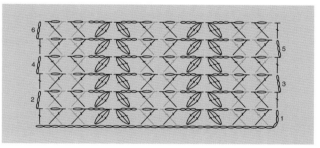

3-Dc Puff st: (Yo, insert hook in next st, yo, draw yarn through st, yo, draw yarn through 2 loops on hook) 3 times in same st, yo, draw yarn through 4 loops on hook.

Chain multiples of 12 plus 10.

Row 1: Dc in 6th ch from hook, ch 1, skip 1 ch to the right, working behind last dc made, dc in next ch to the right (crossed dc made), skip next 2 ch, *dc in next ch, working behind last dc made, dc in last skipped ch (crossed dc made)**, ch 3, 3-dc puff st in next ch, skip next 4 ch, 3-dc puff st in next ch, ch 3, skip next 2 ch, dc in next ch, working behind last dc made, dc in last skipped ch (crossed dc made); rep from * across, ending last rep at **, dc in last ch, turn.

Row 2: Ch 3 (counts as dc), skip first dc, *(skip next dc and ch-1 space, dc in next dc, working behind last dc made, dc in last skipped dc) twice (2 crossed dc made)**, ch 3, 3-dc puff st in each of next 2 ch-3 loops, ch 3; rep from * across, ending last rep at **, dc in top of turning ch, turn.

Rep Row 2 for pattern.

382

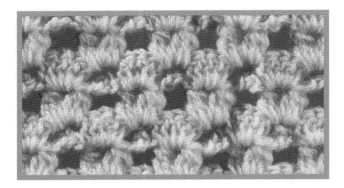

3-Dc Puff st: (Yo, insert hook in next st, yo, draw yarn through st, yo, draw yarn through 2 loops on hook) 3 times in same st, yo, draw yarn through 4 loops on hook.

Chain multiples of 5 plus 4.

Row 1: 3-dc puff st in 4th ch from hook, *ch 4, sl st in 3rd ch from hook for picot, ch 1, skip next 4 ch**, (3-dc puff st, ch 1, 3-dc puff st) in next ch; rep from * across, ending last rep at **, (3-dc puff st, ch 1, dc) in last ch, turn.

Row 2: Ch 3 (counts as dc), 2 dc in first dc, *skip next picot and ch-1 space**, 5 dc in next ch-1 space; rep from * across, ending last rep at **, 3 dc in 3rd ch of turning ch, turn.

Row 3: Ch 3 (counts as dc), skip first 3 dc, (3-dc puff st, ch 1, 3-dc puff st) between last skipped and next dc**, ch 4, sl st in 3rd ch from hook for picot, ch 1, skip next 5 dc; rep from * across, ending last rep at **, skip next 2 dc, dc in 3rd ch of turning ch, turn.

Row 4: Ch 3 (counts as dc), 5 dc in next ch-1 space, *skip next picot and ch-1 space, 5 dc in next ch-1 space; rep from * across to last ch-1 space, dc in top of turning ch, turn.

Row 5: Ch 3 (counts as dc), 3-dc puff st in first dc, *ch 4, sl st in 3rd ch from hook for picot, ch 1, skip next 5 dc**, (3-dc puff st, ch 1, 3-dc puff st) between last skipped and next dc; rep from * across, ending last rep at **, (3-dc puff st, dc) in 3rd ch of turning ch, turn.

Rep Rows 2-5 for pattern.

383

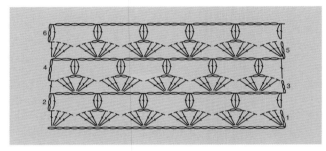

2-Dc Puff st: (Yo, insert hook in next st, yo, draw yarn through st, yo, draw yarn through 2 loops on hook) twice in same st, yo, draw yarn through 3 loops on hook.

3-Dc Puff st: (Yo, insert hook in next st, yo, draw yarn through st, yo, draw yarn through 2 loops on hook) 3 times in same st, yo, draw yarn through 4 loops on hook.

Chain multiples of 6 plus 4.

Row 1: 3 dc in 4th ch from hook, *skip next 5 ch, (3 dc, ch 2, 3 dc) in next ch; rep from * across to within last 6 ch, skip next 5 ch, 4 dc in last ch, turn.

Row 2: Ch 3 (counts as dc), dc in first dc, *ch 5, skip next 6 dc**, 3-dc puff st in next ch-2 space; rep from * across, ending last rep at**, 2-dc puff st in 3rd ch of turning ch, turn.

Row 3: Ch 3 (counts as dc), (3 dc, ch 2, 3 dc) in center ch of each ch-5 loop across, skip next dc, dc in 3rd ch of turning ch, turn.

Row 4: Ch 5 (counts as dc, ch 2), 3-dc puff st in next ch-2 space, (ch 5, 3-dc puff st) in each ch-2 space across to last ch-2 space, ch 2, skip next 3 dc, dc in 3rd ch of turning ch, turn.

Row 5: Ch 3, 3 dc in first dc, (3 dc, ch 2, 3 dc) in center ch of each ch-5 loop across to last ch-5 loop, skip next 2 ch of turning ch, 4 dc in 3rd ch of turning ch, turn.

Rep Rows 2-5 for pattern.

384

2-Dc Puff st: (Yo, insert hook in next st, yo, draw yarn through st, yo, draw yarn through 2 loops on hook) twice in same st, yo, draw yarn through 3 loops on hook.

3-Dc Puff st: (Yo, insert hook in next st, yo, draw yarn through st, yo, draw yarn through 2 loops on hook) 3 times in same st, yo, draw yarn through 4 loops on hook.

4-Dc Cluster: (Yo, insert hook in next st, yo, draw yarn through st, yo, draw yarn through 2 loops on hook) 4 times in designated sts, yo, draw yarn through 5 loops on hook.

Chain multiples of 8 plus 2.

Row 1: Sc in 2nd ch from hook, sc in next ch, *ch 4, 4-dc cluster, working 1 half-closed dc in each of next 2 ch, skip next ch, work next 2 half-closed dc in next 2 ch, yo, complete cluster, ch 4, sc in next ch**, ch 1, skip next ch, sc in next ch; rep from * across, ending last rep at **, sc in last ch, turn.

Row 2: Ch 3 (counts as dc), dc in first dc, *ch 3, sc in next ch-4 loop, ch 1, sc in next ch-4 loop, ch 3**, 3-dc puff st in next ch-1 space; rep from * across, ending last rep at **, skip next sc, 2-dc puff st in last sc, turn.

Row 3: Ch 1, sc in first cluster, *sc in next ch-3 loop, ch 4, 4-dc cluster, working first 2 half-closed dc in same ch-3 loop as last sc worked, skip next ch-1 space, work next 2 half-closed dc in next ch-3 loop, ch 4, sc in same ch-3 loop holding last 2 dc of last cluster**, ch 1; rep from * across, ending last rep at **, sc in 3rd ch of turning ch, turn.

Rep Rows 2-3 for pattern.

385

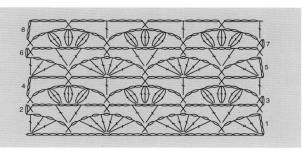

3-Dc Puff st: (Yo, insert hook in next st, yo, draw yarn through st, yo, draw yarn through 2 loops on hook) 3 times in same st, yo, draw yarn through 4 loops on hook.

Chain multiples of 10 plus 5.

Row 1: (Dc, ch 1, dc) in 5th ch from hook, *ch 1, skip next 4 ch, sc in next ch, ch 1, skip next 4 ch**, (dc, ch 1, dc, ch 1, dc, ch 1, dc, ch 1, dc) in next ch; rep from * across, ending last rep at **, (dc, ch 1, dc, ch 1, dc) in last ch, turn.

Row 2: Ch 1, sc in first dc, *ch 3, skip next 3 ch-1 spaces, (dc, ch 3, dc) in next sc, ch 3, skip next 3 ch-1 spaces, sc in next ch-1 space; rep from * across, ending with last sc in 3rd ch of turning ch, turn.

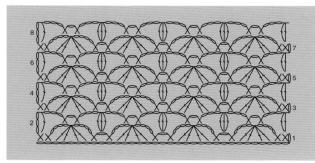

Row 3: Ch 1, sc in first sc, *ch 2, skip next ch-3 loop, (3-dc puff st, ch 2, 3-dc puff st, ch 2, 3-dc puff st) in next ch-3 loop, ch 2, skip next ch-3 loop, sc in next sc; rep from * across, turn.

Row 4: Ch 7 (counts as dc, ch 4), *skip next 2 ch-2 spaces, sc in next puff st, ch 4, skip next 2 ch-2 spaces, dc in next sc**, ch 4; rep from * across, ending last rep at **, turn.

Row 5: Ch 4 (counts as dc, ch 1), (dc, ch 1, dc) in first dc, *ch 1, skip next ch-4 loop, sc in next sc, ch 1, skip next ch-4 loop**, (dc, ch 1, dc, ch 1, dc, ch 1, dc, ch 1, dc, ch 1, dc) in next dc; rep from * across, ending last rep at **, (dc, ch 1, dc, ch 1, dc) in 3rd ch of turning ch, turn.

Rep Rows 2-5 for pattern.

386

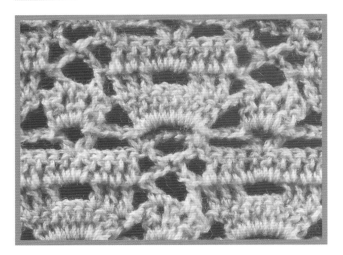

2-Dc Puff st: (Yo, insert hook in next st, yo, draw yarn through st, yo, draw yarn through 2 loops on hook) twice in same st, yo, draw yarn through 3 loops on hook.

Chain multiples of 12 plus 6.

Row 1: Sc in 8th ch from hook, *ch 3, skip next 3 ch, (dc, ch 3, dc) in next ch, ch 3, skip next 3 ch, sc in next ch**, ch 5, skip next 3 ch, sc in next ch; rep from * across, ending last rep at **, ch 2, skip next ch, dc in last ch, turn.

Row 2: Ch 3 (counts as dc), 4 dc in next ch-2 space, *ch 2, skip next ch-3 loop, (2-dc puff st, ch 2) 3 times in next ch-3 loop, skip next ch-3 loop**, 9 dc in next ch-5 loop; rep from * across, ending last rep at **, 4 dc in ch-2 space of turning ch, dc in next ch of turning ch, turn.

Row 3: Ch 4 (counts as dc, ch 1), skip first 2 dc, *dc in each of next 3 dc, skip next ch-2 space, dc in next ch-2 space, ch 5, dc in next ch-2 space, skip next ch-2 space, dc in each of next 3 dc**, ch 3, skip next 3 dc; rep from * across, ending last rep at **, ch 1, skip next dc, dc in 3rd ch of turning ch, turn.

Row 4: Ch 3 (counts as dc), dc in next ch-1 space, *dc in each of next 3 dc, (dc, ch 5, dc) in center ch of next ch-5 loop, skip next dc, dc in each of next 3 dc**, 3 dc in next ch-3 loop; rep from * across, ending last rep at **, dc in ch-1 space of turning ch, dc in 3rd ch of turning ch, turn.

Row 5: Ch 4 (counts as dc, ch 1), dc in first dc, *ch 3, skip next 5 dc, (sc, ch 5, sc) in next ch-5 loop, ch 3, skip next 5 dc**, (dc, ch 5, dc) in next dc; rep from * across, ending last rep at **, (dc, ch 1, dc) in 3rd ch of turning ch, turn.

Row 6: Ch 5 (counts as dc, ch 2), 2-dc puff st in next ch-1 space, ch 2, skip next ch-3 loop, *9 dc in next ch-5 loop, ch 2, skip next ch-3 loop**, (2-dc puff st, ch 2) 3 times in next ch-3 loop, skip next ch-3 loop; rep from * across, ending last rep at **, 2-dc puff st in next ch-1 space of turning ch, ch 2, dc in 3rd ch of turning ch, turn.

Row 7: Ch 5 (counts as dc, ch 2), dc in next ch-2 space, *skip next ch-2 space, dc in each of next 3 dc, ch 3, skip next 3 dc, dc in each of next 3 dc, skip next ch-2 space**, dc in next ch-2 space, ch 5, dc in next ch-2 space; rep from * across, ending last rep at **, dc in ch-2 space of turning ch, dc in 3rd ch of turning ch, turn.

Row 8: Ch 5 (counts as dc, ch 2), dc in first dc, skip next dc, *dc in each of next 3 dc, 3 dc in next ch-3 loop, dc in each of next 3 dc**, (dc, ch 5, dc) in center ch of next ch-5 loop; rep from * across, ending last rep at **, skip next 2 ch of turning ch, (dc, ch 2, dc) in 3rd ch of turning ch, turn.

Row 9: Ch 5 (counts as dc, ch 2), sc in next ch-2 space, *ch 3, skip next 5 dc, (dc, ch 3, dc) in next dc, ch 3, skip next 5 dc**, (sc, ch 5, sc) in next ch-5 loop; rep from * across, ending last rep at **, sc in next ch-2 space of turning ch, ch 2, dc in 3rd ch of turning ch, turn.

Rep Rows 2-9 for pattern.

387

2-Dc Puff st: (Yo, insert hook in next st, yo, draw yarn through st, yo, draw yarn through 2 loops on hook) twice in same st, yo, draw yarn through 3 loops on hook.

Chain multiples of 13 plus 10.

Row 1: Sc in 2nd ch from hook, *ch 3, skip next 3 ch, (dc, ch 1, dc) in next ch, ch 3, skip next 3 ch, sc in next ch**, ch 4, skip next 4 ch, sc in next ch; rep from * across, ending last rep at **, turn.

Row 2: Ch 6 (counts as dc, ch 3), *skip next ch-3 loop, sc in next dc, ch 3, skip next ch-1 space, sc in next dc, ch 3, skip next ch-3 loop**, (2-dc puff st, ch 2, 2-dc puff st, ch 2, 2-dc puff st) in next ch-4 loop, ch 3; rep from * across, ending last rep at **, dc in last sc, turn.

Row 3: Ch 1, sc in first dc, *ch 3, skip next ch-3 loop, (dc, ch 1, dc) in next ch-3 loop, ch 3**, skip next ch-3 loop, sc in next ch-2 space, ch 4, sc in next ch-2 space; rep from * across, ending last rep at **, skip next 3 ch of turning ch, dc in 3rd ch of turning ch, turn.

Rep Rows 2-3 for pattern.

388

2-Dc Puff st: (Yo, insert hook in next st, yo, draw yarn through st, yo, draw yarn through 2 loops on hook) twice in same st, yo, draw yarn through 3 loops on hook.

Chain multiples of 12 plus 11.

Row 1: Sc in 5th ch from hook, *ch 3, skip next 3 ch, sc in next ch; rep from * across to within last 2 ch, ch 1, skip next ch, hdc in last ch, turn.

Row 2: Ch 1, sc in first hdc, skip next ch-1 space, *7 dc in next ch-3 loop**, sc in next ch-3 loop, ch 3, sc in next ch-3 loop; rep from * across, ending last rep at **, skip next ch of turning ch, sc in next ch of turning ch, turn.

Row 3: Ch 5 (counts as dc, ch 2), skip first 3 sts, *sc in next dc, ch 3, skip next dc, sc in next dc**, ch 3, (2-dc puff st, ch 3, 2-dc puff st) in next ch-3 loop, ch 3, skip next 3 sts; rep from * across, ending last rep at **, skip next 2 dc, dc in last sc, turn.

Row 4: Ch 1, sc in first hdc, skip next ch-2 space, *7 dc in next ch-3 loop**, skip next ch-3 loop, sc in next puff st, ch 3, skip next ch-3 loop, sc in next puff st; rep from * across, ending last rep at **, skip next 2 ch of turning ch, sc in next ch of turning ch, turn.

Rep Rows 3-4 for pattern.

389

2-Dc Puff st: (Yo, insert hook in next st, yo, draw yarn through st, yo, draw yarn through 2 loops on hook) twice in same st, yo, draw yarn through 3 loops on hook.

3-Dc Puff st: (Yo, insert hook in next st, yo, draw yarn through st, yo, draw yarn through 2 loops on hook) 3 times in same st, yo, draw yarn through 4 loops on hook.

Chain multiples of 8 plus 3.

Row 1: Dc in 3rd ch from hook, *ch 2, skip next ch, sc in next ch, ch 3, skip next 3 ch, sc in next ch, ch 2, skip next ch**, 3-dc puff st in next ch; rep from * across, ending last rep at **, 2-dc puff st in last ch, turn.

Row 2: Ch 1, sc in first puff st, *ch 1, skip next ch-2 space, (2 dc, ch 2, 2 dc) in next ch-3 loop, ch 1, skip next ch-2 space, sc in next puff st; rep from * across, ending with last sc in 2nd ch of turning ch, turn.

Row 3: Ch 1, sc in first sc, ch 2, skip next ch-1 space, *sc in next dc, ch 2, 3-dc puff st in next ch-2 space, ch 2, skip next dc, sc in next dc**, ch 3, skip next 2 ch-1 spaces; rep from * across, ending last rep at **, ch 2, skip next ch-1 space, sc in last sc, turn.

Row 4: Ch 3 (counts as dc), 2 dc in next ch-2 space, *ch 1, skip next ch-2 space, sc in next puff st, ch 1, skip next ch-2 space**, (2 dc, ch 2, 2 dc) in next ch-3 loop; rep from * across, ending last rep at **, 2 dc in next ch-2 space, dc in last sc, turn.

Row 5: Ch 2 (counts as dc), dc in first dc, *ch 2, skip next dc, sc in next dc, ch 3, skip next 2 ch-1 spaces, sc in next dc**, ch 2, 3-dc puff st in next ch-2 space; rep from * across, ending last rep at **, ch 2, skip next dc, 2-dc puff st in 3rd ch of turning ch, turn.

Rep Rows 2-5 for pattern.

390

2-Dc Puff st: (Yo, insert hook in next st, yo, draw yarn through st, yo, draw yarn through 2 loops on hook) twice in same st, yo, draw yarn through 3 loops on hook.

Chain multiples of 11 plus 6.

Row 1: Sc in 7th ch from hook, *skip next 3 ch, (2-dc puff st, [ch 1, 2-dc puff st] 4 times) in next ch, skip next 3 ch, sc in next ch**, ch 5, skip next 2 ch, sc in next ch; rep from * across, ending last rep at **, ch 2, skip next ch, dc in last ch, turn.

Row 2: Ch 5 (counts as dc, ch 2), sc in next ch-2 space, *ch 1, sc in next ch-1 space, (ch 3, sc) in each of next 3 ch-1 spaces, ch 1**, (sc, ch 5, sc) in next ch-5 loop; rep from * across, ending last rep at **, sc in ch-2 space of turning ch, ch 2, dc in next ch of turning ch, turn.

Row 3: Ch 5 (counts as dc, ch 2), sc in next ch-2 space, *skip next 2 spaces, (2-dc puff st, [ch 1, 2-dc puff st] 4 times) in next ch-3 loop, skip next 2 spaces**, (sc, ch 5, sc) in next ch-5 loop; rep from * across, ending last rep at **, sc in ch-2 space of turning ch, dc in 3rd ch of turning ch, turn.

Rep Rows 2-3 for pattern.

391

2-Tr Puff st: (Yo twice, insert hook in next st, yo, draw yarn through st, [yo, draw yarn through 2 loops on hook] twice) twice in same st, yo, draw yarn through 3 loops on hook.

Chain multiples of 9 plus 4.

Row 1: Dc in 4th ch from hook, *ch 3, skip next 2 ch, sc in next ch, ch 3, skip next ch, sc in next ch, ch 3, skip next 2 ch, dc in each of next 2 ch; rep from * across, turn.

Row 2: Ch 3 (counts as dc), skip first dc, dc in next dc, *ch 4, sl st in 3rd ch from hook for picot, (2-tr puff st, [ch 1, picot, 2-tr puff st] twice) in next ch-3 loop, ch 1, skip next ch-3 loop, dc in each of next 2 dc; rep from * across, ending with last dc in 3rd ch of turning ch, turn.

Row 3: Ch 3 (counts as dc), skip first dc, dc in next dc, *(ch 3, skip next picot, sc in next ch-1 space) twice, ch 3, skip next picot, dc in each of next 2 dc; rep from * across, ending with last dc in 3rd ch of turning ch, turn.

Rep Rows 2-3 for pattern.

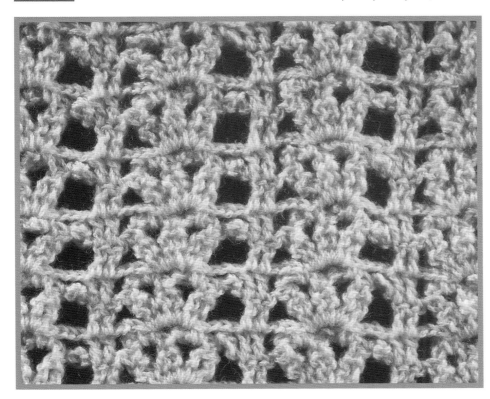

392

2-Dc Puff st: (Yo, insert hook in next st, yo, draw yarn through st, yo, draw yarn through 2 loops on hook) twice in same st, yo, draw yarn through 3 loops on hook.

Chain multiples of 12 plus 4.

Row 1: Sc in 2nd ch from hook, ch 2, skip next ch, sc in next ch, *skip next 3 ch, (3 tr, ch 4, sc) in next ch, ch 2, skip next ch, (sc, ch 4, 3 tr) in next ch, skip next 3 ch, sc in next ch, ch 2, skip next ch, sc in next ch; rep from * across, turn.

Row 2: Ch 4 (counts as dc, ch 1), dc in next ch-2 space, *ch 1, sc in next ch-4 loop, ch 2, 2-dc puff st in next ch-2 space, ch 2, sc in next ch-4 loop, ch 1**, (dc, ch 1, dc) in next ch-2 space; rep from * across, ending last rep at **, dc in next ch-2 space, dc in last sc, turn.

Row 3: Ch 1, sc in first dc, ch 2, skip next ch-1 space, sc in next dc, *skip next ch-1 space, (3 tr, ch 4, sc) in next ch-2 space, ch 2, (sc, ch 4, 3 tr) in next ch-2 space, skip next ch-1 space, sc in next dc, ch 2, skip next ch-1 space, sc in next dc; rep from * across, ending with last sc in 3rd ch of turning ch, turn.

Rep Rows 2-3 for pattern.

393

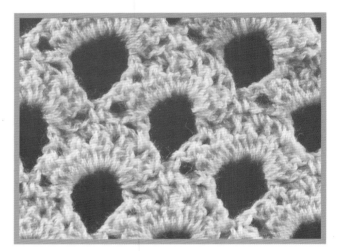

2-Dc Puff st: (Yo, insert hook in next st, yo, draw yarn through st, yo, draw yarn through 2 loops on hook) twice in same st, yo, draw yarn through 3 loops on hook.

3-Dc Puff st: (Yo, insert hook in next st, yo, draw yarn through st, yo, draw yarn through 2 loops on hook) 3 times in same st, yo, draw yarn through 4 loops on hook.

Chain multiples of 12.

Row 1: Sc in 9th ch from hook, sc in each of next 6 ch, *ch 7, skip next 5 ch, sc in each of next 7 ch; rep from * across, ending with sc in each of last 4 ch, turn.

Row 2: Ch 1, sc in first sc, *ch 1, (3-dc puff st, [ch 2, 3-dc puff st] 4 times) in next ch-7 loop, ch 1, skip next 3 sc, sc in next sc; rep from * across to within last 3 sc and turning ch, ch 1, (3-dc puff st, ch 2, 3-dc puff st) in next ch-3 loop of turning ch, ch 2, 2-dc puff st in next ch of turning ch, turn.

Row 3: Ch 1, sc in first puff st, sc in next ch-2 space, ch 2, dc in next ch-2 space, *ch 5, skip next 2 ch-1 spaces, dc in next ch-2 space, (ch 2, sc) in each of next 2 ch-2 spaces, ch 2, dc in next ch-2 space; rep from * across to within last ch-1 space, ch 2, skip next ch-1 space, tr in last sc, turn.

Row 4: Ch 3 (counts as dc), dc in first tr, (ch 2, 3-dc puff st) twice in next ch-2 space, ch 1, *skip next ch-2 space, sc in next ch-2 space, ch 1, (3-dc puff st, [ch 2, 3-dc puff st] 4 times) in next ch-5 loop, ch 1; rep from * across to within last ch-2 space, ch 1, skip next sc, sc in last sc, turn.

Row 5: Ch 6 (counts as tr, ch 2), skip next ch-1 space, *dc in next ch-2 space, (ch 2, sc) in each of next 2 ch-2 spaces, ch 2, dc in next ch-2 space, ch 5, skip next 2 ch-1 spaces; rep from * across to within last 2 ch-2 spaces, dc in next ch-2 space, ch 2, sc in next ch-2 space, skip next dc, sc in 3rd ch of turning ch, turn.

Row 6: Ch 1, sc in first sc, *ch 1, skip next ch-2 space, (3-dc puff st, [ch 2, 3-dc puff st] 4 times) in next ch-5 loop, ch 1, skip next ch-2 space, sc in next ch-2 space; rep from * across to within last ch-2 space and turning ch, ch 1, skip next ch-2 space, (3-dc puff st, ch 2, 3-dc puff st) in next ch-2 space of turning ch, ch 2, 2-dc puff st in 4th ch of turning ch, turn.

Rep Rows 3-6 for pattern.

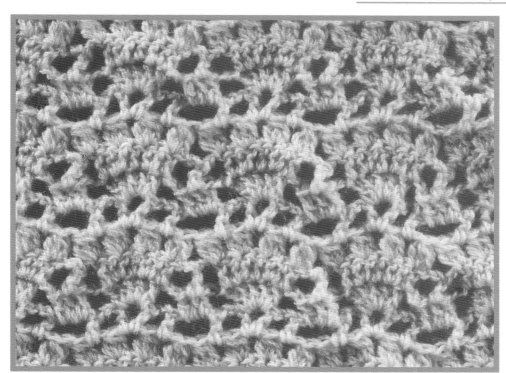

394

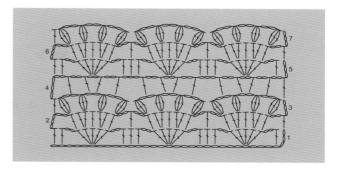

3-Dc Puff st: (Yo, insert hook in next st, yo, draw yarn through st, yo, draw yarn through 2 loops on hook) 3 times in same st, yo, draw yarn through 4 loops on hook.

Chain multiples of 10 plus 3.

Row 1: Dc in 4th ch from hook, *ch 2, skip next 3 ch, 5 dc in next ch, ch 2, skip next 3 ch, dc in each of next 3 ch; rep from * across, ending with dc in each of last 2 ch, turn.

Row 2: Ch 5 (counts as dc, ch 2), *skip next ch-2 space, dc in next dc, (2 dc in next dc, dc in next dc) twice, ch 2, skip next dc**, dc in next dc, ch 2; rep from * across, ending last rep at **, dc in 3rd ch of turning ch, turn.

Row 3: Ch 3 (counts as dc), skip next ch-2 space, *(3-dc puff st in next dc, ch 2, skip next dc) 3 times, 3-dc puff st in next dc**, skip next 2 ch-2 spaces; rep from * across, ending last rep at **, dc in 3rd ch of turning ch, turn.

Row 4: Ch 5 (counts as dc, ch 2), *dc in next ch-2 space, ch 2, (dc, ch 2, dc) in next ch-2 space, ch 2, dc in next ch-2 space**, ch 3; rep from * across, ending last rep at **, ch 2, dc in 3rd ch of turning ch, turn.

Row 5: Ch 3 (counts as dc), dc in next ch-2 space, *ch 2, skip next ch-2 space, 5 dc in next ch-2 space, ch 2, skip next ch-2 space**, 3 dc in next ch-3 loop; rep from * across, ending last rep at **, dc in next ch-2 space of turning ch, dc in 3rd ch of turning ch, turn.

Rep Rows 2-5 for pattern.

395

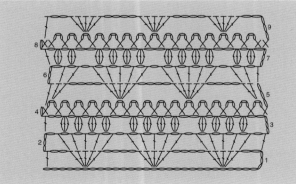

3-Dc Puff st: (Yo, insert hook in next st, yo, draw yarn through st, yo, draw yarn through 2 loops on hook) 3 times in same st, yo, draw yarn through 4 loops on hook.

Chain multiples of 9 plus 6.

Row 1: 5 dc in 10th ch from hook, *ch 4, skip next 8 ch, 5 dc in next ch; rep from * across to within last 5 ch, ch 2, skip next 4 ch, dc in last ch, turn.

Row 2: Ch 4 (counts as dc, ch 1), *skip next ch-2 space, (dc, ch 1) in each of next 5 dc**, skip next ch-4 loop; rep from * across, ending last rep at **, skip next 2 ch of turning ch, dc in next ch of turning ch, turn.

Row 3: Ch 5 (counts as dc, ch 2), skip next ch-1 space, *(3-dc puff st, ch 1) in each of next 3 ch-1 spaces, 3-dc puff st in next ch-1 space, ch 2, skip next ch-1 space; rep from * across, dc in 3rd ch of turning ch, turn.

Row 4: Ch 1, sc in first dc, ch 3, sc in next ch-2 space, ch 3, (sc, ch 3) in each of next 3 ch-1 spaces**, (sc, ch 3, sc) in next ch-2 space, ch 3; rep from * across, ending last rep at **, sc in next ch-2 space of turning ch, ch 3, sc in 3rd ch of turning ch, turn.

Row 5: Ch 3 (counts as dc), 2 dc in next ch-3 loop, *ch 4, skip next 4 ch-3 loops**, 5 dc in next ch-3 loop; rep from * across, ending last rep at **, 2 dc in next ch-3 loop, dc in last sc, turn.

Row 6: Ch 4 (counts as dc, ch 1), skip first dc, (dc, ch 1) in each of next 2 dc, *skip next ch-4 loop, (dc, ch 1) in each of next 5 dc; rep from * across to within last ch-4 loop, skip next ch-4 loop, (dc, ch 1) in each of next 2 dc, dc in 3rd ch of turning ch, turn.

Row 7: Ch 4 (counts as dc, ch 1), 3-dc puff st in next ch-1 space, ch 1, 3-dc puff st in next ch-1 space, *ch 2, skip next ch-1 space, 3-dc puff st in next ch-1 space, (ch 1, 3-dc puff st) in each of next 3 ch-1 spaces; rep from * across to within last 3 spaces, ch 2, skip next ch-1 space, (3-dc puff st, ch 1) in each of next 2 ch-1 spaces, dc in 3rd ch of turning ch, turn.

Row 8: Ch 1, sc in first dc, (sc, ch 3) in each of next 2 ch-1 spaces, *(sc, ch 3, sc) in next ch-2 space, ch 3**, (sc, ch 3) in each of next 3 ch-1 spaces; rep from * across, ending last rep at **, sc in next ch-1 space, ch 3, sc in next ch-1 space of turning ch, sc in 3rd ch of turning ch, turn.

Row 9: Ch 5 (counts as dc, ch 2), skip next 2 ch-3 loops, *5 dc in next ch-3 loop**, ch 4, skip next 4 ch-3 loops; rep from * across, ending last rep at **, ch 2, skip next 2 ch-3 loops, skip next sc, dc in last sc, turn.

Rep Rows 2-9 for pattern.

396

Rows 2-3: Ch 3 (counts as dc), skip first dc, dc in next dc, *ch 1, skip next ch-1 space, dc in each of next 2 dc; rep from * across, ending with last dc in 3rd of turning ch, turn.

Row 4: Ch 5 (counts as tr, ch 1), skip first 2 dc, tr in next ch-1 space, ch 1, skip next dc, tr in next dc, *ch 1, skip next ch-1 space, tr in next dc, ch 3, skip next ch-1 space, (tr, ch 3, tr) in next ch-1 space, ch 3, skip next ch-1 space, skip next dc, tr in next dc, ch 1, skip next ch-1 space, tr in next dc, ch 1, tr in next ch-1 space, ch 1, skip next dc, tr in next dc; rep from * across, ending with last tr in 3rd ch of turning ch, turn.

Row 5: Ch 5 (counts as tr, ch 1), skip next ch-1 space, tr in next tr, ch 1, skip next ch-1 space, tr in next tr, *ch 3, skip next 2 spaces, (3-tr puff st, ch 3, 3-tr puff st, ch 3, 3-tr puff st) in next ch-3 loop, ch 3, skip next 2 spaces, (tr, ch 1) in each of next 2 tr, tr in next tr; rep from * across, ending with last tr in 4th ch of turning ch, turn.

Row 6: Ch 5 (counts as tr, ch 1), skip next ch-1 space, tr in next tr, ch 3, skip next 2 spaces, *(3-tr puff st, ch 3, 3-tr puff st) in next puff st, ch 3, skip next puff st, (3-tr puff st, ch 3, 3-tr puff st) in next puff st, ch 3, skip next 2 spaces, tr in next tr; rep from * across to turning ch, ch 1, tr in 4th ch of turning ch, turn.

Row 7: Ch 6 (counts as tr, ch 2), skip next 2 spaces, *(3-tr puff st, ch 2, 3-tr puff st, ch 2) in each of next 3 ch-3 loops, skip next 2 spaces; rep from * across to turning ch, tr in 4th ch of turning ch, turn.

Row 8: Ch 1, sc in first tr, 2 sc in next ch-2 space, sc in next puff st, *(2 sc in next ch-2 space, sc in next puff st) 5 times**, 3 sc in next ch-2 space, sc in next puff st; rep from * across, ending last rep at **, 2 sc in next ch-2 space of turning ch, sc in 4th ch of turning ch, turn.

Row 9: Ch 3 (counts as dc), skip first sc, dc in next sc, *ch 1, skip next sc, dc in each of next 2 sc; rep from * across, turn.

Rep Rows 2-9 for pattern.

3-Tr Puff st: *(Yo twice, insert hook in next st, yo, draw yarn through st, [yo, draw yarn through 2 loops on hook] twice) 3 times in same st, yo, draw yarn through 4 loops on hook.*

Chain multiples of 18 plus 7.

Row 1: Dc in 4th ch from hook, *ch 1, skip next ch, dc in each of next 2 ch; rep from * across, turn.

397

2-Dc Puff st: (Yo, insert hook in next st, yo, draw yarn through st, yo, draw yarn through 2 loops on hook) twice in same st, yo, draw yarn through 3 loops on hook.

3-Dc Puff st: (Yo, insert hook in next st, yo, draw yarn through st, yo, draw yarn through 2 loops on hook) 3 times in same st, yo, draw yarn through 4 loops on hook.

Chain multiples of 18 plus 3.

Row 1: 2-dc puff st in 3rd ch from hook, *(ch 2, skip next 2 ch, dc in next ch) twice, skip next 2 ch (dc, ch 3, dc) in next ch, skip next 2 ch, (dc in next ch, ch 2, skip next 2 ch) twice**, 3-dc puff st in next ch; rep from * across, ending last rep at **, 2-dc puff st in last ch, turn.

Row 2: Ch 5 (counts as dc, ch 2), skip next ch-2 space, *dc in next dc, ch 2, skip next ch-2 space, 6 dc in next ch-3 loop, ch 2, skip next ch-2 space, dc in next dc, ch 2**, dc in next puff st, ch 2; rep from * across, ending last rep at **, dc in top of turning ch, turn.

Row 3: Ch 5 (counts as dc, ch 2), skip next ch-2 space, dc in next dc, skip next ch-2 space, *(dc, ch 1) in each of next 5 dc, dc in next dc, skip next ch-2 space, dc in next dc**, (ch 2, dc) in each of next 2 dc; rep from * across, ending last rep at **, ch 2, dc in 3rd ch of turning ch, turn.

Row 4: Ch 5 (counts as dc, ch 2), *skip next ch-2 space, skip next dc, 3-dc puff st in next dc, ch 1, (3-dc puff st, ch 1) in each of next 5 ch-1 spaces, 3-dc puff st in next dc, ch 2, skip next ch-2 space**, dc in next dc, ch 2; rep from * across, ending last rep at **, dc in 3rd ch of turning ch, turn.

Row 5: Ch 5 (counts as dc, ch 2), *skip next ch-2 space, (3-dc puff st, ch 1) in each of next 5 ch-1 spaces, 3-dc puff st in next ch-1 space, ch 2, skip next ch-2 space**, dc in next dc, ch 2; rep from * across, ending last rep at **, dc in 3rd ch of turning ch, turn.

Row 6: Ch 5 (counts as dc, ch 2), *skip next ch-2 space, dc in next puff st, ch 1, (3-dc puff st, ch 1) in each of next 5 ch-1 spaces, dc in next puff st, ch 2, skip next ch-2 space**, dc in next dc, ch 2; rep from * across, ending last rep at **, dc in 3rd ch of turning ch, turn.

Row 7: Ch 5 (counts as dc, ch 2), skip next ch-2 space, dc in next dc, ch 2, *skip next ch-1 space, (3-dc puff st, ch 1) in each of next 3 ch-1 spaces, 3-dc puff st in next ch-1 space, ch 2, skip next ch-1 space**, (dc, ch 1) in each of next 3 dc; rep from * across, ending last rep at **, dc in next dc, ch 2, dc in 3rd ch of turning ch, turn.

Row 8: Ch 5 (counts as dc, ch 2), skip next ch-2 space, dc in next dc, ch 2, skip next ch-2 space, (3-dc puff st, ch 1) in each of next 2 ch-1 spaces, 3-dc puff st in next ch-1 space, ch 2, skip next ch-2 space**, (dc, ch 1) in each of next 3 dc; rep from * across, ending last rep at **, dc in next dc, ch 2, dc in 3rd ch of turning ch, turn.

Row 9: Ch 5 (counts as dc, ch 2), skip next ch-2 space, dc in next dc, ch 2, skip next ch-2 space, *dc in next puff st, ch 1, (3-dc puff st, ch 1) in each of next 2 ch-1 spaces, dc in next puff st, ch 2, skip next ch-2 space**, (dc, ch 1) in each of next 3 dc; rep from * across, ending last rep at **, dc in next dc, ch 2, dc in 3rd ch of turning ch, turn.

Row 10: Ch 4 (counts as dc, ch 1), dc in first dc, skip next ch-2 space, *dc in next dc, ch 2, skip next ch-2 space, dc in next dc, ch 2, skip next ch-1 space, 3-dc puff st in next ch-1 space, ch 2, skip next ch-1 space, dc in next dc, ch 2, dc in next dc, skip next ch-2 space**, (dc, ch 3, dc) in next dc, skip next ch-2 space; rep from * across, ending last rep at **, (dc, ch 1, dc) in 3rd ch of turning ch, turn.

Row 11: Ch 3 (counts as dc), 3 dc in next ch-1 space, *(ch 2, skip next ch-2 space, dc in next st) 3 times, ch 2, skip next ch-2 space**, 6 dc in next ch-3 loop, ch 2; rep from * across, ending last rep at **, 3 dc in next ch-1 space of turning ch, dc in 3rd ch of turning ch, turn.

Row 12: Ch 3 (counts as dc), skip first dc, dc in next dc, (ch 1, dc) in each of next 2 dc, *skip next ch-2 space, (dc, ch 2) in each of next 2 dc, dc in next dc, skip next ch-2 space**, (dc, ch 1) in each of next 5 dc, dc in next dc, skip next ch-2 space; rep from * across, ending last rep at **, (dc, ch 1) in each of next 2 dc, dc in next dc, dc in 3rd ch of turning ch, turn.

Row 13: Ch 2 (counts as dc), 2-dc puff st in first dc, (ch 1, 3-dc puff st) in each of next 2 ch-1 spaces, ch 1, 3-dc puff st in next dc, *ch 2, skip next ch-2 space, dc in next dc, ch 2, skip next ch-2 space, skip next dc, 3-dc puff st in next dc, ch 1**, (3-dc puff st, ch 1) in each of next 5 ch-1 spaces, 3-dc puff st in next dc; rep from * across, ending last rep at **, (3-dc puff st, ch 1) in each of next 2 ch-1 spaces, 2-dc puff st in 3rd ch of turning ch, turn.

Row 14: Ch 3 (counts as dc), 3-dc puff st in next ch-1 space, (ch 1, 3-dc puff st) in each of next 2 ch-1 spaces, *ch 2, skip next ch-2 space, dc in next dc, ch 2, skip next ch-2 space**, (3-dc puff st, ch 1) in each of next 5 ch-1 spaces, 3-dc puff st in next ch-1 space; rep from * across, ending last rep at **, (3-dc puff st, ch 1) in each of next 2 ch-1 spaces, 3-dc puff st in next ch-1 space, dc in 2nd ch of turning ch, turn.

Row 15: Ch 2 (counts as dc), 2-dc puff st in first dc, ch 1, (3-dc puff st, ch 1) in each of next 2 ch-1 spaces, *dc in next puff st, ch 2, skip next ch-2 space, dc in next dc, ch 2, skip next ch-2 space, dc in next puff st, ch 1**, (3-dc puff st, ch 1) in each of next 5 ch-1 spaces; rep from * across, ending last rep at **, (3-dc puff st, ch 1) in each of next 2 ch-1 spaces, 2-dc puff st in 3rd ch of turning ch, turn.

Row 16: ch 3 (counts as dc), 3-dc puff st in next ch-1 space, ch 1, 3-dc puff st in next ch-1 space, *ch 2, (dc, ch 2) in each of next 3 dc, skip next ch-1 space**, (3-dc puff st, ch 1) in each of next 3 ch-1 spaces, 3-dc puff st in next ch-1 space; rep from * across, ending last rep at **, 3-dc puff st in next ch-1 space, ch 1, 3-dc puff st in next ch-1 space, dc in 2nd ch of turning ch, turn.

Row 17: Ch 2 (counts as dc), 2-dc puff st in first dc, ch 1, 3-dc puff st in next ch-1 space, ch 2, skip next ch-2 space, *(dc, ch 2) in each of next 3 dc, skip next ch-2 space**, (3-dc puff st, ch 1) in each of next 2 ch-1 spaces, 3-dc puff st in next ch-1 space, ch 2, skip next ch-2 space; rep from * across, ending last rep at **, 3-dc puff st in next ch-1 space, ch 1, 2-dc puff st in 3rd ch of turning ch, turn.

Row 18: Ch 3 (counts as dc), 3-dc puff st in next ch-1 space, ch 1, dc in next puff st, *ch 2, skip next ch-2 space, (dc, ch 2) in each of next 3 dc, skip next ch-2 space, dc in next puff st, ch 1**, (3-dc puff st, ch 1) in each of next 2 ch-1 spaces, dc in next puff st; rep from * across, ending last rep at **, 3-dc puff st in next ch-1 space, dc in 2nd ch of turning ch, turn.

Row 19: Ch 2 (counts as dc), 2-dc puff st in first dc, *ch 2, skip next ch-1 space, dc in next dc, ch 2, skip next ch-2 space, dc in next dc, skip next ch-2 space, (dc, ch 3, dc) in next dc, skip next ch-2 space, (dc, ch 2) in each of next 2 dc, skip next ch-1 space**, 3-dc puff st in next ch-1 space; rep from * across, ending last rep at **, 2-dc puff st in 3rd ch of turning ch, turn.

Rep Rows 2-19 for pattern.

398

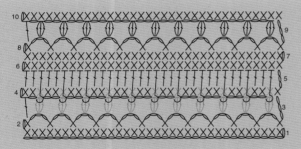

3-Dc Puff st: (Yo, insert hook in next st, yo, draw yarn through st, yo, draw yarn through 2 loops on hook) 3 times in same st, yo, draw yarn through 4 loops on hook.

Front Post Double Crochet (FPdc): Yo, insert hook from front to back to front again around the post of designated st, yo, draw yarn through, (yo, draw yarn through 2 loops on hook) twice.

Chain multiples of 3 plus 2.

Row 1: Sc in 2nd ch from hook, sc in each ch across, turn.

Row 2: Ch 1, sc in first sc, *ch 3, skip next 2 sc, sc in next sc; rep from * across, turn.

Row 3: Ch 3 (counts as dc), *(3-dc puff st, ch 2) in each ch-3 loop across to within last ch-3 loop, 3-dc puff st in last ch-3 loop, ch 1, dc in last sc, turn.

Row 4: Ch 1, sc in first dc, sc in next ch-1 space, sc in next puff st, *2 sc in next ch-2 space, sc in next puff st; rep from * across to turning ch, sc in 3rd ch of turning ch, turn.

Row 5: Ch 3 (counts as dc), skip first sc, *FPdc around the post of next corresponding puff st 2 rows below, skip sc behind post st just made, dc in each of next 2 sc; rep from * across, turn.

Row 6: Ch 1, sc in each dc across, ending with last sc in 3rd ch of turning ch, turn.

Row 7: Ch 1, sc in each sc across, turn.

Rep Rows 2-7 for pattern.

399

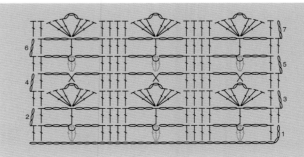

3-Dc Puff st: *(Yo, insert hook in next st, yo, draw yarn through st, yo, draw yarn through 2 loops on hook) 3 times in same st, yo, draw yarn through 4 loops on hook.*

Back Post Double Crochet (BPdc): *Yo, insert hook from back to front to back again around the post of designated st, yo, draw yarn through, (yo, draw yarn through 2 loops on hook) twice.*

Chain multiples of 11 plus 2.

Row 1: Dc in 4th ch from hook, *ch 3, skip next 3 ch, 3-dc puff st in next ch, ch 3, skip next 3 ch, dc in each of next 4 ch; rep from * across, ending with dc in each of last 2 ch, turn.

Row 2: Ch 3 (counts as dc), skip first dc, dc in next dc, *ch 3, skip next ch-3 loop, BPdc around the post of next puff st, ch 3, skip next ch-3 loop**, dc in each of next 4 dc; rep from * across, ending last rep at **, dc in next dc, dc in 3rd ch of turning ch, turn.

Row 3: Ch 3 (counts as dc), skip first dc, dc in next dc, *skip next ch-3 loop, (3 dc, ch 3, 3 dc) in next dc, skip next ch-3 loop**, dc in each of next 4 dc; rep from * across, ending last rep at **, dc in next dc, dc in 3rd ch of turning ch, turn.

Row 4: Ch 3 (counts as dc), skip first dc, dc in next dc, *ch 3, skip next 3 dc, sc in next ch-3 loop, ch 3, skip next 3 dc**, dc in each of next 4 dc; rep from * across, ending last rep at **, dc in next dc, dc in 3rd ch of turning ch, turn.

Row 5: Ch 3 (counts as dc), skip first dc, dc in next dc, *ch 3, skip next ch-3 loop, 3-dc puff st in next sc, ch 3, skip next ch-3 loop**, dc in each of next 4 dc; rep from * across, ending last rep at **, dc in next dc, dc in 3rd ch of turning ch, turn.

Rep Rows 2-5 for pattern.

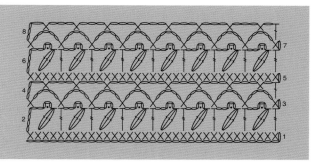

3-Dc Puff st: *(Yo, insert hook in next st, yo, draw yarn through st, yo, draw yarn through 2 loops on hook) 3 times in same st, yo, draw yarn through 4 loops on hook.*

Chain multiples of 4 plus 2.

Row 1: Sc in 2nd ch from hook, sc in each ch across, turn.

Row 2: Ch 6 (counts as tr, ch 2), *ch 3, sl st in 3rd ch from hook for picot, skip first sc, 3-dc puff st in next sc, skip next 2 sc, tr in next sc**, ch 2; rep from * across, ending last rep at **, turn.

Row 3: Ch 1, sc in first tr, *ch 4, skip next (puff st, picot, ch-2 space), sc in next tr; rep from * across, ending with last sc in 4th ch of turning ch, turn.

Row 4: Ch 4 (counts as dc, ch 1), sc in next ch-4 loop, (ch 3, sc) in each ch-4 loop across to last ch-4 loop, ch 1, tr in last sc, turn.

Row 5: Ch 1, sc in first dc, sc in next ch-1 space, sc in next sc, *3 sc in next ch-3 loop, sc in next sc; rep from * across to turning ch, sc in ch-1 space of turning ch, sc in 3rd ch of turning ch, turn.

Rep Rows 2-5 for pattern.

401

2-Tr Cluster: (Yo twice, insert hook in next st, yo, draw yarn through st, [yo, draw yarn through 2 loops on hook] twice) in 2 designated sts, yo, draw yarn through 3 loops on hook.

3-Tr Puff st: (Yo twice, insert hook in next st, yo, draw yarn through st, [yo, draw yarn through 2 loops on hook] twice) 3 times in same st, yo, draw yarn through 4 loops on hook.

4-Tr Cluster: (Yo twice, insert hook in next st, yo, draw yarn through st, [yo, draw yarn through 2 loops on hook] twice) 4 times in designated sts, yo, draw yarn through 5 loops on hook.

Chain multiples of 16 plus 9.

Row 1: Tr in 7th ch from hook, ch 3, *2-tr cluster, working first half-closed tr in same ch at last tr made, skip next 3 ch, work 2nd half-closed tr in next ch, yo, complete cluster, ch 3; rep from * across to within last 2 ch, 2-tr cluster, working first half-closed tr in same ch at last tr made, skip next ch, work 2nd half-closed tr in next ch, yo, complete cluster, turn.

Row 2: Ch 5 (counts as tr, ch 1), 2-tr cluster worked across first 2 clusters, ch 3, *2-tr cluster worked across last cluster (holding last tr made) and next cluster, ch 3; rep from * across to within last ch-3 loop, 2-tr cluster worked across last cluster (holding last tr made) and top of turning ch, ch 1, tr in top of turning ch, turn.

Row 3: Ch 4 (counts as tr), skip next ch-1 space, tr in next cluster, *(ch 3, 2-tr cluster worked across last cluster [holding last tr made] and next cluster) 3 times, 3 tr in same cluster (holding last tr made), 2-tr cluster worked across last cluster (holding last tr made) and next cluster; rep from * across, ch 3, 2-tr cluster worked across last cluster (holding last tr made) and 4th ch of turning ch, turn.

Row 4: Ch 5 (counts as tr, ch 1), *4-tr cluster, working first half-closed tr in first cluster, work last 3 half-closed tr in next cluster, yo, complete cluster**, (ch 1, 3-tr puff st) in each of next 3 tr, ch 1, 4-tr cluster, working first 3 half-closed tr in next cluster, working 4th half-closed tr in next cluster, yo, complete cluster, ch 3, 2-tr cluster worked across next 2 clusters, ch 3; rep from * across, ending last rep at ** in last tr, ch 1, tr in 4th ch of turning ch, turn.

Row 5: Ch 4 (counts as tr), skip next ch-1 space, tr in next cluster, *2-tr cluster working first half-closed tr in last cluster (holding last tr made), skip next 3 sts, work 2nd half-closed tr in next cluster, yo, complete cluster; rep from * across to turning ch, 2-tr cluster worked across last cluster (holding last tr made) and 4th ch of turning ch, turn.

Row 6: Rep Row 2.

Row 7: Ch 4 (counts as tr), skip next ch-1 space, tr in next cluster, *ch 3, 2-tr cluster worked across last cluster [holding last tr made] and next cluster, 3 tr in same cluster (holding last tr made), 2-tr cluster worked across last cluster (holding last tr made) and next cluster, (ch 3, 2-tr cluster worked across last cluster [holding last tr made] and next cluster) twice; rep from * across, ch 3, 2-tr cluster worked across last cluster (holding last tr made) and 4th ch of turning ch, turn.

Row 8: Ch 5 (counts as tr, ch 1), *4-tr cluster, working first 3 half-closed tr in first cluster, work 4th half-closed tr in next cluster, yo, complete cluster**, ch 3, 2-tr cluster worked across next 2 clusters, ch 3, 4-tr cluster, working first half-closed tr in last cluster (holding last tr made), work last 3 half-closed tr in next cluster, yo, complete cluster, (ch 1, 3-tr puff st) in each of next 3 tr, ch 1; rep from * across, ending last rep at **, ch 1, tr in 4th ch of turning ch, turn.

Row 9: Rep Row 5.

Rep Rows 2-9 for pattern.

.27.
Popcorn Stitches

402

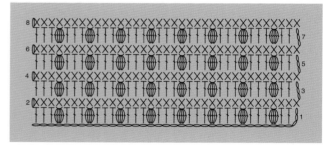

Popcorn (pop): 5 dc in next st, drop loop from hook, insert hook from front to back in first dc of group, pull dropped loop through st.

Chain multiples of 4 plus 1.

Row 1: Dc in 4th ch from hook, dc in next ch, *pop in next ch, dc in each of next 3 ch; rep from * across, turn.

Row 2: Ch 1, sc in each st across, ending with last sc in 3rd ch of turning ch, turn.

Row 3: Ch 3 (counts as dc), skip first sc, dc in each of next 2 sc, *pop in next sc, dc in each of next 3 sc; rep from * across, turn.

Rep Rows 2-3 for pattern.

403

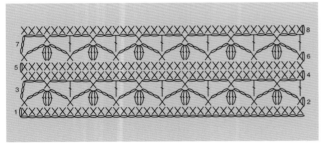

Popcorn (pop): 4 dc in next st, drop loop from hook, insert hook from front to back in first dc of group, pull dropped loop through st.

Chain multiples of 6 plus 2.

Row 1 (WS): Sc in 2nd ch from hook, sc in each ch across, turn.

Row 2: Ch 1, sc in first sc, *ch 3, skip next 2 sc, pop in next sc, ch 3, skip next 2 sc, sc in next sc; rep from * across, turn.

Row 3: Ch 5 (counts as dc, ch 2), skip next ch-3 loop, *sc in next pop, ch 2, skip next ch-3 loop, dc in next sc**, ch 2, skip next ch-3 loop; rep from * across, ending last rep at **, turn.

Row 4: Ch 1, sc in first dc, *2 sc in next ch-2 space, sc in next st; rep from * across, ending with last sc in 3rd ch of turning ch, turn.

Row 5: Ch 1, sc in each sc across, turn.

Rep Rows 2-5 for pattern.

404

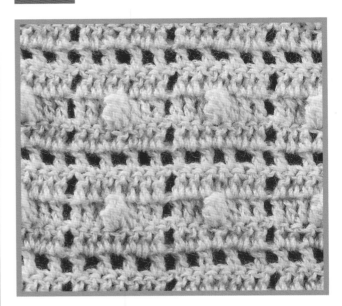

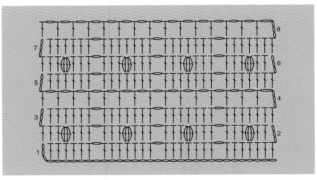

Popcorn (pop): 4 dc in next st, drop loop from hook, insert hook from front to back in first dc of group, pull dropped loop through st.

Chain multiples of 8 plus 1.

Row 1 (WS): Dc in 4th ch from hook, dc in each of next 5 ch, *ch 1, skip next ch, dc in each of next 7 ch; rep from * across, turn.

Row 2: Ch 3 (counts as dc), skip first dc, dc in each of next 2 dc, *pop in next dc, dc in each of next 3 dc**, ch 1, skip next ch-1 space, dc in each of next 3 dc; rep from * across, ending last rep at **, with last dc in 3rd ch of turning ch, turn.

Row 3: Ch 3 (counts as dc), skip first dc, dc in each of next 6 sts, *ch 1, skip next ch-1 space, dc in each of next 7 sts; rep from * across, ending with last dc in 3rd ch of turning ch, turn.

Row 4: Ch 4 (counts as dc, ch 1), skip first 2 dc, *dc in next dc, ch 1, skip next st; rep from * across to turning ch, dc in 3rd ch of turning ch, turn.

Row 5: Ch 3 (counts as dc), skip first dc, *(dc in next ch-1 space, dc in next dc) 3 times**, ch 1, skip next ch-1 space, dc in next dc; rep from * across, ending last rep at **, with last dc in 3rd ch of turning ch, turn.

Rep Rows 2-5 for pattern.

405

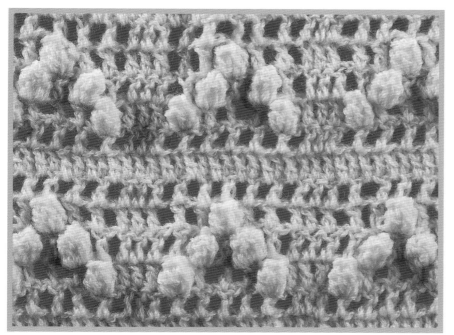

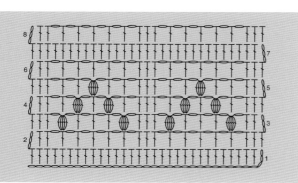

Popcorn (pop) (on RS rows): 5 dc in next st, drop loop from hook, insert hook from front to back in first dc of group, pull dropped loop through st.

Popcorn (pop) (on WS rows): 5 dc in next st, drop loop from hook, insert hook from back to front in first dc of group, pull dropped loop through st.

Chain multiples of 14 plus 5.

Row 1 (RS): Dc in 4th ch from hook, dc in each ch across, turn.

Row 2: Ch 3 (counts as dc), skip first dc, dc in each of next 2 dc, *(ch 1, skip next dc, dc in next dc) 6 times, dc in each of next 2 dc; rep from * across, ending with last dc in 3rd ch of turning ch, turn.

Row 3: Ch 3 (counts as dc), skip first dc, dc in each of next 2 dc, *ch 1, pop in next dc, (ch 1, dc in next dc) 3 times, ch 1, pop in next dc, ch 1, dc in each of next 3 dc; rep from * across, ending with last dc in 3rd ch of turning ch, turn.

Row 4: Ch 3 (counts as dc), skip first dc, dc in each of next 2 dc, *ch 1, dc in next pop, ch 1, pop in next dc, ch 1, dc in next dc, ch 1, pop in next dc, ch 1, dc in next pop, ch 1, dc in each of next 3 dc; rep from * across, ending with last dc in 3rd ch of turning ch, turn.

Row 5: Ch 3 (counts as dc), skip first dc, dc in each of next 2 dc, *ch 1, dc in next dc, ch 1, dc in next pop, ch 1, pop in next dc, ch 1, dc in next pop, ch 1, dc in next dc, ch 1, dc in each of next 3 dc; rep from * across, ending with last dc in 3rd ch of turning ch, turn.

Row 6: Ch 3 (counts as dc), skip first dc, dc in each of next 2 dc, *(ch 1, skip next ch-1 space, dc in next st) 6 times, dc in each of next 2 dc; rep from * across, ending with last dc in 3rd ch of turning ch, turn.

Row 7: Ch 3 (counts as dc), skip first dc, dc in each dc and space across, ending with last dc in 3rd ch of turning ch, turn.

Rep Rows 2-7 for pattern.

406

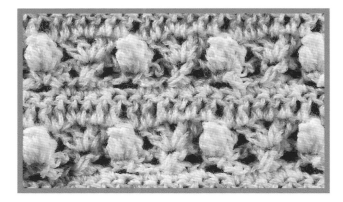

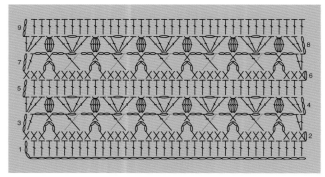

Popcorn (pop): 5 dc in next st, drop loop from hook, insert hook from front to back in first dc of group, pull dropped loop through st.

Chain multiples of 6 plus 3.

Row 1 (WS): Dc in 4th ch from hook, dc in each ch across, turn.

Row 2: Ch 1, sc in first 3 dc, *ch 4, skip next dc**, sc in each of next 5 dc; rep from * across, ending last rep at **, sc in each of next 2 dc, dc in 3rd ch of turning ch, turn.

Row 3: Ch 3 (counts as dc), dc in first sc, *ch 2, sc in next ch-4 loop, ch 2**, skip next 3 sc, dc in next sc, ch 1, working behind last dc made, dc in 2nd skipped sc (crossed dc made); rep from * across, ending last rep at **, skip next 2 sc, 2 dc in last sc, turn.

Row 4: Ch 3 (counts as dc), 2 dc in first dc, *skip next ch-2 space, pop in next sc, skip next ch-2 space**, (2 dc, ch 1, 2 dc) in next ch-1 space; rep from * across, ending last rep at **, skip next dc, 3 dc in 3rd ch of turning ch, turn.

Row 5: Ch 3 (counts as dc), skip first dc, dc in each st and space across, ending with last dc in 3rd ch of turning ch, turn.

Rep Rows 2-5 for pattern.

407

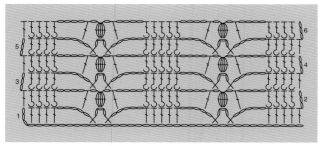

Popcorn (pop): 5 dc in next st, drop loop from hook, insert hook from front to back in first dc of group, pull dropped loop through st.

***Front Post Double Crochet (FPdc):** Yo, insert hook from front to back to front again around the post of designated st, yo, draw yarn through, (yo, draw yarn through 2 loops on hook) twice.*

***Back Post Double Crochet (BPdc):** Yo, insert hook from back to front to back again around the post of designated st, yo, draw yarn through, (yo, draw yarn through 2 loops on hook) twice.*

Chain multiples of 16 plus 7.

Row 1 (WS): Dc in 4th ch from hook, dc in each of next 3 ch, *ch 5, skip next 4 ch, sc in next ch, ch 3, skip next ch, sc in next ch, ch 5, skip next 4 ch, dc in each of next 5 ch; rep from * across, turn.

Row 2: Ch 3 (counts as dc), skip first dc, FPdc around the post of each of next 4 dc, *ch 4, dc in next ch-5 loop, ch 1, pop in next ch-3 loop, ch 1, dc in next ch-5 loop, ch 4**, FPdc around the post of each of next 5 dc; rep from * across, ending last rep at **, FPdc around the post of each of next 4 dc, dc in 3rd ch of turning ch, turn.

Row 3: Ch 3 (counts as dc), skip first dc, BPdc around the post of each of next 4 dc, *ch 6, skip next ch-4 loop, sc in next ch-1 space, ch 3, sc in next ch-1 space, ch 6**, BPdc around the post of each of next 5 dc; rep from * across, ending last rep at **, BPdc around the post of each of next 4 dc, dc in 3rd ch of turning ch, turn.

Rep Rows 2-3 for pattern.

408

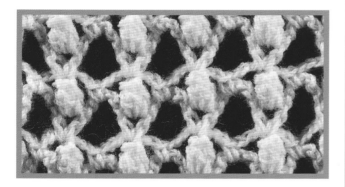

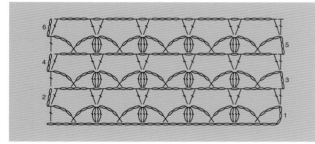

Popcorn (pop): 4 dc in next st, drop loop from hook, insert hook from front to back in first dc of group, pull dropped loop through st.

Chain multiples of 6.

Row 1 (RS): Sc in 9th ch from hook, *ch 3, skip next 2 ch, pop in next ch, ch 3, skip next 2 ch, sc in next ch; rep from * across to within last 3 ch, ch 3, skip next 2 ch, dc in last ch, turn.

Row 2: Ch 3 (counts as dc), dc in first dc, *ch 4, skip next 2 ch-3 loops**, (dc, ch 1, dc) in next pop; rep from * across, ending last rep at **, 2 dc in next ch of turning ch, turn.

Row 3: Ch 6 (counts as dc, ch 3), *sc in next ch-4 loop, ch 3**, pop in next ch-1 space, ch 3; rep from * across, ending last rep at **, skip next dc, dc in 3rd ch of turning ch, turn.

Rep Rows 2-3 for pattern.

409

Popcorn (pop): 4 dc in next st, drop loop from hook, insert hook from front to back in first dc of group, pull dropped loop through st.

2-Dc Puff st: (Yo, insert hook in next st, yo, draw yarn through st, yo, draw yarn through 2 loops on hook) twice in same st, yo, draw yarn through 3 loops on hook.

Chain multiples of 6 plus 2.

Row 1 (RS): Sc in 2nd ch from hook, *ch 3, skip next 2 ch, pop in next ch, ch 3, skip next 2 ch, sc in next ch; rep from * across, turn.

Row 2: Ch 1, sc in first sc, *3 sc in each of next 2 ch-3 loops, sc in next sc; rep from * across, turn.

Row 3: Ch 2 (counts as dc), dc in first sc, *ch 3, skip next 3 sc, sc between last skipped and next sc, ch 3, skip next 3 sc**, pop in next sc; rep from * across, ending last rep at **, skip next 3 sc, 2-dc puff st in last sc, turn.

Row 4: Ch 1, sc in first bauble, *3 sc in next ch-3 loop, sc in next sc, 3 sc in next ch-3 loop; rep from * across, ending with last sc in 2nd ch of turning ch, turn.

Row 5: Ch 1, sc in first sc, *ch 3, skip next 3 sc, pop in next sc, ch 3, skip next 3 sc, sc between last skipped and next sc; rep from * across, ending with last sc in last sc, turn.

Rep Rows 2-5 for pattern.

410

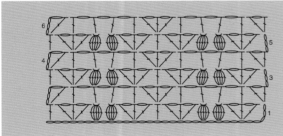

Popcorn (pop): 5 dc in next st, drop loop from hook, insert hook from front to back in first dc of group, pull dropped loop through st.

Chain multiples of 14 plus 3.

Row 1: (Dc, ch 1, dc, ch 1, dc) in 6th ch from hook, *skip next 2 ch, pop in next ch, skip next ch, pop in next ch, skip next 2 ch, (dc, ch 1, dc, ch 1, dc) in next ch, skip next 2 ch, dc in next ch**, skip next 2 ch, (dc, ch 1, dc, ch 1, dc) in next ch; rep from * across, ending last rep at **, turn.

Row 2: Ch 4 (counts as dc, ch 1), dc in first dc, *skip next ch-1 space, dc in next dc, ch 1, skip next dc, (dc, ch 1) in each of next 2 pops, skip next ch-1 space, dc in next dc, skip next dc**, (dc, ch 1, dc, ch 1, dc) in next dc; rep from * across, ending last rep at **, (dc, ch 1, dc) in top of turning ch, turn.

Row 3: Ch 3 (counts as dc), *skip next ch-1 space, skip next dc, (dc, ch 1, dc, ch 1, dc) in next dc, skip next ch-1 space, pop in each of next 2 dc, skip next ch-1 space, (dc, ch 1, dc, ch 1, dc) in next dc, skip next ch-1 space, dc in next dc; rep from * across, ending with last dc in 3rd ch of turning ch, turn.

Rep Rows 2-3 for pattern.

411

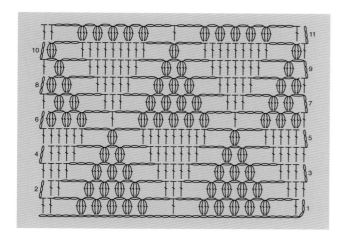

Popcorn (pop) (on RS rows): 4 dc in next st, drop loop from hook, insert hook from front to back in first dc of group, pull dropped loop through st.

Popcorn (pop) (on WS rows): 4 dc in next st, drop loop from hook, insert hook from back to front in first dc of group, pull dropped loop through st.

Chain multiples of 16 plus 5.

Row 1 (RS): Dc in 4th ch from hook, *ch 3, skip next 3 ch, (pop in next ch, ch 1, skip next ch) 4 times, pop in next ch, ch 3, skip next 3 ch, dc in next ch; rep from * across to within last ch, dc in last ch, turn.

Row 2: Ch 3 (counts as dc), skip first dc, dc in next dc, dc in next ch-3 loop, *ch 3, (pop, ch 1) in each of next 3 ch-1 spaces, pop in next ch-1 space, ch 3, dc in next ch-3 loop, dc in next dc, dc in next ch-3 loop; rep from * across, ending with last dc in 3rd ch of turning ch, turn.

Row 3: Ch 3 (counts as dc), skip first dc, dc in each of next 2 dc, *dc in next ch-3 loop, ch 3, (pop, ch 1) in each of next 2 ch-1 spaces, pop in next ch-1 space, ch 3, dc in next ch-3 loop, dc in each of next 3 dc; rep from * across, ending with last dc in 3rd ch of turning ch, turn.

Row 4: Ch 3 (counts as dc), skip first dc, dc in each of next 3 dc, *dc in next ch-3 loop, ch 3, pop in next ch-1 space, ch 1, pop in next ch-1 space, ch 3, dc in next ch-3 loop**, dc in each of next 5 dc; rep from * across, ending last rep at **, dc in each of next 3 dc, dc in 3rd ch of turning ch, turn.

Row 5: Ch 3 (counts as dc), skip first dc, dc in each of next 4 dc, *dc in next ch-3 loop, ch 3, pop in next ch-1 space, ch 3, dc in next ch-3 loop**, dc in each of next 7 dc; rep from * across, ending last rep at **, dc in each of next 4 dc, dc in 3rd ch of turning ch, turn.

Row 6: Ch 3 (counts as dc), skip first dc, (pop in next dc, ch 1, skip next dc) twice, pop in next dc, *ch 3, skip next ch-3 loop, dc in next pop, ch 3, skip next ch-3 loop**, (pop in next dc, ch 1, skip next dc) 4 times, pop in next dc; rep from * across, ending last rep at **, (pop in next dc, ch 1, skip next dc) twice, pop in next dc, dc in 3rd ch of turning ch, turn.

Row 7: Ch 4 (counts as dc, ch 1), pop in next ch-1 space, ch 1, pop in next ch-1 space, *ch 3, dc in next ch-3 loop, dc in next dc, dc in next ch-3 loop, ch 3**, (pop, ch 1) in each of next 3 ch-1 spaces, pop in next ch-1 space; rep from * across, ending last rep at **, (pop, ch 1) in each of next 2 ch-1 spaces, dc in 3rd ch of turning ch, turn.

Row 8: Ch 3 (counts as dc), pop in next ch-1 space, ch 1, pop in next ch-1 space, *ch 3, dc in next ch-3 loop, dc in each of next 3 dc, dc in next ch-3 loop, ch 3**, (pop, ch 1) in each of next 2 ch-1 spaces, pop in next ch-1 space; rep from * across, ending last rep at **, pop in next ch-1 space, ch 1, pop in next ch-1 space, dc in 3rd ch of turning ch, turn.

Row 9: Ch 4 (counts as dc, ch 1), pop in next ch-1 space, *ch 3, dc in next ch-3 loop, dc in each of next 5 dc, dc in next ch-3 loop, ch 3, pop in next ch-1 space, ch 1**, pop in next ch-1 space; rep from * across, ending last rep at **, dc in 3rd ch of turning ch, turn.

Row 10: Ch 3 (counts as dc), pop in next ch-1 space, *ch 3, dc in next ch-3 loop, dc in each of next 7 dc, dc in next ch-3 loop, ch 3, pop in next ch-1 space; rep from * across, dc in 3rd ch of turning ch, turn.

Row 11: Ch 3 (counts as dc), skip first dc, *dc in next pop, ch 3, skip next ch-3 loop, (pop in next dc, ch 1, skip next dc) 4 times, pop in next dc, ch 3, skip next ch-3 loop; rep from * across to turning ch, dc in next pop, dc in 3rd ch of turning ch, turn.

Rep Rows 2–11 for pattern.

412

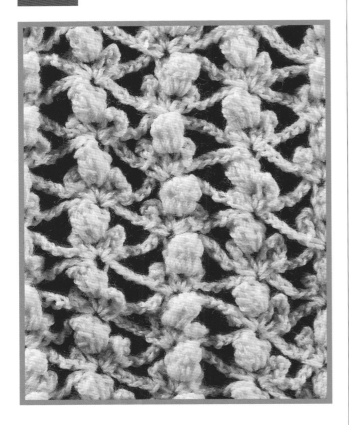

Popcorn (pop) (on RS rows): 4 dc in next st, drop loop from hook, insert hook from front to back in first dc of group, pull dropped loop through st.

Popcorn (pop) (on WS rows): 4 dc in next st, drop loop from hook, insert hook from back to front in first dc of group, pull dropped loop through st.

Chain multiples of 12 plus 2.

Row 1 (RS): (Sc, ch 4, sc) in 2nd ch from hook, *ch 5, skip next 5 ch, pop in next ch, ch 5, skip next 5 ch**, (sc, ch 4, sc, ch 4, sc) in next ch; rep from * across, ending last rep at **, (sc, ch 4, sc) in last ch, turn.

Row 2: Ch 8 (counts as dc, ch 5), *skip next ch-5 loop, (sc, ch 4, sc, ch 4, sc) in next pop, ch 5, skip next ch-5 loop, skip next ch-4 loop**, pop in next sc; rep from * across, ending last rep at **, dc in last sc, turn.

Row 3: Ch 1, (sc, ch 4, sc) in first dc, *ch 5, skip next ch-5 loop, skip next ch-4 loop, pop in next sc, ch 5, skip next ch-5 loop**, (sc, ch 4, sc, ch 4, sc) in next pop; rep from * across, ending last rep at **, (sc, ch 4, sc) in 3rd ch of turning ch, turn.

Rep Rows 2-3 for pattern.

.28.
Dropped Stitches

413

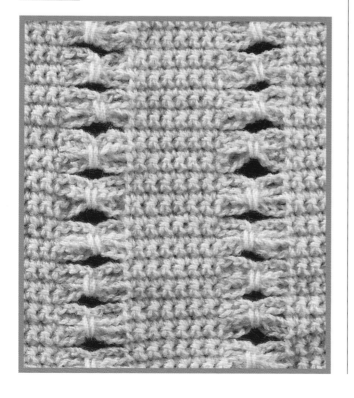

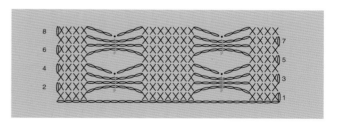

Chain multiples of 14 plus 1.

Row 1: Sc in 2nd ch from hook, sc in each of next 3 ch, *ch 7, skip next 7 ch, sc in each of next 7 ch; rep from * across, ending with sc in each of last 4 ch, turn.

Rows 2-3: Ch 1, sc in each of first 4 sc, *ch 7, skip next ch-7 loop, sc in each of next 7 sc; rep from * across, ending with sc in each of last 4 sc, turn.

Row 4: Ch 1, sc in each of first 4 sc, *ch 3, sl st over next 3 ch-7 loops in last 3 rows, ch 3, sc in each of next 7 sc; rep from * across, ending with sc in each of last 4 sc, turn.

Row 5: Ch 1, sc in each of first 4 sc, *ch 7, skip next 2 ch-3 loops, sc in each of next 7 sc; rep from * across, ending with sc in each of last 4 sc, turn.

Rep Rows 2-5 for pattern.

414

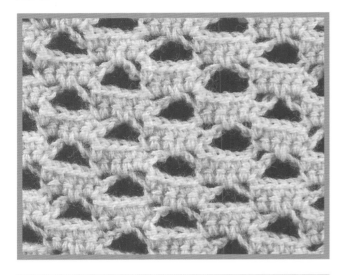

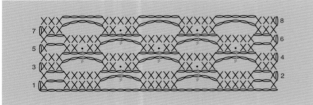

Chain multiples of 10 plus 2.

Row 1 (WS): Sc in 2nd ch from hook, ch 2, skip next 2 ch, *sc in each of next 5 ch**, ch 5, skip next 5 ch; rep from * across, ending last rep at **, ch 2, skip next 2 ch, sc in last ch, turn.

Row 2: Ch 1, sc in first sc, ch 2, skip next ch-2 space, *sc in each of next 5 sc**, ch 5, skip next ch-5 loop; rep from * across, ending last rep at **, ch 2, skip next ch-2 space, sc in last sc, turn.

Row 3: Ch 1, sc in first sc, 2 sc in next ch-2 space, *ch 5, skip next 5 sc**, 2 sc in next ch-5 loop, sl st over 2 ch-5 loops in last 2 rows, 2 sc in same ch-5 in current row; rep from * across, ending last rep at **, 2 sc in next ch-2 space, sc in last sc, turn.

Row 4: Ch 1, sc in each of first 3 sc, *ch 5, skip next ch-5 loop**, sc in each of next 5 sts; rep from * across, ending last rep at **, sc in each of last 3 sc, turn.

Row 5: Ch 1, sc in first sc, ch 2, skip next 2 sc, *2 sc in next ch-5 loop, sl st over 2 ch-5 loops in last 2 rows, 2 sc in same ch-5 in current row**, ch 5, skip next 5 sc; rep from * across, ending last rep at **, ch 2, skip next 2 sc, sc in last sc, turn.

Rep Rows 2-5 for pattern.

415

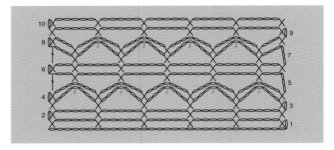

Chain multiples of 6 plus 2.

Row 1: Sc in 2nd ch from hook, *ch 5, skip next 5 ch, sc in next ch; rep from * across, turn.

Row 2: Ch 1, sc in first sc, *ch 5, skip next ch-5 loop, sc in next sc; rep from * across, turn.

Row 3: Ch 1, sc in first sc, *ch 7, skip next ch-5 loop, sc in next sc; rep from * across, turn.

Row 4: Ch 1, sc in first sc, *ch 7, skip next ch-7 loop, sc in next sc; rep from * across, turn.

Row 5: Ch 5 (counts as dc, ch 2), *sc over next 2 ch-7 loop in last 2 rows**, ch 5; rep from * across, ending last rep at **, ch 2, dc in last sc, turn.

Row 6: Ch 1, sc in first dc, ch 2, skip next ch-2 space, sc in next sc, *ch 5, skip next ch-5 loop, sc in next sc; rep from * across to turning ch, ch 2, sc in 3rd ch of turning ch, turn.

Row 7: Ch 6 (counts as dc, ch 3), skip next ch-2 space, sc in next sc, *ch 7, skip next ch-5 loop, sc in next sc; rep from * across to within last ch-2 space, ch 3, skip next ch-2 space, dc in last sc, turn.

Row 8: Ch 1, sc in first sc, ch 3, skip next ch-3 loop, sc in next sc, *ch 7, skip next ch-7 loop, sc in next sc; rep from * across to turning ch, ch 3, sc in 3rd ch of turning ch, turn.

Row 9: Ch 1, sc in first sc, skip next ch-3 loop, *ch 5, sc over next 2 ch-7 loops in last 2 rows; rep from * across, ending with last sc in last sc, turn.

Rep Rows 2-9 for pattern.

Row 4: Ch 5 (counts as dc, ch 2), skip first 3 dc, *working over next ch-2 space in last row, dc in each of next 2 corresponding dc 2 rows below, ch 2, skip next 2 dc; rep from * across to turning ch, dc in 3rd ch of turning ch, turn.

Rep Rows 3-4 for pattern.

416

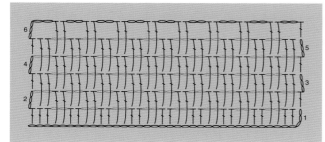

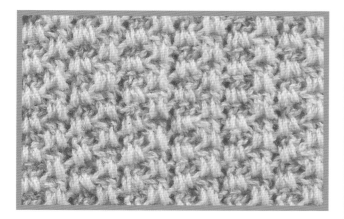

Chain multiples of 4 plus 2.

Row 1: Dc in 4th ch from hook, dc in next ch, *ch 2, skip next 2 ch, dc in each of next 2 ch; rep from * across to within last ch, dc in last ch, turn.

Row 2: Ch 5 (counts as dc, ch 2), skip first 3 dc, *working over next ch-2 space in last row, dc in each of next 2 corresponding ch sts 2 rows below, ch 2, skip next 2 dc; rep from * across to turning ch, dc in 3rd ch of turning ch, turn.

Row 3: Ch 3 (counts as dc), *working over next ch-2 space in last row, dc in each of next 2 corresponding dc 2 rows below**, ch 2, skip next 2 dc; rep from * across, ending last rep at **, dc in 3rd ch of turning ch, turn.

417

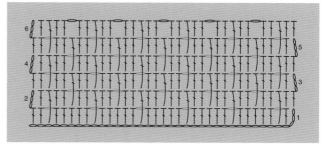

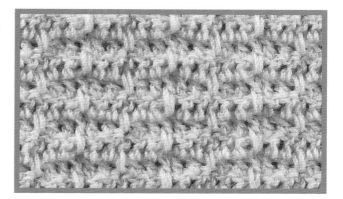

Chain multiples of 6 plus 1.

Row 1: Dc in 4th ch from hook, *ch 1, skip next ch, dc in each of next 5 ch; rep from * across, ending with dc in each of last 2 ch, turn.

Row 2: Ch 3 (counts as dc), skip first dc, dc in next dc, *working over next ch-1 space in last row, dc in next corresponding ch st 2 rows below**, dc in each of next 2 dc, ch 1, skip next dc, dc in each of next 2 dc; rep from * across, ending with last dc in 3rd ch of turning ch, turn.

Row 3: Ch 3 (counts as dc), skip first dc, dc in next dc, *ch 1, skip next dc**, dc in each of next 2 dc, working over next ch-1 space in last row, dc in next corresponding dc 2 rows below, dc in each of next 2 dc; rep from * across, ending last rep at **, dc in next dc, dc in 3rd ch of turning ch, turn.

Rep Rows 2-3 for pattern.

418

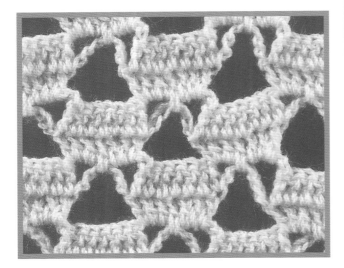

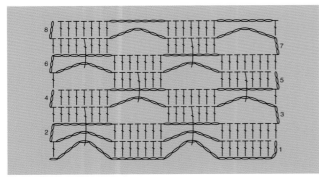

Chain multiples of 14 plus 4.

Row 1: Dc in 4th ch from hook, *dc in each of next 6 ch, ch 7, skip next 7 ch, dc in next ch; rep from * across, turn.

Row 2: Ch 10 (counts as dc, ch 7), skip next ch-7 loop, *dc in each of next 7 dc**, ch 7, skip next ch-7 loop; rep from * across, ending last rep at **, dc in 3rd ch of turning ch, turn.

Row 3: Ch 10 (counts as dc, ch 7), skip first 8 dc, *3 dc in next ch-7 loop, dc over next 3 ch-7 loops in 3 rows below, 3 dc in same ch-7 loop in current row**, ch 7, skip next 7 dc; rep from * across, ending last rep at **, dc in 3rd ch of turning ch, turn.

Row 4: Ch 3 (counts as dc), skip first dc, *dc in each of next 7 dc, ch 7, skip next ch-7 loop; rep from * across to turning ch, dc in 3rd ch of turning ch, turn.

Row 5: Ch 3 (counts as dc), *3 dc in next ch-7 loop, dc over next 2 ch-7 loops in 2 rows below, 3 dc in same ch-7 loop in current row, ch 7, skip next 7 dc; rep from * across to turning ch, dc in 3rd ch of turning ch, turn.

Row 6: Ch 10 (counts as dc, ch 7), *skip next ch-7 loop, dc in each of next 7 dc**, ch 7; rep from * across, ending last rep at **, dc in 3rd ch of turning ch, turn.

Row 7: Ch 10 (counts as dc, ch 7), skip first 8 dc, *3 dc in next ch-7 loop, dc over next 2 ch-7 loops in 2 rows below, 3 dc in same ch-7 loop in current row**, ch 7, skip next 7 dc; rep from * across, ending last rep at **, dc in 3rd ch of turning ch, turn.

Rep Rows 4-7 for pattern.

419

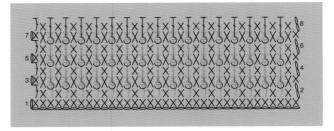

Front Post Double Crochet (FPdc): Yo, insert hook from front to back to front again around the post of designated st, yo, draw yarn through, (yo, draw yarn through 2 loops on hook) twice.

Chain multiples of 2.

Row 1 (WS): Sc in 2nd ch from hook, sc in each ch across, turn.

Row 2: Ch 2 (counts as dc), skip first sc, *sc in next sc, dc in next sc; rep from * across, turn.

Row 3: Ch 1, sc in each st across, ending with sc in 2nd ch of turning ch, turn.

Row 4: Ch 2 (counts as dc), skip first sc, sc in next sc, *FPdc around the post of next corresponding dc 2 rows below, skip sc behind post st just made, sc in next sc; rep from * across to within last sc, dc in last sc, turn.

Rep Rows 3-4 for pattern.

420

Chain multiples of 20 plus 16.

Row 1: Dc in 4th ch from hook, dc in each ch across, turn.

Row 2: Ch 3 (counts as dc), skip first dc, dc in next dc, *ch 10, skip next 10 dc**, dc in each of next 10 dc; rep from * across, ending last rep at **, dc in next dc, dc in 3rd ch of turning ch, turn.

Row 3: Ch 3 (counts as dc), skip first dc, dc in next dc, *ch 10, skip next ch-10 loop**, (dc in each of next 2 dc, ch 2, skip next 2 dc) twice, dc in each of next 2 dc; rep from * across, ending last rep at **, dc in next dc, dc in 3rd ch of turning ch, turn.

Row 4: Ch 3 (counts as dc), skip first dc, dc in next dc, *ch 10, skip next ch-10 loop**, dc in each of next 2 dc, 2 dc in next ch-2 space, ch 2, skip next 2 dc, 2 dc in next ch-2 space, dc in each of next 2 dc; rep from * across, ending last rep at **, dc in next dc, dc in 3rd ch of turning ch, turn.

Row 5: Ch 3 (counts as dc), skip first dc, dc in next dc, *ch 4, work 2 sc over next 3 ch-10 loops in last 3 rows, ch 4**, dc in each of next 2 dc, ch 2, skip next 2 dc, 2 dc in next ch-2 space, ch 2, skip next 2 dc, dc in each of next 2 dc; rep from * across, ending last rep at **, dc in next dc, dc in 3rd ch of turning ch, turn.

Row 6: Ch 3 (counts as dc), skip first dc, dc in next dc, *ch 10, skip next 2 ch-4 loops**, (dc in each of next 2 dc, 2 dc in next ch-2 space) twice, dc in each of next 2 dc; rep from * across, ending last rep at **, dc in next dc, dc in 3rd ch of turning ch, turn.

Row 7: Ch 3 (counts as dc), skip first dc, dc in next dc, *10 dc in next ch-10 loop**, ch 10, skip next 10 dc; rep from * across, ending last rep at **, dc in next dc, dc in 3rd ch of turning ch, turn.

Row 8: Ch 3 (counts as dc), skip first dc, dc in first dc, *(dc in each of next 2 dc, ch 2, skip next 2 dc) twice, dc in each of next 2 dc**, ch 10, skip next ch-10 loop; rep from * across, ending last rep at **, dc in next dc, dc in 3rd ch of turning ch, turn.

Row 9: Ch 3 (counts as dc), skip first dc, dc in next dc, *dc in each of next 2 dc, 2 dc in next ch-2 space, ch 2, skip next 2 dc, 2 dc in next ch-2 space, dc in each of next 2 dc**, ch 10, skip next ch-10 loop; rep from * across, ending last rep at **, dc in next dc, dc in 3rd ch of turning ch, turn.

Row 10: Ch 3 (counts as dc), skip first dc, dc in next dc, *dc in each of next 2 dc, ch 2, skip next 2 dc, 2 dc in next ch-2 space, ch 2, skip next 2 dc, dc in each of next 2 dc**, ch 4, work 2 sc over next 3 ch-10 loops in last 3 rows, ch 4; rep from * across, ending last rep at **, dc in next dc, dc in 3rd ch of turning ch, turn.

Row 11: Ch 3 (counts as dc), skip first dc, dc in next dc, *(dc in each of next 2 dc, 2 dc in next ch-2 space) twice, dc in each of next 2 dc**, ch 10, skip next 2 ch-4 loops; rep from * across, ending last rep at **, dc in next dc, dc in 3rd ch of turning ch, turn.

Rep Rows 2-11 for pattern.

421

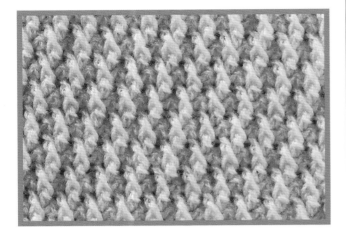

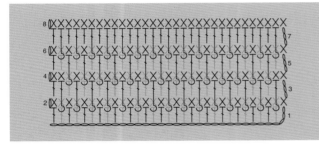

Front Post Double Crochet (FPdc): Yo, insert hook from front to back to front again around the post of designated st, yo, draw yarn through, (yo, draw yarn through 2 loops on hook) twice.

Chain multiples of 2 plus 1.

Row 1 (RS): Dc in 4th ch from hook, dc in each ch across, turn.

Row 2: Ch 1, sc in each st across, ending with sc in 3rd ch of turning ch, turn.

Row 3: Ch 3 (counts as dc), skip first sc, *FPdc around the post of next corresponding dc 2 rows below, skip sc behind post st just made, dc in next sc; rep from * across, turn.

Row 4: Rep Row 2.

Row 5: Ch 3 (counts as dc), skip first sc, dc in next dc, *FPdc around the post of next corresponding dc 2 rows below, skip sc behind post st just made, dc in next sc; rep from * across to tuyrning ch, dc in 3rd ch of turning ch, turn.

Rep Rows 2-5 for pattern.

422

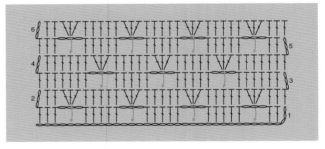

Chain multiples of 8 plus 3.

Row 1: Dc in 4th ch from hook, dc in next ch, *ch 3, skip next 3 ch, dc in each of next 5 ch; rep from * across, ending with dc in each of last 3 ch, turn.

Row 2: Ch 3 (counts as dc), skip first dc, dc in each of next 2 dc, *working over next ch-3 loop, work 3 dc in corresponding center ch st 2 rows below**, dc in each of next 5 dc; rep from * across, ending last rep at **, dc in each of next 2 dc, dc in 3rd ch of turning ch, turn.

Row 3: Ch 3 (counts as dc), skip first dc, dc in each of next 6 dc, *ch 3, skip next 3 dc, dc in each of next 5 dc; rep from * across to within last 2 sts, dc in next dc, dc in 3rd ch of turning ch, turn.

Row 4: Ch 3 (counts as dc), skip first dc, dc in each of next 6 dc, *working over next ch-3 loop, work 3 dc in corresponding center dc 2 rows below, dc in each of next 5 dc; rep from * across, dc in each of next 2 dc, dc in 3rd ch of turning ch, turn.

Row 5: Ch 3 (counts as dc), skip first dc, dc in each of next 2 dc, *ch 3, skip next 3 dc**, dc in each of next 5 dc; rep from * across, ending last rep at **, dc in each of next 2 dc, dc in 3rd ch of turning ch, turn.

Row 6: Ch 3 (counts as dc), skip first dc, dc in each of next 2 dc, *working over next ch-3 loop, work 3 dc in corresponding center dc 2 rows below**, dc in each of next 5 dc; rep from * across, ending last rep at **, dc in each of next 2 dc, dc in 3rd ch of turning ch, turn.

Rep Rows 3-6 for pattern.

Chain multiples of 7 plus 5.

Row 1: 3 dc in 4th ch from hook, *ch 2, skip next 6 ch**, (3 dc, ch 1, 3 dc) in next ch; rep from * across, ending last rep at **, 3 dc in next ch, dc in last ch, turn.

Row 2: Ch 3 (counts as dc), skip first dc, 3 dc in next dc, *ch 2, skip next ch-2 space**, (3 dc, ch 1, 3 dc) in next ch-1 space; rep from * across, ending last rep at **, skip next 2 dc, 3 dc in next dc, dc in 3rd ch of turning ch, turn.

Row 3: Ch 3 (counts as dc), skip first dc, 3 dc in next dc, *ch 1, sl st over next 2 ch-2 spaces in 2 rows below, ch 1**, (3 dc, ch 1, 3 dc) in next ch-1 space; rep from * across, ending last rep at **, skip next 2 dc, 3 dc in next dc, dc in 3rd ch of turning ch, turn.

Row 4: Ch 3 (counts as dc), skip first dc, 3 dc in next dc, *ch 2, skip next 2 ch-1 spaces**, (3 dc, ch 1, 3 dc) in next ch-1 space; rep from * across, ending last rep at **, skip next 2 dc, 3 dc in next dc, dc in 3rd ch of turning ch, turn.

Rep Rows 2-4 for pattern.

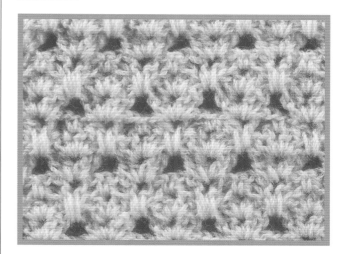

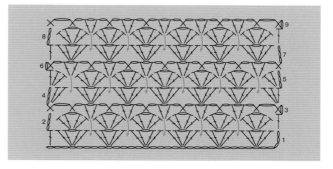

Chain multiples of 5 plus 4.

Row 1: (2 dc, ch 1, 2 dc) in 6th ch from hook, *skip next 4 ch (2 dc, ch 1, 2 dc) in next ch; rep from * across to within last 3 ch, skip next 2 ch, dc in last ch, turn.

Row 2: Ch 3 (counts as dc), skip first 3 dc, (2 dc, ch 1, 2 dc) in each ch-1 space across to last ch-1 space, skip next 2 dc, dc in 3rd ch of turning ch, turn.

Row 3: Ch 1, sc in first dc, *ch 1, sc in next ch-1 space, ch 1**, working over sts in last row, work (dc, ch 1, dc) between next 2 corresponding dc 2 rows below, ch 1; rep from * across, ending last rep at **, skip next 2 dc, sc in 3rd ch of turning ch, turn.

Row 4: Ch 3 (counts as dc), 2 dc in first dc, skip next 2 ch-1 spaces, *(2 dc, ch 1, 2 dc) in next ch-1 space, skip next 2 ch-1 spaces; rep from * across to within last sc, 3 dc in last sc, turn.

Row 5: Ch 3 (counts as dc), 2 dc in first dc, (2 dc, ch 1, 2 dc) in each ch-1 space across to last ch-1 space, skip next 4 dc, 3 dc in 3rd ch of turning ch, turn.

Row 6: Ch 1, sc in first dc, *ch 1, skip next 2 dc, working over sts in last row, work (dc, ch 1, dc) between next 2 corresponding dc 2 rows below, ch 1**, sc in next ch-1 space, ch 1; rep from * across, ending last rep at **, skip next 2 dc, sc in 3rd ch of turning ch, turn.

Row 7: Ch 3 (counts as dc), skip next ch-1 space, *(2 dc, ch 1, 2 dc) in next ch-1 space**, skip next 2 ch-1 spaces; rep from * across, ending last rep at **, skip next ch-1 space, dc in last sc, turn.

Rep Rows 2-7 for pattern.

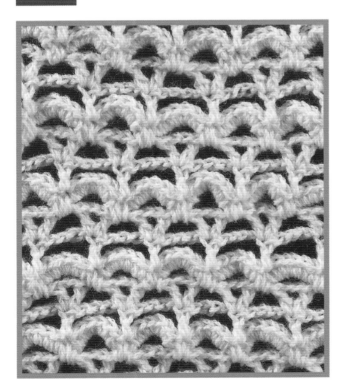

425

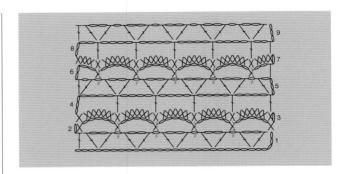

Chain multiples of 5 plus 4.

Row 1: (Dc, ch 2, dc) in 6th ch from hook, *ch 1, skip next 4 ch (dc, ch 2, dc) in next ch; rep from * across to within last 3 ch, skip next 2 ch, dc in last ch, turn.

Row 2: Ch 1, sc in first dc, *ch 5, skip next ch-2 space, sc in next ch-1 space; rep from * across, ending with last sc in 3rd ch of turning ch, turn.

Row 3: Ch 1, sc in first sc, *6 sc in next ch-5 loop, working over sc in last row, sc in next corresponding ch-1 space 2 rows below; rep from * across, ending with last sc in last sc, turn.

Row 4: Ch 7 (counts as dc, ch 4), skip first 7 sc, dc in next sc, *ch 4, skip next 6 sc, dc in next sc; rep from * across, turn.

Row 5: Ch 4 (counts as dc, ch 1), dc in first dc, *ch 1, skip next ch-4 loop**, (dc, ch 2, dc) in next dc; rep from * across, ending last rep at **, (dc, ch 1, dc) in 3rd ch of turning ch, turn.

Row 6: Ch 4 (counts as hdc, ch 2), skip next ch-1 space, sc in next ch-1 space, *ch 5, skip next ch-2 space, sc in next ch-1 space; rep from * across to turning ch, ch 2, hdc in 3rd ch of turning ch, turn.

Row 7: Ch 1, sc in first hdc, 3 sc in next ch-2 space, *working over sc in last row, sc in next corresponding ch-1 space 2 rows below**, 6 sc in next ch-5 loop; rep from * across, ending last rep at **, 3 sc in next ch-2 space of turning ch, sc in 2nd ch of turning ch, turn.

Row 8: Ch 4 (counts as hdc, ch 2), skip first 4 sc, dc in next sc, *ch 4, skip next 6 sc, dc in next sc; rep from * across to within last 4 sc, ch 2, skip next 3 sc, hdc in last sc, turn.

Row 9: Ch 3 (counts as dc), skip next ch-2 space, *(dc, ch 2, dc) in next dc**, ch 1, skip next ch-4 loop; rep from * across, ending last rep at **, skip next 2 ch of turning ch, dc in 2nd ch of turning ch, turn.

Rep Rows 2-9 for pattern.

426

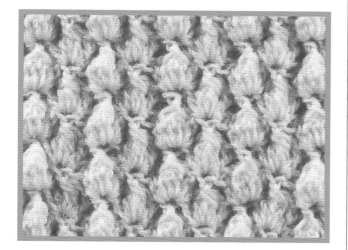

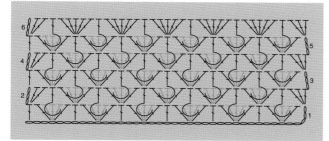

Front Post Double Crochet (FPdc): Yo, insert hook from front to back to front again around the post of designated sts, yo, draw yarn through, (yo, draw yarn through 2 loops on hook) twice.

Back Post Double Crochet (BPdc): Yo, insert hook from back to front to back again around the post of designated sts, yo, draw yarn through, (yo, draw yarn through 2 loops on hook) twice.

Chain multiples of 6 plus 3.

Row 1: 5 dc in 6th ch from hook, *skip next 2 ch, dc in next ch**, skip next 2 ch, 5 dc in next ch; rep from * across, ending last rep at **, turn.

Row 2: Ch 3 (counts as dc), 2 dc in first dc, *skip next dc, BPdc around the posts of next 3 dc, skip next dc**, 5 dc in next dc; rep from * across, ending last rep at **, 3 dc in top of turning ch, turn.

Row 3: Ch 3 (counts as dc), skip first 3 dc, *5 dc in next dc**, skip next dc, FPdc around the posts of next 3 dc, skip next dc; rep from * across, ending last rep at **, skip next 2 dc, dc in 3rd ch of turning ch, turn.

Rep Rows 2-3 for pattern.

427

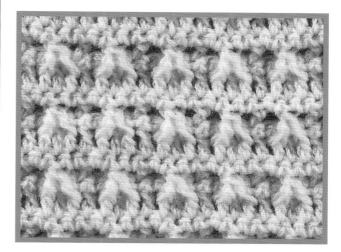

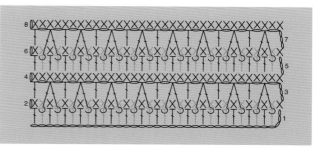

Front Post Double Crochet Cluster (FPdc cluster): (Yo, insert hook from front to back to front again around the post of next designated st, yo, draw yarn through, yo, draw yarn through 2 loops on hook) twice, yo, draw yarn through 3 loops on hook.

Chain multiples of 2 plus 1.

Row 1: Dc in 4th ch from hook, dc in each ch across, turn.

Row 2: Ch 1, sc in each st across, ending with sc in 3rd ch of turning ch, turn.

Row 3: Ch 4 (counts as dc, ch 1), skip first sc, *work FPdc cluster, working first half-closed dc around the post of next corresponding dc 2 rows below, skip next dc, work 2nd half-closed dc around the post of next dc 2 rows below, yo, complete cluster, ch 1, skip 3 sc behind cluster just made, dc in next sc; rep from * across, turn.

Row 4: Ch 1, sc in each st and space across, ending with sc in 3rd ch of turning ch, turn.

Row 5: Ch 3 (counts as dc), skip first sc, dc in each sc across, turn.

Rep Rows 2-5 for pattern.

.29.
Post Stitches

428

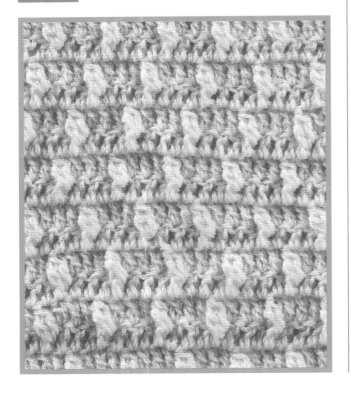

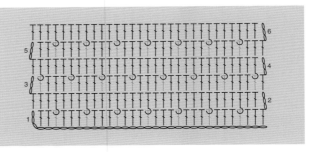

Front Post Double Crochet (FPdc): *Yo, insert hook from front to back to front again around the post of designated st, yo, draw yarn through, (yo, draw yarn through 2 loops on hook) twice.*

Chain multiples of 4 plus 1.

Row 1: (WS): Dc in 4th ch from hook, dc in each ch across, turn.

Row 2: Ch 3 (counts as dc), skip first dc, dc in each of next 2 dc, *FPdc around the post of next dc**, dc in each of next 3 dc; rep from * across, ending with last dc in 3rd ch of turning ch, turn.

Row 3: Ch 3 (counts as dc), skip first dc, dc in each st across, ending with dc in 3rd ch of turning ch, turn.

Row 4: Ch 3 (counts as dc), skip first dc, *FPdc around the post of next dc**, dc in each of next 3 dc; rep from * across, ending last rep at **, dc in 3rd ch of turning ch, turn.

Row 5: Rep Row 3.

Rep Rows 2-5 for pattern.

429

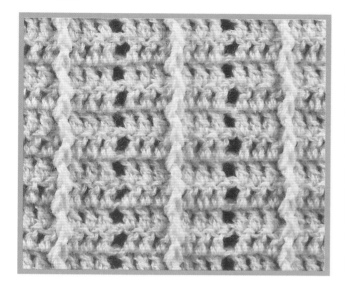

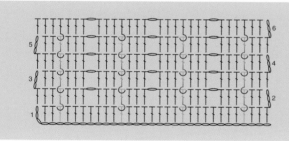

Front Post Double Crochet (FPdc): Yo, insert hook from front to back to front again around the post of designated st, yo, draw yarn through, (yo, draw yarn through 2 loops on hook) twice.

Back Post Double Crochet (BPdc): Yo, insert hook from back to front to back again around the post of designated st, yo, draw yarn through, (yo, draw yarn through 2 loops on hook) twice.

Chain multiples of 8 plus 1.

Row 1 (WS): Dc in 4th ch from hook, dc in each ch across, turn.

Row 2: Ch 3 (counts as dc), skip first dc, dc in each of next 2 dc, *FPdc around the post of next dc, dc in each of next 3 dc**, ch 1, skip next st, dc in each of next 3 dc; rep from * across, ending last rep at **, with last dc in 3rd ch of turning ch, turn.

Row 3: Ch 3 (counts as dc), skip first dc, dc in each of next 2 dc, *BPdc around the post of next dc, dc in each of next 3 dc**, ch 1, skip next ch-1 space, dc in each of next 3 dc; rep from * across, ending last rep at **, with last dc in 3rd ch of turning ch, turn.

Rep Rows 2-3 for pattern.

430

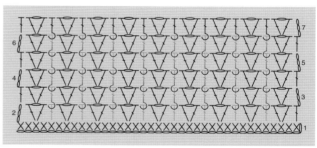

Front Post Double Crochet (FPdc): Yo, insert hook from front to back to front again around the post of designated st, yo, draw yarn through, (yo, draw yarn through 2 loops on hook) twice.

Back Post Double Crochet (BPdc): Yo, insert hook from back to front to back again around the post of designated st, yo, draw yarn through, (yo, draw yarn through 2 loops on hook) twice.

Chain multiples of 4 plus 2.

Row 1: Sc in 2nd ch from hook, sc in each ch across, turn.

Row 2: Ch 3 (counts as dc), skip first 2 sc, *(dc, ch 1, dc) in next sc, skip next sc, dc in next sc**, skip next sc; rep from * across, ending last rep at **, turn.

Row 3: Ch 3 (counts as dc), *(dc, ch 1, dc) in next ch-1 space, skip next dc**, FPdc around the post of next dc; rep from * across, ending last rep at **, dc in 3rd ch of turning ch, turn.

Row 4: Ch 3 (counts as dc), *(dc, ch 1, dc) in next ch-1 space, skip next dc**, BPdc around the post of next dc; rep from * across, ending last rep at **, dc in 3rd ch of turning ch, turn.

Rep Rows 3-4 for pattern.

431

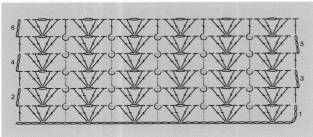

Front Post Double Crochet (FPdc): Yo, insert hook from front to back to front again around the post of designated st, yo, draw yarn through, (yo, draw yarn through 2 loops on hook) twice.

Back Post Double Crochet (BPdc): Yo, insert hook from back to front to back again around the post of designated st, yo, draw yarn through, (yo, draw yarn through 2 loops on hook) twice.

Chain multiples of 6 plus 3.

Row 1: (2 dc, ch 1, 2 dc) in 6th ch from hook, *skip next 2 ch, dc in next ch**, skip next 2 ch, (2 dc, ch 1, 2 dc) in next ch; rep from * across, ending last rep at **, turn.

Row 2: Ch 3 (counts as dc), *(2 dc, ch 1, 2 dc) in next ch-1 space, skip next 2 dc**, BPdc around the post of next dc; rep from * across, ending last rep at **, dc in 3rd ch of turning ch, turn.

Row 3: Ch 3 (counts as dc), *(2 dc, ch 1, 2 dc) in next ch-1 space, skip next 2 dc**, FPdc around the post of next dc; rep from * across, ending last rep at **, dc in 3rd ch of turning ch, turn.

Rep Rows 2-3 for pattern.

432

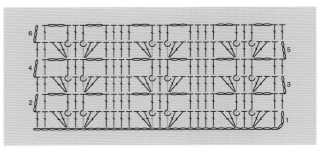

Back Post Double Crochet (BPdc): Yo, insert hook from back to front to back again around the post of designated st, yo, draw yarn through, (yo, draw yarn through 2 loops on hook) twice.

Chain multiples of 11 plus 2.

Row 1: Dc in 4th ch from hook, *skip next 2 ch, 3 dc in next ch, dc in next ch, 3 dc in next ch, skip next 2 ch, dc in each of next 4 ch; rep from * across, ending with dc in each of last 2 ch, turn.

Row 2: Ch 3 (counts as dc), skip first dc, dc in next dc, *ch 2, skip next 2 dc, BPdc around the post of next dc, dc in next dc, BPdc around the post of next dc, ch 2, skip next 2 dc**, dc in each of next 4 dc; rep from * across, ending last rep at **, dc in next dc, dc in 3rd ch of turning ch, turn.

Row 3: Ch 3 (counts as dc), skip first dc, dc in next dc, *skip next ch-2 space, 3 dc in next dc, dc in next dc, 3 dc in next dc, skip next ch-2 space**, dc in each of next 4 dc; rep from * across, ending last rep at **, dc in next dc, dc in 3rd ch of turning ch, turn.

Rep Rows 2-3 for pattern.

433

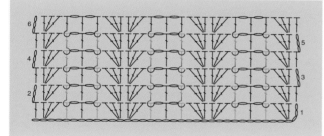

Front Post Double Crochet (FPdc): Yo, insert hook from front to back to front again around the post of designated st, yo, draw yarn through, (yo, draw yarn through 2 loops on hook) twice.

Back Post Double Crochet (BPdc): Yo, insert hook from back to front to back again around the post of designated st, yo, draw yarn through, (yo, draw yarn through 2 loops on hook) twice.

Chain multiples of 11 plus 4.

Row 1: 3 dc in 4th ch from hook, *skip next 2 ch, (dc in next ch, ch 1, skip next ch) twice, dc in next ch, skip next 2 ch, 3 dc in next ch**, 3 dc in next ch; rep from * across, ending last rep at **, dc in last ch, turn.

Row 2: Ch 3 (counts as dc), skip first dc, *3 dc in next dc, skip next 2 dc, BPdc around the post of next dc, ch 1, skip next ch-1 space, dc in next dc, ch 1, BPdc around the post of next dc, skip next 2 dc, 3 dc in next dc; rep from * across to turning ch, dc in 3rd ch of turning ch, turn.

Row 3: Ch 3 (counts as dc), skip first dc, *3 dc in next dc, skip next 2 dc, FPdc around the post of next dc, ch 1, skip next ch-1 space, dc in next dc, ch 1, FPdc around the post of next dc, skip next 2 dc, 3 dc in next dc; rep from * across to turning ch, dc in 3rd ch of turning ch, turn.

Rep Rows 2-3 for pattern.

434

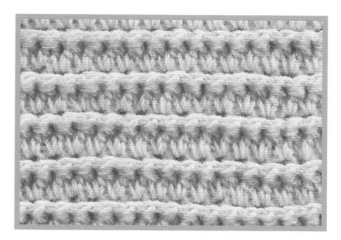

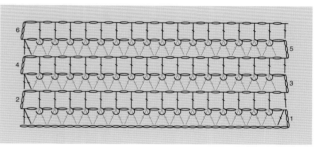

2-Dc Cluster: (Yo, insert hook in next st, yo, draw yarn through st, yo, draw yarn through 2 loops on hook) twice in designated sts, yo, draw yarn through 3 loops on hook.

Front Post Double Crochet (FPdc): Yo, insert hook from front to back to front again around the post of designated sts, yo, draw yarn through, (yo, draw yarn through 2 loops on hook) twice.

Chain multiples of 2.

Row 1: Dc in 5th ch from hook, ch 1, *work 2-dc cluster, working first half-closed dc in same ch holding last dc made, skip next ch, work 2nd half-closed dc in next ch, yo, complete cluster, ch 1; rep from * across to within last ch, work 2-dc cluster across last 2 ch, turn.

Row 2: Ch 4 (counts as dc, ch 1), skip next ch-1 space, *FPdc around the post of next cluster, ch 1, skip next ch-1 space; rep from * across to turning ch, dc in 3rd ch of turning ch, turn.

Row 3: Ch 4 (counts as dc, ch 1), work 2-dc cluster across next 2 ch-1 spaces, *ch 1, starting in same ch-1 space as last dc made, work 2-dc cluster across next 2 ch-1 spaces; rep from * across to turning ch, work 2-dc cluster in ch-1 space of turning ch and in 3rd ch of turning ch, turn.

Rep Rows 2-3 for pattern.

435

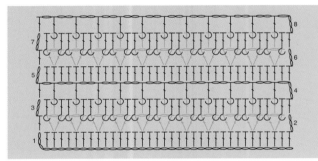

Front Post Double Crochet (FPdc): Yo, insert hook from front to back to front again around the post of designated sts, yo, draw yarn through, (yo, draw yarn through 2 loops on hook) twice.

Back Post Double Crochet (BPdc): Yo, insert hook from back to front to back again around the post of designated st, yo, draw yarn through, (yo, draw yarn through 2 loops on hook) twice.

Chain multiples of 3 plus 1.

Row 1 (WS): Dc in 4th ch from hook, dc in each ch across, turn.

Row 2: Ch 3 (counts as dc), skip first 2 dc, *(dc, ch 1, dc) in next dc**, skip next 2 dc; rep from * across, ending last rep at **, skip next dc, dc in 3rd ch of turning ch, turn.

Row 3: Ch 3 (counts as dc), skip first dc, *BPdc around the post of next dc, dc in next ch-1 space, BPdc around the post of next dc; rep from * across to turning ch, dc in 3rd ch of turning ch, turn.

Row 4: Ch 4 (counts as dc, ch 1), skip first 2 dc, *FPdc around the post of next dc**, ch 2, skip next 2 dc; rep from * across, ending last rep at **, ch 1, skip next dc, dc in 3rd ch of turning ch, turn.

Row 5: ch 3 (counts as dc), skip first dc, dc in next ch-1 space, *dc in next dc, 2 dc in next ch-2 space; rep from * across, ending with last dc in 3rd ch of turning ch, turn.

Rep Rows 2-5 for pattern.

436

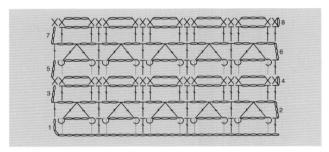

2-FPdc Cluster: (Yo, insert hook from front to back to front again around the post of next designated st, yo, draw yarn through, yo, draw yarn through 2 loops on hook) twice, yo, draw yarn through 3 loops on hook.

Chain multiples of 6 plus 3.

Row 1 (WS): Dc in 4th ch from hook, *ch 3, skip next 3 ch, dc in each of next 3 ch; rep from * across, ending with dc in each of last 2 ch, turn.

Row 2: Ch 5 (counts as dc, ch 2), skip first dc, *2-FPdc cluster, working first half-closed dc around the post of next dc, skip next ch-3 loop, work 2nd half-closed dc around the post of next dc, yo, complete cluster, ch 2**, dc in next dc, ch 2; rep from * across, ending last rep at **, dc in 3rd ch of turning ch, turn.

Row 3: Ch 3 (counts as dc), *dc in next ch-2 space, ch 3, dc in next ch-2 space, dc in next dc; rep from * across, ending with last dc in 3rd ch of turning ch, turn.

Row 4: Ch 1, sc in first dc, *sc in next dc, ch 3, skip next ch-3 loop, sc in each of next 2 dc; rep from * across, ending with last sc in 3rd ch of turning ch, turn.

Row 5: Ch 3 (counts as dc), skip first dc, *dc in next sc, ch 3, skip next ch-3 loop, dc in each of next 2 sc; rep from * across, turn.

Rep Rows 2-5 for pattern.

437

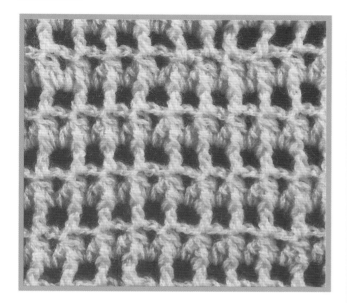

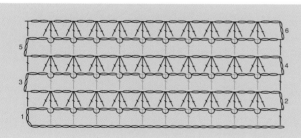

3-Dc Cluster: *Yo, insert hook in next designated space, yo, draw yarn through st, yo, draw yarn through 2 loops on hook, yo, insert hook from front to back to front again around the post of next designated st, yo, draw yarn through, yo, draw yarn through 2 loops on hook, yo, insert hook in next designated space, yo, draw yarn through st, yo, draw yarn through 2 loops on hook, yo, draw yarn through 4 loops on hook.*

Chain multiples of 3 plus 2.

Row 1 (WS): Dc in 8th ch from hook, *ch 2, skip next 2 ch, dc in next ch; rep from * across, turn.

Row 2: Ch 5 (counts as dc, ch 2), *work 3-dc cluster across next (ch-2 space, dc, ch-2 space), ch 2; rep from * across to turning ch, skip next 2 ch, dc in next ch of turning ch, turn.

Row 3: Ch 5 (counts as dc, ch 2), skip next ch-2 space, *dc in next cluster, ch 2, skip next ch-2 space; rep from * across to turning ch, dc in 3rd ch of turning ch, turn.

Rep Rows 2-3 for pattern.

438

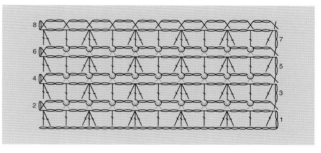

2-Dc Cluster: *(Yo, insert hook in next st, yo, draw yarn through next st, yo, draw yarn through 2 loops on hook) twice, yo, draw yarn through 3 loops on hook.*

3-Dc Cluster: *(Yo, insert hook in next st, yo, draw yarn through next st, yo, draw yarn through 2 loops on hook) 3 times, yo, draw yarn through 4 loops on hook.*

Front Post Double Crochet (FPdc): *Yo, insert hook from front to back to front again around the post of next st, yo, draw yarn through, (yo, draw yarn through 2 loops on hook) twice.*

Dc-FPdc-Dc Cluster: *Yo, insert hook in next designated space, yo, draw yarn through st, yo, draw yarn through 2 loops on hook, yo, insert hook from front to back to front again around the post of next designated st, yo, draw yarn through, yo, draw yarn through 2 loops on hook, yo, insert hook in next designated space, yo, draw yarn through st, yo, draw yarn through 2 loops on hook, yo, draw yarn through 4 loops on hook.*

Chain multiples of 6 plus 3.

Row 1: Dc in 4th ch from hook, *ch 2, skip next ch, dc in next ch, ch 2, skip next ch**, 3-dc cluster worked across next 3 ch; rep from * across, ending last rep at **, 2-dc cluster worked across last 2 ch, turn.

Row 2: Ch 1, sc in first cluster, *ch 2, skip next ch-2 space, sc in next st; rep from * across, ending with last sc in top of turning ch, turn.

Row 3: Ch 2 (counts as dc), dc in next ch-2 space, *ch 2, FPdc around the post of next sc, ch 2**, dc-FPdc-dc cluster worked across next (ch-2 space, dc, ch-2 space); rep from * across, ending last rep at **, 2-dc cluster worked across last ch-2 space and last sc, turn.

Rep Rows 2-3 for pattern.

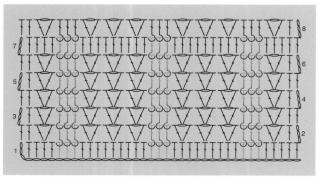

Front Post Double Crochet (FPdc): Yo, insert hook from front to back to front again around the post of designated st, yo, draw yarn through, (yo, draw yarn through 2 loops on hook) twice.

Back Post Double Crochet (BPdc): Yo, insert hook from back to front to back again around the post of designated st, yo, draw yarn through, (yo, draw yarn through 2 loops on hook) twice.

Chain multiples of 12 plus 3.

Row 1: Dc in 4th ch from hook, dc in each ch across, turn.

Row 2: Ch 3 (counts as dc), skip first dc, dc in next dc, skip next dc, (dc, ch 1, dc) in next dc, *skip next dc, FPdc around the post of each of next 3 dc, skip next dc, (dc, ch 1, dc) in next dc**, (skip next 2 dc, [dc, ch 1, dc] in next dc) twice, skip next dc; rep from * across, ending last rep at **, skip next dc, dc in next dc, dc in 3rd ch of turning ch, turn.

Row 3: Ch 3 (counts as dc), skip first dc, dc in next dc, (dc, ch 1, dc) in next ch-1 space, *BPdc around the post of each of next 3 dc**, (dc, ch 1, dc) in each of next 3 ch-1 spaces, skip next dc; rep from * across, ending last rep at **, (dc, ch 1, dc) in next ch-1 space, skip next dc, dc in next dc, dc in 3rd ch of turning ch, turn.

Row 4: Ch 3 (counts as dc), skip first dc, dc in next dc, (dc, ch 1, dc) in next ch-1 space, *skip next dc, FPdc around the post of each of next 3 dc**, (dc, ch 1, dc) in each of next 3 ch-1 spaces; rep from * across, ending last rep at **, (dc, ch 1, dc) in next ch-1 space, skip next dc, dc in next dc, dc in 3rd ch of turning ch, turn.

Rep Rows 3-4 for pattern.

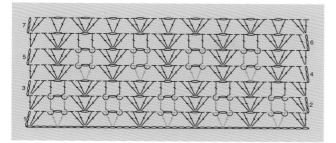

Front Post Double Crochet (FPdc): Yo, insert hook from front to back to front again around the post of designated st, yo, draw yarn through, (yo, draw yarn through 2 loops on hook) twice.

Back Post Double Crochet (BPdc): Yo, insert hook from back to front to back again around the post of designated st, yo, draw yarn through, (yo, draw yarn through 2 loops on hook) twice.

Chain multiples of 8 plus 4.

Row 1 (WS): 2 dc in 4th ch from hook, *skip next 3 ch, (dc, ch 1, dc) in next ch, skip next 3 ch**, (2 dc, ch 1, 2 dc) in next ch; rep from * across, ending last rep at **, 3 dc in last ch, turn.

Row 2: Ch 3 (counts as dc), 2 dc in first dc, *skip next 2 dc, FPdc around the post of next dc, ch 1, skip next ch-1 space, FPdc around the post of next dc**, (2 dc, ch 1, 2 dc) in next ch-1 space; rep from * across, ending last rep at **, skip next 2 dc, 3 dc in 3rd ch of turning ch, turn.

Row 3: Ch 3 (counts as dc), 2 dc in first dc, *skip next 2 dc, BPdc around the post of next dc, ch 1, skip next ch-1 space, BPdc around the post of next dc**, (2 dc, ch 1, 2 dc) in next ch-1 space; rep from * across, ending last rep at **, skip next 2 dc, 3 dc in 3rd ch of turning ch, turn.

Row 4: Ch 3 (counts as dc), dc in first dc, *(2 dc, ch 1, 2 dc) in next ch-1 space**, (dc, ch 1, dc) in next ch-1 space; rep from * across, ending last rep at **, skip next 3 dc, 2 dc in 3rd ch of turning ch, turn.

Row 5: Ch 3 (counts as dc), dc in first dc, *(2 dc, ch 1, 2 dc) in next ch-1 space**, skip next 2 dc, BPdc around the post of next dc, ch 1, skip next ch-1 space, BPdc around the post of next dc; rep from * across, ending last rep at **, skip next 3 dc, 2 dc in 3rd ch of turning ch, turn.

Row 6: Ch 3 (counts as dc), dc in first dc, *(2 dc, ch 1, 2 dc) in next ch-1 space**, skip next 2 dc, FPdc around the post of next dc, ch 1, skip next ch-1 space, FPdc around the post of next dc; rep from * across, ending last rep at **, skip next 3 dc, 2 dc in 3rd ch of turning ch, turn.

Row 7: Ch 3 (counts as dc), 2 dc in first dc, *(dc, ch 1, dc) in next ch-1 space**, (2 dc, ch 1, 2 dc) in next ch-1 space; rep from * across, ending last rep at **, skip next 3 dc, 2 dc in 3rd ch of turning ch, turn.

Rep Rows 2-7 for pattern.

441

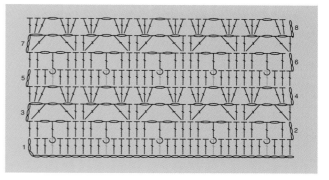

Front Post Double Crochet (FPdc): Yo, insert hook from front to back to front again around the post of designated st, yo, draw yarn through, (yo, draw yarn through 2 loops on hook) twice.

Chain multiples of 7 plus 2.

Row 1 (WS): Dc in 4th ch from hook, dc in each ch across, turn.

Row 2: Ch 3 (counts as dc), skip first dc, dc in next dc, *ch 1, skip next dc, FPdc around the post of next dc, ch 1, skip next dc**, dc in each of next 4 dc; rep from * across, ending last rep at **, dc in next dc, dc in 3rd ch of turning ch, turn.

Row 3: Ch 4 (counts as dc, ch 1), dc in first dc, *ch 1, skip next 2 ch-1 spaces**, (dc, ch 1, dc) in each of next 2 ch-1 spaces; rep from * across, ending last rep at **, (dc, ch 1, dc) in 3rd ch of turning ch, turn.

Row 4: Ch 3 (counts as dc), 2 dc in next ch-1 space, *ch 1, skip next ch-1 space**, 3 dc in each of next 2 ch-1 spaces; rep from * across, ending last rep at **, 2 dc in ch-1 space of turning ch, dc in 3rd ch of turning ch, turn.

Row 5: Ch 3 (counts as dc), dc in first dc, dc in each dc and space across, ending with last dc in 3rd ch of turning ch, turn.

Rep Rows 2-5 for pattern.

442

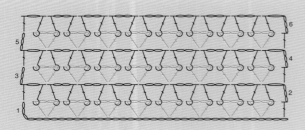

Front Post Double Crochet (FPdc): Yo, insert hook from front to back to front again around the post of designated st, yo, draw yarn through, (yo, draw yarn through 2 loops on hook) twice.

Chain multiples of 4 plus 1.

Row 1 (WS): (Dc, ch 2, dc) in 6th ch from hook, *skip next 3 ch, (dc, ch 2, dc) in next ch; rep from * across to within last 3 ch, skip next 2 ch, dc in next ch, turn.

Row 2: Ch 4 (counts as dc, ch 1), skip first dc, *FPdc around the post of next dc, skip next ch-2 space, FPdc around the post of next dc**, ch 2; rep from * across, ending last rep at **, ch 1, dc in top of turning ch, turn.

Row 3: Ch 3 (counts as dc), skip next ch-1 space, *(dc, ch 2, dc) between next 2 FPdc**, skip next ch-2 space; rep from * across, ending last rep at **, skip next ch of turning ch, dc in 3rd ch of turning ch, turn.

Rep Rows 2-3 for pattern.

443

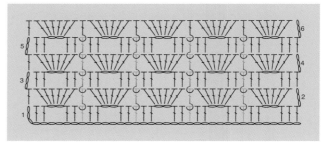

Front Post Double Crochet (FPdc): Yo, insert hook from front to back to front again around the post of designated st, yo, draw yarn through, (yo, draw yarn through 2 loops on hook) twice.

Back Post Double Crochet (BPdc): Yo, insert hook from back to front to back again around the post of designated st, yo, draw yarn through, (yo, draw yarn through 2 loops on hook) twice.

Chain multiples of 7 plus 3.

Row 1 (WS): Dc in 4th ch from hook, dc in next ch, *ch 2, skip next 2 ch, dc in each of next 5 ch; rep from * across, ending with dc in each of last 3 ch, turn.

Row 2: Ch 3 (counts as dc), skip first 3 dc, *6 dc in next ch-2 space, skip next 2 dc**, FPdc around the post of next dc, skip next 2 dc; rep from * across, ending last rep at **, dc in 3rd ch of turning ch, turn.

Row 3: Ch 3 (counts as dc), skip first dc, dc in each of next 2 dc, *ch 2, skip next 2 dc, dc in each of next 2 dc**, BPdc around the post of next dc, dc in each of next 2 dc; rep from * across, ending last rep at **, dc in 3rd ch of turning ch, turn.

Rep Rows 2-3 for pattern.

444

Front Post Single Crochet (FPsc): Insert hook from front to back to front again around the post of designated st, yo, draw yarn through, yo, draw yarn through 2 loops on hook.

Chain multiples of 7 plus 6.

Row 1 (WS): Dc in 8th ch from hook, dc in each of next 2 ch, *ch 4, skip next 4 ch, dc in each of next 3 ch; rep from * across to within last 3 ch, ch 2, skip next 2 ch, dc in next ch, turn.

Row 2: Ch 3 (counts as dc), 3 dc in next ch-2 space, *skip next dc, FPsc around the post of next dc, skip next dc**, 7 dc in next ch-4 loop; rep from * across, ending last rep at **, 3 dc in ch-2 space of turning ch, dc in next ch of turning ch, turn.

Row 3: Ch 3 (counts as dc), skip first 2 dc, *dc in next dc, ch 4, skip next 3 sts, dc in next dc, skip next dc**, dc in next dc, skip next dc; rep from * across, ending last rep at **, dc in 3rd ch of turning ch, turn.

Row 4: Ch 1, FPsc around the post of first dc, *skip next dc, 7 dc in next ch-4 loop, skip next dc**, FPsc around the post of next dc; rep from * across, ending last rep at **, sc in 3rd ch of turning ch, turn.

Row 5: Ch 5 (counts as dc, ch 2), skip first 2 sts, *dc in next dc, (skip next dc, dc in next dc) twice**, ch 4, skip next 3 sts; rep from * across, ending last rep at **, ch 2, skip next dc, dc in last sc, turn.

Rep Rows 2-5 for pattern.

445

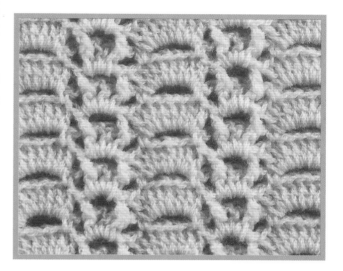

Front Post Double Crochet (FPdc): Yo, insert hook from front to back to front again around the post of designated st, yo, draw yarn through, (yo, draw yarn through 2 loops on hook) twice.

Chain multiples of 13 plus 1.

Row 1 (WS): Sc in 2nd ch from hook, ch 1, skip next ch, sc in next ch, *ch 1, skip next 3 ch, (dc, ch 1, dc, ch 1 dc) in next ch, ch 1, skip next 3 ch, sc in next ch**, ch 4, skip next 4 ch, sc in next ch; rep from * across, ending last rep at **, ch 1, skip next ch, sc in last ch, turn.

Row 2: Ch 3 (counts as dc), 3 dc in next ch-1 space, *skip next ch-1 space, FPdc around the post of next dc, ch 3, skip next 2 ch-1 spaces, FPdc around the post of next dc, skip next ch-1 space**, 9 dc in next ch-4 loop; rep from * across, ending last rep at **, 3 dc in next ch-1 space, dc in last sc, turn.

Row 3: Ch 1, sc in first dc, ch 1, skip next dc, sc in next dc, *ch 1, (dc, ch 1, dc, ch 1, dc) in next ch-3 loop, ch 1, skip next 2 dc, sc in next dc**, ch 4, skip next 4 dc, sc in next dc; rep from * across, ending last rep at **, ch 1, skip next dc, sc in 3rd ch of turning ch, turn.

Rep Rows 2-3 for pattern.

446

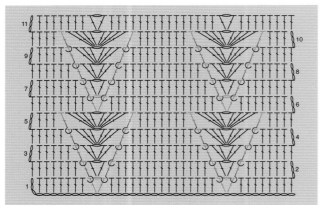

Front Post Double Crochet (FPdc): Yo, insert hook from front to back to front again around the post of designated st, yo, draw yarn through, (yo, draw yarn through 2 loops on hook) twice.

Back Post Double Crochet (BPdc): Yo, insert hook from back to front to back again around the post of designated st, yo, draw yarn through, (yo, draw yarn through 2 loops on hook) twice.

Chain multiples of 18 plus 3.

Row 1 (WS): Dc in 4th ch from hook, dc in of next 6 ch, *skip next ch, (dc, ch 1, dc) in next ch, skip next ch, dc in each of next 15 ch; rep from * across, ending with dc in each of last 8 ch, turn.

Row 2: Ch 3 (counts as dc), skip first dc, dc in each of next 6 dc, *skip next dc, FPdc around the post of next dc, (dc, ch 1, dc) in next ch-1 space, FPdc around the post of next dc, skip next dc**, dc in each of next 13 dc; rep from * across, ending last rep at **, dc in each of next 6 dc, dc in 3rd ch of turning ch, turn.

Row 3: Ch 3 (counts as dc), skip first dc, dc in each of next 5 dc, *skip next dc, BPdc around the post of next dc, (2 dc, ch 1, 2 dc) in next ch-1 space, skip next dc, BPdc around the post of next dc, skip next dc**, dc in each of next 11 dc; rep from * across, ending last rep at **, dc in each of next 5 dc, dc in 3rd ch of turning ch, turn.

Row 4: Ch 3 (counts as dc), skip first dc, dc in each of next 4 dc, *skip next dc, FPdc around the post of next dc, (3 dc, ch 1, 3 dc) in next ch-1 space, skip next 2 dc, FPdc around the post of next dc, skip next dc**, dc in each of next 9 dc; rep from * across, ending last rep at **, dc in each of next 4 dc, dc in 3rd ch of turning ch, turn.

Row 5: Ch 3 (counts as dc), skip first dc, dc in each of next 3 dc, *skip next dc, BPdc around the post of next dc, (4 dc, ch 1, 4 dc) in next ch-1 space, skip next 3 dc, BPdc around the post of next dc, skip next dc**, dc in each of next 7 dc; rep from * across, ending last rep at **, dc in each of next 3 dc, dc in 3rd ch of turning ch, turn.

Row 6: Ch 3 (counts as dc), skip first dc, dc in each of next 7 dc, *skip next dc, (dc, ch 1, dc) in next ch-1 space, skip next dc**, dc in each of next 15 dc; rep from * across, ending last rep at **, dc in each of next 7 dc, dc in 3rd ch of turning ch, turn.

Row 7: Ch 3 (counts as dc), skip first dc, dc in each of next 6 dc, *skip next dc, BPdc around the post of next dc, (dc, ch 1, dc) in next ch-1 space, BPdc around the post of next dc, skip next dc**, dc in each of next 13 dc; rep from * across, ending last rep at **, dc in each of next 6 dc, dc in 3rd ch of turning ch, turn.

Row 8: Ch 3 (counts as dc), skip first dc, dc in each of next 5 dc, *skip next dc, FPdc around the post of next dc, (2 dc, ch 1, 2 dc) in next ch-1 space, skip next dc, FPdc around the post of next dc, skip next dc**, dc in each of next 11 dc; rep from * across, ending last rep at **, dc in each of next 5 dc, dc in 3rd ch of turning ch, turn.

Row 9: Ch 3 (counts as dc), skip first dc, dc in each of next 4 dc, *skip next dc, BPdc around the post of next dc, (3 dc, ch 1, 3 dc) in next ch-1 space, skip next 2 dc, BPdc around the post of next dc, skip next dc**, dc in each of next 9 dc; rep from * across, ending last rep at **, dc in each of next 4 dc, dc in 3rd ch of turning ch, turn.

Row 10: Ch 3 (counts as dc), skip first dc, dc in each of next 3 dc, *skip next dc, FPdc around the post of next dc, (4 dc, ch 1, 4 dc) in next ch-1 space, skip next 3 dc, FPdc around the post of next dc, skip next dc**, dc in each of next 7 dc; rep from * across, ending last rep at **, dc in each of next 3 dc, dc in 3rd ch of turning ch, turn.

Row 11: Rep Row 6.

Rep Rows 2-11 for pattern.

447

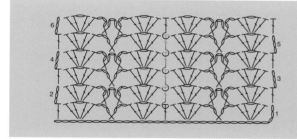

Front Post Double Crochet (FPdc): Yo, insert hook from front to back to front again around the post of designated st, yo, draw yarn through, (yo, draw yarn through 2 loops on hook) twice.

Back Post Double Crochet (BPdc): Yo, insert hook from back to front to back again around the post of designated st, yo, draw yarn through, (yo, draw yarn through 2 loops on hook) twice.

Chain multiples of 14 plus 3.

Row 1: (2 dc, ch 1, 2 dc) in 6th ch from hook, *ch 3, skip next 3 ch, sc in next ch, ch 3, skip next 3 ch, (2 dc, ch 1, 2 dc) in next ch, skip next 2 ch, dc in next ch**, skip next 2 ch, (2 dc, ch 1, 2 dc) in next ch; rep from * across, ending last rep at **, turn.

Row 2: Ch 3 (counts as dc), *(2 dc, ch 1, 2 dc) in next ch-1 space, ch 3, (sc, ch 3) in each of next 2 ch-3 loops, (2 dc, ch 1, 2 dc) in next ch-1 space, skip next 2 dc**, BPdc around the post of next dc; rep from * across, ending last rep at **, dc in 3rd ch of turning ch, turn.

Row 3: Ch 3 (counts as dc), *(2 dc, ch 1, 2 dc) in next ch-1 space, ch 3, skip next ch-3 loop, sc in next ch-3 loop, ch 3, skip next ch-3 loop, (2 dc, ch 1, 2 dc) in next ch-1 space, skip next 2 dc**, FPdc around the post of next dc; rep from * across, ending last rep at **, dc in 3rd ch of turning ch, turn.

Rep Rows 2-3 for pattern.

448

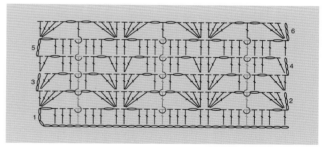

Front Post Double Crochet (FPdc): Yo, insert hook from front to back to front again around the post of designated st, yo, draw yarn through, (yo, draw yarn through 2 loops on hook) twice.

Back Post Double Crochet (BPdc): Yo, insert hook from back to front to back again around the post of designated st, yo, draw yarn through, (yo, draw yarn through 2 loops on hook) twice.

Chain multiples of 11 plus 3.

Row 1 (WS): Dc in 6th ch from hook, dc in each of next 6 ch, *ch 1, skip next ch, dc in each of next 2 ch, ch 1, skip next ch, dc in each of next 7 ch; rep from * across to within last 2 ch, ch 1, skip next ch, dc in last ch, turn.

Row 2: Ch 3 (counts as dc), 3 dc in first dc, *ch 1, skip next 3 dc, FPdc around the post of next dc, ch 1, skip next ch-1 space**, 4 dc in each of next 2 dc; rep from * across, ending last rep at **, skip next ch of turning ch, 4 dc in next ch of turning ch, turn.

Row 3: Ch 3 (counts as dc), 2 dc in first dc, *ch 1, dc in next ch-1 space, BPdc around the post of next dc, dc in next ch-1 space, ch 1, skip next 3 dc**, 3 dc in each of next 2 dc; rep from * across, ending last rep at **, 3 dc in 3rd ch of turning ch, turn.

Row 4: Ch 3 (counts as dc), dc in first dc, *ch 1, dc in next ch-1 space, dc in next dc, FPdc around the post of next next dc, dc in next dc, dc in next ch-1 space, ch 1, skip next 2 dc**, 2 dc in each of next 2 dc; rep from * across, ending last rep at **, 2 dc in 3rd ch of turning ch, turn.

Row 5: Ch 4 (counts as dc, ch 1), *dc in next ch-1 space, dc in each of next 2 dc, BPdc around the post of next dc, dc in each of next 2 dc, dc in next ch-1 space, ch 1, skip next dc**, dc in each of next 2 dc; rep from * across, ending last rep at **, dc in 3rd ch of turning ch, turn.

Rep Rows 2-5 for pattern.

449

Front Post Double Crochet (FPdc): Yo, insert hook from front to back to front again around the post of designated st, yo, draw yarn through, (yo, draw yarn through 2 loops on hook) twice.

Back Post Double Crochet (BPdc): Yo, insert hook from back to front to back again around the post of designated st, yo, draw yarn through, (yo, draw yarn through 2 loops on hook) twice.

Chain multiples of 26 plus 3.

Row 1 (WS): Dc in 4th ch from hook, *skip next 3 ch, dc in each of next 2 ch, ch 3, dc in each of next 2 ch, ch 1, skip next 4 ch, 7 dc in next ch, ch 1, skip next 5 ch, dc in each of next 2 ch, ch 3, dc in each of next 2 ch, skip next 3 ch**, dc in each of next 3 ch; rep from * across, ending last rep at **, dc in each of last 2 ch, turn.

Row 2: Ch 3 (counts as dc), skip first dc, dc in next dc, *ch 3, FPdc around the post of each of next 2 dc, skip next ch-3 loop, dc in each of next 2 dc, ch 1, skip next 3 dc, (dc, ch 1, dc, ch 1, dc, ch 1, dc) in next dc, ch 1, skip next ch-1 space, dc in each of next 2 dc, skip next ch-3 loop, FPdc around the post of each of next 2 dc, ch 3**, dc in each of next 3 dc; rep from * across, ending last rep at **, dc in next dc, dc in 3rd ch of turning ch, turn.

Row 3: Ch 3 (counts as dc), skip first dc, dc in next dc, *skip next ch-3 loop, BPdc around the post of each of next 2 dc, ch 3, dc in each of next 2 dc, ch 1, skip next 2 ch-1 spaces, 7 dc in next ch-1 space, ch 1, skip next 2 ch-1 spaces, dc in each of next 2 dc, ch 3, BPdc around the post of each of next 2 dc, skip next ch-3 loop**, dc in each of next 3 dc; rep from * across, ending last rep at **, dc in next dc, dc in 3rd ch of turning ch, turn.

Rep Rows 2-3 for pattern.

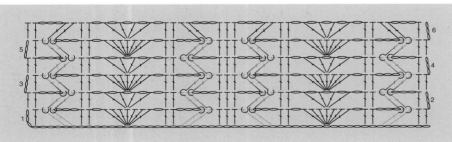

450

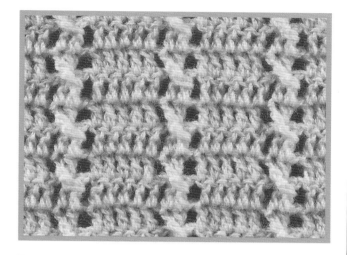

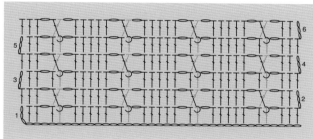

Front Post Double Crochet (FPdc): Yo, insert hook from front to back to front again around the post of designated st, yo, draw yarn through, (yo, draw yarn through 2 loops on hook) twice.

Chain multiples of 9 plus 3.

Row 1 (WS): Dc in 4th ch from hook, dc in next ch, *ch 1, skip next ch, dc in each of next 2 ch, ch 1, skip next ch, dc in each of next 5 ch; rep from * across, ending with dc in each of last 3 ch, turn.

Row 2: Ch 3 (counts as dc), skip first dc, dc in each of next 2 dc, *ch 1, skip next dc, dc in next dc, working in front of last dc made, FPdc around the post of last skipped dc (crossed dc made), ch 1, skip next ch-1 space**, dc in each of next 5 dc; rep from * across, ending last rep at **, dc in each of next 2 dc, dc in 3rd ch of turning ch, turn.

Row 3: Ch 3 (counts as dc), skip first dc, dc in each of next 2 dc, *ch 1, skip next ch-1 space, dc in each of next 2 dc, ch 1, skip next ch-1 space**, dc in each of next 5 dc; rep from * across, ending last rep at **, dc in each of next 2 dc, dc in 3rd ch of turning ch, turn.

Rep Rows 2-3 for pattern.

451

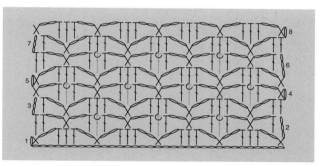

Back Post Double Crochet (BPdc): Yo, insert hook from back to front to back again around the post of designated st, yo, draw yarn through, (yo, draw yarn through 2 loops on hook) twice.

Chain multiples of 8 plus 2.

Row 1 (WS): Sc in 2nd ch from hook, *ch 2, skip next 2 ch, dc in each of next 3 ch, ch 2, skip next 2 ch, sc in next ch; rep from * across, turn.

Row 2: Ch 3 (counts as dc), *dc in next ch-2 space, ch 2, skip next dc, sc in next dc, ch 2, dc in next ch-2 space, dc in next sc; rep from * across, turn.

Row 3: Ch 3 (counts as dc), skip first dc, *dc in next dc, ch 2, skip next ch-2 space, sc in next sc, ch 2, skip next ch-2 space, dc in next dc**, BPdc around the post of next dc; rep from * across, ending last rep at **, dc in 3rd ch of turning ch, turn.

Row 4: Ch 1, sc in first dc, *ch 2, dc in next ch-2 space, dc in next sc, dc in next ch-2 space, ch 2, skip next dc, sc in next dc; rep from * across, ending with last sc in 3rd ch of turning ch, turn.

Row 5: Ch 1, sc in first sc, *ch 2, skip next ch-2 space, dc in next dc, BPdc around the post of next dc, dc in next dc, ch 2, skip next ch-2 space, sc in next sc; rep from * across, turn.

Rep Rows 2-5 for pattern.

452

Front Post Double Crochet (FPdc): Yo, insert hook from back to front to back again around the post of designated st, yo, draw yarn through, (yo, draw yarn through 2 loops on hook) twice.

Chain multiples of 7 plus 2.

Row 1: Dc in 4th ch from hook, *(ch 1, skip next ch, dc in next ch) twice**, dc in each of next 3 ch; rep from * across, ending last rep at **, dc in last ch, turn.

Row 2: Ch 1, sc in first dc, *skip next ch-1 space, (dc, ch 1, 2 dc, ch 1, dc) in next dc, skip next ch-1 space, skip next dc**, sc in each of next 2 dc; rep from * across, ending last rep at **, sc in 3rd ch of turning ch, turn.

Row 3: Ch 3 (counts as dc), skip first sc, *dc in next dc, ch 1, FPdc around the post of next dc, ch 1, skip next ch-1 space**, dc in each of next 4 sts; rep from * across, ending last rep at **, dc in next dc, dc in last sc, turn.

Rep Rows 2-3 for pattern.

453

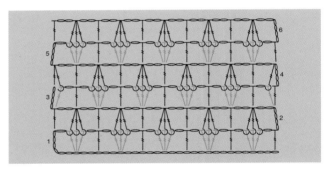

Front Post Treble Crochet (FPtr): Yo twice, insert hook from front to back to front again around the post of next st, yo, draw yarn through, (yo, draw yarn through 2 loops on hook) twice.

FPtr-tr Cluster: Yo twice, insert hook from front to back to front again around the post of next st, yo, draw yarn through, (yo, draw yarn through 2 loops on hook) twice, yo twice, insert hook in next st, yo, draw yarn through st, (yo, draw yarn through 2 loops on hook) twice, yo, draw yarn through 3 loops on hook.

3-FPtr Cluster: (Yo twice, insert hook from front to back to front again around the post of next st, yo, draw yarn through, [yo, draw yarn through 2 loops on hook] twice) 3 times, yo, draw yarn through 4 loops on hook.

Chain multiples of 6 plus 5.

Row 1: 3 tr in 8th ch from hook, *ch 1, skip next 2 ch, tr in next ch**, ch 1, skip next 2 ch, 3 tr in next ch; rep from * across, ending last rep at **, turn.

Row 2: Ch 6 (counts as tr, ch 2), skip next ch-1 space, *work 3-FPtr cluster across next 3 tr, ch 2, skip next ch-1 space, tr in next tr; rep from * across, ending with last tr in top of turning ch, turn.

Row 3: Ch 4 (counts as tr), tr in first tr, *ch 1, skip next ch-2 space, tr in next cluster, ch 1, skip next ch-2 space**, 3 tr in next cluster; rep from * across, ending last rep at **, 2 tr in 4th ch of turning ch, turn.

Row 4: Ch 4 (counts as tr), skip first tr, FPtr around the post of next tr, *ch 2, skip next ch-1 space, tr in next tr, ch 2, skip next ch-1 space**, work 3-FPtr cluster across next 3 tr; rep from * across, ending last rep at **, work FPtr-tr cluster across last tr and 3rd ch of turning ch, turn.

Row 5: Ch 5 (counts as tr, ch 1), *skip next ch-2 space, 3 tr in next tr, ch 1, skip next ch-2 space**, tr in next cluster, ch 1; rep from * across, ending last rep at **, skip next tr, tr in 4th ch of turning ch, turn.

Rep Rows 2-5 for pattern.

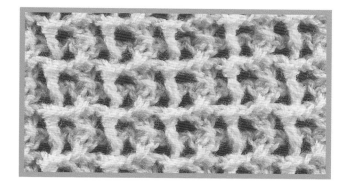

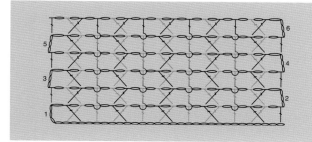

Front Post Double Crochet (FPdc): Yo, insert hook from front to back to front again around the post of designated st, yo, draw yarn through, (yo, draw yarn through 2 loops on hook) twice.

Chain multiples of 6 plus 4.

Row 1 (WS): Dc in 8th ch from hook, ch 1, working over last dc made, skip next ch to the right, dc in next ch to the right (crossed dc made), *ch 1, skip next ch, dc in next ch**, ch 1, skip next 3 ch, dc in next ch, ch 1, working over last dc made, skip next ch to the right, dc in next ch to the right (crossed dc made); rep from * across, ending last rep at **, turn.

Row 2: Ch 4 (counts as dc, ch 1), *skip next 2 ch-1 spaces, dc in next dc, ch 1, working over last dc made, dc in last skipped dc (crossed dc made), ch 1, skip next ch-1 space**, FPdc around the post of next dc, ch 1; rep from * across, ending last rep at **, dc in 3rd ch of turning ch, turn.

Rep Row 2 for pattern.

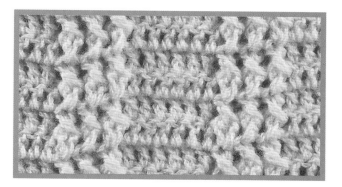

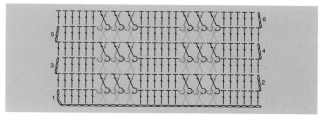

Front Post Double Crochet (FPdc): Yo, insert hook from front to back to front again around the post of designated st, yo, draw yarn through, (yo, draw yarn through 2 loops on hook) twice.

Chain multiples of 12 plus 8.

Row 1: Dc in 4th ch from hook, dc in each of next 4 ch, *(skip next ch, dc in next ch, working over last dc made, dc in last skipped ch [crossed dc made]) 3 times, dc in each of next 6 ch; rep from * across, turn.

Row 2: Ch 3 (counts as dc), skip first dc, dc in each of next 5 dc, *(skip next dc, FPdc around the post of next dc, working in front of last dc made, FPdc around the post of last skipped dc [crossed FPdc made]) 3 times, dc in each of next 6 dc; rep from * across, ending with last dc in 3rd ch of turning ch, turn.

Row 3: Ch 3 (counts as dc), skip first dc, dc in each of next 5 dc, *(skip next dc, dc in next dc, working over last dc made, dc in last skipped dc [crossed dc made]) 3 times, dc in each of next 6 dc; rep from * across, ending with last dc in 3rd ch of turning ch, turn.

Rep Rows 2-3 for pattern.

456

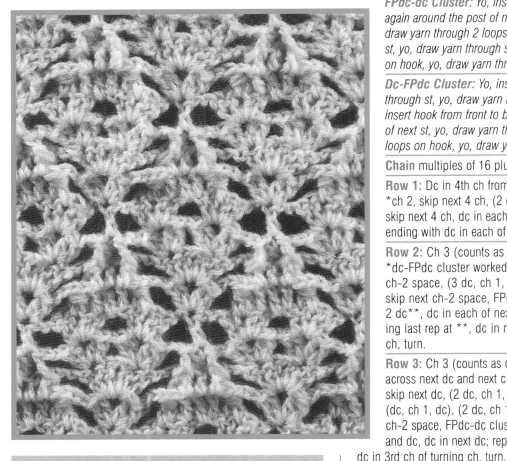

Front Post Double Crochet (FPdc): *Yo, insert hook from front to back to front again around the post of designated st, yo, draw yarn through, (yo, draw yarn through 2 loops on hook) twice.*

FPdc-dc Cluster: Yo, insert hook from front to back to front again around the post of next st, yo, draw yarn through, yo, draw yarn through 2 loops on hook, yo, insert hook in next st, yo, draw yarn through st, yo, draw yarn through 2 loops on hook, yo, draw yarn through 3 loops on hook.

Dc-FPdc Cluster: Yo, insert hook in next st, yo, draw yarn through st, yo, draw yarn through 2 loops on hook, yo, insert hook from front to back to front again around the post of next st, yo, draw yarn through, yo, draw yarn through 2 loops on hook, yo, draw yarn through 3 loops on hook.

Chain multiples of 16 plus 3.

Row 1: Dc in 4th ch from hook, dc in each of next 2 ch, *ch 2, skip next 4 ch, (2 dc, ch 1, 2 dc) in next ch, ch 2, skip next 4 ch, dc in each of next 7 ch; rep from * across, ending with dc in each of last 4 ch, turn.

Row 2: Ch 3 (counts as dc), skip first dc, dc in next dc, *dc-FPdc cluster worked across next 2 dc, ch 2, skip next ch-2 space, (3 dc, ch 1, 3 dc) in next ch-1 space, ch 2, skip next ch-2 space, FPdc-dc cluster worked across next 2 dc**, dc in each of next 3 dc; rep from * across, ending last rep at **, dc in next dc, dc in 3rd ch of turning ch, turn.

Row 3: Ch 3 (counts as dc), *dc-FPdc cluster worked across next dc and next cluster, ch 2, skip next ch-2 space, skip next dc, (2 dc, ch 1, 2 dc) in next dc, ch 1, skip next (dc, ch 1, dc), (2 dc, ch 1, 2 dc) in next dc, ch 2, skip next ch-2 space, FPdc-dc cluster worked across next cluster and dc, dc in next dc; rep from * across, ending with last dc in 3rd ch of turning ch, turn.

Row 4: Ch 5 (counts as dc, ch 2), *skip next ch-2 space, (2 dc, ch 1, 2 dc) in next ch-1 space, ch 1, skip next ch-1 space, (2 dc, ch 1, 2 dc) in next ch-1 space, ch 2, skip next ch-2 space, skip next cluster**, FPdc around the post of next dc, ch 2; rep from * across, ending last rep at **, dc in 3rd ch of turning ch, turn.

Row 5: Ch 3 (counts as dc), 2 dc in first dc, *ch 2, skip next ch-2 space, dc in next ch-1 space, (dc in each of next 2 dc, dc in next ch-1 space) twice, ch 2, skip next ch-2 space**, (2 dc, ch 1, 2 dc) in next dc; rep from * across, ending last rep at **, 3 dc in 3rd ch of turning ch, turn.

Row 6: Ch 3 (counts as dc), 3 dc in first dc, *ch 2, skip next ch-2 space, FPdc-dc cluster worked across next 2 dc, dc in each of next 3 dc, dc-FPdc worked across next 2 dc, ch 2, skip next ch-2 space**, (3 dc, ch 1, 3 dc) in next ch-1 space; rep from * across, ending last rep at **, skip next 2 dc, 4 dc in 3rd ch of turning ch, turn.

Row 7: Ch 3 (counts as dc), skip first 2 dc, *(2 dc, ch 1, 2 dc) in next dc, ch 2, skip next ch-2 space, FPdc-dc cluster worked across next cluster and next dc, dc in next dc, dc-FPdc cluster worked across next dc and next cluster, ch 2, skip next ch-2 space and next dc, (2 dc, ch 1, 2 dc) in next dc**, ch 1, skip next (dc, ch 1, dc); rep from * across, ending last rep at **, skip next dc, dc in 3rd ch of turning ch, turn.

Row 8: Ch 3 (counts as dc), *(2 dc, ch 1, 2 dc) in next ch-1 space, ch 2, skip next ch-2 space, skip next cluster, FPdc around the post of next dc, ch 2, skip next ch-2 space, (2 dc, ch 1, 2 dc) in next ch-1 space**, ch 1, skip next ch-1 space; rep from * across, ending last rep at **, skip next 2 dc, dc in 3rd ch of turning ch, turn.

Row 9: Ch 3 (counts as dc), skip first dc, *dc in each of next 2 dc, dc in next ch-1 space, ch 2, skip next ch-2 space, (2 dc, ch 2, 2 dc) in next dc, ch 2, skip next ch-2 space, dc in next ch-1 space, dc in each of next 2 dc, dc in next ch-1 space; rep from * across, ending with last dc in 3rd ch of turning ch, turn.

Rep Rows 2-9 for pattern.

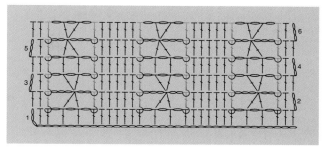

Front Post Double Crochet (FPdc): *Yo, insert hook from front to back to front again around the post of designated st, yo, draw yarn through, (yo, draw yarn through 2 loops on hook) twice.*

2-Dc Cluster: *(Yo, insert hook in next st, yo, draw yarn through st, yo, draw yarn through 2 loops on hook) twice, yo, draw yarn through 3 loops on hook.*

Chain multiples of 12 plus 1.

Row 1 (WS): Dc in 4th ch from hook, dc in next ch, *(ch 1, skip next ch, dc in next ch) 3 times**, dc in each of next 6 ch; rep from * across, ending last rep at **, dc in each of last 2 ch, turn.

Row 2: Ch 3 (counts as dc), skip first dc, dc in next dc, *FPdc around the post of next dc, ch 2, skip next ch-1 space, 2-dc cluster worked across next 2 dc, ch 3, skip next ch-1 space, FPdc around the post of next dc**, dc in each of next 5 dc; rep from * across, ending last rep at **, dc in next dc, dc in 3rd ch of turning ch, turn.

Row 3: Ch 3 (counts as dc), skip first dc, dc in next dc, *FPdc around the post of next dc, ch 1, skip next ch-3 loop, (dc, ch 1, dc) in next cluster, ch 1, skip next ch-2 space, FPdc around the post of next dc**, dc in each of next 5 dc; rep from * across, ending last rep at **, dc in next dc, dc in 3rd ch of turning ch, turn.

Rep Rows 2-3 for pattern.

457

458

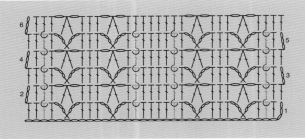

Front Post Double Crochet (FPdc): Yo, insert hook from front to back to front again around the post of designated st, yo, draw yarn through, (yo, draw yarn through 2 loops on hook) twice.

Back Post Double Crochet (BPdc): Yo, insert hook from back to front to back again around the post of designated st, yo, draw yarn through, (yo, draw yarn through 2 loops on hook) twice.

2-Dc Cluster: (Yo, insert hook in next space, yo, draw yarn through st, yo, draw yarn through 2 loops on hook) twice, yo, draw yarn through 3 loops on hook.

Chain multiples of 17 plus 2.

Row 1: Dc in 4th ch from hook, dc in each of next 2 ch, *ch 3, skip next ch, sc in next ch, ch 3, skip next ch, dc in each of next 3 ch, ch 3, skip next ch, sc in next ch, ch 3, skip next ch, dc in each of next 8 ch; rep from * across, ending with dc in each of last 4 ch, turn.

Row 2: Ch 3 (counts as dc), skip first dc, dc in next dc, *BPdc around the post of next dc, dc in next dc, ch 1, 2-dc cluster worked across next 2 ch-3 loops, ch 1, dc in each of next 3 dc, ch 1, 2-dc cluster worked across next 2 ch-3 loops, ch 1, dc in next dc, BPdc around the post of next dc**, dc in each of next 4 dc; rep from * across, ending last rep at **, dc in next dc, dc in 3rd ch of turning ch, turn.

Row 3: Ch 3 (counts as dc), skip first dc, dc in next dc, *FPdc around the post of next dc, dc in next dc, ch 3, skip next ch-1 space, sc in next cluster, ch 3, skip next ch-1 space, dc in each of next 3 dc, ch 3, skip next ch-1 space, sc in next cluster, ch 3, skip next ch-1 space, dc in next dc, FPdc around the post of next dc**, dc in each of next 4 dc; rep from * across, ending last rep at **, dc in next dc, dc in 3rd ch of turning ch, turn.

Rep Rows 2-3 for pattern.

459

Back Post Double Crochet (BPdc): Yo, insert hook from back to front to back again around the post of designated st, yo, draw yarn through, (yo, draw yarn through 2 loops on hook) twice.

Chain multiples of 10 plus 3.

Row 1: Dc in 4th ch from hook, dc in next ch, *ch 3, skip next ch, sc in next ch, (hdc, 3 dc, hdc) in next ch, sc in next ch, ch 3, skip next ch, dc in each of next 5 ch; rep from * across, ending with dc in each of last 3 ch, turn.

Row 2: Ch 3 (counts as dc), skip first dc, BPdc around the post of each of next 2 dc, *ch 3, skip next ch-3 loop, skip next 3 sts, sc in next dc, ch 3, skip next ch-3 loop**, BPdc around the post of each of next 5 dc; rep from * across, ending last rep at **, BPdc around the post of each of next 2 dc, dc in 3rd ch of turning ch, turn.

Row 3: Ch 3 (counts as dc), skip first dc, dc in each of next 2 dc, *ch 3, sc in next ch-3 loop, (hdc, 3 dc, hdc) in next sc, sc in next ch-3 loop, ch 3**, dc in each of next 5 dc; rep from * across, ending last rep at **, dc in each of next 2 dc, dc in 3rd ch of turning ch, turn.

Rep Rows 2-3 for pattern.

460

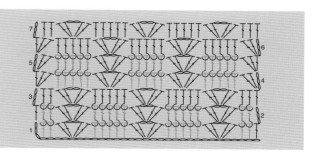

Front Post Double Crochet (FPdc): Yo, insert hook from front to back to front again around the post of designated st, yo, draw yarn through, (yo, draw yarn through 2 loops on hook) twice.

Back Post Double Crochet (BPdc): Yo, insert hook from back to front to back again around the post of designated st, yo, draw yarn through, (yo, draw yarn through 2 loops on hook) twice.

Chain multiples of 10 plus 3.

Row 1: Dc in 4th ch from hook, dc in next ch, *skip next 2 ch, (2 dc, ch 2, 2 dc) in next ch, skip next 2 ch, dc in each of next 5 ch; rep from * across, ending with dc in each of last 3 ch, turn.

Row 2: Ch 3 (counts as dc), skip first dc, FPdc around the post of each of next 2 dc, *(2 dc, ch 2, 2 dc) in next ch-2 space, skip next 2 dc**, FPdc around the post of each of next 5 dc; rep from * across, ending last rep at **, FPdc around the post of each of next 2 dc, dc in 3rd ch of turning ch, turn.

Row 3: Ch 3 (counts as dc), skip first dc, BPdc around the post of each of next 2 dc, (2 dc, ch 2, 2 dc) in next ch-2 space, skip next 2 dc**, BPdc around the post of each of next 5 dc; rep from * across, ending last rep at **, BPdc around the post of each of next 2 dc, dc in 3rd ch of turning ch, turn.

Row 4: Ch 3 (counts as dc), 2 dc in first dc, *skip next 2 dc, dc in each of next 2 dc, dc in next ch-2 space, dc in each of next 2 dc, skip next 2 dc**, (2 dc, ch 2, 2 dc) in next dc; rep from * across, ending last rep at **, 3 dc in 3rd ch of turning ch, turn.

Row 5: Ch 3 (counts as dc), 2 dc in first dc, *skip next 2 dc, BPdc around the post of each of next 5 dc**, (2 dc, ch 2, 2 dc) in next ch-2 space; rep from * across, ending last rep at **, skip next ch-2 space, 3 dc in 3rd ch of turning ch, turn.

Row 6: Ch 3 (counts as dc), 2 dc in first dc, *skip next 2 dc, FPdc around the post of each of next 5 dc **, (2 dc, ch 2, 2 dc) in next ch-2 space; rep from * across, ending last rep at **, skip next ch-2 space, 3 dc in 3rd ch of turning ch, turn.

Row 7: Ch 3 (counts as dc), skip first dc, dc in each of next 2 dc, *skip next 2 dc, (2 dc, ch 2, 2 dc) in next dc, skip next 2 dc, dc in each of next 2 dc**, dc in next ch-2 space, dc in each of next 2 dc; rep from * across, ending last rep at **, dc in 3rd ch of turning ch, turn.

Rep Rows 2-7 for pattern.

461

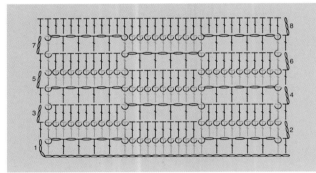

Front Post Double Crochet (FPdc): Yo, insert hook from front to back to front again around the post of designated st, yo, draw yarn through, (yo, draw yarn through 2 loops on hook) twice.

Back Post Double Crochet (BPdc): Yo, insert hook from back to front to back again around the post of designated st, yo, draw yarn through, (yo, draw yarn through 2 loops on hook) twice.

Chain multiples of 20 plus 15.

Row 1 (WS): Dc in 4th ch from hook, *(ch 1, skip next ch, dc in next ch) 5 times**, dc in each of next 10 ch; rep from * across, ending last rep at **, dc in last ch, turn.

Row 2: Ch 3 (counts as dc), skip first dc, *FPdc around the post of next dc, (dc in next ch-1 space, dc in next dc) 4 times, dc in next ch-1 space, FPdc around the post of next dc**, BPdc around the post of each of next 9 dc; rep from * across, ending last rep at **, dc in 3rd ch of turning ch, turn.

Row 3: Ch 3 (counts as dc), skip first dc, *BPdc around the post of each of next 11 dc**, (ch 1, skip next dc, dc in next dc) 4 times, ch 1, skip next dc; rep from * across, ending last rep at **, dc in 3rd ch of turning ch, turn.

Row 4: Ch 3 (counts as dc), skip first dc, *FPdc around the post of next dc, (ch 1, skip next dc, dc in next dc) 4 times, ch 1, skip next dc, FPdc around the post of next dc**, (dc in next ch-1 space, dc in next dc) 4 times, dc in next ch-1 space; rep from * across, ending last rep at **, dc in 3rd ch of turning ch, turn.

Row 5: Ch 3 (counts as dc), skip first dc, *BPdc around the post of next dc, (dc in next ch-1 space, dc in next dc) 4 times, dc in next ch-1 space, BPdc around the post of next dc**, BPdc around the post of each of next 9 dc; rep from * across, ending last rep at **, dc in 3rd ch of turning ch, turn.

Row 6: Ch 3 (counts as dc), skip first dc, *FPdc around the post of next dc, BPdc around the post of each of next 9 dc, FPdc around the post of next dc**, (ch 1, skip next dc, dc in next dc) 4 times, ch 1, skip next dc; rep from * across, ending last rep at **, dc in 3rd ch of turning ch, turn.

Row 7: Ch 3 (counts as dc), skip first dc, *BPdc around the post of next dc, (ch 1, skip next dc, dc in next dc) 4 times, ch 1, skip next dc, BPdc around the post of next dc**, (dc in next ch-1 space, dc in next dc) 4 times, dc in next ch-1 space; rep from * across, ending last rep at **, dc in 3rd ch of turning ch, turn.

Rep Rows 2-7 for pattern.

462

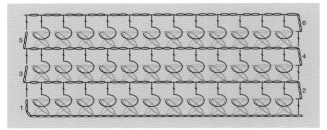

Bobble: (Yo, insert hook in next st, yo, draw yarn through st and up to level of work) twice in same st, yo, draw yarn through 5 loops on hook.

Front Post Double Crochet (FPdc): Yo, insert hook from front to back to front again around the post of designated st, yo, draw yarn through, (yo, draw yarn through 2 loops on hook) twice.

Chain multiples of 3 plus 1.

Row 1: Bobble in 6th ch from hook, ch 1, working over last bobble made, skip 1 ch to the right, bobble in next ch to the right (crossed bobble made), *skip next 2 ch, bobble in next ch, ch 1, working over last bobble made, bobble in first skipped ch (crossed bobble made); rep from * across to within last ch, dc in last ch, turn.

Row 2: Ch 4 (counts as dc, ch 1), skip first dc, FPdc around the posts of next 2 bobbles, *ch 2, FPdc around the posts of next 2 bobbles; rep from * across to turning ch, ch 1, dc in 3rd ch of turning ch, turn.

Row 3: Ch 3 (counts as dc), skip first dc, skip next ch-1 space, *bobble in next ch-2 space, ch 1, working over last bobble made, bobble in last space to the right (crossed bobble made); rep from * across to turning ch, dc in 3rd ch of turning ch, turn.

Rep Rows 2-3 for pattern.

463

Front Post Double Crochet (FPdc): Yo, insert hook from front to back to front again around the post of designated st, yo, draw yarn through, (yo, draw yarn through 2 loops on hook) twice.

Back Post Double Crochet (BPdc): Yo, insert hook from back to front to back again around the post of designated st, yo, draw yarn through, (yo, draw yarn through 2 loops on hook) twice.

Chain multiples of 16 plus 9.

Row 1: Sc in 2nd ch from hook, ch 3, skip next 2 ch, sc in next ch, *ch 3, skip next 3 ch, dc in each of next 2 ch, ch 3, skip next 3 ch, sc in next ch, ch 7, skip next 6 ch, sc in next ch; rep from * across to within last 4 ch, ch 3, skip next 3 ch, dc in last ch, turn.

Row 2: Ch 6 (counts as dc, ch 3), skip next ch-3 loop, *10 dc in next ch-7 loop, ch 3, skip next ch-3 loop, FPdc around the post of each of next 2 dc, ch 3, skip next ch-3 loop; rep from * across to within last ch-3 loop, 4 dc in next ch-3 loop, dc in sc, turn.

Row 3: Ch 6 (counts as dc, ch 3), skip first dc, *(BPdc around the post of next dc, ch 3) twice, skip next ch-3 loop, 2 BPdc around the post of each of next 2 dc, ch 3, skip next ch-3 loop, (BPdc around the post of next dc, ch 3, skip next dc) 5 times, skip next ch-3 loop; rep from * across to turning ch, 2 dc in 3rd ch of turning ch, turn.

Row 4: Ch 3 (counts as dc), 2 FPdc around the post of next dc, *ch 3, skip next ch-3 loop, (sc, ch 3) in each of next 4 ch-3 loops, skip next ch-3 loop, 2 FPdc around the post of next dc, FPdc around the post of each of next 2 dc, 2 FPdc around the post of next dc; rep from * across to within last 3 ch-3 loops, ch 3, skip next ch-3 loop, sc in next ch-3 loop, ch 3, sc in next ch-3 loop, ch 1, dc in 3rd ch of turning ch, turn.

Row 5: Ch 1, sc in first dc, ch 3, skip next ch-1 space, sc in next ch-3 loop, ch 3, skip next ch-3 loop, *2 BPdc around the post of next dc, BPdc around the post of each of next 4 dc, 2 BPdc around the post of next dc, ch 3, skip next ch-3 loop, (sc, ch 3) in each of next 3 ch-3 loops, skip next ch-3 loop; rep from * across to within last 3 sts, 2 BPdc around the post of next dc, BPdc around the post of next dc, dc in 3rd ch of turning ch, turn.

Row 6: Ch 3 (counts as dc), FPdc around the post of each of next 2 dc, 2 FPdc around the post of next dc, *ch 3, skip next ch-3 loop, (sc, ch 3) in each of next 2 ch-3 loops, skip next ch-3 loop, 2 FPdc around the post of next dc, FPdc around the post of each of next 6 dc, 2 FPdc around the post of next dc; rep from * across to within last 2 ch-3 loops, ch 3, skip next ch-3 loop, sc in next ch-3 loop, ch 1, dc in last sc, turn.

Row 7: Ch 1, sc in first dc, ch 3, skip next ch-3 loop, *2 BPdc around the post of next dc, BPdc around the post of each of next 8 dc, 2 BPdc around the post of next dc, ch 3, skip next ch-3 loop, sc in next ch-3 loop, ch 3, skip next ch-3 loop; rep from * across to within last 5 sts, 2 BPdc around the post of next dc, BPdc around the post of each of next 3 dc, dc in 3rd ch of turning ch, turn.

Row 8: Ch 3 (counts as dc), FPdc around the post of each of next 4 dc, 2 FPdc around the post of next dc, *ch 2, skip next 2 ch-3 loops, 2 FPdc around the post of next dc, FPdc around the post of each of next 10 dc, 2 FPdc around the post of next dc; rep from * across to within last ch-3 loop, skip next ch-3 loop, tr in last sc, turn.

Row 9: Ch 3 (counts as dc), *BPdc around the post of each of next 14 dc, ch 2, skip next ch-2 space; rep from * across to within last 7 sts, BPdc around the post of each of next 6 dc, dc in 3rd ch of turning ch, turn.

Row 10: Ch 1, sc in first dc, ch 3, skip next 2 dc, sc in next dc, *ch 3, 2 dc in next ch-2 space, ch 3, skip next 3 dc, sc in next dc, ch 7, skip next 6 dc, sc in next dc; rep from * across to within last 4 sts, ch 3, skip next 3 dc, dc in 3rd ch of turning ch, turn.

Rep Rows 2-10 for pattern.

464

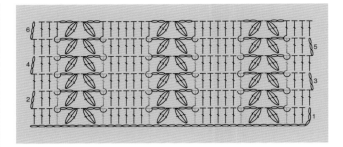

3-Dc Puff st: (Yo, insert hook in next st, yo, draw yarn through st, yo, draw yarn through 2 loops on hook) 3 times in same st, yo, draw yarn through 4 loops on hook.

Front Post Double Crochet (FPdc): Yo, insert hook from front to back to front again around the post of designated st, yo, draw yarn through, (yo, draw yarn through 2 loops on hook) twice.

Back Post Double Crochet (BPdc): Yo, insert hook from back to front to back again around the post of designated st, yo, draw yarn through, (yo, draw yarn through 2 loops on hook) twice.

Chain multiples of 12 plus 3.

Row 1: Dc in 4th ch from hook, dc in each of next 2 ch, *ch 2, 3-dc puff st in next ch, skip next 3 ch, 3-dc puff st in next ch, ch 2, dc in each of next 7 ch; rep from * across, ending with dc in each of last 4 ch, turn.

Row 2: Ch 3 (counts as dc), skip first dc, dc in each of next 2 dc, *BPdc around the post of next dc, ch 2, 3-dc puff st in each of next 2 ch-2 spaces, ch 2, BPdc around the post of next dc**, dc in each of next 5 dc; rep from * across, ending last rep at **, dc in each of next 2 dc, dc in 3rd ch of turning ch, turn.

Row 3: Ch 3 (counts as dc), skip first dc, dc in each of next 2 dc, *FPdc around the post of next dc, ch 2, 3-dc puff st in each of next 2 ch-2 spaces, ch 2, FPdc around the post of next dc**, dc in each of next 5 dc; rep from * across, ending last rep at **, dc in each of next 2 dc, dc in 3rd ch of turning ch, turn.

Rep Rows 2-3 for pattern.

.30.
Horizontal Stripe Patterns

465

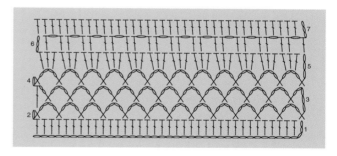

Chain multiples of 3.

Row 1: Dc in 4th ch from hook, dc in each ch across, turn.

Row 2: Ch 1, sc in first dc, *ch 4, skip next 2 dc, sc in next dc; rep from * across, ending with last sc in 3rd ch of turning ch, turn.

Row 3: Ch 5 (counts as dc, ch 2), sc in next ch-4 loop, (ch 4, sc) in each ch-4 loop across to last ch-4 loop, ch 2, dc in last sc, turn.

Row 4: Ch 1, sc in first dc, (ch 4, sc) in each ch-4 loop across, ending with last sc in 3rd ch of turning ch, turn.

Row 5: Ch 3 (counts as dc), 3 dc in each ch-4 loop across, turn.

Row 6: Ch 3 (counts as dc), skip first dc, dc in next dc, *ch 1, skip next dc, dc in each of next 2 dc; rep from * across to within last 2 sts, ch 1, skip next dc, dc in 3rd ch of turning ch, turn.

Row 7: Ch 3 (counts as dc), skip first dc, dc in each dc and each ch-1 space across, ending with dc in 3rd ch of turning ch, turn.

Rep Rows 2-7 for pattern.

466

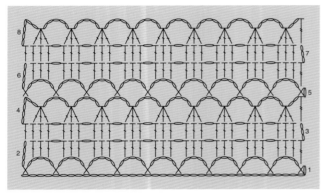

3-Dc Cluster: (Yo, insert hook in next st, yo, draw yarn through st, yo, draw yarn through 2 loops on hook) 3 times, yo, draw yarn through 4 loops on hook.

Chain multiples of 4 plus 2.

Row 1: Sc in 2nd ch from hook, *ch 5, skip next 3 ch, sc in next ch; rep from * across, turn.

Row 2: Ch 4 (counts as tr), 3 dc in next ch-5 loop, (ch 1, 3 dc) in each ch-5 loop across to last ch-5 loop, tr in last sc, turn.

Row 3: Ch 3 (counts as dc), skip first dc, dc in each of next 3 dc, *ch 1, skip next ch-1 space, dc in each of next 3 dc; rep from * across to turning ch, dc in 4th ch of turning ch, turn.

Row 4: Ch 6 (counts as tr, ch 2), skip first dc, *3-dc cluster worked across next 3 dc**, ch 5, skip next ch-1 space; rep from * across, ending last rep at **, ch 2, tr in 3rd ch of turning ch, turn.

Row 5: Ch 1, sc in first tr, (ch 5, sc) in each ch-5 loop across, ending with last sc in 4th ch of turning ch, turn.

Rep Rows 2-5 for pattern.

467

Chain multiples of 4 plus 3.

Row 1: Dc in 4th ch from hook, dc in each ch across, turn.

Row 2: Ch 1, sc in first dc, *ch 5, skip next 3 dc, sc in next dc; rep from * across, ending with last sc in 3rd ch of turning ch, turn.

Row 3: Ch 3 (counts as dc), (dc, ch 1, dc) in next ch-5 loop, *ch 1, (dc , ch 1, dc) in next ch-5 loop; rep from * across to last ch-5 loop, tr in last sc, turn.

Row 4: Ch 5 (counts as dc, ch 2), sc in next ch-1 space, *ch 5, skip next ch-1 space, sc in next ch-1 space; rep from * across to last ch-1 space, ch 2, dc in 3rd ch of turning ch, turn.

Row 5: Ch 1, sc in first dc, skip next ch-2 space, *3 dc in next sc, sc in next ch-5 loop; rep from * across, ending with last sc in 3rd ch of turning ch, turn.

Row 6: Ch 3 (counts as hdc, ch 1), skip first 2 sts, sc in next dc, *ch 3, skip next 3 sts, sc in next dc; rep from * across to within last 2 sts, ch 1, skip next dc, hdc in last sc, turn.

Row 7: Ch 3 (counts as dc), dc in next ch-1 space, dc in next sc, *3 dc in next ch-3 loop, dc in next sc; rep from * across to turning ch, dc in ch-1 space of turning ch, dc in 3rd ch of turning ch, turn.

Rep Rows 2-7 for pattern.

468

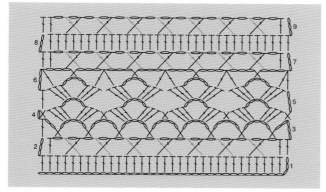

2-Dc Cluster: *(Yo, insert hook in next st, yo, draw yarn through st, yo, draw yarn through 2 loops on hook) twice, yo, draw yarn through 3 loops on hook.*

Chain multiples of 8 plus 3.

Row 1: Dc in 4th ch from hook, dc in each ch across, turn.

Row 2: Ch 3 (counts as dc), skip first dc, dc in next dc, *ch 1, skip next 3 dc, dc in next dc, ch 1, working over last dc made, dc in 2nd skipped dc (crossed dc made); rep from * across to within last 3 sts, ch 1, skip next dc, dc in next dc, dc in 3rd ch of turning ch, turn.

Row 3: Ch 5 (counts as dc, ch 2), sc in next ch-1 space, *ch 5, skip next ch-1 space, sc in next ch-1 space; rep from * across to last ch-1 space, ch 2, skip next dc, dc in 3rd ch of turning ch, turn.

Row 4: Ch 1, sc in first dc, skip next ch-2 space, *(3 dc, ch 5, 3 dc) in next ch-5 loop, sc in next ch-5 loop; rep from * across, ending with last sc in 3rd ch of turning ch, turn.

Row 5: Ch 3 (counts as dc), (3 dc, ch 5, 3 dc) in each ch-5 loop across to last ch-5 loop, skip next 3 dc, dc in last sc, turn.

Row 6: Ch 3 (counts as dc), skip first 2 dc, dc in next dc, *ch 3, sc in next ch-5 loop, ch 3, skip next dc**, 2-dc cluster, working first half-closed dc in next dc, skip next 2 dc, work 2nd half-closed dc in next dc, yo, complete cluster; rep from * across, ending last rep at **, 2-dc cluster, working first half-closed dc in next dc, skip next dc, work 2nd half-closed dc in 3rd ch of turning ch, yo, complete cluster, turn.

Row 7: Ch 3 (counts as dc), dc in next ch-3 loop, *ch 1, dc in next ch-3 loop, ch 1, working over last dc made, dc in last ch-3 loop (crossed dc made); rep from * across to last ch-3 loop, ch 1, dc in same ch-3 loop, skip next dc, dc in 3rd ch of turning ch, turn.

Row 8: Ch 3 (counts as dc), skip first dc, dc in each dc and each ch-1 space across, ending with last dc in 3rd ch of turning ch, turn.

Rep Rows 2-8 for pattern.

469

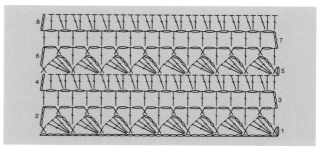

Chain multiples of 4 plus 2.

Row 1: (Sc, ch 3, 3 dc) in 2nd ch from hook, *skip next 3 ch, (sc, ch 3, 3 dc) in next ch; rep from * across to within last 4 ch, skip next 3 ch, sc in last ch, turn.

Row 2: Ch 4 (counts as dc, ch 1), *sc in next ch-3 loop, ch 1, dc in next sc**, ch 1; rep from * across, ending last rep at **, turn.

Row 3: Ch 4 (counts as dc, ch 1), *skip next ch-1 space, dc in next sc, ch 1, skip next ch-1 space**, dc in next dc, ch 1; rep from * across, ending last rep at **, dc in 3rd ch of turning ch, turn.

Row 4: Ch 3 (counts as dc), dc in next ch-1 space, 2 dc in each ch-1 space across to turning ch, dc in 3rd ch of turning ch, turn.

Row 5: Ch 1, (sc, ch 3, 3 dc) in first dc, *skip next 3 dc, (sc, ch 3, 3 dc) in next dc; rep from * across to within last 4 sts, skip next 3 dc, sc in 3rd ch of turning ch, turn.

Rep Rows 2-5 for pattern.

470

Triple Treble Crochet (trtr): Yo (4 times), insert hook in next st, yo, draw yarn through st, (yo, draw yarn through 2 loops on hook) 5 times.

Chain multiples of 7 plus 4.

Row 1: Dc in 4th ch from hook, dc in each ch across, turn.

Row 2: Ch 5 (counts as dc, ch 2), skip first 4 dc, *(3 dc, ch 5, 3 dc) in next dc**, ch 5, skip next 6 dc; rep from * across, ending last rep at **, ch 2, skip next 3 dc, dc in 3rd ch of turning ch, turn.

Row 3: Ch 1, sc in first dc, *(4 dc, ch 5, 4 dc) in next ch-5 loop, sc in next ch-5 loop; rep from * across, ending with last sc in 3rd ch of turning ch, turn.

Row 4: Ch 1, sc in first sc, *ch 3, (4 dc, ch 5, 4 dc) in next ch-5 loop, ch 3, skip next 4 dc, sc in next sc; rep from * across, turn.

Row 5: Ch 7 (counts as trtr, ch 1), skip next ch-3 loop, *5 sc in next ch-5 loop**, ch 2; rep from * across, ending last rep at **, ch 1, skip next ch-3 loop, trtr in last sc, turn.

Row 6: Ch 1, sc in first dc, sc in next ch-1 space, *sc in each of next 5 sc**, 2 sc in next ch-2 space; rep from * across, ending last rep at **, sc in ch-1 space of turning ch, sc in 6th ch of turning ch, turn.

Row 7: Ch 4 (counts as dc, ch 1), skip first 2 sc, dc in next sc, *ch 1, skip next sc, dc in next sc; rep from * across, turn.

Row 8: Ch 1, sc in each dc and ch-1 space across, ending with sc in 3rd ch of turning ch, turn.

Row 9: Ch 3 (counts as dc), skip first dc, dc in each dc across, ending with dc in 3rd ch of turning ch, turn.

Rep Rows 2-9 for pattern.

471

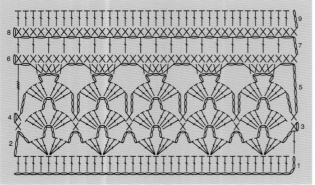

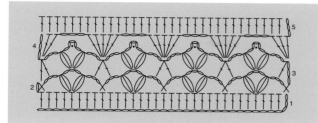

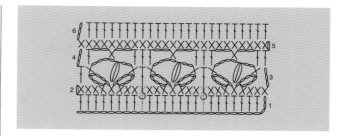

Bobble: *(Yo, insert hook in next st, yo, draw yarn through st and up to level of work) 3 times in same st, yo, draw yarn through 7 loops on hook.*

2-Dc Cluster: *(Yo, insert hook in next st, yo, draw yarn through st, yo, draw yarn through 2 loops on hook) twice, yo, draw yarn through 3 loops on hook.*

Chain multiples of 8 plus 3.

Row 1: Dc in 4th ch from hook, dc in each ch across, turn.

Row 2: Ch 1, sc in first dc, *ch 3, skip next 3 dc, (bobble, ch 3, bobble) in next dc, ch 3, skip next 3 dc, sc in next dc; rep from * across, ending with last sc in 3rd ch of turning ch, turn.

Row 3: Ch 3 (counts as dc), dc in next ch-3 loop, *ch 3, (bobble, ch 4, sl st in 3rd ch from hook for picot, ch 1, bobble) in next ch-3 loop, ch 3**, work 2-dc cluster across next 2 ch-3 loops; rep from * across, ending last rep at **, work 2-dc cluster across next ch-3 loop and last sc, turn.

Row 4: Ch 3 (counts as dc), 2 dc in first cluster, *ch 3, skip next 2 ch-3 loops**, 5 dc in next cluster; rep from * across, ending last rep at **, 3 dc in 3rd ch of turning ch, turn.

Row 5: Ch 3 (counts as dc), skip first dc, dc in each of next 2 dc, *3 dc in next ch-3 loop**, dc in each of next 5 dc; rep from * across, ending last rep at **, dc in each of next 2 dc, dc in 3rd ch of turning ch, turn.

Rep Rows 2-5 for pattern.

472

Front Post Double Crochet (FPdc): *Yo, insert hook from front to back to front again around the post of designated st, yo, draw yarn through, (yo, draw yarn through 2 loops on hook) twice.*

Bobble: *(Yo, insert hook in next st, yo, draw yarn through st and up to level of work) 3 times in same st, yo, draw yarn through 7 loops on hook.*

Chain multiples of 8 plus 3.

Row 1: Dc in 4th ch from hook, dc in each ch across, turn.

Row 2: Ch 1, sc in each of first 4 dc, *ch 7, sl st in 7th ch from hook for picot, sc in next dc, ch 7, sl st in 7th ch from hook for picot**, sc in each of next 7 dc; rep from * across, ending last rep at **, sc in each of next 3 dc, dc in 3rd ch of turning ch, turn.

Row 3: Ch 3 (counts as dc), *sc in next picot, ch 2, bobble in next sc, ch 4, sc in next picot, skip next 3 sc**, FPdc around the post of next corresponding dc 2 rows below; rep from * across, ending last rep at **, dc in last sc, turn.

Row 4: Ch 3 (counts as dc), skip first dc, *dc in next sc, ch 2, sc in next ch-4 loop, ch 2, skip next ch-2 space, dc in next sc, dc in next dc; rep from * across, ending with last dc in 3rd ch of turning ch, turn.

Row 5: Ch 1, sc in first dc, sc in next dc, *2 sc in next ch-2 space, sc in next sc, 2 sc in next ch-2 space**, sc in each of next 3 dc; rep from * across, ending last rep at **, sc in next dc, sc in 3rd ch of turning ch, turn.

Row 6: Ch 3 (counts as dc), skip first sc, dc in each sc across, turn.

Rep Rows 2-6 for pattern.

.31.
Vertical Columns

473

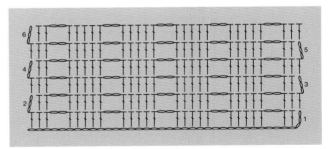

Chain multiples of 7 plus 3.

Row 1: Dc in 4th ch from hook, dc in next ch, *ch 2, skip next 2 ch, dc in each of next 5 ch; rep from * across, ending with dc in each of last 3 ch, turn.

Row 2: Ch 3 (counts as dc), skip first dc, dc in each of next 2 dc, *ch 2, skip next ch-2 space**, dc in each of next 5 dc; rep from * across, ending last rep at **, dc in each of next 2 dc, dc in 3rd ch of turning ch, turn.

Rep Row 2 for pattern.

474

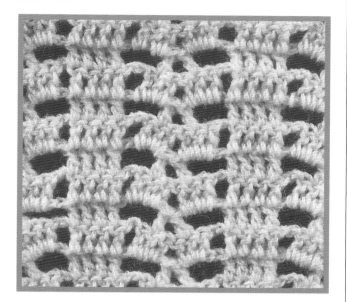

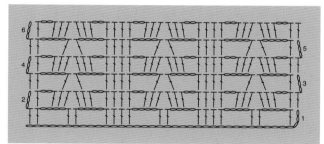

Chain multiples of 12 plus 2.

Row 1: Dc in 4th ch from hook, *ch 4, skip next 3 ch, dc in each of next 2 ch, ch 4, skip next 3 ch, dc in each of next 4 ch; rep from * across, ending with dc in each of last 2 ch, turn.

Row 2: Ch 3 (counts as dc), skip first dc, dc in next dc, *ch 2, 3 dc in each of next 2 ch-4 loops, ch 2**, dc in each of next 4 dc; rep from * across, ending last rep at **, dc in next dc, dc in 3rd ch of turning ch, turn.

Row 3: Ch 3 (counts as dc), skip first dc, dc in next dc, *ch 4, skip next dc, dc in next dc, skip next 2 dc, dc in next dc, ch 4, skip next ch-2 space**, dc in each of next 4 dc; rep from * across, ending last rep at **, dc in next dc, dc in 3rd ch of turning ch, turn.

Rep Rows 2-3 for pattern.

475

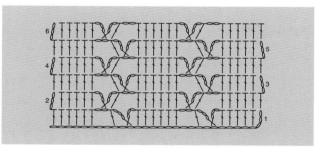

Chain multiples of 11 plus 8.

Row 1: Dc in 4th ch from hook, dc in each of next 4 ch, *ch 3, sc in next ch, ch 3, skip next ch, dc in next ch, ch 2, skip next 2 ch, dc in each of next 6 ch; rep from * across, turn.

Row 2: Ch 3 (counts as dc), skip first dc, dc in each of next 5 dc, *ch 3, sc in next ch-2 space, ch 3, dc in next dc, ch 2, skip next 2 ch-3 loops, dc in each of next 6 dc; rep from * across, ending with last dc in 3rd ch of turning ch, turn.

Rep Row 2 for pattern.

476

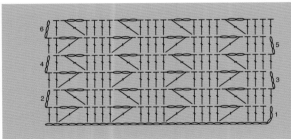

Chain multiples of 7 plus 4.

Row 1: Dc in 4th ch from hook, dc in each of next 2 ch, *skip next 3 ch, (dc, ch 2, dc) in next ch**, dc in each of next 3 ch; rep from * across, ending last rep at **, dc in last ch, turn.

Row 2: Ch 3 (counts as dc), skip first dc, dc in next dc, *skip next ch-2 space, skip next dc, (dc, ch 2, dc) in next dc, dc in each of next 3 dc; rep from * across, ending with last dc in 3rd ch of turning ch, turn.

Rep Row 2 for pattern.

477

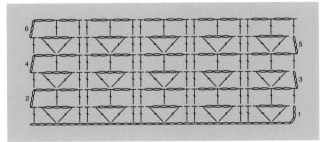

Chain multiples of 7 plus 2.

Row 1: (Dc, ch 3, dc) in 6th ch from hook, skip next 2 ch, *dc in each of next 2 ch, skip next 2 ch, (dc, ch 3, dc) in next ch, skip next 2 ch; rep from * across to within last ch, dc in last ch, turn.

Row 2: Ch 5 (counts as dc, ch 2), *dc in next ch-3 loop, ch 2, skip next dc**, dc in each of next 2 dc, ch 2; rep from * across, ending last rep at **, dc in 3rd ch of turning ch, turn.

Row 3: Ch 3 (counts as dc), *skip next ch-2 space, (dc, ch 3, dc) in next dc, skip next ch-2 space**, dc in each of next 2 dc; rep from * across, ending last rep at **, dc in 3rd ch of turning ch, turn.

Rep Rows 2-3 for pattern.

478

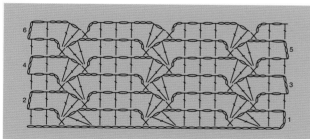

Chain multiples of 11 plus 4.

Row 1: Dc in 6th ch from hook, *ch 3, (dc, ch 1, dc) in next ch, skip next 3 ch, sc in next ch, ch 3, skip next ch**, (dc in next ch, skip next ch) twice, dc in next ch; rep from * across, ending last rep at **, dc in next ch, ch 1, skip next ch, dc in last ch, turn.

Row 2: Ch 4 (counts as dc, ch 1), skip next ch-1 space, dc in next dc, *ch 3, skip next ch-3 loop, (dc, ch 1, dc) in next sc, skip next ch-1 space, sc in next ch-3 loop, ch 3**, (dc, ch 1) in each of next 2 dc, dc in next dc; rep from * across, ending last rep at **, dc in next dc, ch 1, skip next ch of turning ch, dc in next ch of turning ch, turn.

Rep Row 2 for pattern.

479

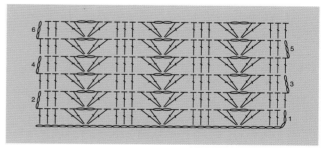

Chain multiples of 10 plus 5.

Row 1: Dc in 4th ch from hook, dc in next ch, *skip next 3 ch, (2 dc, ch 2, 2 dc) in next ch, skip next 3 ch, dc in each of next 3 ch; rep from * across, turn.

Row 2: Ch 3 (counts as dc), skip first dc, dc in each of next 2 dc, *(2 dc, ch 2, 2 dc) in next ch-2 space, skip next 2 dc, dc in each of next 3 dc; rep from * across, ending with last dc in 3rd ch of turning ch, turn.

Rep Row 2 for pattern.

480

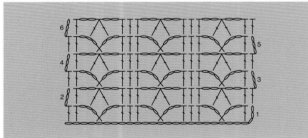

2-Dc Cluster: (Yo, insert hook in next st, yo, draw yarn through st, yo, draw yarn through 2 loops on hook) twice, yo, draw yarn through 3 loops on hook.

Chain multiples of 8 plus 3.

Row 1: Dc in 4th ch from hook, dc in next ch, *ch 3, skip next 2 ch, sc in next ch, ch 3, skip next 2 ch, dc in each of next 3 ch; rep from * across, ending with dc in each of last 2 ch, turn.

Row 2: Ch 3 (counts as dc), skip first dc, dc in next dc, *ch 2, 2-dc cluster worked across next 2 ch-3 loops, ch 2**, dc in each of next 3 dc; rep from * across, ending last rep at **, dc in next dc, dc in 3rd ch of turning ch, turn.

Row 3: Ch 3 (counts as dc), skip first dc, dc in next dc, *ch 3, skip next ch-2 space, sc in next cluster, ch 3, skip next ch-2 space**, dc in each of next 3 dc; rep from * across, ending last rep at **, dc in next dc, dc in 3rd ch of turning ch, turn.

Rep Rows 2-3 for pattern.

481

Chain multiples of 16 plus 3.

Row 1: Dc in 4th ch from hook, dc in next ch, *(ch 3, skip next 3 ch, sc in next ch) twice, ch 3, skip next 3 ch, dc in each of next 5 ch; rep from * across, ending with dc in each of last 3 ch, turn.

Row 2: Ch 3 (counts as dc), skip first dc, dc in each of next 2 dc, *ch 3, sc in next ch-3 loop, 7 dc in next ch-3 loop, sc in next ch-3 loop, ch 3**, dc in each of next 5 dc; rep from * across, ending last rep at **, dc in each of next 2 dc, dc in 3rd ch of turning ch, turn.

Row 3: Ch 3 (counts as dc), skip first dc, dc in each of next 2 dc, *ch 1, sc in next ch-3 loop, (dc, ch 1) in each of next 6 dc, dc in next dc, sc in next ch-3 loop, ch 1**, dc in each of next 5 dc; rep from * across, ending last rep at **, dc in each of next 2 dc, dc in 3rd ch of turning ch, turn.

Row 4: Ch 3 (counts as dc), skip first dc, dc in each of next 2 dc, *skip next ch-1 space, skip next sc, *(dc in next dc, dc in next ch-1 space) 6 times, dc in next dc, skip next ch-1 space**, dc in each of next 5 dc; rep from * across, ending last rep at **, dc in each of next 2 dc, dc in 3rd ch of turning ch, turn.

Row 5: Ch 3 (counts as dc), skip first dc, dc in each of next 2 dc, *ch 3, skip next 4 dc, sc in next dc, ch 3, skip next 3 dc, sc in next dc, ch 3, skip next 4 dc**, dc in each of next 5 dc; rep from * across, ending last rep at **, dc in each of next 2 dc, dc in 3rd ch of turning ch, turn.

Rep Rows 2-5 for pattern.

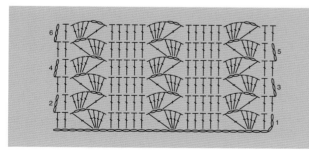

Chain multiples of 10 plus 2.

Row 1: Dc in 4th ch from hook, *skip next ch (4 dc, ch 2, dc) in next ch, skip next 3 ch, dc in each of next 5 ch; rep from * across, ending with dc in each of last 2 ch, turn.

Row 2: Ch 3 (counts as dc), skip first dc, dc in next dc, *(4 dc, ch 2, dc) in next ch-2 space, skip next 4 dc**, dc in each of next 5 dc; rep from * across, ending last rep at **, dc in next dc, dc in 3rd ch of turning ch, turn.

Rep Row 2 for pattern.

Chain multiples of 15 plus 2.

Row 1: Dc in 4th ch from hook, dc in each of next 2 ch, *skip next 3 ch, (dc, ch 2, 2 dc, ch 2, dc) in next ch, skip next 3 ch, dc in each of next 8 ch; rep from * across, ending with dc in each of last 4 ch, turn.

Row 2: Ch 5 (counts as dc, ch 2), skip first 3 dc, dc in next dc, *(ch 3, sc) in each of next 2 ch-2 loops, ch 3, dc in next dc, ch 2, skip next 2 dc**, dc in each of next 2 dc, ch 2, skip next 2 dc, dc in next dc; rep from * across, ending last rep at **, dc in 3rd ch of turning ch, turn.

Row 3: Ch 3 (counts as dc), *2 dc in next ch-2 space, dc in next dc, skip next ch-3 loop, (dc, ch 2, 2 dc, ch 2, dc) in next ch-3 loop, skip next ch-3 loop, dc in next dc, 2 dc in next ch-2 space**, dc in each of next 2 dc; rep from * across, ending last rep at **, dc in 3rd ch of turning ch, turn.

Rep Rows 2-3 for pattern.

484

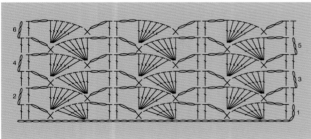

Chain multiples of 12 plus 4.

Row 1: Dc in 4th ch from hook, *ch 2, skip next 2 ch, 6 dc in next ch, skip next 4 ch, sc in next ch, ch 2, skip next 2 ch, dc in each of next 2 ch; rep from * across, turn.

Row 2: Ch 3 (counts as dc), skip first dc, dc in next dc, *ch 2, skip next ch-2 space, 6 dc in next sc, skip next 5 dc, sc in next dc, ch 2, skip next ch-2 space, dc in each of next 2 dc; rep from * across, ending with last dc in 3rd ch of turning ch, turn.

Rep Row 2 for pattern.

485

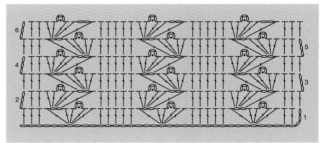

Chain multiples of 12 plus 3.

Row 1: Dc in 4th ch from hook, dc in next ch, *skip next 3 ch, (2 dc, ch 3, sl st in 3rd ch from hook for picot, 2 dc, ch 2, dc) in next ch, skip next 3 ch, dc in each of next 5 ch; rep from * across, ending with dc in each of last 3 ch, turn.

Row 2: Ch 3 (counts as dc), skip first dc, dc in each of next 2 dc, *(2 dc, ch 3, sl st in 3rd ch from hook for picot, 2 dc, ch 2, dc) in next ch-2 space, skip next 4 dc**, dc in each of next 5 dc; rep from * across, ending last rep at **, dc in each of next 2 dc, dc in 3rd ch of turning ch, turn.

Rep Row 2 for pattern.

486

Chain multiples of 10 plus 7.

Row 1: Dc in 4th ch from hook, dc in each of next 3 ch, *ch 5, skip next 2 ch, sc in next ch, ch 5, skip next 2 ch, dc in each of next 5 ch; rep from * across, turn.

Row 2: Ch 3 (counts as dc), skip first dc, dc in each of next 4 dc, *ch 3 (sc, ch 3) in each of next 2 ch-5 loops, dc in each of next 5 dc; rep from * across, ending with last dc in 3rd ch of turning ch, turn.

Row 3: Ch 3 (counts as dc), skip first dc, dc in each of next 4 dc, *skip next ch-3 loop, 7 dc in next ch-3 loop, skip next ch-3 loop, dc in each of next 5 dc; rep from * across, ending with last dc in 3rd ch of turning ch, turn.

Row 4: Ch 3 (counts as dc), skip first dc, dc in each of next 4 dc, *ch 5, skip next 3 dc, sc in next dc, ch 5, skip next 3 dc, dc in each of next 5 dc; rep from * across, ending with last dc in 3rd ch of turning ch, turn.

Rep Rows 2-4 for pattern.

487

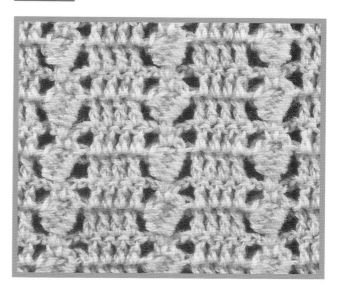

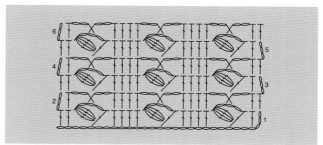

4-Dc Puff st: (Yo, insert hook in next st, yo, draw yarn through st, yo, draw yarn through 2 loops on hook) 4 times in same st, yo, draw yarn through 5 loops on hook.

Chain multiples of 9 plus 2.

Row 1: Dc in 4th ch from hook, *skip next 2 ch, dc in next ch, ch 3, 4-dc puff st worked around the post of last dc made, skip next 2 ch, dc in each of next 4 ch; rep from * across, ending with dc in each of last 2 ch, turn.

Row 2: Ch 3 (counts as dc), skip first dc, dc in next dc, *ch 2, sc in next ch-3 loop, ch 2, skip next dc**, dc in each of next 4 dc; rep from * across, ending last rep at **, dc in next dc, dc in 3rd ch of turning ch, turn.

Row 3: Ch 3 (counts as dc), skip first dc, dc in next dc, *skip next ch-2 space, dc in next sc, ch 3, 4-dc puff st worked around the post of last dc made, skip next ch-2 space**, dc in each of next 4 dc; rep from * across, ending last rep at **, dc in next dc, dc in 3rd ch of turning ch, turn.

Rep Rows 2-3 for pattern.

488

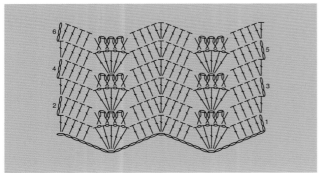

Chain multiples of 14 plus 4.

Row 1: Dc in 4th ch from hook, *dc in each of next 3 ch, skip next 3 ch, (dc, ch 1, dc, ch 1, dc, ch 1, dc, ch 1, dc) in next ch, skip next 3 ch, dc in each of next 3 ch**, 3 dc in next ch; rep from * across, ending last rep at **, 2 dc in last ch, turn.

Row 2: Ch 3 (counts as dc), dc in first dc, *dc in each of next 3 dc, (sc, ch 3) in each of next 3 ch-1 spaces, sc in next ch-1 space, skip next 2 dc, dc in each of next 3 dc**, 3 dc in next dc; rep from * across, ending last rep at **, 2 dc in 3rd ch of turning ch, turn.

Row 3: Ch 3 (counts as dc), dc in first dc, *dc in each of next 3 dc, skip next ch-3 loop, (dc, ch 1, dc, ch 1, dc, ch 1, dc, ch 1, dc) in next ch-3 loop, skip next (ch-3 loop, sc and dc), dc in each of next 3 dc**, 3 dc in next dc; rep from * across, ending last rep at **, 2 dc in 3rd ch of turning ch, turn.

Rep Rows 2-3 for pattern.

489

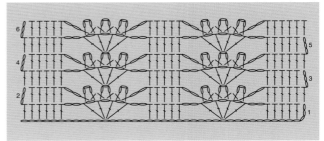

Chain multiples of 16 plus 9.

Row 1: Dc in 4th ch from hook, dc in each of next 4 ch, *ch 2, skip next 5 ch, (dc, ch 1, dc, ch 1, dc, ch 1, dc) in next ch, ch 2, skip next 5 ch, dc in each of next 5 ch; rep from * across to within last ch, dc in last ch, turn.

Row 2: Ch 3 (counts as dc), skip first dc, dc in each of next 5 dc, *ch 2, skip next ch-2 space, (sc, ch 3, sc) in each of next 3 ch-1 spaces, ch 2, skip next ch-2 space, dc in each of next 5 dc; rep from * across to turning ch, dc in 3rd ch of turning ch, turn.

Row 3: Ch 3 (counts as dc), skip first dc, dc in each of next 5 dc, *ch 2, skip next 2 spaces, (dc, ch 1, dc, ch 1, dc, ch 1, dc) in next ch-3 loop, ch 2, skip next 2 spaces, dc in each of next 5 dc; rep from * across to turning ch, dc in 3rd ch of turning ch, turn.

Rep Rows 2-3 for pattern.

490

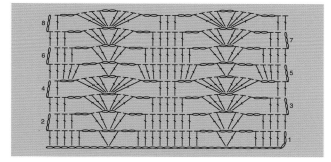

Chain multiples of 16 plus 3.

Row 1: Dc in 4th ch from hook, dc in each of next 3 ch, *ch 2, skip next 3 ch, (dc, ch 2, dc) in next ch, ch 2, skip next 3 ch, dc in each of next 9 ch; rep from * across, ending with dc in each of last 5 ch, turn.

Row 2: Ch 3 (counts as dc), skip first dc, dc in each of next 3 dc, *ch 2, skip next ch-2 space, (2 dc, ch 2, 2 dc) in next ch-2 space, ch 2, skip next ch-2 space, skip next dc**, dc in each of next 7 dc; rep from * across, ending last rep at **, dc in each of next 3 dc, dc in 3rd ch of turning ch, turn.

Row 3: Ch 3 (counts as dc), skip first dc, dc in each of next 2 dc, *ch 2, skip next ch-2 space, (3 dc, ch 2, 3 dc) in next ch-2 space, ch 2, skip next ch-2 space, skip next dc**, dc in each of next 5 dc; rep from * across, ending last rep at **, dc in each of next 2 dc, dc in 3rd ch of turning ch, turn.

Row 4: Ch 3 (counts as dc), skip first dc, dc in next dc, *ch 2, skip next ch-2 space, (4 dc, ch 2, 4 dc) in next ch-2 space, ch 2, skip next ch-2 space, skip next dc**, dc in each of next 3 dc; rep from * across, ending last rep at **, dc in next dc, dc in 3rd ch of turning ch, turn.

Row 5: Ch 3 (counts as dc), skip first dc, dc in next dc, *3 dc in next ch-2 space, ch 2, (dc, ch 2, dc) in next ch-2 space, ch 2, 3

dc in next ch-2 space**, dc in each of next 3 dc; rep from * across, ending last rep at **, dc in next dc, dc in 3rd ch of turning ch, turn.

Rep Rows 2-5 for pattern.

491

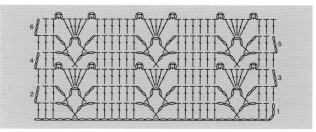

Chain multiples of 11 plus 2.

Row 1: Dc in 4th ch from hook, dc in next ch, *ch 3, skip next 2 ch, sc in next ch, ch 3, skip next 2 ch, dc in each of next 6 ch; rep from * across, ending with dc in each of last 3 ch, turn.

Row 2: Ch 3 (counts as dc), skip first dc, dc in each of next 2 dc, *ch 2, sc in next ch-3 loop, ch 3, sc in next ch-3 loop, ch 2**, dc in each of next 6 dc; rep from * across, ending last rep at **, dc in each of next 2 dc, dc in 3rd ch of turning ch, turn.

Row 3: Ch 3 (counts as dc), skip first dc, dc in each of next 2 dc, *ch 3, sl st in 3rd ch from hook for picot, skip next ch-2 space, 5 dc in next ch-3 loop, picot, skip next ch-2 space**, dc in each of next 6 dc; rep from * across, ending last rep at **, dc in each of next 2 dc, dc in 3rd ch of turning ch, turn.

Row 4: Ch 3 (counts as dc), skip first dc, dc in each of next 2 dc, *ch 3, skip next 2 dc, sc in next dc, ch 3, skip next picot**, dc in each of next 6 dc; rep from * across, ending last rep at **, dc in each of next 2 dc, dc in 3rd ch of turning ch, turn.

Rep Rows 2-4 for pattern.

.32.
Multi-Stitches

492

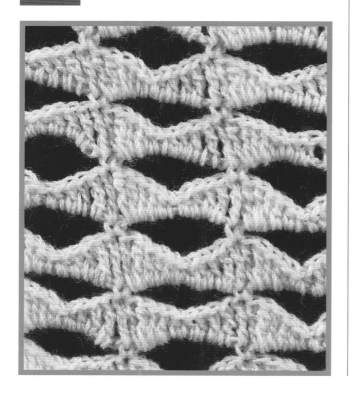

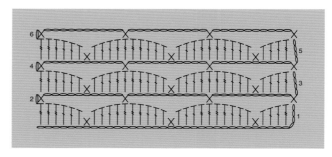

Chain multiples of 11 plus 4.

Row 1: Tr in 5th ch from hook, dc in each of next 2 ch, hdc in next ch, *sc in next ch, hdc in next ch, dc in each of next 2 ch**, tr in each of next 4 ch, dc in each of next 2 ch, hdc in next ch; rep from * across, ending last rep at **, tr in each of last 3 ch, turn.

Row 2: Ch 1, sc in first tr, *ch 10, skip next 10 sts, sc in next tr; rep from * across, ending with last sc in 4th ch of turning ch, turn.

Row 3: Ch 4 (counts as tr), *(tr, 2 dc, hdc, sc, hdc, 2 dc, 2 tr) in next ch-10 loop, tr in next sc; rep from * across, turn.

Rep Rows 2-3 for pattern.

493

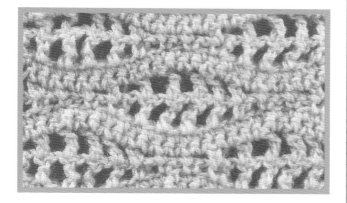

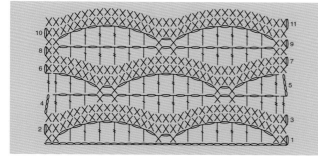

Chain multiples of 16 plus 2.

Row 1: Sc in 2nd ch from hook, *sc in next ch, ch 1, skip next ch, hdc in next ch, ch 1, skip next ch, dc in next ch, (ch 1, skip next ch, tr in next ch) twice, ch 1, skip next ch, dc in next ch, ch 1, skip next ch, hdc in next ch, ch 1, skip next ch, sc in next ch**, ch 1, skip next ch; rep from * across, ending last rep at **, sc in last ch, turn.

Row 2: Ch 1, sc in each st and ch-1 space across, turn.

Row 3: Ch 1, sc in each sc across, turn.

Row 4: Ch 4 (counts as tr), skip first sc, *tr in next sc, ch 1, skip next sc, dc in next sc, ch 1, skip next sc, hdc in next sc, (ch 1, skip next sc, sc in next sc) twice, ch 1, skip next sc, hdc in next sc, ch 1, skip next sc, dc in next sc, ch 1, skip next sc, tr in next sc**, ch 1, skip next sc; rep from * across, ending last rep at **, tr in last sc, turn.

Row 5: Ch 4 (counts as tr), skip first tr, *tr in next tr, ch 1, skip next ch-1 space, dc in next dc, ch 1, skip next ch-1 space, hdc in next hdc, (ch 1, sc) in each of next 2 sc, ch 1, skip next ch-1 space, hdc in next hdc, ch 1, skip next ch-1 space, dc in next dc, ch 1, skip next ch-1 space, tr in next tr**, ch 1, skip next ch-1 space; rep from * across, ending last rep at **, tr in 4th ch of turning ch, turn.

Rows 6-7: Rep Rows 2-3.

Row 8: Ch 1, sc in first 2 sc, *ch 1, skip next sc, hdc in next sc, ch 1, skip next sc, dc in next sc, (ch 1, skip next sc, tr in next sc) twice, ch 1, skip next sc, dc in next sc, ch 1, skip next sc, hdc in next sc, ch 1, skip next sc, sc in next sc**, ch 1, skip next sc, sc in next sc; rep from * across, ending last rep at **, sc in last sc, turn.

Row 9: Ch 1, sc in first 2 sc, *ch 1, skip next ch-1 space, hdc in next hdc, ch 1, skip next ch-1 space, dc in next dc, (ch 1, tr) in each of next 2 tr, ch 1, skip next ch-1 space, dc in next dc, ch 1, skip next ch-1 space, hdc in next hdc, ch 1, skip next ch-1 space, sc in next sc**, ch 1, skip next ch-1 space, sc in next sc; rep from * across, ending last rep at **, sc in last sc, turn.

Rep Rows 2-9 for pattern.

494

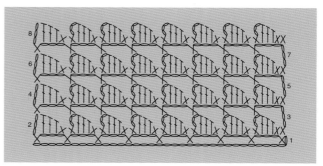

Chain multiples of 4 plus 2.

Row 1: Sc in 2nd ch from hook, *ch 3, skip next 3 ch, sc in next ch; rep from * across, turn.

Row 2: Ch 3 (counts as dc), (2 dc, hdc, sc) in next ch-3 loop, (sc, ch 3, 2 dc, hdc, sc) in each ch-3 loop across to last ch-3 loop, sc in last sc, turn.

Row 3: Ch 6 (counts as dc, ch 3), skip first 5 sts, (sc, ch 3) in each ch-3 loop across to last ch-3 loop, sc in 3rd ch of turning ch, turn.

Rep Rows 2-3 for pattern.

495

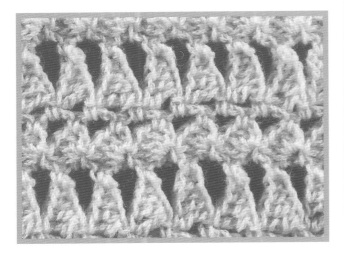

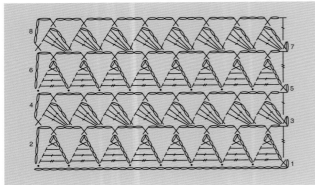

Chain multiples of 4 plus 2.

Row 1: Sc in 2nd ch from hook, *ch 6, sc in 3rd ch from hook, hdc in next ch, dc in next ch, tr in next ch, skip next 3 ch, sl st in next ch; rep from * across, turn.

Row 2: Ch 5 (counts as tr, ch 1), (sc, ch 3) in ch-2 space at top of each triangle across to within last ch-2 space, sc in next ch-2 space, ch 1, tr in last sc, turn.

Row 3: Ch 1, (sc, ch 3, 3 dc) in first tr, skip next ch-1 space, (sc, ch 3, 3 dc) in each ch-3 loop across to turning ch, sc in 4th ch of turning ch, turn.

Row 4: Ch 4 (counts as dc, ch 1), (sc, ch 3) in each ch-3 loop across to within last ch-3 loop, sc in next ch-3 loop, ch 1, dc in last sc, turn.

Row 5: Ch 1, sc in first dc, *ch 6, sc in 3rd ch from hook, hdc in next ch, dc in next ch, tr in next ch, sl st in next ch-3 loop; rep from * across, ending with last sl st in 3rd ch of turning ch, turn.

Rep Rows 2-5 for pattern.

496

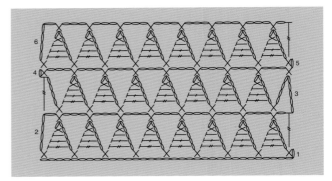

Chain multiples of 4 plus 2.

Row 1: Sc in 2nd ch from hook, *ch 6, sc in 3rd ch from hook, hdc in next ch, dc in next ch, tr in next ch, skip next 3 ch, sc in next ch; rep from * across, turn.

Row 2: Ch 5 (counts as tr, ch 1), (sc, ch 3) in ch-2 space at top of each triangle across to within last ch-2 space, sc in next ch-2 space, ch 1, tr in last sc, turn.

Row 3: Ch 9 (counts as tr, ch 4), skip next ch-1 space, sc in next sc, *ch 6, sc in 3rd ch from hook, hdc in next ch, dc in next ch, tr in next ch, skip next ch-3 loop, sc in next sc; rep from * across to turning ch, ch 4, tr in 4th ch of turning ch, turn.

Row 4: Ch 1, sc in first tr, (ch 3, sc) in ch-2 space at top of each triangle across, ending with last sc in 5th ch of turning ch, turn.

Row 5: Ch 1, sc in first sc, *ch 6, sc in 3rd ch from hook, hdc in next ch, dc in next ch, tr in next ch, skip next ch-3 loop, sc in next sc; rep from * across, turn.

Rep Rows 2-5 for pattern.

.33.
Miscellaneous

497

Chain multiples of 6 plus 5.

Row 1: (Tr, ch 4, tr) in 7th ch from hook, *work 2-tr cluster working first half-closed tr in next ch, skip next 4 ch, work 2nd half-closed tr in next ch, yo, complete cluster, ch 4, tr in same ch as last tr of last cluster; rep from * across to within last 3 ch, work 2-tr cluster working first half-closed tr in next ch, skip next 2 ch, work 2nd half-closed tr in last ch, yo, complete cluster, turn.

Row 2: Ch 6 (counts as tr, ch 2), tr in first cluster, *work 2-tr cluster working first half-closed tr in next tr, skip next ch-4 loop, work 2nd half-closed tr in next cluster, yo, complete cluster**, ch 4, tr in same cluster holding last tr of last cluster; rep from * across, ending last rep at **, ch 2, tr in top of turning ch, turn.

Row 3: Ch 4 (counts as tr), skip next ch-2 space, (tr, ch 4, tr) in next cluster, *work 2-tr cluster working first half-closed tr in next tr, skip next 4 ch, work 2nd half-closed tr in next cluster, yo, complete cluster, ch 4, tr in same cluster as last tr of last cluster; rep from * across to turning ch, work 2-tr cluster working first half-closed tr in next tr, skip next 2 ch of turning ch, work 2nd half-closed tr in 4th ch of turning ch, yo, complete cluster, turn.

Rep Rows 2-3 for pattern.

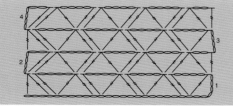

498

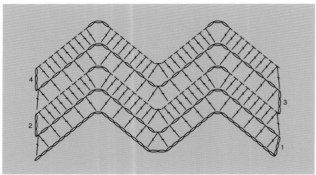

2-Dc Cluster: *(Yo, insert hook in next st, yo, draw yarn through st, yo, draw yarn through 2 loops on hook) twice, yo, draw yarn through 3 loops on hook.*

Chain multiples of 19 plus 4.

Row 1: Dc in 5th ch from hook, *(ch 1, skip next ch, dc in next ch) 3 times, ch 1, skip next ch, (dc, ch 3, dc) in next ch, (ch 1, skip next ch, dc in next ch) 3 times, ch 1, skip next ch**, work 2-dc cluster working first half-closed dc in next ch, skip next 2 ch, work 2nd half-closed dc in next ch, yo, complete 2-dc cluster; rep from * across, ending last rep at **, work 2-dc cluster working first half-closed dc in next ch, skip next ch, work 2nd half-closed dc in last ch, yo, complete cluster, turn.

Row 2: Ch 3 (counts as dc), skip next ch-1 space, *dc in next dc, (dc in next ch-1 space, dc in next dc) 3 times, (2 dc, ch 3, 2 dc) in next ch-3 loop, (dc in next dc, dc in next ch-1 space) 3 times**, work 2-dc cluster working first half-closed dc in next dc, skip next 3 sts, work 2nd half-closed dc in next dc, yo, complete cluster; rep from * across, ending last rep at **, work 2-dc cluster working first half-closed dc in next dc, skip next 2 sts, work 2nd half-closed dc in top of turning ch, yo, complete 2-dc cluster, turn.

Row 3: Ch 3 (counts as dc), skip first 2 sts, dc in next dc, *(ch 1, skip next dc, dc in next dc) 3 times, ch 1, (dc, ch 3, dc) in next ch-3 loop, ch 1, (dc in next dc, ch 1, skip next dc) 3 times**, work 2-dc cluster working first half-closed dc in next dc, skip next 3 sts, work 2nd half-closed dc in next dc, yo, complete cluster; rep from * across, ending last rep at **, work 2-dc cluster working first half-closed dc in next dc, skip next 2 sts, work 2nd half-closed dc in top of turning ch, yo, complete cluster, turn.

Rep Rows 2-3 for pattern.

499

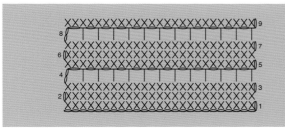

Chain multiples of 2.

Row 1: Sc in 2nd ch from hook, sc in each ch across, turn.

Rows 2-3: Ch 1, sc in each sc across, turn.

Row 4: Ch 3 (counts as hdc, ch 1), skip first 2 sc, hdc in next sc, *ch 1, skip next sc, hdc in next sc; rep from * across, turn.

Row 5: Ch 1, sc in each hdc and each ch-1 space across, ending with last sc in 2nd ch of turning ch, turn.

Rep Rows 2-5 for pattern.

500

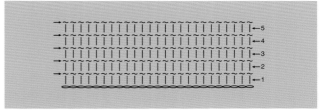

Use an Afghan or Tunisian crochet hook.

Chain any multiple.

Row 1: Insert hook in 2nd ch from hook, yo, draw yarn through st, *insert hook in next ch, yo, draw yarn through st; rep from * across keeping all loops on hook, (first half of Row 1 complete), begin 2nd half of row, yo, draw yarn through 1 loop on hook, **yarn over, draw yarn through 2 loops on hook; rep from ** across (1 loop remains on hook and counts as first loop of next row).

Row 2: *Insert hook from front to back to front again under next vertical st, yo, draw yarn through st; rep from * across to last st, insert hook under next vertical st and vertical st behind it, yo, draw yarn through 2 vertical sts (first half of Row 2 complete), begin 2nd half of row, yo, draw yarn through 1 loop on hook, **yarn over, draw yarn through 2 loops on hook; rep from ** across (1 loop remains on hook and counts as first loop of next row).

Rep Row 2 for pattern.

Acknowledgments

I would like to thank Anna Kunz-Schapper who, when I was a very young girl, welcomed me into her family in Wetzikon, Switzerland, and passed on to me her techniques, patterns, and her love of crochet, and also Charles Nurnberg, president of Sterling Publishing Company in New York, who very kindly remembered me from 20 years ago, when I wrote my first crochet stitch book, and gave me the wonderful opportunity of reprising it with Lark Books and passing on again these timeless techniques and my own love of crochet.

Author Biography

Linda Schapper's artistic vision is expressed in a wide range of media, from patchwork quilts and crochet, to painting and liturgical textiles, all of which are characterized by a folk-art style. She has traveled and taught extensively around the world in more than 30 countries, speaks four languages, and has had some 100 exhibits of her patchwork quilts. She has written eight books, four of them on crochet. She now divides her time between painting and writing about her liturgical work.